PRAISE FOR GREY WOLF

"Remarkable detail."—Sir David Frost, *Frost Over the World*

"Stunning Account of the Last Days of the Reich."—Parapolitical.com

"Describes a ghastly pantomime played out in the names of the Führer and the woman who had been his mistress."—*The Sun*

"Laid out in lavish detail."—*Daily Mail*

"Stunning saga of intrigue."—*Pravda*

"I thought the book was hugely thought-provoking and explores some of the untold, murky loose ends of World War Two."—Dan Snow, broadcaster and historian, *The One Show*, BBC One

"*Grey Wolf* is more than a conspiracy yarn. . . . Its authors show Hitler's escape was possible. . . . It's a gripping read."—*South China Morning Post*

GREY WOLF

The Escape of
ADOLF HITLER

SIMON DUNSTAN AND GERRARD WILLIAMS

STERLING
New York

STERLING
New York

An Imprint of Sterling Publishing
1166 Avenue of the Americas
New York, NY 10036

© 2011 by Simon Dunstan, Gerrard Williams, Spitfire Recovery Ltd.
Project sources through Greene Media Ltd. (info@greenemedia.co.uk)
For picture credits, see page 352
Book design and layout: Buoy Point Media (www.buoypoint.com)

ISBN 978-1-4027-9619-7

Library of Congress Cataloging-in-Publication Data

Dunstan, Simon.
  Grey wolf: the escape of Adolf Hitler / Simon Dunstan and Gerrard Williams.
    p. cm.
  Includes bibliographical references and index.
  ISBN 978-1-4027-8139-1 (alk. paper)—ISBN 978-1-4027-8933-5 (e-book)
  1. Hitler, Adolf, 1889–1945—Death and burial. 2. Hitler, Adolf, 1889–1945—Exile. 3. Heads of
state—Germany—Biography. I. Williams, Gerrard. II. Title.
  DD247.H5D76 2011
  943.086092—dc22
      2011014763

Distributed in Canada by Sterling Publishing
c/o Canadian Manda Group, 664 Annette Street
Toronto, Ontario, Canada M6S 2C8
Distributed in the United Kingdom by GMC Distribution Services
Castle Place, 166 High Street, Lewes, East Sussex, England BN7 1XU
Distributed in Australia by Capricorn Link (Australia) Pty. Ltd.
P.O. Box 704, Windsor, NSW 2756, Australia

For information about custom editions, special sales, and premium and corporate purchases, please contact
Sterling Special Sales at 800-805-5489 or specialsales@sterlingpublishing.com.

Manufactured in the United States of America

8   10   9   7

FRONTISPIECE: HITLER ON the terrace of his holiday retreat, the Berghof,
at Obersalzberg in Bavaria, undated.

Publisher's Note

When we were first presented with the idea for *Grey Wolf: The Escape of Adolf Hitler,* our initial reaction was to dismiss it as just another conspiracy theory. Everyone knows that Hitler and Eva Braun took their lives in the bunker to escape the humiliation and certain execution that awaited them. However, we agreed to give it serious consideration due to the stellar reputations of the authors, Simon Dunstan and Gerrard Williams. We were also encouraged by the recent independent discovery that the remains recovered at the bunker were not those of Hitler or Eva Braun. Upon reading the proposal and challenging the authors over a period of several months, we were convinced that they had raised serious questions that called the conventional wisdom into question, and we therefore decided to publish the book.

The authors have spent the last five years researching this subject—traveling the globe, interviewing eyewitnesses, unearthing documents, and piecing together a mountain of evidence that has convinced them of a fact almost too horrible to contemplate: that Adolf Hitler escaped punishment and lived out his life in relative tranquility in Patagonia until his death in 1962.

This prospect is so despicable that we contemplated not publishing the book out of concern for those who would be offended by the mere prospect of Hitler's escape, whether or not they found the argument credible. However, after much consideration, and a lengthy editorial process during which the authors were challenged to support their facts, we believe it is possible they may have uncovered the truth behind one of the greatest deceptions in history.

This book raises many intriguing questions, but it does not conclusively settle the issue. Perhaps this is a mystery that will never be solved, as with so many other moments in time. Or perhaps, once this issue is in the public arena, other facts will come to light that will bring us closer to a definitive answer. The authors wrote this book in a search for the truth, and they may have found it. Inevitably, you, the reader, will be the ultimate judge.

CONTENTS

PART III: THE ESCAPE

PART IV: THE GREY WOLF OF PATAGONIA

DRAMATIS PERSONAE

This listing of significant characters who appear in this book omits unnecessary explanations of major historical figures such as Adolf Hitler, Martin Bormann, Hermann Göring, Franklin D. Roosevelt, Dwight D. Eisenhower, and Winston Churchill. Its main purpose is to help readers keep track of less familiar personalities who recur in these pages. Capitalized names within entries refer to individuals who appear elsewhere in the dramatis personae.

GERMAN AND AUSTRIAN

ABS, HERMANN JOSEF: Chairman of the board of Deutsche Bank AG. (1957–67). Member of the board of directors (1938–45).

ALVENSLEBEN, GEN. LUDOLF VON: SS and police general, and wanted war criminal, later governor of Nazi settlement at Inalco, Río Negro province, Argentina.

ARENSTORFF, GERDA VON: Colleague of DIETRICH NIEBUHR at German embassy in Buenos Aires (1938–44), who recruited EVA DUARTÉ as an agent.

BARSCH, 1ST LT. FRANZ: Commander of submarine U-1235.

BAUMBACH, LT. COL. WERNER: Luftwaffe (air force) officer commanding special-duties wing Kampfgeschwader 200, who supervised flight of Hitler's party from Travemünde, Germany, to Reus, Spain, on April 29, 1945.

BAUMGART, CAPT. PETER ERICH: South African-born Luftwaffe and SS officer, who flew Hitler's party from Berlin to Tønder, Denmark, on April 28, 1945.

BETHE, HEINRICH: German sailor from warship *Admiral Graf Spee*, who became Hitler's last servant.

BRAUN, WERNHER VON: Technical director of V-2 ballistic missile program; employed in America after the war.

CANARIS, ADM. WILHELM: Head of Abwehr military intelligence organization.

DOERGE, HEINRICH: Reichsbank official seconded to Argentina as aide to LUDWIG FREUDE, and financial adviser to Argentine government.

FAUPEL, GEN. WILHELM VON: Former military adviser to Argentine Army, and, in 1930s–40s, intelligence chief for Spain and South America as head of Ibero-American Institute.

FEGELEIN, GEN. HERMANN: Heinrich Himmler's SS adjutant to Hitler's headquarters, who became Hitler's brother-in-law and a confidant of Martin Bormann.

FLICK, FRIEDRICH: Steel industry magnate and supporter of Nazi Party, a director of Vereinigte Stahlwerke AG (United Steelworks) (1933–45).

HOHENLOHE-LANGENBURG, PRINCE MAXIMILIAN EGON ZU: German aristocrat and intermediary between Heinrich Himmler and ALLEN DULLES.

HUDAL, BISHOP ALOIS: Martin Bormann's main pro-Nazi contact in the Vatican, who helped organize escape of many war criminals to South America.

HUMMEL, LT. COL. HANS HELMUT VON: SS adjutant to Martin Bormann, and Bormann's intermediary to ALLEN DULLES.

HÖTTL, MAJ. WILHELM: SS officer, intermediary between SS GEN. KALTENBRUNNER and ALLEN DULLES.

KALTENBRUNNER, GEN. ERNST: SS and police general commanding Reich Main Security Office (RSHA), coordinating police, Gestapo (Secret Police), and SS intelligence and counterintelligence branch (SD).

KAY, CAPT. WALTER: Former first officer of warship *Admiral Graf Spee*, later energetic in Nazi intelligence activities in Argentina and Uruguay.

KOEHN, WILLI: Head of Latin America desk in German Foreign Office based in Madrid, and active intelligence agent.

LANTSCHNER, COL. FRIEDRICH: SS officer, later owner of construction business at San Carlos de Bariloche, Río Negro province, Argentina.

LEHMANN, OTTO (POSSIBLE PSEUDONYM): Medical officer at Nazi settlement at Inalco, Argentina, and later Hitler's personal physician at his La Clara retreat.

MEYNEN, OTTO: Senior intelligence agent at German embassy in Buenos Aires (1939–44), replacing DIETRICH NIEBUHR.

MÜLLER, GEN. HEINRICH "GESTAPO": SS and police general in command of the Gestapo.

NIEBUHR, CAPT. DIETRICH: Naval attaché at German embassy in Buenos Aires (1939–41), and intelligence agent for GEN. VON FAUPEL.

OFFERMANN, 1ST LT. HANS-WERNER: Commander of submarine U-518.

PUTTKAMER, ADM. KARL-JESCO VON: Hitler's navy adjutant in the Führerbunker, who assisted Martin Bormann with secure radio communications.

ROSENBERG, ALFRED: Nazi Party artistic "commissar," and head of ERR (Einsatzstab Reichsleiter Rosenberg für die Besetzen Gebiete— Special Staff of National Leader Rosenberg for the Occupied Territories) organization in charge of looting artworks from occupied countries.

RUDEL, COL. HANS-ULRICH: Stuka dive-bomber pilot who was most highly decorated officer in the German military, later active in Nazi community around San Carlos de Bariloche, Argentina.

SANDSTEDE, GOTTFRIED: Press attaché at German embassy in Buenos Aires (1939–41), senior intelligence agent for GENERAL VON FAUPEL, and executive of Delfino shipping line.

SCHACHT, HJALMAR: One-time president of Reichsbank and economics minister of Reich, and a principal director of Bank for International Settlements in Basel, Switzerland.

SCHAUMBURG-LIPPE, PRINCE STEPHAN ZU: Consular officer in Chile (1936–41), also active in affairs of Buenos Aires embassy.

SCHELLENBERG, GEN. WALTER: SS general commanding the Sicherheitsdienst (SD) intelligence agency, and would-be intermediary between Heinrich Himmler and ALLEN DULLES.

SCHMITZ, HERMANN: Chairman of the board of IG Farben conglomerate; funder and supporter of Nazi Party.

SCHÖTZAU, LT. CDR. GERHARD: Commander of submarine U-880.

SCHRÖDER, BARON KURT VON: Leading banker and supporter of Nazi Party.

THERMANN, BARON EDMUND VON: German ambassador to Argentina (1938–41).

THYSSEN, FRITZ: Steel industry magnate and supporter of Nazi Party; chairman of Vereinigte Stahlwerke AG (United Steelworks).

VOSS, ADM. HANS-ERICH: Naval liaison officer at the Führer's headquarters.

WINTER, GUSTAV: Agent of the Abwehr, who established a secret intelligence base on Fuerteventura in the Canary Islands.

WOLFF, GEN. KARL: SS military governor of northern Italy, who negotiated with ALLEN DULLES for surrender of German forces in Operation Sunrise.

AMERICAN

DONOVAN, GEN. WILLIAM J.: Director of Office of the Coordinator of Information (COI) (1941) and Office of Strategic Services (OSS) (1942–45).

DULLES, ALLEN WELSH: Corporate lawyer with extensive prewar contacts in Germany; from October 1941 head of operations of COI and then OSS station chief in Bern, Switzerland (1942–45); after the war, director of Central Intelligence Agency (CIA) (1953–61).

FORD, HENRY: Automobile industry magnate, decorated by Nazi Party for his support.

GROVES, GEN. LESLIE R.: Director of Manhattan Project, and instigator of U.S. efforts to locate and neutralize German nuclear research.

LANSDALE JR., LT. COL. JOHN: Head of security for Manhattan Project, and second-in-command of Alsos Mission to neutralize Germany's nuclear research program.

LESLIE, EDGEWORTH M.: OSS officer, intermediary between ALLEN DULLES and SS GEN. KALTENBRUNNER.

MORGENTHAU, HENRY J.: U.S. Secretary of the Treasury (1934–45).

PASH, COL. BORIS T.: Commander of Alsos Mission.

WALLACE, HENRY: Vice president of the United States (1941–45).

BRITISH

DALZEL-JOB, LT. CDR. PATRICK: Royal Navy officer commanding Team 4 of 30 Assault Unit (AU).

FLEMING, LT. CDR. IAN: Officer in Royal Naval Volunteer Reserve, and personal assistant to Admiral John Henry Godfrey, Director of Naval Intelligence; later, author of best-selling James Bond spy novels.

NORMAN, SIR MONTAGUE: Governor of Bank of England (1920–44), and a principal director of Bank for International Settlements in Basel, Switzerland.

ARGENTINE

EICHHORN, WALTER AND IDA: Leading supporters and fund-raisers for Nazi Party, friends of Hitler, and owners of Hotel Eden, La Falda, Córdoba province, Argentina.

FREUDE, LUDWIG: Banker and construction-industry millionaire, who acted as Nazis' chief financial representative and agent of influence in Argentina.

FREUDE, RODOLFO: Son of LUDWIG, who became private secretary and intelligence coordinator to PRESIDENT PERÓN.

LEUTE, RICARDO VON: General manager of German-founded Lahusen trading conglomerate.

PAHLKE, MAX: German-born director of Mannesmann company's Argentine subsidiary, and owner of Gran Hotel Viena clinic and spa, Miramar, Córdoba province.

PERÓN, COL. JUAN DOMINGO: Member of Grupo de Oficiales Unidos (GOU)—United Officers' Group military junta, who became vice president, later president, of Argentina.

PERÓN, EVA "EVITA" DUARTÉ: Mistress, later wife, of COL. PERÓN, and agent of influence for Nazi intelligence.

SANTANDER, SILVANO: Deputy for Entre Ríos province (1936–44), active and vocal opponent of Nazi links with Argentine government.

TABORDA, RAÚL DAMONTE: Chairman of Argentine congressional committee investigating Nazi activities.

OTHER

BRUGGMANN, CHARLES: Swiss ambassador to the United States (1939–45).

DODERO, ALBERTO: Uruguayan-Argentine millionaire shipping magnate and confederate of the Peróns.

MASSON, GENERAL ROGER: Director of the Swiss secret service (1939–45).

WALLENBERG, MARCUS: Swedish industrial and banking magnate.

TREATMENT OF
MILITARY RANKS

Since this book is not primarily a work of military history, we have not distinguished between the different grades of generals and flag officers in any of the Axis and Allied armed forces.

We have translated German SS and navy ranks, as below, and have simplified the former. The complexity of the SS structure meant that general officer ranks held by individuals were often qualified by suffixes differentiating rank within the basic organization or Allgemeine-SS, the military branch or Waffen-SS, and parallel rank in the police. Apart from key individuals with dual titles, such as "SS and Police Gen. Kaltenbrunner," we have felt it unnecessary to make most of these distinctions.

SS RANKS	FORMS USED IN TEXT
SS-Oberstgruppenführer	
SS-Obergruppenführer	
SS-Gruppenführer	SS General (Gen.)
SS-Brigadeführer	
SS-Oberführer	
SS-Standartenführer	SS Colonel (Col.)
SS-Obersturmbannführer	SS Lieutenant Colonel (Lt. Col.)
SS-Sturmbannführer	SS Major (Maj.)
SS-Hauptsturmführer	SS Captain (Capt.)
SS-Obersturmführer	SS Lieutenant (Lt.)
SS-Untersturmführer	
SS-Hauptscharführer	SS Staff Sergeant (S/Sgt.)

NAVY RANKS	FORMS USED IN TEXT
Kapitän zur See	Captain (Capt.)
Fregattenkapitän	Captain junior grade (Capt. jg)
Korvettenkapitän	Commander (Cdr.)
Kapitänleutnant	Lieutenant Commander (Lt. Cdr.)
Oberleutnant zur See	First Lieutenant (1st Lt.)

ABBREVIATIONS

AU	Assault Unit
CAFT	Consolidated Advance Field Team
CAO	Civil Affairs Office
CIOS	Combined Intelligence Objectives Sub-Committee
COI	Coordinator of Information
CU	Commando Unit
EPES	Enemy Personnel Exploitation Section
ERR	Einsatzstab Reichsleiter Rosenberg für die Besetzen Gebiete (Special Staff of National Leader Rosenberg for the Occupied Territories)
ETH	Eidgenossische Technische Hochschule
FEA	Federal Economic Administration
FFI	French Forces of the Interior
LRDG	Long Range Desert Group
MFA&A	Monuments, Fine Arts and Archives
NID	Naval Intelligence Division
NSDAP	Nationalsozialistische Deutsche Arbeiterpartei (National Socialist German Workers' Party or Nazi Party)
OKW	Oberkommando der Wehrmacht (Supreme Command of the Armed Forces)
OSS	Office of Strategic Services
RAF	Royal Air Force
RM	Royal Marines
RN	Royal Navy
RSHA	Reich Main Security Office
SA	Sturmabteilung (the Nazi Party's uniformed part-time activists, the "brownshirts")
SAS	Special Air Service
SD	Security Service (or Sicherheitsdienst)
SHAEF	Supreme Headquarters Allied Expeditionary Force
SS	Schutzstaffel (literally, "protection squad")
TICOM	Target Intelligence Committee
USAAF	United States Army Air Forces

LIST OF MAPS
AND DIAGRAMS

PREFACE

WE NEVER WANTED THIS STORY TO BE TRUE. It was originally intended to be a quixotic but thought-provoking "conspiracy theory" television documentary. However, extensive research in Argentina, Poland, Germany, Great Britain, and the Canary Island of Fuerteventura produced a compelling dossier of details—backed up by the testimonies of many eyewitnesses—that told a completely different story from the accepted "history" of World War II. In the words of Winston S. Churchill, "History is written by the victors." Never has this been more true than the untold account of Hitler's escape from the ruins of the Third Reich in April 1945.

The horrifying reality, we believe, is that at the end of World War II the most evil man in the world, Adolf Hitler, escaped from Germany and lived out his life in Argentina—and that his deputy, Reichsleiter Martin Bormann, and Heinrich "Gestapo" Müller, a key figure in the planning of the Final Solution, also escaped justice and joined him there. Equally disturbing is the evidence that America and Britain facilitated the flight of hundreds of erstwhile Nazis, such as the rocket scientist Wernher von Braun and the sadistic torturer Klaus Barbie, the Butcher of Lyon. Both were employed by U.S. government agencies in the postwar years while others were allowed to avoid prosecution and flee to the far corners of the world. Even as this book goes to press in the summer of 2011, a ninety-one-year-old Ukrainian, Ivan "John" Demjanjuk, has been convicted as an accessory to the murder of 28,060 Jews in the Sobibor death camp in Poland some sixty-eight years after the event. For years he lived a comfortable life as an autoworker for the Ford Motor Company in Cleveland, Ohio, before being extradited to Germany in 2009 for trial as a war criminal.

There is no concrete forensic evidence that it was Adolf Hitler and Eva Braun who died in the Führerbunker—no eyewitness to the moment of death. The famous "Hitler Skull" fragment held in Moscow for decades has finally been DNA-tested. It is that of a woman under the age of forty and it is not Eva Braun. There is also no absolutely accepted forensic evidence for Martin Bormann's supposed death; in 1998 German officials claimed that a skeleton buried near the Reichstag matched the DNA of an elderly relative of Bormann's, who remains nameless; the cremated ashes of the remains were scattered at sea. Bormann's family refused to accept the findings. Meanwhile, the bones found in Müller's grave, when exhumed in 1963, were found to be those of three other people.

We show for the first time that the "last official pictures of Hitler," with Artur Axmann and his Hitler Youth on March 20, 1945, are actually of Hitler's double. Modern science has proved beyond reasonable doubt that the man in the film and still pictures of the event, although bearing a striking resemblance to Hitler, was in fact not him, but one of several doubles. Alf Linney, professor of medical physics at University College London and a noted facial recognition expert witness, reviewed the picture for us and is convinced that it is not Hitler. Hitler was not alone in his use of plausible stand-ins. Stalin had numerous doubles; Churchill at least one. Field Marshall Bernard Montgomery—"Monty"—used one in a successful ruse to mislead the Germans about his movements prior to D-Day in 1944.

Magicians have known the trick for hundreds of years. People expect to see what they are shown. It's called sleight of hand. Martin Bormann carried out the most incredible trick in history on April 28, 1945. The Reichsleiter replaced Hitler with the double from the March 20 appearance. An actress from Propaganda Minister Joseph Goebbels's cinematic "stable" of film actresses—aided by the best makeup artists the Reich could find—stood in for Eva Braun. The look-alikes took their places in the Führerbunker as Hitler and Eva made their escape. Bormann carried on the charade for two days until he was sure that the real Hitler was safe. He then staged the fake double suicide of Hitler and his new bride and then callously had Hitler's double and his bogus bride murdered, almost certainly by "Gestapo" Müller.

The escape route into the Berlin subway system is still there. There are similar tunnels in London from the cellars of Buckingham Palace and 10 Downing Street, the residence of the British prime minister, to the London Tube, which would have been used by the British royal family and senior members of the government and military if London had ever fallen to Nazi invaders.

The Associated Press and Reuters reported the testimony of the pilot Peter Baumgart, who flew the couple out of Berlin along with Eva's brother in-law, Gen. Hermann Fegelein, extensively from Warsaw in 1947. But researchers have ignored this until today. Having worked for both of these illustrious press agencies as a lifelong journalist, Gerrard Williams knows how difficult it is to get copy onto the wire. It passes through many subeditors in an exacting process before it can end up in a newspaper column. Newspapers around the world carried the story, although curiously no one ever followed up with Peter Baumgart and he simply disappeared from history after his release in 1951 from Warsaw's Mokotów Prison (also known as Rakowiecka Prison).

Historians have preferred to accept the "masterful" account of British historian, Oxford professor, and former intelligence officer Hugh Trevor-Roper, which insists that Hitler committed suicide in the Führerbunker on April 30, 1945. It was vital to the Allied cause that Hitler should be demonstrably dead, to allow a new Germany to emerge from the ashes of the old. Trevor-Roper's work, which was published in 1947 as a book called *The Last Days of Hitler*, is intrinsically flawed, from the testimony of Hanna Reitsch—"Hitler's favorite pilot"—who denied ever meeting Trevor-Roper or saying what he quoted of her, to Hitler's Luftwaffe adjutant, Nicolaus von Below, who later stated that he had lied to the Oxford don and had a good laugh every time he saw his lies repeated. Hitler's chauffeur, Erich Kempka, was interrogated repeatedly but subsequently admitted in 1974, "I told American and British interrogators just about anything or everything I thought they wanted to hear."

Accepted as fact, Trevor-Roper's book has never been out of print. The acclaimed historian—who in 1983 identified the pathetic "Hitler Diaries" forgeries as real—had created his own sophisticated "forgery." He had never been given access to those Germans who had been in the bunker and were captured by the Soviets while trying to escape Berlin; these escapees were subsequently held prisoner, some for many years. Similarly, Trevor-Roper received only written accounts from those held by the Americans. All were anxious to save their own skins and invariably related whatever their captors wished to hear—that Hitler was dead.

There are other much better descriptions of the final days; the account by James O'Donnell in his 1978 book *The Bunker* is a thorough investigative report, with interviews from all the surviving people. But O'Donnell, like Trevor-Roper, was fooled by one thing. The corpses that were said in the accepted "history" to be taken up to the garden and burned were not those of the two main actors in the appalling final death throes of the Third Reich, but their doppelgängers. Hitler's double was likely an unfortunate stand-in named Gustav Weber, but the name of Eva's look-alike may never be known. They will go down in history as the world's unluckiest body doubles.

Stalin never believed Hitler was dead, insisting at the Potsdam Conference on July 17, 1945, that he had escaped—probably to "Spain or Argentina." Stalin's top general, Marshal Georgi Zhukov, said on August 6, 1945: "We found no corpse that could be Hitler's."

Gen. Dwight D. Eisenhower stated publicly on October 12, 1945, "There is every *assumption* that Hitler is dead, but *not a bit of conclusive proof* that he is dead." He told the Associated Press that "Russian friends" had informed him that they had been "unable to unearth any tangible evidence of his death." One U.S. senator went as far as offering one million U.S. dollars for proof of Hitler's death. It has never been claimed.

Uncovering Hitler's escape has not been simple. Our New York agent, Bill Corsa, gave us what seemed to be the best analogy for this work. He described it as similar to the tracking of an animal; you never get to see all the traces left and sometimes there are gaps where the trail seems to go cold, but if you persevere you will pick it up again until you find the final lair.

For the authors, the trail began in Buenos Aires in Argentina in 2006 and led us later to the windswept beaches of Patagonia and the city of San Carlos de Bariloche in the foothills of the Andes, where, to our amazement, no one we talked to seemed surprised at all that Hitler had lived there after the Nazi defeat in 1945. Prior to this research, two Argentine investigators whom we met, Capt. Manuel Monasterio and Abel Basti, had followed and uncovered trails of many "sightings" of

Hitler in Argentina. Capt. Monasterio published his book, *Hitler murío en la Argentina (Hitler Died in Argentina),* in 1987, and although he admits he made part of it up—to avoid trouble with the Argentine authorities at the time—he insists that the most salient points are true.

Much of Basti's work is more difficult to accept. Basti's website and books carry a picture of a man alleged to be Hitler in old age. It was sent to him by an unidentified source who had found it on the Internet. Basti presents this photo as proof of Hitler's survival. The same expert who spotted the March 20, 1945, fake has checked the photo scientifically for us. Although superficially an aged look-alike, the facial features do not stand up to scrutiny; it is not Hitler. The same is true about a passport alleged by Basti to be that of Martin Bormann. Of Uruguayan origin and issued in Genoa, Italy, it was in the name of Ricardo Bauer—a known alias of Bormann in the postwar era. It carried a thumbprint and a picture of a man who looked superficially like Bormann. We had the print checked against Bormann's known fingerprints from the Interpol files by a police expert, and we had the picture tested. Neither belonged to Hitler's faithful right-hand man.

However, video interviews with eyewitnesses filmed in the 1990s while Basti was working for *Ambito Financiero,* one of Argentina's most respected daily newspapers, are compelling. It is the words of these witnesses, on a tape given to us by the paper's editorial director Ricardo D'Aloia, that have contributed to the findings published in this book.

In over twenty research trips to Argentina, a beautiful country full of wonderful people, one thing has always surprised us: everyone we spoke to about the possibility of Hitler living there after the war believes it was eminently possible and in many cases definitely true.

It is often dropped into conversation quite innocently. On one investigative trip, we were in the city of Córdoba planning a foray to the dilapidated Hotel Viena on the shores of Mar Chiquita, a large inland salt lake. We asked the young receptionist at our hotel for the best route from Argentina's second city to Mar Chiquita. Without knowing why we were going to Mar Chiquita, she took our map and politely showed our interpreter the best route to get there. After we had finished with the map, she said to us, "Oh, you must try the fish—it's sea fish in the middle of Argentina! And then if you're bored you can visit the Hotel Viena where Hitler and his wife used to stay after the war."

Similar stories greeted us throughout our trips. On April 20, 2007, we were in San Carlos de Bariloche smoking cigarettes outside the town's casino. A man in his seventies approached us and asked for a light and then, somewhat incongruously, inquired if we were South African. Explaining that Gerrard was Welsh and Simon English, we asked him where he was from. "Chile," he replied, explaining that he ran a fish-farming business there. We offered him a cigarette and commented that Bariloche felt very German—there were a lot of German speakers everywhere, much of the food, architecture, and culture was Germanic, and many of the street names were in German. He replied that the place was full of Nazis, particularly tonight, the anniversary of the Führer's birthday. He should know, he said; his father was the gauleiter (Nazi Party regional leader) of Hamburg, Germany, and when Hitler visited Hamburg he would always stay at their home. With a cheerful auf Wiedersehen, he then walked off into the night. We had scores of similar encounters in the deepest reaches of Patagonia, but that is a story in itself.

There is no proof that Adolf Hitler and his "wife" Eva Braun killed themselves in the bunker, and yet the wider world has always believed this. Not everyone seems to have taken it as fact: the Federal Bureau of Investigation under Director J. Edgar Hoover kept files of reports on every sighting of Hitler into the 1960s; the relevant Argentine ones are to be seen in this book. However, many of the FBI's files on Hitler and Eva Braun after the war have not been released, and the same is true of those of the British security services. It should be remembered that Bormann's ruse fooled almost everyone and that Hitler subsequently lived among fellow Nazis and collaborators, many of them also on the run for war crimes. The government of Juan Domingo Perón—and the Peróns themselves—benefited massively from the influx of looted money as well as German experts and scientists. Argentina is a huge country—about the size of the entire United States east of the Mississippi River—and in 1945 there were fewer than 20 million people. Today there are still only 42 million—slightly more than the state of California—approximately 3 million of whom are of German origin. It was easy for Nazis to lose themselves in places where being German was completely normal.

Why did none of the world's intelligence organizations or the Israeli government continue searching for Hitler? The simplest answer is, "Why bother? He was dead." To their lasting shame, the Allied Powers employed numerous Nazi war criminals for their supposed knowledge of the Red Army and Soviet capabilities in the emerging Cold War of the late 1940s. Men such as Klaus Barbie, the Butcher of Lyon, were hired by Western intelligence agencies for years after the war: an inconvenient fact that was suppressed for decades. Most proved to be of little value in the Cold War confrontation with the Soviet Union. Equally troubling, many Nazis were allowed to find new lives in North and South America as well as Australia under government-sponsored emigration schemes in return for their services.

In the case of Israel, the young Jewish state was surrounded by enemies, and its overriding priority was simply survival as a nation. As an indication, the most comprehensive history of Israel's formidable intelligence services runs to 634 pages, yet only three pages are concerned with Nazi hunting in South America. Mossad's eventual capture of Adolf Eichmann came only after repeated requests from concentration camp survivor Lothar Hermann in Argentina, whose daughter had dated one of Eichmann's sons. Hermann had been trying to get both the German and Israeli governments to investigate for a number of years. It has now been proved—after a lengthy court battle in Germany— that the West German intelligence service knew that Eichmann was in Argentina—indeed, knew his address and his pseudonym of Ricardo Klement—as early as 1952, eight years before he was seized and taken to Israel, where he was tried and hanged.

West Germany under Chancellor Konrad Adenauer had good reason to remain quiet on the matter. Adenauer's chief of staff, Hans Globke, had not only helped to draft the 1935 anti-Semitic Nuremberg Laws but had also worked with Eichmann in the Department for Jewish Affairs. Any revelations by Eichmann during his trial in Jerusalem would have been extremely embarrassing to West Germany, since many other government posts, both federal and local, were held by former Nazis who had been cleared of complicity in the Third Reich after a perfunctory "denazification" program in the late 1940s. Many of the most odious Nazi war criminals had found employment in the CIA-funded and SS-dominated "Gehlen Organization," led by former Nazi general Reinhard Gehlen. Indeed, to the British intelligence services the Gehlen Organization was known as the "Gestapo Boys." Such an organization had little vested interest in revealing the whereabouts of other high-ranking Nazis around the world. On the front line of the Cold War, what the West Germans knew, so did the United States and Britain. What other details lurk in the still-secret files of the Gehlen Organization, the forerunner of the West German foreign intelligence agency, the BND? We may never know.

If Eichmann could have been a considerable embarrassment, what would the fact of Hitler's, Bormann's, and Müller's survival do to the West? The world was a dangerous place in the days of two diametrically opposed nuclear-armed superpowers, and Argentina was not high on the intelligence-gathering list of the Soviet Union or the United States, let alone Israel. On the other side of the world, away from important "spheres of influence," Hitler was able to live out his life helped, hidden, and harbored by Perón's fascist friends and thousands of die-hard Nazis who fled to South America after the war.

But probably the most telling comment in our hunt for Hitler and the U-boats that brought him and his stolen loot to Argentina came from the-then Argentine minister of justice and human rights, Señor Aníbal Fernández. As we left his Buenos Aires ministerial office in 2007 after a lengthy interview, he politely shook our hands and said, "In 1945, in Argentina, anything was possible." He was right.

INTRODUCTION

"Who controls the past controls the future."

—GEORGE ORWELL, *1984,* 1949

There is an old saying in police work that applies to most crimes—
"Follow the money."

When Adolf Hitler returned from the Western Front to Munich
ten days after the Armistice of November 11, 1918, his bank account
contained the sum total of 15 marks and 30 pfennigs (pennies)—the
equivalent of less than two U.S. dollars. Despite a public persona of
austerity and selfless service to Germany, Hitler was the wealthiest man
in Europe by 1945. His fortune was based on plunder and extortion.
From the earliest days, Hitler attracted monetary contributions from
German nationalists and industrialists anxious to counter the threat
of communism in the weak and decadent Weimar Republic in the
aftermath of World War I. Once Hitler became chancellor in 1933,
Germany embarked on a massive rearmament program to reconstruct
the German armed forces, denied by the humiliating Treaty of Versailles
of 1919 at the conclusion of World War I. Germany soon became an
attractive prospect for capitalists in America and Britain keen to make
profits and to create a strong Germany as a bulwark in Central Europe
against the threat posed by the communist Soviet Union.

For many years, Hitler's closest and most loyal acolyte was Head
of the Party Chancellery and Reichsleiter (Reich leader) Martin
Bormann. Since Hitler was totally disinterested in administrative matters, Bormann soon ran the Führer's day-to-day diary and his personal
affairs. As an astute businessman and bureaucrat, Bormann quickly
devised numerous schemes to enhance revenues both for the Nazi
Party and Adolf Hitler himself. Long before today's soccer and bas-
ketball players realized the value of their image rights, Bormann raised
a levy on every use of the Führer's likeness, from posters to postage

stamps—Hitler personally obtained several pfennigs for every stamp issued throughout the Third Reich. Similarly, Hitler received a bounty on every ton of steel and barrel of oil produced by the grateful industrialists making fortunes from German rearmament. Both Wall Street and the City of London (London's financial district) were eager to invest in the resurgent German economy despite the excesses of the Nazi regime, and this collusion continued even after war was declared in September 1939.

The Nazi war machine bulldozed all before it in the victorious days of the blitzkrieg campaigns of 1939–41 that reached from the Atlantic Ocean to the gates of Moscow. Most of the nations of Europe were crushed beneath the Nazi jackboot and the tracks of the all-powerful panzers. Once occupied, these countries were unmercifully plundered of their wealth and cultural heritage to feed the coffers of Nazi Germany and satisfy the greed of its corrupt leadership. Between them, Adolf Hitler and Field Marshal Hermann Göring acquired the most extensive and valuable art collections of any individuals ever in history. Similarly, the national treasuries of the occupied countries were looted of their gold bullion and coinage to pay for the raw materials necessary to sustain Germany's war effort. First and foremost, the Nazi Party was a criminal organization and its hierarchy acquired much of this wealth for its own dubious ends, let alone the gold and money extracted from the victims of the Holocaust before they were butchered in the gas chambers of the death camps. Large quantities of gold and precious gems were processed through the neutral countries of Switzerland, Sweden, and Spain, with considerable individual fortunes secreted in the numbered accounts of Swiss banks. There is an old German saying that "Money does not bring happiness unless you have it in a Swiss bank."

By 1943, Martin Bormann realized that the war was lost and the Nazi Party doomed to extinction. He instituted Aktion Adlerflug (Project Eagle Flight) to smuggle gold bullion, gems, and other valuables out of Germany to safe havens around the world, especially in South America. The amount of money was staggering. There was to be no repeat of the Treaty of Versailles, when Germany was stripped of all its possessions and wealth. At the same time, Bormann devised Aktion Feuerland (Project Land of Fire) to secure a safe refuge for the

Nazi leadership. The chosen bolt-hole was in the depths of deepest Patagonia in Argentina. The price was high, but Nazi gold was a powerful inducement. Argentine gold reserves grew from 346 tons in 1940 to 1,173 in 1945—a sum of some $1.4 billion. Brazil's grew from 50 tons to 346 in the same period—an increase of $350 million. As a comparison, the cost of gold in 1945 was $37 an ounce: it is now, at this writing, $1,360 an ounce. Similarly, the purchasing power of the U.S. dollar in 1945 was approximately twelve times what it is today, so all sums quoted in this book must be multiplied by at least a factor of ten to appreciate their true value.

By 1944, the Western Allies were poised for the invasion of northwest Europe with the largest amphibious landings in history on the coastline of Normandy in France. The Allies were well aware of the superiority of German military technology, from the Tiger 1 heavy tank to the Messerschmitt 262 jet fighter, as well as the world's first ballistic missile—the V-2 "Vengeance Weapon." Similarly, the Allies were highly fearful that the Germans might develop the first atomic bomb. Evidence of the extermination of the Jews and other minorities was becoming apparent, as was the plunder of Europe's wealth and famous works of art. Accordingly, the Allies created a host of elite Special Forces units to address each of these problems. Teams of warriors and experts, such as 30 Advance Unit, Monuments Men, TICOM, and the Alsos Mission, were at the vanguard of every Allied army to uncover German military technology, loot, and hidden treasures. Their work was so secret that their extraordinary exploits can be revealed only now after many years hidden in classified documents. These elite units were crucial in the defeat of Germany, and with the subsequent emergence of the Cold War their roles became integral in the struggle against communism. Their quest for Nazi weapons and research projects proved invaluable in the postwar space race and the development of intercontinental ballistic missiles, advanced submarines, and biological warfare agents.

With defeat looming, members of the Nazi hierarchy, such as Reichsführer-SS Heinrich Himmler, tried desperately to achieve a separate peace with the Western Allies, whereby the democratic powers would join forces with Germany to fight the threat of communism as the Red Army rampaged through Eastern Europe. Most of these peace feeler forays were conducted through neutral countries with agents of the British Secret Service, MI6, or the U.S. Office of Strategic Services (OSS). The main OSS center in Europe was in Switzerland and run by Allen Dulles, later director of the Central Intelligence Agency (CIA) between 1953 and 1961. From his offices in Bern, Dulles coordinated hundreds of agents, including several Nazi diplomats, across occupied Europe. In early 1945, Dulles was in direct communication with various Nazi factions and Wehrmacht generals to arrange a separate peace in Italy and Austria in order to shorten the war and end the suffering of millions.

To the end, Bormann was determined to save the looted wealth of Germany for his own nefarious ends and to sustain a select band of Nazis following military defeat and the fall of Berlin. Massive funds were channeled abroad while large stashes of bullion and stolen artworks were hidden underground in deep mines across the Third Reich. These were primed with explosives for demolition, which Bormann considered preferable to allowing them to fall into the hands of the Bolshevik hordes. But to Bormann, the artworks were also a bargaining tool. It seems evident that Bormann offered the OSS a Faustian pact: the fruits of one thousand years of Western art together with the secrets of Nazi Germany's advanced military technology in exchange for the escape of one man—Adolf Hitler. The alternative was the total destruction of the jewels of Western civilization. This was the key to Aktion Feuerland. The deal was done and on the night of April 28, 1945, the plan was put into place. Grey Wolf was on the run.

GREY WOLF

The name Adolf derives from the Old High German for "noble wolf." From early on, Adolf Hitler used the nom de guerre of Wolf. It was a title he used throughout his life. His first mistress, Mitzi Reiter, called him Wolf and it was as Herr Wolf that he was introduced to Eva Braun. To intimates such as the Wagner family, heirs of composer Richard Wagner, he was known as Uncle Wolf. As Hitler became more famous, he had the surname of his younger sister Paula changed to Wolf so that she could live quietly in Vienna while running an arts and crafts shop; she was buried as Paula Wolf at Berchtesgaden when she died in 1960. Hitler's yacht was called *Seewolf* (Sea Wolf) and his personal plane *Fliegende Wolf* (Flying Wolf). His field headquarters in East Prussia was the Wolfschanze (Wolf's Lair); in the Ukraine it was Wehrwolf (Werewolf), while for the battle for France it was the Wolfsschlucht (Wolf's Gorge). Among the most potent of Hitler's weapons during World War II were the wolf packs of U-boats that preyed on Allied shipping. U-boats themselves were known as grey wolves and it was in one of them from a wolf pack code-named Gruppe Seewolf that Hitler escaped to Argentina, where he spent his declining years as the proverbial Grey Wolf.

PART I

THE NAZIS TRIUMPHANT

Chapter 1

FUELING THE BEAST

AT THE BEGINNING OF OCTOBER 1942, the Third Reich was at the zenith of its success. The empire occupied by Hitler's armies stretched from the Arctic Sea of northern Norway all the way south to the deserts of North Africa, and from the Atlantic coast of France eastward to the Volga River, deep inside the Soviet Union. On the North African front of the Wehrmacht (German armed forces), Field Marshal Erwin Rommel's Deutsches Afrika Korps was poised on the border of Egypt for a final offensive to capture the Suez Canal—the vital jugular vein of the British Empire. On the Volga, Gen. von Paulus's Sixth Army was fighting its way yard by yard into the city of Stalingrad in savage street fighting. If the Suez Canal and Stalingrad were to fall to the Germans, then the oil fields of the Middle East and the Caucasus would be theirs for the taking, fueling the German war machine with the essential lifeblood of warfare to sustain itself for decades.

Meanwhile, the ships from Canada and the United States carrying the fuel, the munitions, and the very food that beleaguered Britain needed to sustain itself after three exhausting years of war were being sent to the bottom of the Atlantic in appalling numbers by German submarines. From their bases on the Atlantic coast of France,

Adm. Karl Dönitz's U-boats ranged out to gather in "wolf packs" astride the western sea-lanes. Since January 1940, British experts at the Government Code and Cypher School at Bletchley Park had been increasingly successful in cracking intercepted German signals traffic generated by the "Enigma" encryption machine, producing the stream of priceless top-secret intelligence—code-named "Ultra"—that would give the Allies an extraordinary insight into the intentions and capabilities of Hitler's armed forces. Nevertheless, it was May 1941 before the capture of an Enigma machine and its operating manuals from a U-boat allowed the breaking of the Kriegsmarine (German navy) codes. For a while, British antisubmarine successes had increased encouragingly, but, in February 1942, a modification of the Enigma code-setting system—code-named "Shark" by Bletchley Park—once more denied the Royal Navy its invaluable access to Dönitz's operational orders to his U-boat commanders at sea. The cost of this denial was about to be demonstrated yet again.

ON THE EARLY MORNING of November 2, 1942, a convoy of forty-two ships designated SC-107, heading eastbound out of New York, was approaching the "Black Pit"—the seven-hundred-mile gap in the mid-Atlantic where shipping could not as yet be protected by Allied aircraft. Closing in on the convoy were thirteen U-boats of Gruppe Veilchen (Group Viola). At this time many Allied naval assets had been diverted far south to take part in Operation Torch, the invasion of French North Africa. Convoy SC-107 was protected only by Canadian Escort Group C4, with just one destroyer and four corvettes. Under the cover of darkness and bad weather, two U-boats slipped through the widely stretched cordon of escorts and maneuvered into attack positions. Cdr. Baron Siegfried von Forstner's U-402 fired a salvo of torpedoes at a range of four hundred yards and one struck the freighter SS *Empire Sunrise* amidships, damaging it badly. It would later be finished off by Lt. Cdr. Horst Uphoff's U-84. Lt. Cdr. Herbert Schneider's U-522 also penetrated the escort screen and sank no fewer than four vessels. By dawn, Gruppe Veilchen had sunk eight ships and damaged two more. The U-boats then slipped away to avoid detection but had to remain on the surface in order to keep up with the convoy.

Throughout the following day, convoy SC-107 tried to evade the wolf pack by changing course whenever fog or snowstorms provided any fleeting cover. Soon after the early sunset of November 3, U-89 (Cdr. Dietrich Lohmann) slipped into the center of the convoy and launched five torpedoes. Two of them struck their targets, including the convoy commodore's ship, the 5,318-ton SS *Jeypore*, laden with ammunition. Around midnight, U-132 (Lt. Cdr. Ernst Vogelsang) unleashed a fan of five torpedoes toward the starboard flank of SC-107. Three ships were hit. Thirty minutes later one of these vessels, carrying munitions, exploded with such ferocity that surface ships some six miles away felt the blast and U-boats at depths of two hundred feet were jolted by the shock wave—indeed U-132 and her crew were never heard from again. On November 5, a Royal Air Force B-24 Liberator long-range bomber of No. 120 Squadron arrived overhead and further naval escorts from Iceland rendezvoused with SC-107. When U-89 was damaged by air attack, Gruppe Veilchen broke off the battle. It had won a significant victory: in all, fifteen merchantmen out of forty-two were sunk and four damaged, for a total of 107,958 tons of shipping lost.

During the month of November 1942 alone, a total of 730,000 tons of Allied shipping was sunk. During the whole of 1942, the Allies lost an estimated 1,661 ships and 6.5 million tons of cargo to U-boat attack. About 87 U-boats were sunk but 238 new boats were commissioned and that year saw Dönitz's fleet increased from 91 to 212 boats. Famously, British prime minister Winston Churchill wrote, "The only thing that ever really frightened me during the war was the U-boat peril." He declared, "On their defeat hung the outcome of World War II."

IF THE COSTS OF A WORLD WAR in blood and misery are almost incalculably huge, so they are in treasure—but for the canny and the farsighted, vast deficits also create vast opportunities.

The terms imposed on Germany by the Treaty of Versailles after her defeat in World War I were draconian. Articles 231 to 248, the "war guilt" clauses, stipulated that Germany alone bore complete responsibility for the war and therefore must pay immense reparations to France, Belgium, Britain, and other countries. The sums involved amounted to 132 billion gold marks ($31.4 billion). When Germany defaulted on payments, the French and Belgian armies occupied the Rhineland. The mark collapsed and the economy was saved only by massive loans through Wall Street and other international banks.

In August 1924, the Dawes Plan brokered by the U.S. government imposed a moratorium on reparations and provided a $200 million loan to allow German industrial reconstruction. This elegant solution allowed American money to finance German industry through loans, whereby the German government was able to make reparation payments to Britain and France and they in turn were able to repay America for the loans they had incurred to finance their colossal military expenditures during World War 1. In the decade between 1921 and 1931, international banks provided Germany with some 27 billion marks in loans while the Allies received some 19.1 billion marks in reparations. Created in 1930 specifically for the task, the Bank for International Settlements (BIS) in Basel, Switzerland, staffed by representatives from all the participating nations, supervised the process of reparations.

Two of the American corporate lawyers who were actively engaged in the flow of funds from the United States into Germany were brothers named John Foster and Allen Welsh Dulles. They worked for the prestigious New York law firm of Sullivan & Cromwell. They acted for business clients wishing to invest in German industry or to enter into partnership with established companies. The Dulles brothers, scions of a patrician East Coast family with a tradition of public service, had enviable background experience and contacts for this role. Their uncle was Robert Lansing, who had been U.S. secretary of state under President Woodrow Wilson. During World War I, Allen had served as a State Department attaché in Berlin, Vienna, and Bern in neutral Switzerland, gathering intelligence on the Central Powers. At the invitation of "Uncle Bert" Lansing, both the Dulles brothers had been members of the U.S. commission at the Paris Peace Conference (1919–20) that had culminated in the Treaty of Versailles.

American corporations such as the Aluminum Company of America (Alcoa), DuPont, International Business Machines (IBM), General Motors, International Telephone & Telegraph (ITT), the Ford Motor Company, and General Electric made significant investments in Germany. Joint enterprises were created to exchange technical innovations and to divide market shares around the world. This led to the merging of existing German companies into powerful and influential conglomerates, such as Interessen-Gemeinschaft Farbenindustrie (IG Farben), which was founded in 1925. IG Farben was a market leader in the manufacture of chemicals, dyes, pharmaceuticals, explosives, rubber, and a host of other products—indeed, IG Farben was the prototypical "military-industrial complex." In April 1929, Standard Oil of New Jersey joined forces with IG Farben to develop a hydrogenation process for converting coal to oil. Again, American money funded the research and development in Germany while the world markets were to be shared between the two companies. In return, IG Farben promised to provide the technical specifications for its new "buna" process for the production of synthetic rubber, a vital strategic resource for both countries. As America's stake in Germany expanded, so U.S. government officials were less inclined to support the repeated demands for reparations by France and Britain, for fear of jeopardizing American investments.

EVERYTHING CHANGED WITH THE WALL STREET CRASH of 1929. That October, America's financial system collapsed and the world was plunged into the Great Depression. With its mountain of international debt and its weak and unstable political institutions, Germany's Weimar Republic was especially vulnerable. In 1929, the National Socialist German Workers' Party (NSDAP or Nazi Party) boasted just 120,000 members. As the economic situation deteriorated, the party's popularity grew as a strident force promising the frightened petite bourgeoisie protection against hunger, anarchy, and the perceived menace of communism. In the elections of 1932, the Nazis won a majority of seats in the Reichstag (Parliament) with a popular vote of 37.3 percent. As a result, Adolf Hitler became Reichskanzler (national chancellor or prime minister) on January 30, 1933.

During that month the Dulles brothers were in Germany on behalf of clients of Sullivan & Cromwell, both American and German. The latter included IG Farben, Robert Bosch GmbH, and Vereinigte Stahlwerke AG (United Steelworks), which was run by the leading

German industrial families of Fritz Thyssen and Friedrich Flick. The steel magnate Fritz Thyssen had been a major contributor to Nazi funds during the 1932 elections. In early 1933, the Dulles brothers met Hitler to determine business prospects under the prospective government. Hitler's determination to embark on a massive rearmament program provided even more opportunities for America to do business in the Third Reich. Later, at a Berlin reception given by Thyssen, Allen Dulles met Martin Bormann, an ambitious Nazi bureaucrat assiduously seeking favor with the Führer. He later recalled that Bormann was not the "grubby, uncivilized man" he had been led to expect: "He was soft-spoken and direct, but while he talked to you his eyes continued to keep watch on Hitler and those surrounding him. I felt he was a man of strength who might one day best his more colorful rivals in the Nazi hierarchy." It was a remarkably prescient observation.

Within weeks of Hitler's appointment as chancellor, an attempt to burn down the Reichstag building gave him the excuse to rush through emergency legislation suspending civil liberties, freedom of the press, and regional autonomy. The last multiparty election, held on March 5, 1933, returned the Nazi Party with 44 percent of the vote. The first concentration camp for political prisoners was opened on March 22, at Dachau near Munich. On the following day, an enabling act was passed that allowed Hitler to rule Germany by decree as an unfettered dictator. In an irony too gross to need stressing, the act's full title, Gesetz zur Behebung der Not von Volk und Reich, literally meant "The Law to Remedy the Distress of the People and the Nation."

In the same month, Franklin D. Roosevelt became the thirty-second president of the United States. The country was still mired in the Depression. America's focus turned inward as President Roosevelt launched his "New Deal" with a raft of legislation and executive orders to promote jobs for the unemployed and recovery for the economy. Germany followed suit with a program of public works, including the construction of an extensive arterial highway system known as *Autobahnen*. The autobahns also had a significant military purpose, as they greatly enhanced the vital process of rapidly moving supplies and equipment from the interior of Germany to support military forces on the country's frontiers in time of war. However, because rearmament was the major priority in German industry there were very few automobiles on the new highways, despite Hitler's pledge to manufacture a car for the people—the Volkswagen.

The Ford Motor Company and General Motors were happy to fill the gap in the market. Henry Ford greatly expanded the supply of components sent from America to the Ford Motor Company AG in Cologne, and between 1934 and 1938 its revenues soared by 400 percent. The Nazi regime was so impressed that the company was officially recognized as a German rather than a foreign-owned firm; as Ford-Werke AG it became eligible for government contracts. Since 1936, when Hermann Göring was appointed head of the Four-Year Plan to prepare the German economy for war, rearmament had shifted into high gear. Just prior to the occupation of the Czech Sudetenland in October 1938, when Ford-Werke AG was unable to meet the demands of the Wehrmacht for military trucks, Ford Motor Company dispatched vehicles from America to Cologne in kit form to be assembled during extra night shifts. Hitler was a great admirer of Henry Ford. For his services to Nazi Germany, in 1938 the American magnate was presented with the Grand Cross of the Order of the German Eagle, the Third Reich's highest civilian award for which foreigners were eligible, of which only fourteen were ever awarded.

Another recipient of the German decoration in 1938 was James Mooney, the chief executive of overseas operations for General Motors, who was awarded the Order of the German Eagle, First Class. In 1931, General Motors had acquired Opel, Germany's largest automobile manufacturer, in its entirety. By 1935, Opel AG of Russelsheim was producing more than 100,000 cars a year and almost 50 percent of the new trucks in Germany at a plant in Brandenburg. The most important of these products was the range of trucks known as the Opel Blitz (Lightning)—which would in fact be the Wehrmacht's most numerous workhorse during the victorious years of blitzkrieg. By the late 1930s, car production for the masses was no longer a priority. In addition to truck production, many Opel factories were converted to the production of Junkers Jumo aircraft engines and the complex "pistol" detonators for naval torpedoes such as those that sank the ships of convoy SC-107.

FORD AND GENERAL MOTORS were only two of the foreign companies that invested heavily in Germany and thus ultimately aided the Nazi war effort. Oil was always to be the Achilles' heel of Hitler's war machine. During the 1930s, the British-owned Anglo-Persian Oil Company (later British Petroleum, or BP) and the Royal Dutch Shell conglomerate were extensively involved in oil refining in Germany, while the British tire company Dunlop had extensive investments in the German rubber industry. There was already a fine line between taking advantage of sound business opportunities and aiding the possible future enemy. The Ethyl Gasoline Corporation (owned jointly by General Motors and Standard Oil) developed a critical additive to increase the octane rating of aviation fuel. It was against the specific wishes of the U.S. War Department regarding the transfer of strategic materials and technical knowledge that an agreement was reached between IG Farben and Ethyl Gasoline; production began in 1935 at a jointly owned factory, IG Ethyl GmbH. This product was of immense value to the Luftwaffe (German air force) in boosting the performance of its aircraft engines—some of which were built by a subsidiary of General Motors, fitted to airframes made of metals manufactured by Alcoa, in aircraft using radios and electronic equipment built by ITT, and flying on fuel derived by the hydrogenation process funded by Standard Oil of New Jersey. These were the aircraft that would devastate Guernica, Warsaw, Rotterdam, and Coventry.

As Britain fought for her life in 1940, some 300 American companies continued doing business as usual with Germany, and they did not automatically stop even after Germany declared war on the United States on December 11, 1941. In that year, 171 U.S. corporations still had over $420 million invested in German industry. It was only after the promulgation of the Trading with the Enemy Act of 1942 that most companies ceased direct business with Germany, but the profits to be made from the trade in oil and other strategic materials were still too tempting for some. The cartels created in the aftermaths of World War I and the Great Depression were now more powerful than many governments, and these international corporations were so deeply intertwined that national identity became increasingly opaque. This would be a major factor in the later German execution, under the direction of Martin Bormann, of Aktion Feuerland—Project Land of Fire.

ON THE SAME DAY THAT CONVOY SC-107 was first attacked by Gruppe Veilchen, a minor diplomat left Washington, D.C., bound for the American legation in Bern, Switzerland. Like the capitals of the other neutral European countries—Lisbon, Madrid, and Stockholm—Bern was a hotbed of espionage and multinational intrigue. The American diplomat's circuitous journey took him by air to the Azores and then via Lisbon and Madrid to the border of Vichy France; he arrived in neutral Switzerland two days after Operation Torch put Allied troops ashore in Algeria and Morocco on November 8, 1942. The American was the aforementioned Allen Welsh Dulles and his appointment was as the special assistant for legal affairs to Ambassador Leland Harrison. His real role was as the head of the newly formed Special Intelligence branch of the Office of Strategic Services (OSS)—in effect, America's master spy inside Nazi-occupied Europe. Within weeks, Swiss newspapers were declaring that Allen Dulles was "the personal representative of President Roosevelt, charged with special duties"—a thin veil of euphemism for espionage.

At the outbreak of war in September 1939, the United States had no central foreign intelligence service that reported directly to the executive office of the president in the White House. The original U.S. government code-breaking operation had been run by the MI-8 section of the State Department, but that had been shut down in 1929 by Secretary of State Henry Stimson with the comment that "gentlemen do not read each other's mail."

Each of the armed services had its own intelligence branch, as did the State Department, but coordination of information was almost nonexistent before the creation of the Joint Intelligence Committee on December 9, 1941, two days after Pearl Harbor. As a case in point, when American cryptanalysts unraveled the intricacies of the Japanese diplomatic cipher known as "Purple," neither the U.S. Army's G-2 Signals Intelligence Service nor the U.S. Navy's Office of Naval Intelligence OP-20-G section was willing or capable of cooperating in the decryption of this vital intelligence source. Such was the interservice rivalry that the army exclusively decoded material on even days of the month and the navy on odd days. Similarly, the world itself was divided up into spheres of influence that were specific to a particular service. Thus the U.S. Navy was charged with intelligence-gathering in the Pacific region and Far East while the U.S. Army was entrusted with Europe, Africa, and the Panama Canal Zone. The whole of continental America, including Canada, the United States, Central America (except Panama), and South America, was the responsibility of the Federal Bureau of Investigation (FBI) under J. Edgar Hoover.

On July 11, 1941, with war looming, President Roosevelt created the first civilian-run agency tasked with gathering foreign diplomatic and military intelligence worldwide. The first director of this Office of the Coordinator of Information (COI) was one of Roosevelt's old classmates from Columbia Law School, William J. Donovan. A recipient of the Medal of Honor in World War I, "Wild Bill" Donovan was a successful Wall Street lawyer who had traveled extensively in Europe during the interwar years, meeting several foreign leaders, including Adolf Hitler. On a mission from Roosevelt in July 1940, he had been given extraordinary access to Britain's leaders and security agencies, including the secret code-breaking establishment at Bletchley Park.

After America's entry into World War II, there was a thorough reappraisal of the U.S. armed forces and particularly the intelligence services that had failed to forewarn of the attack on Pearl Harbor. Accordingly, the COI was split. Its propaganda wing, the Foreign Information Service, passed to the new Office of War Information, while the remainder became the Office of Strategic Services, coming directly under the control of the U.S. Joint Chiefs of Staff—a group of high command staff newly formed of necessity but not formally established until 1947. The OSS was created, under Donovan's directorship, by a military order of June 13, 1942. Now with greater access to military support and resources, the OSS was given equal status to the other armed services. Its principal roles were to gather military, diplomatic, and commercial intelligence, to conduct psychological warfare, to support friendly resistance and partisan movements in Axis-occupied countries, and to launch covert operations, both in Europe and in the China-Burma-India theater.

Donovan immediately set about obtaining new recruits for the OSS. As happens so often with elite organizations, among the many highly motivated men and women attracted by the prospect of adventure were a significant number drawn from the higher echelons of society. These volunteers included Morgans, Mellons, Du Ponts, Roosevelts, and Vanderbilts—indeed, the OSS soon achieved such a cachet that it was dubbed "Oh So Social, Oh So Secret." The service also attracted several left-wing sympathizers, such as the German immigrant and Marxist philosopher Herbert Marcuse. When challenged, however, Donovan responded forcefully, "I'd put Stalin on the OSS payroll if I thought it would help defeat Hitler." One of the first recruits was Donovan's old friend and collaborator Allen Dulles, who had formerly been his head of operations in the COI.

ON OCTOBER 30, 1942, a week before Allen Dulles arrived in Bern, the badly damaged German submarine U-559 (Lt. Cdr. Hans Heidtmann) was abandoned by its crew under the guns of the Royal Navy destroyer HMS *Petard* off the coast of Egypt. A British officer and two seamen swam across and risked their lives to clamber down inside. Two of them were dragged down to their deaths when the U-boat sank, but a sixteen-year-old canteen assistant named Tommy Brown survived—and with him, vital operating manuals for the latest four-rotor Enigma machine. This act of sacrificial courage won for Bletchley Park the means to begin breaking, on December 13, 1942, the Shark codes that had defied the cryptanalysts since February. Their success was far from immediate and for months they could only decrypt U-boat signals after long delays, but by September 1943 they would be producing Ultra intelligence at their former speed. At the outset, the British were reluctant to share such sensitive information with their American counterparts in the OSS, but in time their cooperation gave birth to a massive signals intelligence-gathering organization that became one of the great Anglo-American achievements of the war.

Chapter 2

THE TURNING TIDE

ALLEN DULLES ONCE WROTE, in a letter to his mother, "Bern is the diplomatic and spy center. . . . I now hobnob with all sorts of outlandish people—Czechs, Yugoslavs, Albanians, Montenegrins, Ukrainians. . . . There is a chance to do as much here as if one were shooting personally a whole regiment of Bosche [sic]." That letter was dated Christmas 1917, when Dulles was twenty-four. A quarter of a century later Dulles was once again in Bern at Christmas, back in the business of cultivating "all sorts of outlandish people."

He had reached Switzerland just in time. On November 11, 1942, the Germans retaliated for the halfhearted French resistance to the Allied landings in North Africa by occupying the remainder of France, previously ruled by Marshal Pétain's Vichy government. Thereafter, all France's borders were sealed. Switzerland was now a vulnerable island, surrounded by Nazi and Italian Fascist territory. This made the task of communicating with London or Washington much more difficult. All diplomatic mail ceased, all telephone lines and radio communications were monitored, and Dulles lacked the staff for efficient encryption of messages.

Originally, "Wild Bill" Donovan had asked Dulles to go to London to coordinate between the OSS and British intelligence. Dulles had demurred and instead suggested that he set up a Special Intelligence station for the OSS in Switzerland. His motives were mixed. Obviously, he knew the city and the country well and he spoke very passable German. On a personal level, Bern held much more attraction than blitzed London for a bon vivant who enjoyed fine food and wines and the company of young women. Furthermore, Switzerland was the nexus of clandestine business and banking activities in occupied Europe. As a successful lawyer for Sullivan & Cromwell, Dulles was well qualified to monitor such activities both for the U.S. government and for his corporate clients. But above all, Bern was the ideal location to conduct espionage. It provided Dulles with what he later described as his "big window" into the Nazi world.

Dulles was often to be found taking lunch at the Theater Café or dining at the Hotel Bellevue Palace, where foreign diplomats and Swiss officials liked to congregate and exchange gossip or intelligence. At the age of fifty, he had the air of a college professor, with his tweed jackets, bow ties, and briar pipes, and his easy charm made him congenial company. He had time for everyone, whatever the time of day. In his own words, his open attitude had the result of "bringing to my door purveyors of information, volunteers and adventurers of every sort, professional and amateur spies, good and bad." At night, he held court in the book-lined study of his comfortable residence at Herrengasse 23, offering a discreet welcome to any furtive visitor wishing anonymity.

Despite his talent for being all things to all men, however, Dulles did have considerable antipathy toward the British. After leaving Princeton in 1914, he had briefly worked as a teacher in India, where he had acquired a visceral loathing for the British Empire—a sentiment shared by many in the American establishment. The British intelligence community, for its part, was somewhat suspicious of his casual manner and lavish lifestyle, but, as professionals, both parties were willing to cooperate when their interests coincided. Even so, as Dulles later recalled, he was never averse to "putting one over the Brits."

DULLES SOON ACHIEVED some notable successes. After the occupation of Vichy France, all the local agents of the Deuxième Bureau (French secret service) agreed to work with him provided that they were financed by the OSS. Dulles thus enjoyed a constant flow of intelligence from occupied France that would be much prized by Allied planners during the preparations for the Normandy landings and the subsequent liberation of Western Europe. He learned of the existence of Hitler's program to produce "Vengeance Weapons"—the V-1 and V-2 missiles—and when this information was combined with intelligence from Polish and Scandinavian sources and the RAF Photographic Interpretation Unit, it allowed the RAF to bomb the German research and testing facility at Peenemünde in August 1943 (see Chapter 8).

Allen Dulles was a master at cultivating people as potential spies across all sectors of society and nationalities. His sources included diplomats, financiers, clergymen, journalists, and intelligence agents from around the world. At one end of the spectrum, he gained information from the bargemen plying the River Rhine through Germany and Switzerland. At the other, he met regularly with Carl Jung, the famous Swiss psychiatrist who provided psychological profiles of the Nazi leadership and applied his innovative concept of the "collective unconscious" to an analysis of the German people. However, it was Dulles's contacts with disaffected Germans that proved the most profitable.

Not the least of these was Fritz Kolbe, a senior diplomat in the Reich Foreign Ministry who was code-named "George Wood" by the OSS. Kolbe was rejected by the British as an obvious plant. Dulles cultivated him assiduously and, over time, obtained some 1,600 Foreign Ministry policy documents that gave invaluable insights into Hitler's war plans and the Third Reich's international relationships. Among the intelligence provided by Kolbe was a highly detailed sketch of Hitler's field headquarters in a forest near Rastenburg, East Prussia (present-day Kętrzyn, Poland)—the Wolfschanze or Wolf's Lair—including the exact locations of the antiaircraft defenses and the buildings used by Göring and Goebbels. Although Hitler spent a large proportion of his time at the Wolfschanze during the war, the Allies did not bomb it once.

On January 15, 1943, Dulles was visited by an old acquaintance, Prince Maximilian Egon zu Hohenlohe-Langenburg, whose Liechtenstein passport allowed him to travel the world unimpeded. The prince had innumerable contacts with high officials across Europe, especially in Berlin, and most notably with Reichsführer-SS Heinrich Himmler, who orchestrated the prince's meeting with Dulles. The proposition that the prince wished to float before Dulles was simple, if startling: in the name of civilization, Himmler's SS would eliminate Hitler, after which Germany would join forces with the Western democracies in a global war against Soviet communism. True to his methods, Dulles allowed himself to appear interested but made no commitment, keeping his options open for future dialogue with the SS and the Nazi hierarchy.

Among his other SS contacts was an Austrian aristocrat, SS Capt. Reinhard Spitzy, who was SS adjutant to Foreign Minister Joachim von Ribbentrop. Spitzy subsequently served with the Amt Ausland/ Abwehr im Oberkommando der Wehrmacht (Foreign Affairs/ Supreme Command of the Armed Forces or OKW), or Abwehr—the German military intelligence organization, headed until February 1944 by the formidable Adm. Wilhelm Canaris. However, it was through the German vice-consul in Zurich, Hans Bernd Gisevius, that Dulles gained a channel to the Abwehr. Canaris, known as the "Old Fox," had been the head of the Abwehr since 1935 and was one of the most enigmatic figures of the Third Reich. Fluent in several languages, he had been involved in intelligence work throughout his long naval career. He was a brilliant spymaster but he also ensured that his closest colleagues were not members of the Nazi Party. Since before the outbreak of war, Canaris had been active in the resistance movement of Germans attempting at first to frustrate and then to overthrow Hitler—a group known to the Gestapo as the Schwarze Kappelle (Black Orchestra) and to the OSS as "Breakers."

Canaris, like Heinrich Himmler, sought to discover the probable attitude of the Western Allies if and when Hitler was removed or killed. Canaris needed to know what support might be forthcoming for the conspiracy itself or in the political aftermath once the deed was done. Mindful of Dulles's proclivities, he directed one of his resident agents in Switzerland, Halina Szymańska, the widow of a Polish officer, to develop a relationship with the American. Providentially, she was Canaris's close companion during his visits to Switzerland, so pillow talk proved beneficial to both sides. Szymańska was also Canaris's liaison with British intelligence—it was through her that Canaris had informed the British in late 1940 of Hitler's plans for the invasion of the Soviet Union. However, Canaris's attempts to sound out Washington and London about a possible future for a Germany without the Führer came to nothing. Neither leadership was willing to support any resistance movement inside Germany or any plot to kill Hitler and neither had any sympathy for conspirators whom President Roosevelt dismissed as "these east German Junkers."

For months, the British code-breakers at Bletchley Park had been deciphering Dulles's cables, and the transcripts were in the hands of the British Foreign Office's Secret Intelligence Service or MI6. In disparaging reports, Dulles was described as "a Yankee Doodle Dandy blow-in who has little to provide in real intelligence" and "seems to get too excited about small successes." But one MI6 officer took a different view of the transcripts—the British traitor Kim Philby. He immediately dispatched a report on Dulles's activities to his controller in Moscow. The response he received was clear: Dulles and his informers must be discredited—Moscow was paranoid about any possibility of the Western Allies negotiating a separate peace.

Some time thereafter, Dulles received a telegram from his superiors in the OSS: "It has been requested of us to inform you that 'all news from Berne these days is being discounted 100 percent by the War Department.' It is suggested that Switzerland is an ideal location for plants, tendentious intelligence and peace feelers, but no details are given." Dulles was mortified that policy-makers in Washington were dismissing his intelligence-gathering operations, and when he discovered the part played by MI6, his distrust of the British intensified. He became determined that his future operations would exclude any meaningful British participation. Nevertheless, he continued building up his web of contacts across Europe and in the Middle East. Bern remained an important center of OSS operations in Europe and Allen Dulles remained at the center of the web.

OPERATION TORCH, THE ANGLO-AMERICAN INVASION of French North Africa, began on November 8, 1942, when 100,000 Allied troops landed in Morocco and Algeria against spasmodic French resistance. Under the command of Gen. Dwight D. Eisenhower, the landings were a complete success and a ceasefire was arranged on November 11—the same day that Hitler responded with the occupation of Vichy France. Operation Torch coincided with the first major British land victory of the war, at El Alamein on the Libyan-Egyptian frontier, where Gen. Bernard Montgomery's Eighth Army inflicted a major defeat on Rommel and forced his Afrika Korps into headlong retreat. As the New Year of 1943 dawned, the German forces in North Africa were confined to a diminishing enclave centered on Tunisia, with the British Eighth Army advancing from the east and the U.S. Fifth and British First armies from the west. Heavy fighting would continue over the following months as the German-Italian Armeegruppe Afrika fought to the last, but surrender became inevitable. On May 12, 1943, a last radio message was transmitted: "All ammunition spent. Weapons and equipment destroyed. In accordance with its orders, the Afrika Korps has battled on until it can fight no more. We shall rise again." The message signed off with the Swahili battle cry that had been adopted by the Afrika Korps—"*Heia Safari!*" (roughly translating as "Tallyho!"). In this last African campaign, some 60,000 Axis soldiers had died and 240,000 went into captivity. Despite the brave words about rising again, the German troops dubbed this disaster "Tunisgrad."

ON THE DAY THAT VICHY FRANCE WAS OCCUPIED, the German Sixth Army's last assault through the rubble of Stalingrad ground to a halt in the appalling conditions of the Wehrmacht's second Russian winter. At the end of their enormously extended lines of supply, ammunition and all other essentials were running short. One week later, on November 19, Gen. Georgi Zhukov launched Operation Uranus with major offensives to the north and south of Stalingrad. By November 22, the Sixth Army was surrounded. Out of bravado or sheer ignorance, Marshal Hermann Göring promised Hitler that his Luftwaffe could supply the trapped army by air. The daily minimum requirement of supplies needed to sustain the Sixth was 550 tons, but the Luftwaffe rarely exceeded 300 tons and, as the weather worsened, with temperatures dropping to −22°F in mid-January, deliveries diminished to just 30 tons a day. The freezing German soldiers subsisted on a few slices of bread and a small hunk of horse meat daily and were soon suffering from dysentery and typhoid. The fighting continued until February 2, when the last defenders inside the Red October Factory laid down their arms. The German forces suffered 750,000 casualties over that dreadful Russian winter, and of the 94,000 who were captured at Stalingrad just 5,000 would ever see Germany again.

The Red Army had paid an immense price for the defense, encirclement, and final recapture of Stalingrad, losing almost 500,000 killed or missing and a staggering 650,000 wounded—to say nothing of a further 40,000 civilians dead. Yet these horrendous sacrifices had bought the Soviet Union a genuinely pivotal victory. For the first time, a whole German army had been decisively beaten and then destroyed on the battlefield. To mark this unprecedented reverse on the Eastern Front, Radio Berlin played somber music for three days, but it would take much longer than that for the German people to come to terms with the catastrophe. The prestige of the Red Army soared, both in the Motherland and in the Western democracies. Basking in the glory of the victory at the city named after him, Stalin grew in stature both at home and abroad—and his repeated demands for the opening of a second front in Europe by the Western Allies, to relieve the pressure on the Soviet Union, became more insistent.

IN JANUARY 1943, ALL THE GREAT POWER LEADERS had been invited to attend a conference in the Moroccan coastal city of Casablanca. Stalin declined, since the battle for Stalingrad was then reaching its climax. Between January 14 and 24, President Roosevelt and Prime Minister Churchill, together with the Combined Chiefs of Staff, met at the Anfa Hotel to decide the future strategy for the war in the West and in the Pacific. Churchill was anxious for the war in Europe to be given top priority and his view prevailed. More resources were to be allocated to fight the Battle of the Atlantic, since Britain's very survival and America's ability to deploy armies in Europe depended on defeating the U-boat threat. Despite Stalin's urgings, the outcome of the disastrous Dieppe raid in August 1942 had confirmed that a major landing on the coast of mainland Northwest Europe simply was not feasible during 1943. Instead, once the anticipated victory in North Africa was achieved, Allied forces were to invade first the island of Sicily and then Italy.

In order to mollify Stalin, the Western Allies issued the Casablanca Directive, which dealt with the closer coordination of the strategic bombing offensive against Germany by the Royal Air Force and the U.S. Army Air Force. The objective set for the Joint Bombing Program was "the progressive destruction and dislocation of the German military, industrial, and economic system, and the undermining of the morale of the German people to the point where their capacity for armed resistance is fatally weakened." The priority targets were U-boat construction yards and operating bases, followed by the German aircraft industry, the transportation system, and all oil-producing facilities. The USAAF retained its faith in daylight precision-bombing missions against specific point targets while the RAF preferred area bombing by night. This combined Operation Pointblank would condemn Germany to round-the-clock aerial bombardment on an unprecedented scale, testing the will of the German people to the utmost.

However, there was one aspect of the Casablanca Conference that did not meet with full accord. President Roosevelt retained a deep disgust for the German military caste that he dismissed as "the Vons," and he would not countenance any sort of deal with a German government short of unconditional surrender. Neither Churchill nor the Combined Chiefs of Staff were at ease with such a strategy, but Roosevelt remained adamant and in this his will prevailed, just as Churchill's had over the planned Italian campaign. Citing the implacable resolve of Ulysses S. Grant—"Unconditional Surrender Grant"—during the American Civil War, Roosevelt required a complete and unequivocal victory over Germany. There was to be no repeat of the armistice that had ended the Great War with German troops still on French soil. Its result had been a widespread illusion during the interwar years that the German army had remained undefeated on the battlefield and that Germany was only forced to capitulate by devious politicians.

Objections to the policy of unconditional surrender were advanced by, among others, Roosevelt's U.S. Army chief of staff, Gen. George C. Marshall, and his rising field commander Gen. Eisenhower, on the grounds that it would inevitably increase the resolve of German armies on the battlefield. The intelligence community recognized that the policy would effectively scupper any real dialogue with or support for the resistance movement inside Germany, since its leaders would know that even the death of Hitler would not spare their country from utter ruin and humiliation. As Allen Dulles wrote, "We rendered impossible internal revolution in Germany, and thereby prolonged the war and the destruction." Apart from Stalin, the only belligerent leaders whose interests were served by this decision were the Nazi hierarchy.

Chapter 3

THE BROWN EMINENCE

AFTER THE STAGGERING SETBACKS of Stalingrad and North Africa, it was vital to galvanize the dispirited German people for a protracted war. Hitler's complete military strategy had been predicated on a short conflict of conquest before the material superiority of his opponents—France and Britain, then the Soviet Union—became overwhelming. The era of rapid victories in 1938–42 had allowed Germany to loot raw materials, agricultural production, and industrial capacity from Czechoslovakia, Poland, Denmark, Norway, Holland, Belgium, France, Yugoslavia, Greece, and the western USSR. These years of pillage had delayed the tipping point after which the imbalance of resources between the Allies and the Axis became at first chronic and then terminal; but they had gained Germany only capital—not a revenue stream—and the point of no return had now been reached.

Nazi Germany entered spring 1943 with no coherent overall military strategy to prosecute the war further. The failure of the invasion of the USSR was already obvious for the world to see. In May 1943, due to a combination of Allied technical and operational advances, the monthly losses suffered by U-boats in the Atlantic suddenly tripled. This forced Adm. Dönitz to withdraw his wolf packs from the convoy lanes for three months; they would never recover their dominance. In June and July 1943, the first RAF Thousand-Bomber raids devastated cities such as Essen, Cologne, and Hamburg, and during that summer USAAF daylight raids penetrated deep into Germany to hit industrial targets, drawing Luftwaffe fighter squadrons back from other fronts. In July, the defeat of a new German offensive around Kursk in the Ukraine finally crushed any hope of regaining the initiative on the Eastern Front. Also in July, the Western Allies successfully invaded Sicily, and in September, Italy became the first of the Axis nations to sue for peace. In the coming winter nights the RAF's baleful focus would shift to Berlin itself—in November alone, 400,000 Berliners were rendered homeless. Despite occupying most of Europe, German forces were now wholly on the defensive and trapped in a war of attrition, reduced to waiting, with dwindling resources, for the Allies to unleash new offensives in the east, the south, and the west. Moreover, there was simply no coherent mechanism for addressing Germany's situation. The Führer's word was absolute and there was no one in the Nazi hierarchy or the armed forces to contradict him.

The German regime's response to the disaster of Stalingrad and President Roosevelt's demand for unconditional surrender was a call for "total war." In a widely reported speech given to the Berlin Nazi Party in the Sportpalast (Sports Palace) on February 18, 1943, the Reich minister of propaganda, Dr. Joseph Goebbels, demanded of his audience and the German people their complete commitment to "*der totaler Krieg*." Warning that "two thousand years of Western history are in danger," Goebbels called for even greater sacrifices in support of the Wehrmacht, the last defenders against the Bolshevik hordes that were threatening the territory and the very cultural identity of Europe. To this end, he called for the full mobilization of the German economy and the German people for the exclusive support of the war effort. On the podium with Goebbels was Albert Speer, Reich minister of armaments and war production. Speer was desperate to put the mismanaged German economy on a proper war footing, but was frustrated by a lack of skilled workers. In the face of ever-wider military conscription and Hitler's reluctance to mobilize Germany's women for the same sort of effort that Britain and America had made, much of industry was dependent upon slave labor from the East and conscripted workers from the occupied countries of Europe.

Hermann Göring, that great collector of titles, had proved equally incompetent in the position of Reich commissioner for the Four-Year Plan as he was in strategic command of the Luftwaffe. Sensing that Göring—after the failure of his boast that he could sustain the Sixth Army at Stalingrad—was falling out of favor with Hitler, Goebbels and Speer tried to persuade Hitler to dismiss him so they could take over control of the domestic economy for more efficient war production. This attempt soon failed, however, in a welter of other plots. In the turmoil following Stalingrad, pent-up rivalries among the hierarchy came boiling to the surface.

Having the ear of Hitler, Party Chief Reichsleiter Martin Bormann suggested that a triumvirate representing the state, the party, and the armed forces be established as a Council of Three with dictatorial powers to control the economy—exactly what Goebbels and Speer were proposing for themselves. They immediately changed tack and now sought an alliance with Göring and Himmler to thwart Bormann. But Himmler was in a separate plot with Bormann to gain more power at the expense of Göring. As the controller of Hitler's personal finances, Bormann finessed the plotters by giving Göring six million reichsmarks to indulge himself away from Hitler's court. In the end, none of these plots succeeded in its object since Hitler was indifferent to such ploys beyond creating divisions among his acolytes.

IN THE WORDS OF DR. OTTO DIETRICH, the Reich press chief, "Hitler created in the political leadership of Germany the greatest confusion that has ever existed in a civilized state." The plots and counterplots of 1943 were a prime example of how Hitler exercised his absolute power by fomenting fierce rivalries among his immediate subordinates so that none could ever acquire sufficient power or influence to challenge the Führer himself. Indeed, such episodes represent the whole Nazi regime in microcosm.

The popular perception holds that the Third Reich was a monolithic totalitarian state that controlled a reluctant population through terror and Teutonic efficiency. While the reign of terror was real enough, the government institutions of the Third Reich were in fact massively inefficient, hampered by conflicts of interest and muddled chains of command and absurdly wasteful of money, time, and manpower. Hitler showed little interest in or talent for administration; he preferred to wield power through many competing organizations that owed their very existence to his good offices. In line with his conception of creative chaos, different individuals and agencies were given ill-defined responsibilities in closely related fields of activity in everything from postal administration to weapons development. The price demanded for Hitler's support in the resulting turf wars was total personal loyalty. This might earn supplicants a loosely expressed general directive that they could interpret as endorsing their particular agendas. In pursuit of these rivalries, empire building and bureaucratic obstruction were rife and were deliberately encouraged by Hitler, according to his simplistic view that the strongest would prevail through competition.

The architecture of the Nazi state machinery defied all logical explanation. Before the war, the operations of government were nominally entrusted to seventeen ministries, yet the last actual cabinet meeting had taken place in November 1937. On August 30, 1939, the Ministerial Council for the Defense of the State had been formed. It was composed of six of Hitler's closest followers and bureaucrats; this body, chaired by Göring, could enact laws at Hitler's will. Commissioners were appointed with broadly defined powers within various areas of government activity, but there was no actual machinery for coordinating their work. Worse, there was at every level a divisive duplication of authority caused by the parallel prerogatives of state and Nazi Party functionaries. Virtually every state body was replicated with a party equivalent, with each vying for resources and favor.

Heinrich Himmler, as national leader of the SS and chief of German police, was already ruler of the entire security and police apparatus, but his ambitions for expanding his SS empire knew no bounds. The whole machinery of government was interpenetrated by Himmler's practice of awarding parallel SS ranks to functionaries of every kind. Adm. Canaris's Abwehr military intelligence department, answerable to the Armed Forces Supreme Command, was a particular target for Himmler's ambition. Its activities were mirrored by the intelligence and counterintelligence branch of the SS, the Security Service—Sicherheitsdienst. This was commanded until June 1942 by Himmler's deputy, SS and Police Gen. Reinhard Heydrich, the head of the Reich Main Security Office. Each agency scrabbled for supremacy at the expense of efficient operations against the common enemy.

Canaris and Heydrich, who shared a mutual love of riding and of music, maintained an ostensibly cordial relationship. They sometimes dined together *en famille*. The cold-blooded killer Heydrich was also an accomplished violinist and he often played for Canaris's wife. When the professional rivalry became too intense, however, Canaris betrayed Heydrich's movements in Czechoslovakia to Britain's MI6. Two parachutists of the Czech Brigade, Jan Kubis and Jozef Gabcik, threw an antitank grenade at Heydrich's open-top Mercedes in a Prague street on May 27, 1942. Several fragments and bits of horsehair seat upholstery entered Heydrich's back. He was at first expected to recover from the operation to extract the debris, but the wounds became infected and he died a week later. The death of the central architect of the "Final Solution"— which he had unveiled at the Wannsee conference that January—led to mass reprisals that killed about 5,000 Czech men, women, and children.

AMONG THE ABHORRENT FIGURES at the pinnacle of the Nazi hierarchy, popular history recalls in particular the flamboyant, drug-addicted Luftwaffe commander in chief Hermann Göring, the occultist security overlord Heinrich Himmler, and the odious propaganda minister and de facto interior minister Joseph Goebbels. In truth, however, the most devious of them all, and the master of palace intrigue, was the relatively faceless party chief Martin Bormann. Hitler's shadow and gatekeeper for much of the Third Reich, Bormann was a figure forever lurking in the background at the Führer's elbow. His battlegrounds were the card-index file and the double-entry ledger. His principal weapon was the teleprinter, through which he issued a torrent of instructions to his ubiquitous regional gauleiters (district leaders). To these party officials, Bormann was known behind his back as the "Telex General."

Bormann had come to the Nazi Party relatively late, joining only in 1926, so the *Alte Kämpfer* ("Old Fighters") who had supported Hitler in the Munich putsch attempt tended to dismiss him. Nevertheless, he held the party membership number 6088 and was therefore eligible for the Gold Party Badge, awarded to party members with a registration number under 100,000. Bormann's first job was to run the relief fund for the storm troopers of the Sturmabteilungen (SA—the party's brown-shirted uniformed part-time activists) who were injured in brawls and riots. He cannily negotiated reduced premiums to the insurance company concerned while at the same time increasing the contributions from NSDAP members by 50 percent; furthermore, the payment of dues was now compulsory, while any payment of benefits was at Bormann's sole discretion. In short order, this scheme raised 1.4 million reichsmarks in a single year—much to Hitler's delight. The Führer moved Bormann and the SA fund into the NSDAP proper. Bormann now worked at the Brown House, the party headquarters in Munich, where he aspired to taking over the post of party treasurer from Franz Xaver Schwarz.

Meanwhile, he progressed to controlling the finances of the Adolf Hitler Spende der Deutsche Wirtschaft, the "Adolf Hitler Fund of German Business." This AH Fund was originally established as "a token of gratitude to the leader" in order to provide campaign funds and finance for cultural activities within the NSDAP. In reality it became Hitler's personal treasure chest, with revenues gathered from many sources. The most important were the contributions made by industrialists—such as Krupp and Thyssen and of course IG Farben—who were benefiting enormously from German rearmament. In essence, this was a tax amounting to one-half percent of a company's payroll, payable directly to the Führer. In its first year alone, 30 million reichsmarks poured into the coffers of the AH Fund.

In 1929, Bormann married Gerda Buch, the daughter of a senior party official, and on July 3, 1933, he was appointed chief of staff to the deputy Führer, Rudolf Hess. Hess was as uninterested as Hitler in paperwork, so Bormann's skill in turning Hitler's spontaneous verbal directives into coherent orders was invaluable. The Führer would comment approvingly that "Bormann's proposals are so precisely worked out that I have only to say 'yes' or 'no.' With him, I deal in ten minutes with a pile of documents for which with another man I should need hours." On October 10, 1933, Hitler appointed Bormann as a party

Reichsleiter or national leader, making him fourth in the Nazi hierarchy behind Hitler, Göring, and Hess. The intertwining of party and state authority, as described above, would henceforth give Bormann all the freedom of maneuver that he needed.

BORMANN'S ABILITY TO INGRATIATE HIMSELF with the Führer was uncanny. He altered his sleeping pattern to coincide with Hitler's and even mimicked his master by eating vegetarian food and avoiding alcohol when they were dining together—although in private he gorged himself on schnitzel, wurst, and schnapps. As one regional gauleiter commented, "Bormann clung to Hitler like ivy around an oak, using him to get to the light and to the very summit." This he achieved after Deputy Führer Hess—already a marginalized figure—embarked on his bizarre solo flight to Scotland on May 10, 1941, apparently to seek a peace agreement with opponents of the British government. Hess's departure from the scene allowed Bormann to get even closer to Hitler. He was now entirely responsible for arranging the Führer's daily schedule, appointments, and personal business. He was always at his master's side and never took a vacation for fear of losing influence. His reward came in April 1943, when he was appointed secretary to the Führer and chief of the party chancellery. The latter post gave him immense influence over the gauleiters who controlled every district (*Gau*) across the Third Reich. He was now so indispensable that the Führer was prompted to say, "To win this war, I need Bormann."

He also needed Bormann to control his personal finances. At a dinner party with Himmler in October 1941, Hitler had declaimed, "As far as my own private existence is concerned, I shall always live simply, but in my capacity as Führer and Head of State I am obliged to stand out clearly from amongst all the people around me. If my close associates glitter with decorations, I can distinguish myself from them only by wearing none at all." This claim of monkish asceticism was not strictly true. Hitler enjoyed a lavish lifestyle at his Bavarian residence, the Berghof, in the mountain village retreat of Berchtesgaden in Obersalzburg municipality. Besides the Berghof itself, separate villas were provided at Obersalzberg for all the notables of the Nazi hierarchy. This compound had all been created for the Führer by Bormann and financed from the AH Fund to the tune of about 100 million reichsmarks. With its splendid views of the Bavarian Alps, the Berghof was Hitler's favorite retreat. This was where he spent time with his mistress, Eva Braun, and entertained foreign visitors and his close and trusted associates—his *Berg Leute*, or mountain people.

As Otto Dietrich would write,

> Bormann then assumed economic and financial direction of the entire "household of the Führer." He was especially attentive to the lady of the house, anticipating her every wish and skillfully helping her with the often rather complicated arrangements for social and state functions. This was all the more necessary, since she herself tactfully kept in the background as much as possible. Bormann's adroitness in this matter undoubtedly strengthened his unassailable position of trust with Hitler, who was extraordinarily sensitive about Eva Braun.

There was, however, no love lost between Bormann and Braun; behind his back she called him an "oversexed toad."

With his brilliant business acumen, Bormann found many ways to bolster Hitler's personal fortune. Apart from the considerable income derived from royalties on *Mein Kampf*—which, since it was required reading in German schools, sold millions of copies—Bormann devised a scheme to capitalize on image rights whereby Hitler received a payment for every use of his likeness, be it on a postcard or even a postage stamp. These monies were paid into a separate Adolf Hitler Cultural Fund to support the performing arts and to purchase paintings for the Führer's personal collection. By the outbreak of war in 1939, Hitler's annual income was immense, but—thanks to a deal that Bormann had arranged with the authorities—he paid no income tax. Like other Nazi leaders, Hitler had foreign bank accounts, including one with the Union Bank of Switzerland in Bern and another in Holland. These accounts received the royalties earned on Hitler's book sales abroad and, more importantly, allowed him to indulge the one passion in his life besides politics—his obsession with art.

Chapter 4

THE RAPE OF EUROPE

AS A YOUNG MAN IN VIENNA before World War I, Hitler had nurtured ambitions to be an artist and an architect, despite the fierce objections of his overbearing father, Alois Schicklgruber. In 1907, he applied to the Academy of Fine Arts but failed the entrance examination. Desolated, he applied again the following year but was rejected again, his portfolio winning only a cursory glance. This was a turning point in Hitler's life. Attributing his rejection to the panel of academicians being Jews, he nursed a deep embitterment toward the Jewish race, although, ironically, on the few occasions that Hitler ever sold any of his paintings, it was through the Jewish Hungarian art dealer Josef Neumann.

For the next few years Hitler lived a vagrant's life "of hardship and misery," as he later recalled in *Mein Kampf.* His only solace was found in Vienna's many art museums and the city's deep tradition of classical music. His musical tastes were catholic—Beethoven, Bruckner, Chopin, Grieg, Schubert, Schumann, and even Mahler and Mendelssohn—but his abiding favorite was Richard Wagner and he knew the opera *Die Meistersinger von Nürnberg* by heart. Hitler gave up painting after World War 1 as his political career progressed, but he retained an illusion of himself as a great artist throughout his life and his interest in architecture never diminished.

Once in office as chancellor, Hitler pursued his obsession of "racial purity" with ruthless zeal, in parallel with a breakneck program of centralizing all power in the party's hands. The Nazis' election in 1933 was followed almost immediately by their virtual destruction of the German constitution in response to the Reichstag fire and, on the death of President Paul von Hindenburg in August 1934, by Hitler's assumption of the dual leadership of the Nazi Party and the state as Führer (leader)—a coup d'état endorsed in a plebiscite by 38 million German citizens. Once parliament and the courts were castrated, the regime enjoyed unfettered power and was free to institute a policy of *Gleichschaltung* (enforced conformity), consolidating its hold over the nation by the elimination or neutering of any organized bodies that were outside the complete control of the Nazi Party. A spate of decrees revoked individual liberties and rights of association, silenced the media, banned rival political parties and free labor unions, and destroyed the independence of regional governments and the judiciary. The death penalty was introduced for a wide range of politically defined "crimes," and there were mass arrests not only of communist, social democratic, and Jewish activists but also of freemasons, gypsies, homosexuals, and any others deemed deviant in the eyes of Nazi orthodoxy. Most of these "pariahs" were incarcerated in the fifty concentration camps that were opened during the Nazis' first year in power.

In April 1933, Julius Streicher, the notorious Jew-baiter and editor of the Nazi weekly newspaper *Der Stürmer* (*The Attacker*), orchestrated an economic boycott of Jewish businesses. Dr. Joseph Goebbels, head of the newly founded Reich Ministry for Public Enlightenment and Propaganda, called for the "cleansing by fire" of "un-German" books, particularly those by authors of Jewish background such as Einstein, Freud, Kafka, and Marx—and even the works of the revered German nineteenth-century poet Heinrich Heine, whose tragedy *Almansor* contains the warning "Where they burn books, they will in the end also burn people." On May 10, a crowd of 40,000 watched the burning of 25,000 books in Berlin's Opernplatz. In November 1933 a national referendum showed that 95 percent of the population approved of Nazi policies, even as their rights and freedoms were being systematically destroyed.

IN THE HEADY DAYS following their electoral victory, the Nazis concentrated on eliminating political opponents of the center and left. Now they had the opportunity to turn on the Jews. By 1934, all Jewish shops were prominently daubed with the word "*Juden*" or the Star of David, and storm troopers of the SA frequently hung around outside them to discourage customers from entering. Increasingly, Jewish business people were forced to close down as they lost their livelihood. Soon, German Jews were being forced out of the professions and government employment as doctors, lawyers, teachers, scientists, and civil servants. Shops and restaurants refused to serve Jews and they were banned from public parks, swimming pools, and even public transport. German children were imbued with anti-Semitism during school lessons and even during playtime—the object of a popular children's board game was to render particular areas of Germany *Juden Frei* or "Jew-free."

A major step in the process of "Aryanization" of all aspects of German society was taken on September 15, 1935, with the enactment of the so-called Nuremberg Laws. Henceforth, marriage or sexual intercourse between Jews and Aryans was expressly forbidden, and Jews were deprived of their political rights as citizens. Increasingly, Jews attempted to emigrate to France, Switzerland, and further afield, but they were rarely made welcome and many were refused entry. Out of a total Jewish population of some 525,000, about 170,000 had already left Germany before October 5, 1938, when a decree invalidated their passports. The Swiss insisted that German Jews who needed traveling documents for emigration purposes be reissued passports with a large "J" for ready identification and rejection at the border. Many Jews could not afford the ever-increasing cost of emigration. Those who could were not permitted to take any capital with them, and few had any money left after being forced to sell their homes and businesses at greatly discounted prices to pay the *Reichsfluchtsteuer* ("escape tax"). Dealers in art and antiquities were specifically targeted, and this enforced liquidation of about 80 percent of such businesses in Germany caused a glut on the market and a sharp slump in prices.

On November 9, 1938, racial violence—sparked by the assassination of a German diplomat in Paris by a young Jewish Pole whose family had been deported from Germany—reached new heights. That night Jewish homes, properties, and synagogues across Germany and parts of Austria and the Sudetenland were attacked and burned in the orgy of destruction known as *Kristallnacht*—"Crystal Night" or the Night of Broken Glass—from the amount of broken glass it left carpeting the streets. At least ninety-one Jews lost their lives; another 30,000 were arrested and largely consigned to concentration camps. The survivors were actually forced to pay the material price of this pogrom. Replacing all the broken windows would cost some 25 million reichsmarks, and since almost all plate glass was imported from Belgium this had to be paid in scarce foreign currency. By now, the avaricious Hermann Göring was in charge of the "Program to Eliminate Jews from German Economic Life" and he decreed that all Jews remaining in Germany were to provide the Reich exchequer with "atonement payments," totaling 1 billion reichsmarks, to cover the costs of repairing the damage. In addition, any insurance payments made to German Jews were confiscated by the state.

KRISTALLNACHT WAS THE CLEAREST WARNING YET to German Jewry of their perilous situation, and, between then and the outbreak of war in September 1939, approximately 100,000 Jews somehow found ways to leave the Reich. Another Nazi legislative novelty was about to suggest that any who were unable or unwilling to do so might find themselves at the mercy of a state prepared to commit mass murder.

Among the plague of new legislation enacted in 1933 was a law for the compulsory sterilization of people suffering "congenital mental defects, schizophrenia, manic-depressive psychosis, hereditary epilepsy, and severe alcoholism." Germans were not alone in their enthusiasm for the pseudoscience of eugenics, which in the 1920s–30s was widely espoused across Europe and America in the interests of "racial hygiene." One of its advocates was John D. Rockefeller, the founder of Standard

Oil of New Jersey. It was his Rockefeller Foundation that provided much of the funding for the Kaiser Wilhelm Institute, Germany's most prestigious medical school, to carry out studies on "anthropology, eugenics, and human heredity" under the direction of a Swiss psychiatrist and fervent Nazi, Ernst Rüdin. A mass program of sterilization of both the mentally ill and social misfits, as determined by 220 district "hereditary health courts," was instituted. Among the several hundred thousand victims were such undesirables as convicts, prostitutes, and even children as young as ten from orphanages.

By inexorable Nazi logic, the next step was euthanasia or "mercy killing." This program began in 1938 under the auspices of Hitler's personal physician, Dr. Karl Brandt. At first the victims were limited to mentally and physically handicapped children who were killed by lethal injection. But the program was soon extended to handicapped adults and to anyone judged an incorrigible social deviant. When lethal injection proved time-consuming and less than efficient, a bureaucracy of murder was established; this was designated the T4 program after the address of its headquarters at Tiergartenstrasse 4 in Berlin. The program was codified in law by decree of the Führer in October 1939. At every mental institution false bathhouses were built, where the victims were killed at first by carbon monoxide and later by poison gas.

SOON AFTER KRISTALLNACHT, Göring devised yet more devious schemes from which to profit by forcing German Jews to leave the country. By a decree dated January 1, 1939, all their property and possessions were essentially confiscated by the state. Public Acquisition Offices were set up for "the safekeeping of works of art belonging to Jews," and a subsequent decree demanded the surrender of "any objects in their ownership made of gold, platinum, or silver, as well as precious stones and pearls." This expropriation of Jewish property was the first foreshadowing of the Nazis' future plundering of Europe. After Göring had made his choice of artworks and trinkets, the proceeds from the loot went directly to the coffers of the AH Fund or the Adolf Hitler Cultural Fund. With such resources at his disposal, Hitler was able to indulge his passion for paintings.

The Führer's personal taste was bourgeois in the extreme. He loathed all nonrepresentational art and his eye for quality was completely inconsistent. In 1934 he purchased a portrait of his great hero Frederick the Great of Prussia by the Swiss painter Anton Graff (1736–1813) for the then-considerable sum of 34,000 reichsmarks. It was Hitler's favorite painting and it traveled with him everywhere. As an example of his more prosaic taste, Hitler paid 120,000 reichsmarks to Hermann Gradl, a painter of idyllic landscapes, to make six large oils for the dining hall of the New Reich Chancellery between 1939 and 1941. Their conventional character may be guessed from Hitler's instructions that this commission was to illustrate "the typical appearance of the German Land, in its intertwining of Nature and Culture and its many different guises as Motherland of the German Nation." To adorn the New Chancellery the Führer spent nearly 400,000 reichsmarks on other contemporary artworks of very mixed quality. Although he bought for his own collection paintings by Rubens, Canaletto, van Dyck, and Watteau at the behest of his art adviser, Dr. Hans Posse, his favorite painters were actually somewhat obscure German nineteenth- and early twentieth-century artists such as Franz Stuck and Carl Spitzweg, neither of whom has stood the test of time. One of his all-time favorites was Eduard von Grützner, whose particular specialty was portraits of drunken monks. In a conversation with Albert Speer, Hitler declaimed, "Look at those details—Grützner is greatly underrated. It's simply that he hasn't been discovered yet. Some day he'll be worth as much as a Rembrandt." This has not proved to be the case.

In one of his first acts as chancellor, Hitler ordered the construction of the House of German Art in Munich to display the finest examples of Germanic painting and sculpture. The task was entrusted to Alfred Rosenberg, the Nazi Party ideologue and chief racial theorist, who was given the grandiose title of "Führer's Delegate for the Entire Intellectual and Philosophical Education and Instruction of the National Socialist Party." The fundamental contradiction was, of course, that the Nazi Party was profoundly anti-intellectual and as totally opposed to freedom in the arts as it was to any other sort of independent thinking. Nevertheless, the leadership devoted an inordinate amount of time to cultural matters—as the character Wilhelm Furtwängler says in

Ronald Harwood's modern play *Taking Sides*, "Only tyrannies under-stand the power of art." But Rosenberg's role was twofold; besides finding and glorifying politically acceptable German art, he was to root out all art that did not conform to Nazi ideology or Hitler's personal taste. For fear of losing their jobs, museum directors and cura-tors across Germany were obliged to surrender to the state "purging" committees all works by artists suspected of "degeneracy"—Cubists, Impressionists, Futurists, German Expressionists, Dadaists—and other "un-German" art.

In all, some 16,000 works of art were confiscated from museums across the country. As the new arbiter of artistic merit, Hitler dis-missed the works of masters such as Georges Braque, Paul Cézanne, Henri Matisse, and Pablo Picasso as "twaddle," and a new office was set up to implement his demands in the "unrelenting war of purifica-tion." All active artists had to submit their work to this Committee for the Assessment of Inferior Works of Art; any works deemed sub-standard were confiscated without compensation, and artists who ran afoul of the committee were forbidden to purchase painting materials on pain of imprisonment, thus ending their careers. Many artworks were destroyed; for example, on March 20, 1939, 1,004 paintings and sculptures as well as 3,825 drawings, watercolors, and other items were burned during a practice exercise for the Berlin Fire Department.

Predictably, Hermann Göring turned the situation to his pecu-niary advantage. All the confiscated works of art from the nation's museums were stored in a warehouse on Kopernikusstrasse in Berlin, and when Göring sent his art agent to forage through this Aladdin's cave he came away with a veritable feast of Impressionist paintings, including four by Vincent van Gogh. A single Cézanne and two van Goghs, including *Portrait of Dr. Gachet*, were sold to a Dutch banker for 500,000 reichsmarks. (In 1990, *Portrait of Dr. Gachet* sold for $82.5 million.) With the money raised, Göring purchased more Old Masters and his favorite Gobelin tapestries to adorn the walls of his country mansion Carinhall.

Following Göring's example, the other Nazi leaders now profited from the activity of a Commission for the Exploitation of Degenerate Art that released purged artworks onto the international market.

Despite their greed, however, the sales of Germany's heritage that were held in London, Paris, and Switzerland from 1937 until early 1939 effectively dumped these despised works. Some extraordinary bargains were to be had: a Paul Klee for $300, now in the Museum of Modern Art in New York; a Kandinsky for $100, now in the Guggenheim Museum in New York; and Henri Matisse's *Bathers with a Turtle*, purchased by Joseph Pulitzer for 9,100 Swiss francs, which now resides in the St. Louis Art Museum.

The Austrian *Anschluss* of March 12, 1938, saw Hitler's native country annexed to the Third Reich, to the rapturous enthusiasm of a large part of the Austrian people. Within hours, every public building was bedecked with swastika flags, while gangs of thugs rampaged through the streets hunting down Jews. Two days later, Hitler made a triumphal progress through Vienna. In the meantime, SS officers were pillaging Jewish homes in search of artworks and valuables. They knew exactly where to look since German scholars had been commissioned to prepare catalogs and inventories of private collections across Europe in anticipation of Hitler's conquests. The art collections of the Rothschild banking family were primary targets; Baron Alphonse de Rothschild was stripped of 3,444 artworks from his Hohe Warte villa in Vienna and his country estate at Schloss Reichenau, while his elder brother Baron Louis lost 919 pieces to the Nazis. All such items were carefully cataloged and photographed and an extensive inventory was prepared before the chosen pieces were transferred to Germany and the residue to Austrian museums. In the month following the Anschluss, Hitler decided to create the greatest art museum in the world in the city of Linz, close to his birthplace. The Führermuseum was planned to become the repository for all the great works of art looted during the Nazi wars of conquest—except, of course, for those pieces diverted to the private collections of Adolf Hitler, Hermann Göring, and a select few others of the Nazi elite.

ON JUNE 23, 1940, THE DAY FOLLOWING France's humiliating armistice, Hitler conducted a triumphal tour of Paris. He was accompanied by his favorite sculptor Arno Breker, his architect Albert Speer, and several general staff officers, traveling in three G4 Mercedes six-wheel touring cars. Speer recalled that when they visited the famed nineteenth-century Paris Opera house, Hitler "seemed fascinated by the Opera, went into ecstasies about its beauty, his eyes glittering with an excitement that struck me as uncanny." The entourage sped past Madeleine church and the Arc de Triomphe, down the Champs-Élysées, past the Eiffel Tower, and on to Les Invalides, where Hitler spent a considerable time at Napoleon's tomb, communing with the previous great European tyrant. At the conclusion of his tour of the City of Light, he stated, "It was the dream of my life to be permitted to see Paris. I cannot say how happy I am to have that dream fulfilled today."

That dream had cost the lives of 27,074 Germans and left another 111,034 wounded, but Allied casualties in the Battle of France were a staggering 2.292 million. The greatest toll was paid by the French, with 97,300 killed and missing, 120,000 wounded, and 1.54 million captured. The latter were doomed to become forced laborers for the German war effort. After this colossal victory, achieved in just six weeks, continental Western Europe lay helpless and ripe for plunder. A galaxy of the world's great art museums had fallen into the hands of the Nazis—the Musées Royaux des Beaux-Arts in Brussels, the Rijksmuseum in Amsterdam, and the Louvre in Paris, as well as a host of provincial galleries and private collections. The greatest hoard in the history of military conquest since the time of Napoleon Bonaparte now became subject to the greatest art theft in recorded history.

THE TASK OF PERFORMING this grandest of larcenies fell to Alfred Rosenberg and an organization named after him, the Einsatzstab Reichsleiter Rosenberg für die Besetzen Gebiete (Special Staff of National Leader Rosenberg for the Occupied Territories) or ERR for short. Rosenberg's role, defined in a personal directive from Hitler, was to comb every public and private collection in the occupied countries and "to transport to Germany cultural goods which appear valuable to him, and to safeguard them there." France, Belgium, and Holland were the responsibility of ERR Dienststelle (Agency) Western, headquartered in Paris. Within a few weeks, a fabulous body of art had been assembled at the Louvre and the German embassy awaiting a decision as to final disposal. This included twenty-six "Jewish-owned works of degenerate art," comprising fourteen Braques, seven Picassos, four Légers, and a Rouault, which were retained for "trading for artistically valuable works."

Even as his Luftwaffe was fighting in the skies over England during the Battle of Britain, Göring was scouring the museums of the Low Countries in his insatiable quest for artistic loot. By October 1940, he had lost his "Channel War," and the contemplated invasion of Britain was canceled. On November 3, he consoled himself with a trip to Paris to view the accumulated treasures that had been gathered in the Jeu de Paume museum. The haul was so extensive that it took Göring two full days to make his choices—mostly French and Dutch masters from the Rothschild and Wildenstein collections. Above all, he craved the painting titled *The Astronomer* by Jan Vermeer, stolen from Baron Alphonse de Rothschild; but as the Führer's collection lacked a Vermeer, Göring was out of luck. In the pecking order of plunderers, Hitler had first choice through his chief art procurer, Dr. Hans Posse, both for his personal collection and for the planned museum at Linz. The diligent and resourceful Posse wrote to Martin Bormann almost every day, in great detail, about his various acquisitions for the Führer and the state of the art market. Second came Reichsmarschall Göring, and after he had taken his pick, then sundry German museums received the remaining spoils.

While the search for Jewish valuables continued tirelessly, with the ready cooperation of officials in Vichy France—even individual safety deposit boxes were opened—the harvesting of conquered Europe was not confined to items of obvious value. In the occupied countries, millions more Jews were now at the disposal of the Nazis, to be registered by their national authorities and to await the bureaucracy of genocide. At any time they were subject to deportation to Germany and on to the concentration camps that spread like plague pits across Eastern Europe. At first, Jewish homes were simply abandoned and then ransacked by neighbors, but the Nazis soon realized that this was a waste of resources. However humble and mundane, furniture and household items could be of benefit to the Reich, where the manufacture of most domestic goods was seriously curtailed in favor of war production.

Accordingly, the ERR set up another division tasked with expropriating all Jewish belongings once their owners had been dispatched to the death camps. This new organization, known as Aktion-M (Project M) for *Möbel* (furniture), operated across Europe. Once a Jewish family had been expelled from their home, local police under the direction of the Nazis would arrange for vans to collect all the furniture and kitchen appliances, which were taken to a central repository to await shipment to Germany. The Dutch even invented a word for the process—*pulsen*—after the name of the Amsterdam moving company Abraham Puls & Sons, which was employed by the Dutch police for this task. In one year alone, Project M was responsible for the clearing of 17,235 Dutch homes of items totaling loads of almost 17 million cubic feet; these were crated for dispatch to Germany or to the ethnic German populations living in the occupied Eastern Territories. During 1942, 40,000 tons of furniture were also shipped from France to Germany. A report by ERR Dienststelle Western dated August 8, 1944, records that after 69,512 Jewish homes had been stripped of household goods, it took 674 trains with 26,984 freight cars to carry the plunder to Germany.

THE NAZIS SYSTEMATICALLY LOOTED artworks—using that term to embrace everything from ceramics to church bells and from sculptures to silverware—from every country they occupied, while also inflicting untold destruction on cultural buildings. The Soviet Union lost 1.148 million artworks as the Germans ransacked 400 museums, 2,000 churches, and 43,000 libraries inside Soviet territory. In Poland, some 516,000 individual pieces of art were looted, representing about 43 percent of the country's cultural heritage. Much of this plunder was intended to reside in the Führermuseum at Linz, the symbol of Hitler's artistic vision and the cultural center of the Thousand-Year Reich, which would finally expunge his rejection at the hands of the Academy of Fine Arts in Vienna. In the meantime, however, the Führermuseum existed only in blueprint and tabletop models, and it was essential to protect Hitler's loot from the ever more destructive Allied bombing campaign.

Across Germany, numerous repositories were created in cave complexes and salt mines where the appropriate conditions of humidity and temperature could be maintained. Thanks to the meticulous records of the ERR and Dr. Hans Posse, Martin Bormann knew the location of every single crate of plunder across the length and breadth of the Third Reich. He was therefore able to inform the Führer of the exact whereabouts of any particular piece, should Hitler wish to view or display it at any time. Bormann himself had little interest in the subject, but he realized the potential value of even "degenerate art" on the world market. He arranged for many pieces to be sold at international auctions held in Switzerland; the funds from these sales were deposited in Hitler's personal account at the Union Bank of Switzerland or in a separate account to purchase essentials for the war effort. Unlike other Nazi leaders, however, Bormann never appropriated state funds for his own personal ends. The rewards he craved were power and control.

Following the occupation of Vichy France in November 1942, this avenue for art sales closed, since international dealers were unable to visit Switzerland and U.S. customs regulations forbade trading with the occupied countries of Europe. Bormann promptly established bogus art dealerships in Latin American locations ranging from Buenos Aires to Mexico City. Degenerate art was now transported to the Americas from Genoa, Italy, on ships sailing under the flags of neutral countries. Many pieces thus continued to reach the American market, and Bormann had the proceeds from these sales salted away in the Banco Alemán Transatlántico and the Banco Germánico in Buenos Aires. The shipping companies involved included the Argentine firm Delfino S.A. and the Spanish line Compañia Naviera Levantina; the latter was purchased by a German front company to make supply voyages under the Spanish flag to the beleaguered German forces in Tunisia during the winter of 1942–43. On their return trips from South America, these vessels brought back much-needed foodstuffs and strategic materials—such as vanadium from Argentina, which was crucial for the production of synthetic fuels. In addition, many crewmen from the Kriegsmarine pocket battleship *Admiral Graf Spee*, who had been interned in Argentina and Uruguay since their ship was scuttled off Montevideo in December 1939, were carried home to Germany.

The flow of confiscated art from France to Germany continued right up until the Allied advance was threatening Paris in July 1944.

By then, 29 major shipments of artworks had been undertaken since 1941, involving 137 freight cars carrying some 4,174 crates of plunder, comprising about 22,000 objects from 203 different collections.

Similar streams of plunder continued to flow from all the other occupied countries of Europe and from the Soviet Union, and even from Italy after its surrender to the Allies in September 1943. Under orders from their titular chief, the Luftwaffe's Hermann Göring Panzer Division plundered artworks from Naples and all points northward as the German forces gradually retreated up the length of Italy. This industrial-scale looting provided a massive infusion of funds to the Third Reich and amassed for both Hitler and Göring the finest individual collections of art ever known. The plundered art was also to become a vital element in the master plan that Martin Bormann developed as the tides of war turned against Germany: Aktion Feuerland.

Chapter 5

NAZI GOLD

FROM THE TIME THAT HITLER assumed power, rearmament was his top priority, both to reduce unemployment among the German people and to pursue his plans for a short, sharp war of conquest. From as early as 1933, the president of the Reichsbank, Dr. Hjalmar Schacht, created several phantom accounts where gold acquisitions by the Reichsbank were hidden in order to finance German rearmament without alerting the outside world. By the following year, the published gold accounts revealed that the Reichsbank had $80.5 million while the hidden accounts held $27 million. By 1939 this situation had almost been reversed, with published gold reserves down to $28.6 million while the hidden accounts had risen to $83 million. Between September 1, 1939, and June 30, 1945, however, Germany's gold transactions for the purchase of vital raw materials from overseas amounted to the staggering sum of $890 million. The eightfold difference between this amount and the Reichsbank holdings represented the gold bullion and coinage ransacked from every country conquered by the Germans.

During the 1930s, Germany was able to attract credit from many foreign banks and countries to underwrite the modernization of its industry and, by extension, the program of rearmament (see Chapter 1). Similarly, up to the outbreak of war, most countries were willing to accept payment for goods and services in reichsmarks, which were then often used to buy manufactured products from Germany. However, once the U.S. Treasury Department severed financial and commercial links with Germany and occupied Europe after December 1941, payment was demanded in more attractive currencies such as British pounds, U.S. dollars, or Swiss francs. But the most attractive currency of all—then as now—was gold.

By the end of 1942, following its conquest of most of Europe, Germany had an abundance of gold. The central banks of every occupied country were plundered for the benefit of the Third Reich, starting with that of Austria following its annexation in March 1938. The gold reserves of the Austrian National Bank divulged 200,765 pounds of gold bars and coinage, of which some 49,254 pounds were held in the Bank of England; the total value in U.S. dollars was $102,689,215. Czechoslovakia rendered $44 million; the Free City of Danzig, $4.1 million; Holland, $163 million; Luxembourg, nearly $4.858 million; Belgium, $223.2 million; and Italy after September 1943, some $80 million. The amount of gold taken from Greece is not recorded, while that of Yugoslavia was shared between Italy and Germany, some of it being used to establish the Ustaše fascist regime in the puppet state of Greater Croatia. Denmark, Norway, and France had made the wise provision of transferring most of their gold reserves to England, America, or Canada before the Nazis invaded.

POLAND'S GOLD WAS SAVED by chance and by the indefatigable efforts of Stefan Michalski, the director of the Bank of Poland. In September 1939, just as the Germans were invading Poland, he personally escorted the gold via train and truck from Warsaw through Romania and Turkey to Lebanon, where it was loaded on a ship bound for Marseille in France. It arrived in Paris by train in October 1939. The gold was then moved to the port of Lorient in Brittany and shipped aboard the French cruiser *Victor Schoelcher* to Dakar in French West Africa (in the region that is now the country of Senegal). After May 1940, Dakar was also the refuge for the residual gold holdings of France and Belgium's reserves; the latter had been transferred to the Bank of France for safekeeping early in 1940. German demands for the surrender of the Polish and Belgian gold under the terms of the armistice with Vichy France met with months of delay and prevarication. Eventually the French agreed to hand over the Belgian gold, but not the Polish, on the grounds that since that country had been carved up between Nazi Germany and the Soviet Union it was no longer a sovereign state and could not currently honor the credit France had extended to it previously. The diligent Stefan Michalski guarded his charge until the Allied invasion of North Africa in November 1942, when he arranged for a U.S. warship to transport the sixty-five tons of Polish gold to New York to be deposited in the U.S. Federal Reserve Bank.

The saga of the Belgian gold was one of the most extraordinary tales of World War II. On September 23, 1940, the British and Gen. de Gaulle's Free French launched Operation Menace, an unsuccessful attack on Dakar to capture the remaining French gold reserves. Before this fiasco, the Belgian gold—comprising 4,944 sealed boxes weighing some 270 tons—had been moved inland by Vichy French operatives to Kayes, where it arrived on September 20. From there it went by train to Bamako on the Niger River and was transported by riverboats and light trucks upriver to Timbuktu and Gao. The long haul across the Sahara Desert was accomplished by camel train to the railhead at Colomb-Béchar in French Algeria. Once the gold reached Algiers, 120 aircraft flights were needed to transport it to Marseille. It arrived at the Reichsbank in Berlin in May 1942, after a journey lasting twenty months.

ANY GOLD BULLION STOLEN from the central banks of the occupied countries was easily recognized on the international market, due to particular stampings on each gold bar that revealed its provenance. Accordingly, all looted gold was processed through the Precious Metals Department of the Reichsbank, where it was carefully weighed, cataloged, and stored, either centrally in Berlin or in one of some twenty other branches. When necessary, the bullion was re-smelted at the Prussian State Mint into new bars that were stamped with prewar German markings to disguise their true origins.

Similarly, all the gold items taken from the victims in the extermination camps, such as gold teeth and jewelry, were either sold or melted down and cast into gold bars by the firm of Degussa—Deutsche Gold und Silber Scheideanstalt. The company even had its own smelter at Auschwitz, where it processed on average twenty-four pounds of gold per day: with a hideous symmetry, Degussa and IG Farben jointly owned the chemical production firm Degesch, which manufactured the Zyklon-B tablets used in the gas chambers. The first shipment of prisoners' valuables from the death camps to the Reichsbank was made on August 26, 1942, under the supervision of SS Capt. Bruno Melmer. In November 1942, the tenth shipment to the Reichsbank was the first to include dental gold, and the deliveries continued until the end of the war; some seventy-eight in all. The Reichsbank realized the market value of all the bullion and currency, and the proceeds were deposited in a special SS account under the name of Melmer. Funds were then transferred to an account in the name of Max Heiliger; this account was controlled by SS and Police Gen. Ernst Kaltenbrunner, the successor to Reinhard Heydrich as head of the Reich Main Security Office, and by SS Gen. Oswald Pohl, the chief administrator of the concentration camps. This became a slush fund for the SS leadership, which made large deposits and investments in Switzerland, mainly through the Bank for International Settlements.

Despite its newfound hoards of looted gold, Nazi Germany had no direct mechanism of paying for foreign goods, and the transfer of funds or gold bullion to another country required the cooperation of the international banking community. The solution lay on Germany's doorstep, in the financial institutions of neutral Switzerland, which had been quick to recognize the commercial opportunities of what was happening in Germany. As early as 1934, Swiss banks had introduced a system of numbered bank accounts to guard the privacy of depositors—particularly Jews wishing to move their wealth out of Germany—from the scrutiny of the Nazi regime. Only the most senior bank officials knew the true identities of the account holders. In August 1939 alone, just weeks ahead of the German invasion, some 17,000 transfers were made from Poland for safekeeping in Swiss bank accounts, and once war broke out large numbers of European Jews or their appointed agents came to deposit their savings and valuables in the banks of Basel and Zurich despite Swiss border restrictions to inhibit the entry of Jews. But these Swiss transactions with the prey were small beer compared to the trade in gold that was conducted with the predators.

AT THE OUTSET, THE GERMANS FAVORED the Bank for International Settlements (BIS) based in Basel. As already mentioned, this bank was founded in 1930 for the purpose of overseeing the transfer of German reparation payments to various recipient countries under the provisions of the Treaty of Versailles, but those provisions were repudiated by Germany in 1932. Lacking any form of governmental control, the BIS was owned and run by the central banks of the member countries, including the U.S. Federal Reserve Bank, the Reichsbank, and the Bank of England. Its role was "to promote the cooperation of central banks and to provide additional facilities for international financial operations." By its own charter, it was immune from seizure or prosecution even in times of war. It acted as the prototypical world bank, but was run purely for the benefit of its own members. Indeed, it became a useful club where central bankers and their staffs met once a month in the agreeable surroundings of Basel.

The membership of the BIS board of management was intriguing. The two principal directors were Hjalmar Schacht, former president of the Reichsbank and Reich economic minister, and Sir Montagu Norman, the governor of the Bank of England. These two were long-standing close friends given to extended walks in the woods together. The chairman was the affable Thomas H. McKittrick, a New York banker-cum-lawyer, whose sympathies with the Nazis were well known. The German bias of the BIS was further confirmed by the presence on its board of Dr. Walter Funk, president of the Reichsbank (1939–45), and his deputy Emil Puhl; Hermann Schmitz, chairman of IG Farben; and Baron Kurt von Schröder, banker to Adolf Hitler and owner of the J.H. Stein Bank of Cologne, whose most noted client was the SS—accordingly, one of the Stein bank's directors was Gen. Ernst Kaltenbrunner.

Baron von Schröder, himself an SS brigadier, was the director of more than thirty other companies, including ITT in Germany.

Schröder's Bank of Hamburg was affiliated with the J. Henry Schröder & Co. of London, which acted as the German government's financial agent in Britain from 1938. The latter in its turn owned the J. Henry Schröder Banking Corporation of New York; this concern went into partnership with the Rockefellers in 1936 to become the Schroder Rockefeller & Co. investment bank, of which Allen Welsh Dulles—the future OSS station chief in Bern—was a director. Such was the fraternity of international banking, united in the belief that business must continue even in the depths of a world war.

Up to the outbreak of war in 1939, the BIS channeled funds totaling some 294 million Swiss francs from foreign investors into Nazi Germany, and it continued to assist the Nazis throughout the war. At the time of the German annexation of the Czech Sudetenland in October 1938, the National Bank of Czechoslovakia in Prague held some $26 million of gold in the BIS account held by the Bank of England in London. In March 1939, after the whole of Czechoslovakia had been occupied, the Germans laid claim to this amount for the Reichsbank. The BIS immediately bowed to German demands, but required the agreement of the Bank of England for completion of the transaction, and Sir Montagu Norman duly arranged this. When the Soviet Union tried the same ploy after occupying the Baltic states of Estonia, Latvia, and Lithuania in 1939–40, its claim was refused.

DESPITE CLAIMING NEUTRALITY and total probity, the BIS was of vital assistance to Nazi Germany in its quest for strategic resources—such as rubber from Japanese-occupied Malaya, paid for with funds transferred to Japan via the BIS. It was Germany's need for essential raw materials that fueled the money-laundering operations of the BIS and the Swiss banks. Coincidentally, some of the most critical resources were to be found in Europe's neutral countries—Swedish iron ore, Turkish chromium, and Portuguese and Spanish wolfram—the latter being essential for the manufacture of tungsten, which was used to make machine tools and armor-piercing ammunition. Both Portugal and Spain were ruled by fascist dictators sympathetic to the Nazi cause.

António de Oliveira Salazar of Portugal played a canny game, trading with both the Allies and Germany. His regime depended on

America for oil and wheat but was willing to sell wolfram by a strict quota system on a cash-and-carry basis that inevitably inflated the cost of the ore—by 1943, wolfram commanded eight times the prewar price, and the Allies alone paid $170 million for wolfram to Portugal and Spain during World War II. While Britain and America paid respectively in pounds sterling and U.S. dollars, Germany was obliged to pay in gold. At the outbreak of the war, Salazar had declared that Portugal would remain strictly neutral and would "adhere to an iron principle— we shall not try to exploit the conflict for pecuniary gain." In 1939 the Banco Nacional de Portugal held 63 tons of gold; by October 1945, its reserves stood at 356.5 tons.

In 1939 the Spain of Gen. Francisco Franco—*El Caudillo* (The Leader)—was indebted to Germany to the tune of $212 million for its military and financial support during the Spanish Civil War of 1936–39. Although Spain deployed the "Blue Division" of fascist volunteers to fight with the German army against "Bolsheviks" on the Russian Front, it maintained its neutrality with both Germany and the Western Allies. Spain was a ready source of wolfram and other high-grade ores, such as pyrite, as well as lead, mercury, phosphates, and zinc, and foodstuffs, particularly citrus fruits. Germany paid for all of them with gold, manufactured goods, and weapons. Equally important was Spain's role as a conduit for illicit trade with South America, particularly Argentina, which continued throughout the war despite the Allies' illegal naval blockade of the Iberian Peninsula. Portugal, in its turn, provided a similar conduit to Brazil.

Both America and Britain placed a high priority on sustaining Spain's neutrality. If Franco joined the Axis powers, then British Gibraltar would inevitably be captured and the western gate of the Mediterranean Sea closed, forcing Allied oil tankers to sail all the way around Africa via the Cape of Good Hope. To keep Franco amenable, the Allies provided Spain with large quantities of grain and petroleum products. Indeed, Spain's complete tanker fleet was kept busy throughout the war transporting oil from Venezuela to Spain, courtesy of Standard Oil and the Texas Oil Company, which charged the U.S. government accordingly. For a simple agrarian society such as Spain, this traffic provided a significant surplus of oil over the country's needs and the difference was sold on to Germany. By the end of the war, Spain had paid off all its debts to Germany and Madrid's gold reserves had grown from $42 million in 1939 to $110 million in 1945.

PORTUGAL AND SPAIN ESPOUSED fascist ideologies similar to Nazi Germany's. It is more difficult to justify the wartime dealings of a liberal democracy such as neutral Sweden. Sweden possessed a mineral resource that was absolutely vital to the Nazi war machine—iron ore, the key ingredient of steel. Sweden's vast Kiruna-Gällivare mines in Lapland held almost 90 percent of Europe's high-grade iron ore; Swedish ore exports had underwritten the German steel industry for years and continued to do so until November 1944. One of the fundamental reasons for the German invasions of Denmark and Norway in 1940 was to protect the coastal sea-lanes carrying this continuous supply of iron ore, which amounted to some 10 million tons a year. Sweden was also a major producer of the ball bearings that were essential to every modern weapon system. U.S. intelligence calculated that the German war machine would have ground to a halt within six months if denied Swedish iron ore and the ball bearings manufactured by Svenska Kullagerfabriken (SKF)—a company owned by the Stockholms Enskilda Bank. Of the 100 million ball bearings used each year by German war industries, 60 percent were produced in the SKF subsidiary plants at Schweinfurt and Cannstatt in Germany and most of the remainder came from factories in Sweden.

All these products were paid for in gold or Swiss francs. During World War II, Sweden received 65.7 tons of gold, including 6.6 tons that came from Holocaust victims. The mechanism was simple. Looted gold was moved to Switzerland in diplomatic bags to avoid Swiss customs regulations and deposited in the Swiss National Bank in Bern, BIS, Union Bank of Switzerland, Swiss Bank Corporation, Crédit Suisse, and other financial institutions. These banks then charged commission—commonly 5 percent—for storage prior to dispatch to the central bank of the recipient country. This involved transporting the gold by aircraft, truck convoys, or ship, while insured by Swiss insurance companies. For instance, between May 1942 and February 1943, a series of convoys totaling some 280 trucks marked with Swiss national flags conveyed gold bars with a value of up to $400 million across occupied France to Spain and Portugal.

During the second half of the war, all the neutral countries came under intense pressure from the Allies not to accept payment for any goods or services in Nazi gold. A senior official at the Swiss National Bank (SNB) came up with an ingenious scheme to avoid such censure. Now the Reichsbank would simply sell its gold to Swiss banks in exchange for currency, usually Swiss francs. This money was then deposited in the account of the recipient country at the Swiss National Bank. The country in question was then at liberty to transfer these funds home or else to buy "cleansed" gold from the SNB—which, of course, took a commission on every transaction. Of the $890 million in gold that financed the Nazi war machine, $388 million was processed through the Swiss National Bank and a similar amount, $378 million, through the Bank for International Settlements.

Many other Swiss financial institutions benefited from the Nazi connection. Nazi officials and SS leaders secreted untold millions of dollars' worth of gold, currency, and artworks in Switzerland. There, the plunder was hidden in numbered accounts that were immune to scrutiny, thanks to the Swiss banking laws originally enacted in 1934 to give anonymity to Jewish depositors fleeing the clutches of the Nazi regime. As the French writer and diplomat François-René de Chateaubriand (1768–1848) once observed, "The Swiss, neutral during the great revolutions in the countries surrounding them, have enriched themselves on the destitution of others, and founded a bank on the misfortune of nations."

Chapter 6

EAGLE FLIGHT
AND LAND OF FIRE

BY THE SUMMER OF 1943, the manufacturing capacity of the Soviet Union had recovered from the devastating effects of Hitler's Operation Barbarossa two years earlier. In the face of the remorseless advance of the Wehrmacht in the summer of 1941, whole armaments factories were moved eastward behind the Ural Mountains and beyond the reach of the invaders. Tanks and aircraft were now being produced in unprecedented numbers while lend-lease supplies from America, Britain, and Canada added significantly to the fighting powers of the Red Army.

In July 1943, the Wehrmacht, painfully rebuilt after the losses of Stalingrad, launched a major offensive code-named Operation Citadel against the Kursk salient in central Ukraine, where almost two-thirds of all Soviet armored fighting vehicles, aircraft, and artillery assets were concentrated. In a grueling battle of attrition lasting eight days, the German and Soviet forces fought each other to a standstill. The German Army Groups Center and South lost nearly three hundred tanks and the Soviets three times as many—but the Red Army was left in control of the battlefield and could more easily replace such losses.

Germany's hopes of defeating the Soviet Union had finally failed. Despite German propaganda proclaiming many "defensive triumphs" in the months to come, the *Ostheer* or Eastern Army was never again to mount a major offensive on the Russian Front. From now on, the Red Army would begin its inexorable advance westward toward the borders of Germany.

In the same month as the battle of Kursk, the Western Allies made the first invasion of Europe by amphibious landings in Sicily; Operation Husky cleared the island of German troops by late August, opening the way to the Italian mainland. Reichsleiter Martin Bormann recognized that while the war would continue, these military defeats sounded the death knell of the Third Reich. It was time to plan for the formerly unthinkable—how to save something from the eventual defeat of Nazi Germany. The first requirement was money.

SINCE HE HAD JOINED THE PARTY in 1926, Bormann had raised many millions of reichsmarks for the NSDAP and for the various funds that supported the lavish lifestyle of the Führer. It was a skill he never lost in all his many years of service to Adolf Hitler. His business acumen was legendary and he was quick to recognize any moneymaking opportunity. It was Bormann who organized some of the sales of "degenerate art," of which one was an auction held on June 30, 1939, at the Grand Hotel National in the Swiss lakeside town of Lucerne. Some 126 paintings and sculptures were on offer, including works by Georges Braque, Paul Klee, Vincent van Gogh, Henri Matisse, and Pablo Picasso that had been stripped from museums in Berlin, Bremen, Cologne, Dresden, Essen, Frankfurt, and other collections. Pablo Picasso's masterpiece from his Blue Period, *The Absinthe Drinker*, which had been looted from the Jewish Schoeps family, was auctioned for just 12,000 Swiss francs (equal to US$2,700 in 1939, equivalent to about $42,000 today; in June 2010, the Andrew Lloyd Webber Art Foundation sold it for $52.5 million). All the proceeds from this Swiss auction, about 500,000 Swiss francs, were converted into pounds sterling and deposited in the J. Henry Schröder & Co. bank in London for Bormann's exclusive use; the German art museums did not receive a single pfennig.

With the outbreak of war, Bormann was determined that the Nazi Party should receive its fair share of any plunder from the occupied countries. Following the invasion of the Low Countries, the diamond district of Amsterdam fell into the hands of the Wehrmacht. Some 940,000 carats of cut and industrial diamonds, with a further 290,000 carats of diamonds from Belgium, were confiscated and processed through Johann Urbanek & Co. of Nuremberg. Such high-value, low-volume items were especially useful for Bormann's plans to spread the party's tentacles around the world. In particular, they allowed him to exert complete control over the NSDAP Auslands-Organisation (Foreign Organization) of party members living in countries outside the German Reich, such as the Iberian Peninsula and Latin America. The Foreign Organization also provided excellent cover for intelligence-gathering and the means to manipulate or bribe foreign politicians to support the Nazi cause.

To this end, Bormann acquired his own air and shipping lines to disperse his peddlers of influence and financial assets around the world. These included the previously mentioned Spanish shipping line Compañia Naviera Levantina and the Italian airline Linee Aeree Transcontinentali Italiane (LATI). The latter had run a prewar service to South America from Rome, via Seville in Spain to Villa Cisneros in the Spanish Sahara, then on to Sal in the Portuguese Cape Verde islands, and across the Atlantic to Natal or Recife in Brazil, with final legs to Rio de Janeiro and Buenos Aires. By these means, Bormann acquired a regular pipeline for people and freight to Iberia and South America without using Luftwaffe aircraft or compromising the national airline, Lufthansa. The aircraft of choice was the trimotor Savoia-Marchetti 75 GA (for *grande autonomia* or "long range"), with a payload of a little over one ton and a range of 4,350 miles. This made it an ideal carrier for such items as artworks, gemstones, or large consignments of cash for the German embassies and consulates in South America. On their return flights the aircraft carried high-value minerals and other resources.

Much of the money sent to German embassies around the world to underwrite Bormann's conspiracies was, in fact, in the form of counterfeit British five-, ten-, twenty-, and fifty-pound notes that were less likely to be identified as fakes when circulated in far-flung places. The counterfeit notes were produced from December 1942 to February 1945 during Operation Andreas by 142 Jewish prisoners in Blocks 18 and 19 at the Sachsenhausen concentration camp near Berlin. The program was also known as Operation Bernhard after the man in charge of the scheme, SS Maj. Bernhard Krueger. Once the requisite type of paper was finally obtained, various denomination pound notes were forged, with a face value of £134,609,945, equivalent to $377 million in 1944 or $4.6 billion today, representing some 10 percent of all British banknotes in circulation. The original scheme was to drop bundles of counterfeit notes from aircraft over the British Isles in order to destabilize the British economy, but from 1943 Germany had insufficient aircraft available for the operation. Instead, the notes were laundered through Swiss banks or foreign companies, particularly in Holland, Italy, and Hungary.

The imperative for Bormann was now to transfer monies in every shape and form—counterfeit, stolen, or even legitimate government funds—to safe havens abroad. This was achieved as part of an operation code-named Aktion Adlerflug—Project Eagle Flight—which involved setting up innumerable foreign bank accounts and investing funds in foreign companies that were controlled by hidden German interests. For example, between 1943 and 1945 more than two hundred German companies set up subsidiaries in Argentina. Money and other assets, such as industrial patents, were transferred through shell companies in Switzerland, Spain, and Portugal to the Argentine branches of German banks such as the Banco Alemán Transatlántico. The funds were then channeled to the German companies operating in Argentina, such as the automobile manufacturer Mercedes Benz—the first Mercedes Benz factory to be built outside Germany. These companies were in turn charged by their German head office higher production costs for products made in Argentina; for instance, the true production cost of a Mercedes truck might be $5,000, but Mercedes Benz Argentina was required to pay Mercedes Benz Germany $6,000 for the components. The difference between the actual cost and the prices paid was then secreted in Argentine bank accounts to be drawn upon after the war, without any fear of scrutiny by the Argentine authorities, let alone the Allies. These same companies became a source of employment for fleeing Nazi war criminals after 1945. For example, Adolf Eichmann worked in the Mercedes Benz factory at González Catán in the suburbs of Buenos Aires under the name of Riccardo Klement from 1959 until agents from Mossad, the Israeli national intelligence agency, abducted him on May 11, 1960.

Bormann's money-laundering process was repeated with companies in Portugal, Spain, Sweden, and Turkey as well. By 1945, he had amassed some $18 million in Swedish kroner and $12 million in Turkish lira, with major deposits in the Stockholms Enskilda Bank and in the Deutsche Bank and the Deutsche Orientbank, both in Istanbul.

Another major aspect of Project Eagle Flight was the acquisition of shares or equity in foreign companies, especially in North America. For this, Bormann turned to the past master of the game, IG Farben. Since the time of its formation in 1926, IG Farben had acquired numerous American companies as part of its worldwide cartel. By the time Germany declared war on the United States shortly after Pearl Harbor, IG Farben held a voting majority in 170 American companies and minority holdings in another 108. Bormann turned for advice to its president, Hermann Schmitz, and to the former Reich economics minister, Dr. Hjalmar Schacht. Together they were able to coordinate the transfer of Nazi funds through Swiss banks, via the Bank for International Settlements, or through third parties and companies. As a case in point, through their Stockholms Enskilda Bank (SEB), the Swedish brothers Jacob and Marcus Wallenberg purchased the American Bosch Corporation, the U.S. subsidiary of Robert Bosch GmbH of Stuttgart, on behalf of the Bormann "Organization" but with the Wallenbergs as nominal owners. For their pains, they were paid with 2,350 pounds of gold bullion deposited in a Swiss numbered account on behalf of SEB. This Stockholm bank also bought stocks and bonds for Bormann on the New York Stock Exchange and made substantial loans to the Norsk Hydro ASA plant in Rjukan, Norway, which was crucial in the manufacture of "heavy water" for the Nazi atomic weapons program. Needless to say, IG Farben was the majority shareholder in Norsk Hydro ASA.

By these means, Bormann was able to create some 980 front companies, with 770 of these in neutral countries, including 98 in Argentina,

58 in Portugal, 112 in Spain, 233 in Sweden, 234 in Switzerland, and 35 in Turkey—no doubt there were others whose existence has never been revealed. Every single one was a conduit for the flight of capital from Germany, just waiting for Bormann to give the order when the time was right. In the best IG Farben tradition, ultimate title to the companies was a closely guarded secret maintained through a number of subterfuges, as described succinctly by the celebrated CBS Radio journalist Paul Manning, author of *Martin Bormann: Nazi in Exile*: "Bormann utilized every known device to disguise their ownership and their patterns of operations: use of nominees, option agreements, pool agreements, endorsements in blank, escrow deposits, pledges, collateral loans, rights of first refusal, management contracts, service contracts, patent agreements, cartels, and withholding procedures." The most important of these instruments were bearer bonds. These are securities issued by banks, companies, or even by governments, often in times of crisis, in any given value. They are unregistered; no records are kept of the owners or of any transactions involved, so they are highly attractive to investors who wish to remain anonymous. Whoever physically held the paper on which the bond was issued owned the investment security, so a bearer bond issued in Zurich could be cashed in Buenos Aires or elsewhere with impunity. As Hitler declared to Bormann: "Bury your treasure deep, as you will need it to begin the Fourth Reich."

INSEPARABLE FROM SECURING THE FINANCIAL ASSETS of the Third Reich was the need to preserve the Nazi leadership, in particular Adolf Hitler and his immediate entourage. Any refuge for Hitler had to be chosen with care. When the British were faced with a similar situation in the summer of 1940, it had been a relatively simple matter; if the threat of invasion from across the Channel had become a reality and the plans for containing the German beachhead had failed, then the powerful Royal Navy would have transported the royal family and the government to Canada, to continue the war from the dominions and colonies. Germany, on the other hand, no longer had an overseas empire, since the Treaty of Versailles had stripped her of her few colonies in Africa and the Pacific in 1919.

However, there was still a kind of de facto German overseas colony in Latin America, where many thousands of Germans had emigrated in previous generations. These communities were cohesive and commercially active, and Bormann had access to them through the NSDAP Auslands-Organisation. A file was brought to his attention that had been written during World War I by the young naval intelligence officer Wilhelm Canaris, describing his escape in 1915 from internment in Chile via Patagonia—the vast, sparsely inhabited region of southern Chile and Argentina that had a predominantly German settler population.

Lt. Canaris had been sheltered by the German community around a small town in the foothills of the Argentine Andes. Its isolation and the strongly patriotic German influence among the local population were significant factors. However, if this place was to be selected for such an all-important and top-secret project, then the attitude of the Argentine national government would be equally important. Fortunately, a military coup d'état in Buenos Aires in June 1943 brought to power a regime sympathetic to Nazi Germany—indeed, a highly placed member of the new government, Col. Juan Domingo Perón, had already been on the German intelligence payroll for two years. With massive funds already deposited in Argentina, a cooperative regime in power, and a significant part of the nation's industry and commerce owned by people of German extraction, the pieces were now in place for the execution of a concerted plan.

Bormann's scheme was code-named Aktion Feuerland (Project Land of Fire) in reference to Patagonia's southern tip, the archipelago Tierra del Fuego (Spanish for "Land of Fire"). The plan's object was to create a secret, self-contained refuge for Hitler in the heart of a sympathetic German community, at a chosen site near the town of San Carlos de Bariloche in the far west of Argentina's Río Negro province. Here the Führer could be provided with complete protection from outsiders since all routes in by road, rail, or air were in the hands of Germans. In mid-1943, Bormann's chief agent in Buenos Aires, a banking millionaire named Ludwig Freude, put the work in hand.

PART II

THE
HUNTERS

Chapter 7

RED INDIANS
AND PRIVATE ARMIES

AMONG THE BRITISH FORCES that landed in French North Africa during Operation Torch in November 1942 was a new unit on its first major operation—30 Commando Unit (CU). Primarily, 30 CU was tasked with gathering military intelligence documents and items of enemy weapons technology before they could be hidden or destroyed. The unit had been conceived in the British Admiralty, and the Royal Navy was particularly anxious to gather any intelligence concerning the sophisticated Enigma encryption machines that were used to communicate with Adm. Dönitz's U-boats at sea. The Naval Intelligence Commando Unit was the brainchild of Lt. Cdr. Ian Fleming of the Royal Naval Volunteer Reserve (RNVR)—the future creator of the quintessential fictional spy James Bond. Fleming was recruited in 1939 by Vice Adm. John Godfrey, director of naval intelligence, as his personal assistant. On March 24, 1942, Fleming's proposal for the new unit landed on the admiral's desk.

Fleming had been influenced by the exploits of the Abwehrkommando—German clandestine special forces, often disguised in Allied or neutral uniforms. The Abwehrkommando had performed most effectively against the Allies during the invasions of Holland, Yugoslavia, Greece, Crete, and the USSR. Formed on October 15, 1939, as part of Adm. Canaris's Abwehr, the obscurely titled Lehr und Bau Kompanie zbV 800 (Special Duty Training and Construction Company No. 800) was commanded by Capt. Theodor von Hippel and based at the Generalfeldzeugmeister-Kaserne barracks in Brandenburg, Prussia. Thereafter the unit adopted the name of that town as its informal title—the Brandenburgers. On May 20, during the initial German paratroop drop at Maleme airfield during Germany's airborne invasion of the island of Crete, a special forces unit led the assault on the British headquarters, with the specific task of capturing military intelligence documents and codebooks—fortunately, it found nothing related to Ultra intelligence (see Chapter 1, page 4). It was reports of this mission that prompted Ian Fleming to write his missive to Godfrey proposing a similar raiding force.

At the outset, Fleming's "Red Indians," as he liked to call them, were given the cover name of the Special Engineering Unit of the Special Service Brigade, which was under the operational control of the Chief of Combined Operations, Adm. Lord Louis Mountbatten. Accordingly, after completing training, its personnel were entitled to wear the coveted green beret, as well as drawing a daily special-service allowance to enhance their pay. Subsequently, the group's title was changed to 30 Commando Unit; the "30" related to the room number at the Admiralty in Whitehall, London, occupied by Fleming's legendary secretary Miss Margaret Priestley, a history don from Leeds University and the inspiration for Miss Moneypenny in his James Bond novels.

The unit comprised three elements: No. 33 Royal Marine Troop, which provided the fighting element during operations; No. 34 Army Troop; and No. 36 Royal Navy Troop. Originally there was to have been a No. 35 RAF Troop, but the Royal Air Force never seconded the necessary personnel. Like all such special forces units, 30 CU attracted some extraordinary characters. Its first commanding officer was Cdr. Robert "Red" Ryder, Royal Navy, who had just been awarded the Victoria Cross, Britain's supreme decoration for gallantry in battle, for his exceptional valor and leadership in the destruction of the vital lock gates of the Normandie dock at St. Nazaire during Operation Chariot earlier in the year. This brilliant but costly raid denied the Kriegsmarine any docking facilities on the Atlantic coast for its capital ships such as the *Tirpitz.*

Despite coming under Combined Operations, 30 CU reported directly to Fleming in his capacity as personal assistant to the director of naval intelligence. The unit was first deployed during Operation Jubilee, the ill-fated Dieppe raid on August 12, 1942, but their gunboat HMS *Locust* was struck several times by gunfire on entering the harbor and was forced out to sea before any troops could be landed. One of the primary reasons for the failure of Operation Jubilee was the fact that German signals intelligence had broken Royal Navy codes and had full knowledge of the planned raid some five days before it was launched.

FOR OPERATION TORCH, 30 Commando Unit landed from HMS *Malcolm* on November 8, 1942, at Sidi Ferruch in the Bay of Algiers, together with an assault force of American troops from the U.S. 34th Infantry Division. Advancing with the leading infantry, No. 33 Troop, commanded by Lt. Dunstan Curtis, RNVR, captured several buildings in their quest for intelligence. Because of the peculiar terms of the armistice that was soon concluded with the Vichy French authorities, Curtis and his men needed all their ingenuity to uncover material from places guarded by the French police. In addition, 30 CU captured an Abwehr officer named Maj. Wurmann, who, already disillusioned by the war, provided a mass of information on the structure and organization of the Abwehr, as well as character assessments of its key personnel. This intelligence was rapidly disseminated throughout MI6 and the OSS. In all, some two tons of documentation were collected and shipped back to London. Most importantly, another Enigma encryption machine was captured, which proved immensely helpful to Station X at Bletchley Park in the long task of cracking the Shark U-boat cipher.

The unit's Nos. 33 and 34 Troops were sent back into the line in February 1943 during the middle of the Tunisian campaign—courtesy of Cdr. Fleming, the Royal Marines troop now had jeeps to increase their mobility. During the following months, they met up with several other colorful special forces units that had been operating throughout the North African campaign, including Col. David Stirling's Special Air Service (SAS), the Long Range Desert Group (LRDG), and Popski's Private Army. The jeeps of No. 33 Troop were soon bristling with multiple machine guns in the manner of the SAS, and 30 CU also copied the LRDG in obtaining supply trucks to increase their radius of action and independence of movement.

While 30 CU was now able and ready to fight for the spoils of war, the British First Army in Tunisia had created its own ad hoc intelligence-gathering unit, known as S-Force. This had no permanent organization but was commonly configured around a company of infantry and a military police detachment, with any other miscellaneous attachments judged necessary for the task in hand. Accordingly, S-Force was slow to deploy and cumbersome in action. The quicker reactions of the self-sufficient 30 CU were graphically demonstrated on the night of April 21, 1943. During that day a German Tiger heavy tank—a formidable new threat to Allied armor that was the subject of much fearful speculation—was disabled at Medjez-el-Bab. Any captured example would be of immense value for technical analysis, as neither Britain nor the United States had any comparable tank even on the drawing board. As dusk fell, British troops attempted to drag away the fifty-six-ton behemoth but were driven off by German forces with the same intention. The recovery team called for infantry support but none was forthcoming; S-Force was alerted but was slow to react. Fortunately, 30 Commando Unit was on hand. They arrived quickly in their heavily armed jeeps, recaptured the Tiger, and protected the troops as they hauled their trophy away. This Tiger, undoubtedly the greatest technical prize of the Tunisian campaign, provided stark proof of the superiority of German weapons technology.

Following the Axis surrender in Tunisia, elements of 30 CU went on to serve during Operation Corkscrew on the island of Pantelleria in the Strait of Sicily, on Sicily itself during Operation Husky, on the Greek islands, in Corsica, and in occupied Norway. In November 1943, the unit returned to Britain to begin preparing for the next year's landings in Normandy. The following month it was renamed 30 Assault Unit, Royal Navy. This decision was in reaction to Hitler's infamous

October 1942 *Kommandobefehl* (commando order), which demanded the immediate execution after interrogation of all British commandos captured by German forces under any circumstances, even if surrendering. The mere change of title was not, of course, recognized by the SS as legitimate protection. Nevertheless, 30 Assault Unit was now ready for its most extraordinary campaign of the war.

ON JANUARY 11, 1943, DURING THE ASSAULT on Tripoli in North Africa, a pair of British Eighth Army armored cars of the 11th Hussars slowed to a halt at the center of the Roman amphitheater at Leptis Magna. There was just time for a photograph of the crews against the extraordinary backdrop of one of the world's most magnificent classical ruins. However, Lt. Col. R. Mortimer Wheeler of the Royal Artillery looked on in dismay as the heavy armored vehicles cracked the ancient Roman flagstones under their weight. As a peacetime archaeologist and keeper of the London Museum, Mortimer Wheeler winced at the damage that was being inflicted on one of the wonders of antiquity. He immediately consulted Brig. Maurice Lush, a civil affairs officer (CAO) at the British Military Administration in Tripolitania. Although Lush was baffled that anyone should be concerned about the "broken buildings," he prudently delegated the protection of the site to Mortimer Wheeler and another gunner officer and colleague from the London Museum, Maj. John Bryan Ward-Perkins. This decision proved to be the genesis of an extraordinary organization consisting of specially qualified British and American officers with the remit to identify and, if possible, prevent the destruction of cultural buildings and monuments in the path of the Allied armies. They would be known as the "Monuments Men."

In the same month, George Stout, an art conservator at the Fogg Art Museum at Harvard, wrote a letter to Kenneth Clark, director of the National Gallery in London, suggesting the creation of a "conservation corps" to accompany the frontline troops and forestall the destruction of important historical buildings and monuments. This letter coincided with the arrival on the desk of Lt. Col. Sir Charles Woolley—a world-famous archaeologist and a former colleague of T. E. Lawrence (Lawrence of Arabia)—of a report by Wheeler and

Ward-Perkins about their efforts to protect Leptis Magna. Woolley approached senior figures at the Casablanca Conference, urging the formation of a conservation unit before the next campaign was undertaken. In Woolley's words:

> Prior to this war, no army had thought of protecting the monuments of the country in which and with which it was at war and there were no precedents to follow. . . . All this was changed by a general order issued by [Gen. Eisenhower] just before he left Algiers, an order accompanied by a personal letter to all Commanders. . . . The good name of the Army depended in great measure on the respect which it showed to the art heritage of the modern world.

On June 23, 1943, President Roosevelt established the American Commission for the Protection and Salvage of Artistic and Historical Monuments in War Areas—later known more succinctly as the Roberts Commission after its chairman, U.S. Supreme Court Justice Owen Roberts. At the outset, equipment and transport were sorely lacking, and the aim of accompanying the frontline troops was not achieved during the invasion of Sicily on the night of July 9–10, 1943. The first of the Monuments Men, Capt. Mason Hammond, USAAF—a classics professor from Harvard—landed on July 29. Fortunately, the damage to most of the classical sites had been slight; Gen. George S. Patton, commanding the U.S. Tenth Army and himself a keen military historian, had taken Hammond's directives seriously. Dismayed by the sight of the roofless Greek temples at Agrigento, Patton demanded to know if this damage had been caused by American firepower. A local farmer replied through an interpreter that this was not the case—it had happened during "the last war." When Patton asked which war he meant, the interpreter said that the farmer was referring to the Second Punic War of 218–201 BCE.

On September 3, 1943, the Allies landed on mainland Italy. The Fascist regime was simultaneously overthrown and Italy capitulated, but the country was immediately occupied by German troops under Field Marshal Albert Kesselring. After fierce resistance, the Allies entered Naples on October 1, 1943, at a cost of much damage to the city. Both the Allies and the Germans now accused each other of atrocities and cultural vandalism, but it was the Hermann Göring Panzer Division that had looted many of the greatest Neapolitan works of art.

The Allies' eighteen-month advance northward would be delayed repeatedly by a succession of skillfully sited and stubbornly held defensive lines in difficult mountainous terrain. By January 1944, the Allied armies were stalled in front of the Gustav Line that guarded the approaches to Rome. The defensive emplacements were dotted along the ridgelines and mountaintops where the ancient Benedictine abbey of Monte Cassino towered over the strategic Rapido valley and Highway 6 to Rome. Built in 529 CE, the abbey was a symbol of everything that the Monuments Men were trying to protect from destruction, but their hopes were to be dashed. Although not actually incorporated into the Gustav Line, the dominating heights of Monte Cassino allowed observation over many miles. Despite pleas from the Vatican and after two major ground assaults had failed to capture it, the abbey was pulverized by 1,400 tons of bombs by the U.S. Fifteenth Army Air Force. This was greatest failure of the Monuments Men during the war. Despite the sacrifice of the abbey, it still took several more months of heavy fighting before the position finally fell to Polish and French North African troops on May 18, 1944.

With the breaking of the Gustav Line, Rome was now within reach of the Allies, but there seemed to be every likelihood that the city and its millennia of treasures would be destroyed in costly street fighting. Uncharacteristically, Hitler declared both Rome and Florence "open cities"—meaning that Germany would abandon its defensive if necessary to prevent the destruction of those cities, which he held in cultural awe. Florence, the birthplace of the Renaissance, was the inspiration for his vision of Linz, and in May 1938, he had spent over three hours in the Uffizi Gallery in the company of his Axis partner Benito Mussolini. The Führer was utterly enraptured but Il Duce less so. As he trailed behind Hitler, he was heard to mutter *"Tutti questi vaffunculi quadri!"* ("All these fucking paintings!")

With the Allied landings in France now imminent, it would be the task of the Monuments Men not just to protect Europe's historic heritage but also to find Hitler's immense hoard of artistic plunder and return it to its rightful owners. In the spring of 1944, the Monuments, Fine Arts, and Archives (MFA&A) teams congregated at Shrivenham in southwest England in readiness for D-Day. Other specialized units of military hunters were also being prepared to cross the Channel; in the fog of war, the trails they followed would eventually cut across those of Bormann's conspiracies at several points. One of these organizations would be searching for signs of Hitler's atomic weapons program and another for his looted gold.

IN AUGUST 1939, A MONTH BEFORE THE OUTBREAK of World War II, a group of concerned scientists, including Albert Einstein, had written to President Roosevelt to warn him of the dangers inherent in Germany's lead in the field of theoretical physics. Their expressed concern that "extremely powerful bombs of a new type may thus be constructed" led to the formation of the Uranium Committee to undertake nuclear research, but progress was dilatory. On October 9, 1941, Roosevelt was apprised of the findings of the British nuclear research program, code-named the MAUD Committee, later Tube Alloys, on the feasibility of the use of uranium for a bomb. The U.S. government displayed little interest until Pearl Harbor wrenched it into the war in December 1941. The Office of Scientific Research and Development was established the following month, resulting in the creation of the Manhattan Project into which the researches of the MAUD Committee were subsumed.

The first experimental nuclear reactor, built at the University of Chicago and named Chicago Pile-1, achieved a successful self-sustaining chain reaction on December 2, 1942, under the direction of Enrico Fermi, an émigré from Fascist Italy. By now, the scale of the scientific and industrial effort required to devise and construct an atomic weapon was recognized by the military director of the program, Gen. Leslie R. Groves, and his scientific director, J. Robert Oppenheimer. Numerous universities across the United States, Canada, and Great Britain embarked upon pure and applied research into the separation of uranium isotopes to produce weapons-grade material capable of nuclear fission and to investigate the properties of plutonium for an alternative type of atomic bomb. Over three years, some $2 billion and

130,000 personnel were devoted to the Manhattan Project, the largest military and industrial undertaking of World War II. It was comparable in size to the entire American automobile industry at that time.

Meanwhile, Gen. Groves and other military leaders were increasingly concerned as to the pace of atomic weapons development in Germany. At the instigation of Gen. George C. Marshall, an intelligence-gathering unit was established to determine the level of German progress and to disrupt any atomic weapons program. By early 1943, OSS sources in Europe were reporting rumors that German *Wunderwaffen* or "wonder weapons" would soon enter service, so it was logical to assume that the Germans were at the forefront of atomic weapons technology. For much of World War II, those entrusted with the direction of the Manhattan Project firmly believed that the Allies and Germany were engaged in a life-or-death race to develop the atomic bomb. There was no doubt that if Germany won, then London would be the first target for nuclear annihilation.

In reality, the Germans lagged far behind, due largely to the divisive nature of Nazi governance (see Chapter 3). Unlike the Manhattan Project, with its strictly centralized control under Gen. Groves, German nuclear researchers were overseen by several bodies, including the Army Ordnance Office, the National Research Council, and even the Postal Ministry. Furthermore, the scant resources were divided between nine competing development teams all pursuing different agendas. Before the war, Germany had been the world leader in theoretical physics, culminating in the discovery of the theory of nuclear fission in December 1938, but since many of the leading figures in this field were Jewish, their work was increasingly dismissed as "Jewish physics." Of about twenty-six nuclear physicists at work in 1933, more than half would soon emigrate, including fourteen past or future Nobel laureates. Several of these Jewish refugees joined the Manhattan Project.

By January 1944, Bletchley Park had deciphered several messages concerning ballistic rocket development, but none referring to a uranium bomb. Taking these together with information from their other assets on the continent, MI6 and the Directorate of Tube Alloys (which had superseded the MAUD committee in late October 1941) concluded that there were no concerted plans for a German atomic bomb, but the Americans were not convinced. Understandably, as Groves later wrote,

> Unless and until we had positive knowledge to the contrary, we had to assume that the most competent German scientists and engineers were working on an atomic program with the full support of their government and with the full capacity of German industry at their disposal. Any other assumption would have been unsound and dangerous.

Lt. Col. John Lansdale Jr., head of security for the Manhattan Project, appointed Col. Boris T. Pash to form an intelligence-gathering unit that was designated Alsos—the Greek word for "grove" and thus a play on words of Gen. Groves's name. Born to a Russian émigré family and a fluent Russian speaker with a visceral loathing for the Soviet Union, Pash worked for the U.S. Army's G-2 intelligence division. Samuel A. Goudsmit, a Dutch-born Jewish physicist at the University of Michigan, was chosen as the scientific director of the Alsos Mission, and the team was in place in London by the time of the Allied landings in Normandy in June 1944.

ALTHOUGH CDR. FLEMING'S 30 Assault Unit (30 AU)—had worked alongside other British and American special units during the Sicilian and Italian campaigns, the groups had never had a truly harmonious relationship, and before the invasion of France all parties reassessed the roles of their respective units. Significant changes in operating methods were implemented, but, above all, cooperation rather than competition was now the watchword. The priority was the identification of potential targets in northwest Europe, itemized in "black books" carried by 30 AU. The most pressing problem in the early summer of 1944 was to discover the launch ramps for V-1 flying bombs—the real inspiration for the rumors about German "wonder weapons." These sites were now proliferating in northern France despite a concerted Allied bombing and interdiction campaign to destroy them.

The individual training of 30 AU personnel was intense, embracing many skills, including languages, parachuting, demolitions, photography, street fighting, and even lock-picking and safecracking, courtesy of special courses at Scotland Yard. By now, 30 AU was privy to all the plans for Operation Overlord and the invasion of France. Prior to D-Day, all the 30 AU field troops were issued with a "get-out-of-jail-free" card signed "By command of the Supreme Allied Commander Europe, General Eisenhower"—the overall commander for the invasion of Normandy—and bearing in bold block capitals the order that "The bearer of this card will not be interfered with in the performance of his duty by the Military Police or by other military organization."

After the disappointing performance of the ad hoc S-Force units in North Africa and Italy, a new organization was created with the task of securing specific targets of military or scientific importance and safeguarding documents, equipment, and any other objects of strategic value before the enemy destroyed them—or, more commonly, before they were looted by liberated foreign slave workers or even by Allied troops. For this purpose, specialized Consolidated Advance Field Teams (CAFT) were formed from experts in particular areas of science and technology, to form part of a new Target Force or T-Force organization. Each of the American, British, and Canadian armies committed to the liberation of northwest Europe would have its own T-Force. Their organization incorporated a truck-mounted infantry unit to capture and secure the chosen targets, while the CAFT investigation teams or "assessors" searched each location for items of scientific interest or technological value.

While military and scientific technology was the primary objective of the T-Forces, the Supreme Headquarters Allied Expeditionary Forces (SHAEF) also established teams to search for Nazi gold and other valuables. Known as "Gold Rush" or "Klondike" teams, these came under the control of the formidable Col. Bernard Bernstein, the financial adviser to Gen. Eisenhower for civil affairs and military government. There was hardly a high-ranking officer from Eisenhower downward who did not defer to Col. Bernstein when it came to Nazi loot and his scrupulous procedures for dealing with its correct disposal. All these measures were part of the meticulous planning for the invasion of Hitler's Fortress Europe in the summer of 1944.

Chapter 8

THE HUNTING TRAIL
TO PARIS

AMONG THE FIRST GROUPS TO LAND on the coast of
Normandy on June 6, 1944, D-Day, were elements of both 30 Assault
Unit and the British Second Army's T-Force.

On June 10, Woolforce—named after the commanding officer of
30 AU, Lt. Col. A. R. Woolley, Royal Marines—landed in the American
sector on Utah Beach at Varreville and moved inland toward St. Mère
Église, where the troops encamped in a field without digging protec-
tive trenches. An enemy aircraft flew over and dropped two devices
that exploded overhead, dispensing submunitions that made

> a peculiar fluttering noise in the air. . . . For a while nothing else
> happened; then the whole field was lit by sharp flashes and explo-
> sions, like heavy machine cannons firing sporadically around us.
> The explosions did not last more than half a minute. In that time,
> the Unit lost 30 percent of its strength in killed and wounded. The
> aerial weapon was a large canister that burst in mid-air to release a
> quantity of "butterfly bombs" that then fluttered down to land all
> over the field before exploding in a vicious shower of splinters.

These casualties were caused by the SD2 *Sprengbombe Dickwandig*—the first cluster bomb munition ever to be deployed on the battlefield and typical of the advanced German weapons technology that 30 AU was established to uncover.

Besides pursuing their customary task of searching out naval intelligence in the ports of Le Havre and Cherbourg, one of the primary missions of 30 AU was to capture a V-1 launch pad. Intelligence reports indicated that the rumored *Vergeltungswaffe* 1 (V-1 Vengeance Weapon) was almost ready for deployment—the first of several advanced weapons systems that Hitler believed could still win the war for Germany. Sketches and information had reached the British authorities in November 1943 from the OSS via the MI6 staff at the embassy in Bern, thanks to the courageous efforts of a French Resistance fighter, Michel Hollard. They showed the construction of a concrete launch pad in northern France, with a "ski-ramp" for an unidentified weapon. By December 1943, aerial reconnaissance had identified 103 "ski-ramps," all of them pointing ominously toward London. These were the first visible portent of Hitler's *Unternehmen Eisbär*—Operation Polar Bear.

A concerted bombing campaign against all targets believed to be associated with the V-weapons program had begun with Operation Hydra in August 1943—raids on the V-weapon design center at Peenemünde on the Baltic Sea—followed that November by Operation Crossbow against the heavily protected V-2 bunkers at Watten and the V-3 "supergun" site at Mimoyecques, both in France. After November 15, 1943, all bombing sorties against the V-weapons program came under Operation Crossbow. Despite a massive effort, the ski-ramps proved difficult to hit, let alone destroy. By the summer of 1944, the whole northern tip of the Cherbourg (Cotentin) Peninsula was thick with launching sites, many of them pointing toward the invasion ports of Plymouth, Portsmouth, and Southampton. Fortunately, Operation Crossbow was sufficiently successful to disrupt Polar Bear and postpone its scheduled start date of March 1, 1944, when it could have seriously disrupted preparations for the Normandy landings.

In the early morning of June 13, 1944, Team 4 of 30 AU, led by Lt. Cdr. Patrick Dalzel-Job, Royal Navy, crept out through the

American front lines to find a V-1 launch site that had been identified by the French Resistance some fifteen miles beyond the American
beachhead. As the patrol moved out into the French countryside, the
very first V-1 flying bomb landed on Bethnal Green, East London, at
4:18 a.m. Once the ski-ramp was secured, technical experts were able
to inspect the site and captured examples of the flying bombs, so that
new countermeasures could be implemented. These included the acti-
vation of the Diver air-defense plan for southern England, combining
interception by high-speed fighters and antiaircraft guns aided by new
American radar technology. By July 1944, almost half of all flying
bombs that passed over the Diver defenses were being destroyed. By
the end of August, that figure rose to 83 percent with the first Gloster
Meteor jet fighters of No. 616 Squadron RAF coming into action
against the V-1s.

On the day before, June 16, Hitler's Operation Polar Bear had
begun in earnest, with 244 flying bombs launched from across northern
France. Of these, 45 crashed on takeoff, 144 reached England, and 73
actually fell on London. The British population had stoically borne the
Blitz of 1940–41 and nuisance raids up to 1943, but this attack was different. Quickly nicknamed the "buzz bomb" or "doodlebug," the V-1
carried a warhead of 1,870 pounds of amatol, which caused massive
blast damage. This was compounded by the traumatic psychological
effect when the loud spluttering noise of its pulse-jet engine suddenly
cut out over the target: there was then just twelve seconds of silence

Another target for 30 AU was the crucial German radar installation around Douvres-la-Délivrande to the south of Caen. The Germans
defended the facility with fierce determination for more than ten days,
even receiving a nighttime parachute drop of ammunition and supplies
by the Luftwaffe. It was finally captured, at the cost of heavy casualties,
on June 17, after a combined assault by 41 Royal Marine Commando,
divisional artillery, and tanks. 30 AU was quickly on the scene and
recovered not only much useful intelligence on the capabilities of the
radar system itself, but also a map showing the location of all radar stations across Europe and their exact specifications. A subsequent intelligence report stated that this was "assessed in the Admiralty as the
greatest single technical capture of the war."

On the day before, June 16, Hitler's Operation Polar Bear had
begun in earnest, with 244 flying bombs launched from across northern
France. Of these, 45 crashed on takeoff, 144 reached England, and 73
actually fell on London. The British population had stoically borne the
Blitz of 1940–41 and nuisance raids up to 1943, but this attack was different. Quickly nicknamed the "buzz bomb" or "doodlebug," the V-1
carried a warhead of 1,870 pounds of amatol, which caused massive
blast damage. This was compounded by the traumatic psychological
effect when the loud spluttering noise of its pulse-jet engine suddenly
cut out over the target: there was then just twelve seconds of silence

before the bomb crashed to earth, and that sudden silence meant that someone, somewhere in London, was going to die. After five years of deprivation and rationing, the morale of Londoners suffered severely under this new threat. Many left the city, while the government organized the evacuation of 360,000 women and children as well as the elderly and infirm. It was the dawn of a new era in warfare—the birth of the cruise missile—and the Germans were once more at the forefront of weapons technology.

Over the coming months, 30 AU spent much of their time in pursuit of the V-1 and V-2, often working in concert with local Resistance fighters who provided much valuable intelligence. Before the last V-1 launch site within range of London was overrun in October 1944, 2,515 flying bombs—or only one-quarter of those launched—had actually hit the target area, causing 22,892 casualties, including 6,184 deaths. Each one was a personal tragedy. However, at just 1.39 deaths per bomb launched, the V-1 bomb was hardly going to tilt the balance of the war back in Germany's favor, given the inexorable buildup of Allied forces on both the Western and Eastern Fronts.

The Western Allies now enjoyed a superiority of 20 to 1 in tanks and 25 to 1 in aircraft; their air forces possessed 5,250 bombers, capable of delivering some 20,000 tons of bombs in a single lift. Germany was fighting on three fronts, while its cities and industries were being pulverized from the air. Between June and October 1944, the Royal Air Force and the U.S. Army Air Forces would drop half a million tons of bombs on Germany—more than the entire amount during the war up to that time.

AFTER THE MILITARY DISASTERS OF 1943, Hitler had assumed the mantle of supreme war leader and was increasingly contemptuous of his Oberkommando der Wehrmacht (Supreme Command of the Armed Forces or OKW). His immediate military staff was by now reduced to compliant sycophants, headed by Field Marshal Wilhelm Keitel, commander in chief of OKW, and Gen. Alfred Jodl, chief of the operations staff. The Führer became increasingly dismissive and intolerant of any questioning of his military decisions—decisions that were ultimately disastrous for the Wehrmacht due to Hitler's impatience with the necessary staff work, his poor grasp of the realities on the ground, and his obsession with holding territory at all costs regardless of tactical considerations.

To Martin Bormann, such matters were of little concern, and he was usually excluded from military briefings or conferences. He was thus saved from death or serious injury when, at 12:40 p.m. on July 20, 1944, German Resistance leader Col. Claus von Stauffenberg placed a briefcase carrying a bomb under the oak table around which Adolf Hitler was holding a military conference at his Wolfschanze headquarters near Rastenburg in East Prussia. The bomb exploded as planned, killing three staff officers and a stenographer and wounding several others, but Hitler survived, despite burns, numerous wooden splinters driven into his legs and face, and a perforated eardrum. Operation Valkyrie, the latest of several plots to assassinate Hitler, had come the closest to success, and after its failure the regime exacted a terrible revenge. Some 5,000 people were arrested and nearly 200 executed; under the new laws of *Sippenhaft* or "blood guilt," the Gestapo swept up relatives and even friends of the plotters on the grounds of guilt by association. Hitler ordered that the conspirators were to be "hanged like cattle," and many of them died by slow strangulation while suspended from meat hooks in Plötzensee Prison in Berlin. The Allies did nothing while every vestige of the resistance movement in Germany was ruthlessly eradicated. Since the leading figures in the plot had been old-school military officers, Hitler's lack of confidence in the traditional Wehrmacht leadership class turned to actual suspicion. Henceforward, he would withhold his trust from all but the SS and his immediate circle—and particularly, Reichsleiter Martin Bormann.

Despite the Allies' material superiority, their progress in Normandy was dispiritingly slow and costly; they had hoped to break out of the beachhead within two weeks of D-Day, but in fact it took two months. On the same day that Col. von Stauffenberg's briefcase bomb exploded, Operation Goodwood, Gen. Bernard Montgomery's offensive around Caen at the east of the beachhead, failed with heavy losses. Operation Cobra, Gen. Omar Bradley's planned American breakout from the west of the beachhead, had been scheduled for July 20, but was postponed for five days. On the Eastern Front, however, the largest land battle of World War II was bleeding the Wehrmacht to death.

ON JUNE 22, 1944, THE THIRD ANNIVERSARY of Hitler's Operation Barbarossa, the Red Army launched its greatest offensive of the war so far. This Operation Bagration was a brilliant example of *maskirovka*—literally, "deception through camouflage": a system of sophisticated signals procedures whereby whole phantom armies were created to deceive the Germans thanks to bogus radio traffic, false troop movements, and disinformation via Red Army "deserters." The Soviets covertly assembled a force of 118 rifle divisions, eight tank and mechanized corps with 4,080 tanks and assault guns, six cavalry divisions to negotiate the treacherous Pripyat Marshes, and thirteen artillery divisions with some 10,563 guns and 2,306 Katyusha multiple rocket launchers. These combined armies of 2.3 million troops were covered and supported by 2,318 fighters, 1,744 *Shturmovik* ground-attack aircraft, and 1,086 assorted bombers, with another 1,007 in reserve.

Because of the success of *maskirovka*, the Germans had no real intelligence as to the time or place of this Soviet summer offensive. It was thought that the main assault would strike their Army Group North Ukraine, but the target was in fact Army Group Center in Byelorussia. This command had some 800,000 troops supported by 9,500 artillery pieces but only 553 tanks and assault guns. Worse still, only 20 percent of the Luftwaffe was now deployed on the Eastern Front, since the bulk of its fighters were needed for air defense over Germany. Army Group Center had just 839 aircraft in support. The battle raged for two months and ended with the destruction of Army Group Center in Byelorussia and the arrival of the Red Army at the gates of Warsaw. German casualties rose from 48,363 in May 1944 to 169,881 in July and a staggering 277,465 in August—higher even than the slaughter at the Battle of Verdun in 1916. Bagration was the most calamitous defeat suffered by the Wehrmacht in World War II; it lost more men in three months than it had in the whole of 1942.

On August 15, 1944, the Allies conducted a successful amphibious assault in the south of France—Operation Dragoon. On the following day, Hitler finally gave permission for Army Group B to withdraw from

Normandy, but it came too late. The bulk of the army group's forces were surrounded in the Falaise Pocket, where resistance ceased on August 22 after a sustained bombardment by Allied tactical airpower.

THE DAY BEFORE THE BOMB ATTEMPT on Hitler's life, on Sunday, July 19, 1944, Lt. Cdr. Dalzel-Job's Team 4 from 30 AU entered the ruins of Caen on the hunt for enemy documents and equipment. Approaching the Bassin Saint-Pierre (St. Peter's Basin), Team 4 came across a group of armed Frenchmen and a man in rough peasant clothes who spoke excellent English. The man proved to be S.Sgt. Maurice "Jock" Bramah of the Glider Pilot Regiment, whose aircraft had crashed into an orchard behind enemy lines on the night of June 5–6. Bramah had been shot through the lungs by a German machine gunner and left for dead, but was found by some Frenchmen and cared for in a local village. The Germans learned of his whereabouts and sent two soldiers to capture the wounded pilot on June 16. Bramah killed them both, escaped, and joined the French Forces of the Interior (FFI). Now, just three weeks later, Bramah introduced 30 AU to the FFI and the wider French Resistance network.

Their assistance and local intelligence would prove extremely valuable in the later stages of the French campaign. In particular, their knowledge of the German dispositions in and around Paris allowed 30 AU to enter the city undetected from the east. On August 25, 1944, Woolforce was able to travel via unguarded roads and streets indicated by the French Resistance on a mission to attack the Kriegsmarine headquarters in the Rothschild mansion on the Boulevard Lannes. Marine "Bon" Royle began systematically to blow open the various safes with plastic explosives. As he recalled,

> I had blown over 80 safes by now and was running short of plastic and fuse and I'd been using potato masher [German hand grenade] detonators for some time. . . . The safes were proving disappointing and yielding very little. One had a pair of black dress shoes inside that actually fit. I got married wearing them. Another contained a list of German admirals' birthdays but beyond revealing that some of them were octogenarians it did little else for the cause.

Other targets were more productive. At the torpedo store at Houilles outside of Paris, 30 AU discovered a new experimental eight-bladed torpedo propeller, a revolutionary powered aircraft gun turret, high-speed Morse and burst-transmission radios, and cipher equipment. In September 1944, 30 AU moved to the Pas-de-Calais in its continuing quest for V-1 and V-2 sites and to track down French scientists who had worked on the V-3 *Fleissiges Lieschen* (Busy Lizzie) supercannons at Mimoyecques; these were designed to bombard London with 300-pound high explosive shells at a rate of 300 an hour. By then 30 AU had recovered some 12,000 documents dealing with innumerable subjects, from the complete order of battle of the Kriegsmarine to the capabilities of revolutionary new U-boats, and from the latest communications equipment to maps of German minefields in the North Sea.

AS 30 AU WAS APPROACHING PARIS from the east, Col. Boris Pash and the Alsos Mission were entering the city from the west, at 8:55 a.m. on August 25. So keen was Pash to reach his objective that his jeep was the first American vehicle into the city, following closely behind the tanks of the Free French 2nd Armored Division. Under sporadic sniper fire, Pash's unarmed jeep was the fifth vehicle in a column of tanks that rolled into the center of Paris. In the late afternoon, Pash reached his destination, the Radium Institute on rue Pierre Curie, where he met the man he desperately wished to interview. Frédéric Joliot-Curie, a Nobel Prize winner in chemistry and the son-in-law of the Curies, was in charge of the only cyclotron—particle accelerator—in Europe and was also a leading authority on nuclear chain reactions. Over a celebratory bottle of champagne that evening, Pash learned that Joliot-Curie knew remarkably little about German research into uranium, but he did disclose that there was a research facility at the University of Strasbourg in Alsace-Lorraine, then still far behind enemy lines.

Paris also saw the debut of a joint Anglo-American T-Force of some fourteen inspection teams attached to the U.S. 12th Army Group; a comprehensive, coordinated intelligence-gathering organization would become ever more important as the Allied forces approached Germany itself. In Paris, T-Force activities were compromised by the fierce rivalries between Gaullist and communist factions that on occasion bordered on shooting wars. A further problem was a lack of infantry to secure the targets, as the French population was bent on "*les arrestations et l'epuration*" (arrests and purges) of perceived collaborators, ransacking many properties in the process.

Yet another of the specialized search units to enter Paris on August 25 were the Monuments Men. Second Lt. James Lorimer of the MFA&A program was attached to the logistical units of the U.S. 12th Army Group, so he was able to enter Paris that day with the first U.S. Army supply convoy to reach the city. Lorimer immediately went to the Louvre, where he stared in despair at the museum's long, empty galleries, now quite bare of paintings and sculptures. It was there that he met Mademoiselle Rose Valland, a true heroine of the French Resistance.

Throughout the Nazi occupation, this forty-six-year-old art historian had played on her dowdy appearance to remain in the background at the Jeu de Paume, where she acted as curator. This outstation of the Louvre was used as the main repository for all the artworks looted by Alfred Rosenberg's ERR (see Chapter 4, page 39) in France, where every item was meticulously cataloged and photographed before shipment to Germany. Every night, Rose Valland removed the negatives, which were then printed by a colleague in the Resistance while she transcribed the notes on every item and its proposed destination in Germany. Early each morning she returned the negatives before the start of the working day. Accordingly, she was able to pass to the Free French government in London lists of almost all the looted treasures that left for Germany. The regular flow of information from the various Resistance movements across Europe was routinely acknowledged by cryptic messages broadcast over the BBC radio service—for instance, a typical communication for Rose Valland might be "*La Joconde a le sourire*"—"The Mona Lisa is smiling." She herself had little to smile about: discovery of her activities would result in certain death, either by firing squad or by lingering maltreatment in a concentration camp.

Even as the Allies were approaching Paris, hundreds of artworks were still being packed into crates at the Jeu de Paume for onward shipment. On August 2, 1944, 148 crates of looted paintings were loaded aboard freight cars attached to Train No. 40044 at Aubervilliers railroad station. As usual, Valland had details of the shipment orders and the destinations in Germany. She provided these to the Resistance and asked if there might be some way to delay the train's departure, hopefully until the arrival of the Allies.

By August 10, Train No. 40044 was fully laden and ready to start its journey to Germany. Coincidentally, the French railroad workers in the area went on strike that day. Within forty-eight hours they were cajoled back to work. The train departed only to be mysteriously shunted into a siding. There the engine inexplicably developed mechanical problems; these were eventually rectified, but then broken couplings and seized brakes caused a further forty-eight-hour delay. Eventually, Train No. 40044 got on the move again—only to be halted when two engines collided and became derailed at a notorious bottleneck in the railroad system. The art train was trapped, never to leave Paris.

Chapter 9

CASH, ROCKETS, AND URANIUM

THE SIMULTANEOUS DESTRUCTION of Army Group Center in Byelorussia and Army Group B in Normandy convinced Martin Bormann of the need to accelerate his projects Eagle Flight and Land of Fire. He accordingly convened an extraordinary meeting of German industrialists, business leaders, and selected party officials that took place on August 10, 1944, at the Hôtel Maison Rouge on the rue des France-Bourgeois in the eastern French city of Strasbourg. Bormann was not present in person, since he needed to be at the Führer's side, but the conference was chaired by his personal emissary, SS Gen. Dr. Otto Scheid. Among those present were representatives of Krupp, Messerschmitt, Rheinmetall, Büssing, Volkswagen, and a host of other companies—including, of course, IG Farben.

In an opening statement, Dr. Scheid announced that

the steps to be taken as a result of this meeting will determine the post-war future of Germany. German industry must realize that the war cannot now be won and must take steps to prepare for a post-war commercial campaign, which will in time ensure the economic resurgence of Germany, with each industrial firm making new contacts and alliances with foreign firms. This must be done individually and without attracting suspicion. However, the NSDAP and the Third Reich will stand behind every firm with permissive and financial support.

The shifting of capital abroad was to ratchet into high gear and the "permissive" support took the form of Bormann's declaring some provisions of the 1933 Treason Against the Nation Act null and void. This law had mandated the death penalty for violation of foreign exchange regulations, for the export of capital, and even for concealing foreign currency. The steel magnate Fritz Thyssen had actually fallen victim to this legislation, but, unsurprisingly, had escaped execution; he and his wife had been detained in Sachsenhausen and Dachau, but in some comfort. In January 1950, Thyssen and his wife would emigrate to Buenos Aires, from where he controlled his business empire until his death in 1951.

With exquisite hypocrisy, Bormann made use of the Thyssen family's private bank in Rotterdam, Bank Voor Handel en Scheepvaart N.V., which had originally been founded by August Thyssen in 1918 in order to send illicit funds out of the Kaiser's Germany as defeat in World War I approached. Money was channeled from this bank to the Union Banking Corporation of New York, which was wholly owned by Fritz Thyssen's Vereinigte Stahlwerke AG (United Steelworks). From there it was disbursed to accounts in other American banks, including National City Bank, Chase National Bank, and Irving Trust, and used to buy stocks in U.S. companies and corporations. The flow of capital from Germany now became a flood, as massive amounts of the reserve equity of German industry were routed through the Deutsche Bank AG to Switzerland and beyond. Hoards of precious metals, gems, stocks, patents, and bearer bonds were transferred to anonymous bank accounts and safety deposit boxes around the world, from Ankara to Andorra and from Vigo to Valparaiso. In 1938 the number of industrial and commercial patents registered to German companies was 1,618. After the Maison Rouge conference, this figure rose to 3,377. These patents were transferred to foreign shell companies so they were beyond the reach of the Allies but still valid to protect the merchandise and production processes of German companies. There was to be no repeat of the 1919 Treaty of Versailles, when Germany's national assets had been laid bare to the victors as spoils of war.

At a later session of the Maison Rouge conference, Dr. Kurt Bosse of the Reich armaments ministry advised the industrialists that the military situation was grave and the war effort faltering "but that it would be continued by Germany until certain goals to ensure the economic resurgence of Germany after the war had been achieved." Dr. Bosse continued, "From this day, German industrial firms of all ranks are to begin placing their funds—and, wherever possible, key manpower—abroad, especially in neutral countries." In closing the meeting, he observed that "after the defeat of Germany, the Nazi Party recognizes that certain of its best-known leaders will be condemned as war criminals. However, in cooperation with the industrialists, it is arranging to place its less conspicuous but most important members with various German factories, as technical experts or members of research and design bureaux."

AMONG THE KEY FIGURES involved in Project Eagle Flight was the chairman of Deutsche Bank AG, Dr. Hermann Josef Abs, with whom Martin Bormann maintained a cordial relationship. Another was the former president of the Reichsbank and current director of the Bank for International Settlements, Dr. Hjalmar Schacht. He was a leading coordinator of the export of capital through various Swiss banks, particularly Schweizerische Kreditanstalt of Zurich, Basler Handelsbank, and of course BIS. As part of the dispersal of personnel, a director of IG Farben, Baron Georg von Schnitzler, was sent to Madrid. His cover story was that he was fleeing arrest by the Gestapo, but Schnitzler's true role was to coordinate the movement of monies and company assets via Spain to South America. This was achieved through the good offices of the Spanish banks Banco Alemán Transatlántico and Banco Germánico, both of which were owned by Deutsche Bank. It is estimated that some $6 billion flowed to Buenos Aires by this means, for investment throughout Latin America. Particular funds set aside for the personal benefit of the Nazi leadership were transferred to South America as gold bullion, precious stones, and other valuables in the diplomatic bags of the Reich foreign ministry. Göring, Goebbels, Ribbentrop, and other Nazi officials all had deposit accounts in Argentina, but in fact Bormann had no intention of ever allowing them to enjoy the fruits of their kleptocracy—in his view this was money that belonged to the Nazi Party.

Similarly, Bormann orchestrated the placement of all the financial officials, scientists, technicians, and security personnel associated with Eagle Flight. The powerful companies that attended the Maison Rouge conferences, and their subsidiaries, provided Bormann with information concerning all their research programs and the innovative weapons technology then coming into service or under development. These weapons programs were documented as to viability, location, and associated key personnel. Nothing was to be left to chance in order to preserve the Nazi Party. As early as November 7, 1942, the day before the Allied landings in French North Africa, Himmler and Bormann had met—in spite of their intense personal rivalry—to discuss the future of the party. Himmler later recounted their conclusions to his closest associates: "It is possible that Germany will be defeated on the military front. It is even possible that she may have to capitulate. But never must the National Socialist German Workers' Party capitulate. That is what we have to work for from now on." It was soon after this meeting that Himmler extended his first peace feelers to Allen Dulles in Bern through his intermediary Prince Hohenlohe (see Chapter 2, page 17)—a fact duly noted by Bormann.

IN THE SUMMER OF 1944, THE RIVALRY between Bormann and Himmler was as acute as ever. The SS—soon to be basking in its enhanced status after the July assassination plot—was already muscling in on some of the most prestigious weapons programs. Now that Himmler was also Reich minister of the interior, his empire-building was insatiable, and on August 8, 1944, the SS took over the V-2 rocket program from the army. This was a severe blow to Bormann, since he wished to control the major Nazi weapons programs and their personnel for his own devious ends—as possible bargaining tools for negotiations with the Allies as part of Aktion Feuerland. This development also marked a significant shift in the power balance within the Nazi hierarchy, with Himmler now firmly allied with Albert Speer, the minister of armaments and war production. Speer, who never lost Hitler's favor until the very last days, was determined to reverse the fortunes of war by the mass production of "wonder weapons."

Exactly a month after the SS annexed the V-2 program, the first of these rockets fell on an Allied city, heralding the start of Hitler's *Unternehmen Pinguin* (Operation Penguin). At 11:03 a.m. on September 8, 1944, a deafening explosion occurred near the Porte d'Italie metro station in southeastern Paris. It was followed by the roaring noise of a rocket engine and then, a fraction of a second later, by the sound of a double thunderclap. This was the sonic boom of a ballistic missile reentering the Earth's atmosphere from space at three times the speed of sound, leaving a vertical, lingering vapor trail to mark its flight. Six Parisians were killed and thirty-six others were injured.

At 6:37 that evening, Artillerie Abteilung (battalion) 485 fired two more V-2 missiles from a launch site in the prosperous, leafy suburb of Wassenaar in the Dutch seat of government, The Hague. Their aiming point was London Bridge railroad station in the British capital. One fell into Epping Forest some thirteen miles northeast of London at 6:40; sixteen seconds later the second struck Staveley Road in Chiswick, West London. The explosion burst gas and water mains, collapsed eleven houses, and seriously damaged twelve others. Three people were killed and seventeen others seriously hurt. There was a complete news blackout; to explain this mysterious explosion without any prior warning sound of an engine, the national press was told that the cause was a ruptured gas main. London suffered 22 more V-2 attacks that month, 85 in October 1944, and 154 in November. It was not until November 8 that the Germans finally announced the bombardment of Allied cities with the *Vergeltungswaffe* 2. Two days later Prime Minister Winston Churchill stood up in the House of Commons and admitted to Parliament that "Britain had been under rocket attack for some weeks."

IN 1931, THE GERMAN ARMY WEAPONS OFFICE had established a rocket research facility at Kummersdorf near Berlin, since rocket development was not specifically excluded by the terms of the

Treaty of Versailles. At that time, artillery officers dominated the army and much effort was devoted to improving the range and explosive effects of weapons to supersede the most powerful World War I technology. The first civilian allowed to work at Kummersdorf was the twenty-year-old Wernher von Braun, who began working there in late 1932. In May 1937, a secret test site was opened at Peenemünde on the island of Usedom off the Baltic coast. At the same time, Braun joined the Nazi Party; three years later he became a major in the SS. Development of long-range rockets continued apace, under the command of Gen. Dr. Walter Dornberger, with Braun as his technical director. Typical of the divisive organization of Nazi programs, the air force was in charge of the design of the *Vergeltungswaffe* 1 jet-propelled flying bomb, while the army was responsible for what became the *Vergeltungswaffe* 2 rocket. The rocket's specification called for a range of 170 miles with a payload of one ton, and it was envisaged that it would enter service in 1943. Initially Hitler was lukewarm, but Albert Speer recognized its potential and surreptitiously channeled funds to Peenemünde.

The first full-size A-4 test missile was launched on March 18, 1942; it failed, as did the second and the third. On October 3 the fourth prototype gained an altitude of fifty-three miles before landing some 120 miles away in the Baltic, only two miles from its intended target. It had also reached just three miles into space itself—the first rocket ever to achieve this goal, prompting Gen. Dornberger to declare, "We have invaded space with our rocket. For the first time we have used space as a bridge between two points on the earth. . . . This third day of October 1942 is the first of a new era . . . that of space travel." On November 22, Hitler gave permission for series production to begin.

Such activity did not escape RAF photoreconnaissance; the first actual record on film was taken on June 12, 1943, showing both a rocket lying horizontally and one standing vertically. By then British intelligence was receiving information about the rocket-testing facility from various sources. In December 1942, a Danish chemical engineer had passed to MI6 the broad specifications of a "large rocket." This was confirmed on March 22, 1943, by a conversation between two German tank generals captured in North Africa—Wilhelm Ritter von Thoma and Ludwig Crüwell—that was secretly recorded by MI19 at the Combined Services Detailed Interrogation Centre at Trent Park in England. Thoma revealed many details of the rocket program, and by now more information was filtering in from MI6 and the OSS in Switzerland.

In April 1943, two Polish workers with the Organisation Todt, the Third Reich's civil engineering and construction group, smuggled photographs and plans of Peenemünde to the Polish Home Army. These documents reached the Polish government in exile in London. On May 20, 1944, Polish Home Army partisans actually captured an almost intact V-2 that landed in the soft ground of the Sarnaki marshes, some eighty miles east of Warsaw, after a test flight. After the crew of an RAF transport aircraft undertook a perilous mission into Poland to collect the parts, the precious cargo arrived in London on July 28, to be reconstructed at the Royal Aircraft Establishment (RAE), Farnborough, together with other parts obtained from Sweden. On June 13, 1944, another rocket went out of control during a test flight over the Baltic Sea and exploded over the town of Bäckebo, Sweden. After some negotiation, the Swedes provided the British with a technical report and wreckage in exchange for a consignment of Spitfire fighter aircraft. Unfortunately, RAE Farnborough discovered nothing about the V-2 that could suggest effective countermeasures.

Nevertheless, the British war cabinet's Defense Committee (Operations) authorized Operation Hydra, a strike by RAF Bomber Command on the night of August 17–18, 1943, when 1,875 tons of incendiaries and high explosives were dropped on the rocket production buildings and living quarters at Peenemünde. This raid probably delayed full-scale deployment by three to four months, and both Speer and Hitler realized that production at Peenemünde itself was no longer feasible. It was decided to establish an assembly plant in an underground gypsum mine, near Nordhausen in the Harz Mountains of Thuringia, which was currently used for the storage of fuel reserves and poison gas munitions. The task of converting the mine for missile assembly was given to SS Gen. Dr. Hans Kammler of the SS Economic and Administrative Main Office. Kammler was an engineer who had been involved in the construction of several concentration and extermination camps, including the gas chambers and cremation ovens at

Auschwitz-Birkenau, and also in the destruction of the Warsaw Ghetto in April–May 1943. Kammler now presided over the building of the underground rocket assembly facilities, known as Mittelwerk (Central Works), using slave laborers—mostly French, Polish, and Russian—provided by the SS from the nearby Buchenwald concentration camp. Construction began on August 23, 1943; the laborers were treated with great brutality, living and working in inhuman conditions, and the work went on around the clock. Soon epidemics of dysentery, typhus, and tuberculosis, as well as widespread pneumonia from the damp conditions, were contributing to a death toll averaging twenty-five slave workers every day.

Rocket production began on December 10, 1943. Both Himmler and Speer were highly impressed, and Speer wrote to Kammler on December 17 with ringing praise for his accomplishment, one "that far exceeds anything ever done in Europe and is unsurpassed even by American standards." Production was originally projected at a rate of 900 rockets a month, at a cost of 100,000 reichsmarks each—ten times the cost of a V-1 flying bomb. However, peak production only reached 690 units, in January 1945; a total of 6,422 V-2s were built.

Hitler authorized Operation Penguin on August 29, 1944. By late March 1945, the German had launched 3,172 V-2s, of which 1,402 were fired at cities in England, 1,664 at targets in Belgium, 76 at France, 19 at Holland, and 11 against the Ludendorff Bridge after it was captured by American troops. It is estimated that Operation Penguin killed some 7,250 people over a period of seven months. Again, though the toll in human misery was immense, this average of 2.28 deaths per rocket launched at Allied targets was a remarkably low return for the investment. Of course, to that total must be added the deaths of some 20,000 slave workers at Mittelwerk and about 2,000 Allied airmen who were killed during Operations Crossbow and Big Ben in the hunt for V-weapons facilities and launching sites. At the peak of Operation Penguin in March 1945, about sixty missiles per week were striking England, carrying a grand total of 250 tons of explosives that randomly destroyed suburban streets. In the same month, the Allied air forces dropped 133,329 tons of bombs on Germany, laying waste whole cities.

The true money cost of the *Vergeltungswaffen* program is impossible to ascertain, but a postwar U.S. intelligence assessment put the price at almost $2 billion—about the same amount as the Manhattan Project. For the same cost as 6,422 V-2 missiles, German industry could have produced 6,000 Panther tanks or 12,000 Focke-Wulf Fw 190 fighter aircraft that would have been immeasurably more useful in the defense of the Reich. Nevertheless, the Americans were quick to appreciate the significance of the ballistic missile. It was technology they wanted for themselves at any price.

FOLLOWING THE LIBERATION OF PARIS in August 1944, the Allied armies fanned out across France in headlong pursuit of the retreating German forces. The British Second Army liberated Brussels on September 3 and the port of Antwerp the day after, just as the U.S. First Army reached Luxembourg and Patton's Third Army arrived at the Moselle River. Confidence was so high that Gen. Marshall even advised President Roosevelt that the war in Europe would be over "sometime between September 1 and November 1, 1944." The various specialized Allied search units tried to keep up with the advancing armor and infantry. The Germans' retreat was so rapid that their army was rarely able to implement the scorched-earth policy demanded by Hitler. Nevertheless, many bridges and buildings were mined and booby-trapped, among them Chartres Cathedral, the twelfth-century Gothic masterpiece in Chartres, France. Capt. Walker Hancock, the "Monuments Man" for the U.S. First Army, was quickly on the scene with MFA&A demolitions specialist Capt. Stewart Leonard. With infinite patience, Leonard defused the twenty-two separate demolition charges. When asked by another Monuments Man whether it was right to risk his life for art, Leonard responded, "I had that choice. I chose to remove the bombs. It was worth the reward." "What reward?" "When I finished, I got to sit in Chartres Cathedral—the cathedral I helped save—for almost an hour. Alone."

But the Monuments Men were not always able to reach their objectives in time. On the night of September 7, just hours before the arrival of the Allies, the Bruges Madonna sculpture by Michelangelo was stolen from the Cathedral of Notre Dame in Bruges and shipped off to

Germany. The task of the MFA&A teams was immense; the U.S. First, Third, Ninth, and Fifteenth Armies, with some 1.3 million troops, had just nine frontline MFA&A personnel, and in all there were only 350 people working for the organization in the whole European theater of operations.

Moreover, in the fall of 1944, the Allied advance faltered due to a lack of supplies—particularly gasoline—reaching the frontline troops. The railroad system of northern Europe had been completely destroyed by Allied bombing, and the failure to capture a major port intact was proving critical; the approaches to Antwerp from the sea were still in German hands and the city was now under constant bombardment by V-1 and V-2 missiles. Lacking the resources to advance on a broad front, but heartened by the apparent imminence of German defeat, SHAEF embarked on Operation Market Garden, a bold strategy of using the three divisions of the First Allied Airborne Army to seize vital bridges along a narrow corridor through Holland and on to the River Rhine, the last natural obstacle protecting the Ruhr and the heartlands of Germany. Despite worrisome Ultra decrypts, aerial reconnaissance photos, and warnings from the Dutch Resistance suggesting that major SS tank units stood in the path of this attempt, the high command went ahead with Operation Market Garden on September 17, 1944. Despite the skill and bravery of the American, British, and Polish paratroopers, the operation failed, ending in the destruction of the British 1st Airborne Division at Arnhem.

By October 1944, the mood of the Allied high command had switched from euphoria to despondency, just as the weather turned foul. In the north, the British and Canadians fought a wretched, muddy campaign to clear the banks of the Scheldt Estuary in order to open Antwerp to Allied shipping. The U.S. First Army was to be held up by the battle for the Hürtgen Forest from September 1944 to February 1945. Further south, the U.S. Third Army ground to a halt in Alsace-Lorraine, just short of Metz on the Moselle River, purely due to a lack of fuel; this delay allowed the Germans to reinforce that heavily fortified city for another grueling battle. In the breakout from Normandy, Patton's Third Army had advanced 500 miles in less than a month, and suffered just 1,200 casualties; over the next three months it would advance one-tenth that distance and suffer forty times the casualties. The war would by no means be over by Christmas.

GEN. LESLIE GROVES, THE DIRECTOR of the Manhattan Project, remained highly concerned as to the whereabouts of 1,200 tons of uranium ore belonging to the Union Minière—a Belgian uranium mining company based in the Congo—that the Germans had captured in 1940. Once processed into the isotope uranium-235, such an amount was sufficient to make several viable atomic bombs, which required about 140 pounds of enriched uranium each. After their foray into Paris in late August 1944, Col. Boris Pash and the Alsos team traveled to Toulouse in southern France to follow up on a tip-off. There they found 31 tons of the uranium ore stored in a French naval arsenal. The haul was immediately shipped to the Manhattan Project's production facility in Oak Ridge, Tennessee, to be processed through the electromagnetic separation calutrons into enriched uranium for "Little Boy," the uranium bomb being developed at the project's massive laboratory in Los Alamos, New Mexico.

Back in southern France, Col. Pash had procured several half-tracks, armored cars, and armed jeeps; thus mounted and armed, the Alsos unit followed the advance of the Allied forces toward the German border. In November 1944, the team arrived in newly liberated Strasbourg, in whose university they found a nuclear physics laboratory and bundles of documents. These revealed that the German nuclear weapons development program—known as Uranverein, the "Uranium Club"—was not only in its infancy, but based on flawed science. This confirmed the earlier British intelligence assessment, but Gen. Groves was still not satisfied. Fortuitously, other documents revealed the locations of all laboratories working with Uranverein, greatly simplifying Col. Pash's mission once the Allies advanced into Germany.

Groves was equally determined to forestall the chance of any Uranium Club scientists or their documents falling into the hands of the Soviet Union—whose own nuclear program, as we now know, was only a matter of months behind the U.S. research, thanks to the comprehensive penetration of the Manhattan Project by Soviet spies.

Germany's leading theoretical physicist was Werner Heisenberg, who occasionally traveled to occupied Denmark or neutral Switzerland to give scientific papers and lectures. Groves proposed that Heisenberg be kidnapped during one of these trips and interrogated to ascertain the extent of German progress. If that was not possible, then Heisenberg should be assassinated—in Groves's telling words, "Deny the enemy his brain." The task was given to an OSS agent named Morris "Moe" Berg, a former catcher and coach with the Boston Red Sox. Berg was also a graduate of Princeton who had studied seven languages, including Sanskrit. Now he immersed himself in the theory and practice of nuclear physics so that he would be able to follow Heisenberg's next university lecture, to be held on December 18, 1944, at the Physics Institute of the Eidgenössische Technische Hochschule (ETH) in Zurich, Switzerland.

During the last week of November, Moe Berg arrived in Bern to be briefed by the OSS station chief, Allen Dulles. Like Groves, Dulles was now firmly convinced that the Soviet Union posed a greater threat to Western interests than the death throes of the Third Reich, so, given the danger that the former might inherit the latter's resources in this field, he was happy to assist. It seems that by this time the kidnapping mission had turned into an assassination mission. Berg noted at the time, "Nothing spelled out, but Heisenberg must be rendered hors de combat. Gun in my pocket." This was a .22-caliber Hi-Standard automatic with a sound suppressor; he was also given a cyanide pill in case escape became impossible after the assassination. Admission to Heisenberg's lecture was not a problem, since one of Dulles's innumerable contacts was Dr. Paul Scherrer, the director of the Physics Institute at ETH. Scherrer had organized many such lectures and always passed on any pertinent information to the OSS and MI6.

Heisenberg's presentation concerned quantum mechanics rather than nuclear physics; it did nothing to help Berg decide his course of action so he arranged to have dinner with Heisenberg at Scherrer's home. During the course of the conversation, Heisenberg reveled in the success of the ongoing German offensive in the Ardennes, but when asked if Germany was going to lose the war, he replied, "Yes—but it would have been so good if we had won." This comment probably saved his life, as it showed that Germany did not possess any weapons of mass destruction that might contribute to another outcome. The pistol remained in Moe Berg's pocket.

A YOUNG ALLEN WELSH DULLES in his office at the State Department, 1924. Allen Dulles joined the OSS in 1942 before moving to Bern in Switzerland in October, where he became one of the most successful spymasters of World War II, with numerous contacts across occupied Europe and with the Nazi high command.

ALLEN WELSH DULLES [left] greets his brother John Foster Dulles after a flight on October 4, 1948. After the war, Allen Dulles became the director of the Central Intelligence Agency while John Foster Dulles became secretary of state during the Eisenhower administration. Together, they were among the most influential American officials of the immediate postwar period and leading figures in the Cold War confrontation with the Soviet Union.

REICHSLEITER MARTIN BORMANN stood in the
shadow of his beloved Führer, Adolf Hitler, and served
him faithfully from 1933 for the rest of his life. It was
Bormann's business acumen that made Hitler immensely
wealthy and allowed the creation of Aktion Feuerland to
effect the escape of the Führer to Argentina.

WILHELM "OLD FOX" CANARIS headed up the Abwehr, the
German military intelligence organization, from 1935–44.
He was a brilliant spymaster but he also ensured that his closest
colleagues were not members of the Nazi Party. Since before
the outbreak of war, Canaris had been active in the resistance
movement of Germans attempting at first to frustrate and then
to overthrow Hitler—a group known to the Gestapo
as the Schwarze Kappelle (Black Orchestra) and to the OSS
as "Breakers."

HEINRICH HIMMLER AND
HERMANN GÖRING shake
hands at a Nazi Party event,
April 1934. By 1943, the two
would be embroiled in a plot
with Joseph Goebbels and
Albert Speer to thwart Bormann's
Council of Three plan; at the
same time Himmler would
take part in a separate plot with
Bormann to gain more power
at the expense of Göring.
Such divisions in the Nazi
hierarchy allowed Hitler to rule
the Third Reich with undisputed
absolute power.

A BERLIN STREET after Kristallnacht, November 9, 1938: One of the many Jewish businesses with shattered storefronts. That night Jewish homes, properties, and synagogues across Germany and parts of Austria were attacked in an orgy of destruction—the clearest warning yet to German Jewry of their peril.

HEINRICH HIMMLER, center, briefs SS commanders Reinhard Heydrich, Heinrich Müller, Artur Nebe, and Franz Josef Huber on the day's work at Gestapo headquarters, Berlin, c. 1939. These Nazis were among the principal architects of the Final Solution— the extermination of European Jews, together with other "*untermensch*," a term the Nazis used to refer to what they called "inferior peoples."

AFTER THE FALL of France, Adolf Hitler made a triumphal tour of Paris on June 23, 1940. Here he poses for the camera in front of the Eiffel Tower in company with his favorite architect, Albert Speer (left), and his favorite sculptor, Arno Breker. His visit to Paris marked the start of the Nazi rape of artworks from France and the Low Countries to feed Hitler's lust for the greatest works of art of Western civilization.

ADOLF HITLER RELAXES at his favorite mountain retreat at the Berghof in the Bavarian Alps together with his mistress Eva Braun and their dogs, c. 1940. Hitler holds the leash of his German shepherd, Blondi. Hitler declared that "a woman must be a cute, cuddly, naive little thing—tender, sweet, and dim." Eva Braun was all of these.

Ursula "Uschi" Hitler was the daughter of Hitler and Eva Braun. Here, Hitler and Uschi pose for a picture taken at the Berghof, c. 1942. The press was told that this girl was Uschi Schneider, the daughter of Herta Schneider, a close childhood friend of Eva Braun's. Frau Schneider and her "children" spent a great deal of time at the Berghof, Hitler's Bavarian estate.

ADOLF HITLER, WITH BORMANN behind him as always, stands surrounded by officers after the failed assassination attempt on July 20, 1944, at Wolfschanze or Wolf's Lair, the Führer's field headquarters in East Prussia. Gen. Alfred Jodl, with a bandage around his head, is on the right.

A GROUP OF senior Nazi officials congregate in 1944 at Wolfschanze. On the far left is Foreign Minister Joachim von Ribbentrop. Next to him is Luftwaffe Gen. Bruno Loerzer, a friend of Field Marshal Hermann Göring, who is standing in the center. Next to him is Adm. Karl Dönitz, who became Reich president following Hitler's departure for Argentina. Key to the escape plan was Gen. Hermann Fegelein, shown with his arms crossed at the far right, and displaying the sleeve band of the Waffen SS unit he commanded in summer 1943, the 8th SS Cavalry Division "Florian Geyer."

THE BIG THREE— Winston Churchill, Franklin D. Roosevelt, and Joseph Stalin—at the Yalta Conference in the Crimea during February 1945. By now Roosevelt was gravely ill and still did not realize the dangers posed by the Soviet Union and its destructive communist regime to Europe and the world, in spite of the warnings of Churchill and others such as Allen Dulles.

IAN FLEMING, 1960. Fleming, popularly known as the creator of the fictional spy James Bond, was a British naval intelligence officer during the war. 30 Commando Unit (30 CU), which was tasked with gathering military intelligence documents and items of enemy weapons technology before they could be hidden or destroyed, was another Fleming brainchild.

GEN. DWIGHT D. EISENHOWER, Supreme Allied Commander, accompanied by Gen. Omar N. Bradley and Lt. Gen. George S. Patton Jr., inspects some of the paintings from the salt mine stash, April 1945. In February 1945, the bulk of the remaining German gold reserves and monetary assets, including one billion reichsmarks, had been transferred to the salt mine at Merkers. The rest remained in the Reichsbank in Berlin, where it was ransacked by Gen. Ernst Kaltenbrunner in the largest bank robbery in history.

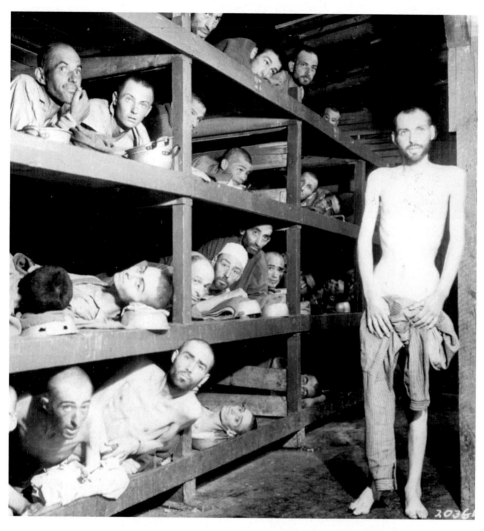

INMATES IN A slave labor barracks at Buchenwald, photographed April 16, 1945, when the camp was liberated by American troops. The concentration camp at Buchenwald provided slave labor for the construction of V-2 rockets at the Mittelwerk underground assembly lines at Nordhausen. Between 20,000 and 30,000 workers died under conditions of the utmost bestiality making Hitler's vengeance weapons. Of particular note, the prisoner in the second row from the bottom and sixth from the left is Elie Wiesel, the Jewish-American winner of the Nobel Peace Prize in 1986, renowned as a "messenger to mankind."

Chapter 10

THE FOG OF WAR

WHILE THE ALLIED ARMIES were still rampaging across
northwest Europe, creating the deceptive prospect of peace before
Christmas 1944, the Roosevelt administration was laying plans for
the structure of a postwar Germany. Both President Roosevelt and his
longtime secretary of the treasury, Henry J. Morgenthau Jr., were vehemently anti-Nazi and had little regard for the Germans as a nation. For
months they had deliberated over a plan for a demilitarized Germany
that would never again be able to wage war. The country was to be
divided into northern and southern zones that were to be completely
"deindustrialized" and turned over solely to agriculture in order to feed
the German people on a subsistence level. In Roosevelt's words, "There
is no reason why Germany couldn't go back to 1810, where they would
be perfectly comfortable, but wouldn't have any luxury." The industrial
Ruhr was to be administered as an international zone, with its products
benefiting those countries that had suffered at the hands of the Nazis.

The Morgenthau Plan was presented to Winston Churchill at the
Second Quebec Conference on September 16, 1944. Churchill yielded
to no one in his loathing for the Nazis, but he did have an instinc-
tive understanding of history and he dismissed this more draconian

repetition of the Treaty of Versailles as "unnatural, unchristian and unnecessary." However, after the secretary of the treasury extended another line of credit to Britain to the tune of $6 billion, Churchill agreed to consider a somewhat modified version of the plan.

Details of the Morgenthau Plan were soon in the hands of both the Soviets and the Abwehr. Moscow was informed immediately, since the author of the plan was Morgenthau's deputy, Dr. Harry Dexter White—a Soviet spy, code-named "Jurist." By reducing Germany to an impotent pastoral society, the plan would render the country more vulnerable to a communist takeover in the near future. The information reached Adm. Canaris by a more devious route. Two of the Abwehr agents he had activated in Switzerland in 1940 were "Habakuk," in the Swiss Foreign Ministry, and "Jakob" in the Swiss Secret Service. Both organizations received a mass of high-value intelligence via the Swiss ambassador to Washington, Dr. Charles Bruggmann. Yet Bruggmann was no spy: his source was his brother-in-law, Henry Wallace—who happened to be the vice president of the United States. Wallace was a popular, left-wing New Dealer; privy to many of America's most important secrets, he was also notoriously indiscreet.

By autumn of 1944, Canaris had long been dismissed as chief of the Abwehr and was being held under house arrest under suspicion of involvement in the July bomb plot against Hitler. Nevertheless, as a German patriot, he was horrified at the prospect of his country being reduced deliberately to abject poverty after unconditional surrender and he quickly passed details of the Morgenthau Plan to Martin Bormann and Joseph Goebbels. The propaganda minister used the information to galvanize the German people to greater resistance, to avoid their country being turned into a "potato field," in Goebbels's telling phrase.

Soon afterward, details of the plan appeared in the *Wall Street Journal*; this revelation caused serious divisions within the Roosevelt administration and in corporate America, whose investments in Germany were now at further risk. Both Gen. Marshall and Gen. Eisenhower complained bitterly that German resistance stiffened appreciably, with the result that the front lines became stabilized along the Siegfried Line just as winter was closing in. Roosevelt's opponent in the presidential election of November 1944, Thomas E. Dewey, said that the Morgenthau Plan was worth "ten fresh German divisions" to the enemy. In a cable from Bern, Allen Dulles was barely able to contain his indignation at the scheme's propaganda value to the Nazis:

> [The average German] now trembles at the idea of what the foreign workers and prisoners of war would do, when disorder comes, and these millions of aliens are let loose to plunder and ravage the cities and land. . . . The soldiers at the front, the workers in the ammunition factories, and the inhabitants of the bombed cities are holding out because they feel that they have no choice, and their existence is at stake. The Nazis are profiting by this state of mind for their own purposes. . . . So far, the Allies have not offered the opposition [inside Germany] any serious encouragement. On the contrary, they have again and again welded together the people and the Nazis by statements published, either out of indifference or with a purpose.

HENRY MORGENTHAU'S TREASURY DEPARTMENT was also the architect of Operation Safehaven. The Bretton Woods Agreement of July 1944, intended to establish a liberal capitalist economic system throughout the industrial nations in the aftermath of the war, had also called on neutral countries to cease the transfer of assets across occupied Europe. In order to choke off the flight of capital from the Third Reich, on August 14 the United States and Britain brought severe pressure to bear on Switzerland to sign a trade agreement that would reduce its dealings with Nazi Germany. Now that the tide of war had turned in favor of the Allies, Switzerland was willing to comply, but in reality, the process of money-laundering was so pervasive that little was achieved to halt it. Furthermore, almost two-thirds of Switzerland's trade was with Nazi Germany and in the midst of a world war it was difficult to judge what was illegal and what was legitimate.

Operation Safehaven was implemented on December 6, 1944, with the aim of tracking the movement of Nazi loot and assets around the world and locating those hidden in neutral countries. However, for Roosevelt and Morgenthau this plan had a wider purpose. They needed concrete evidence of illegality to bring against the major American corporations that had traded with Nazi Germany and those members of the political establishment who were sympathetic to the Nazis: men such as the crypto-Nazi Henry Ford; Joseph P. Kennedy Sr., former U.S. ambassador to London; and John D. Rockefeller Jr., son of John D. Rockefeller Sr., the founder of Standard Oil and advocate of eugenics. Some of these corporations and individuals had tried to undermine the New Deal and destabilize Roosevelt's administration during the 1930s.

This ambitious operation sought the prosecution as war criminals of all those who ran the Nazi war machine and the industrial concerns that sustained it. Bankers and industrialists such as Abs, Schacht, Schröder, Krupp, Flick, Schmitz, and a legion of others were to stand in the dock of an international tribunal and be judged for their actions. Once they were in open court, Morgenthau would reveal years of intercepted documentation, wiretap evidence, and decrypts of Swiss bank codes and cables, courtesy of Ultra intelligence via MI6. In order to redeem themselves, the defendants would have to reveal their dealings with American corporations such as Ford Motor Company, General Motors, and Standard Oil. All the companies and banks found to have traded with the enemy would then face the full rigor of the law in the United States. It was an elegant plan for revenge, legitimized by the victory of good over evil on the battlefield.

Since Morgenthau was distrustful of both the Justice Department and the State Department, Safehaven was entrusted to a select handful of personnel in the Federal Economic Administration (FEA) of the Treasury Department. The president, through the FEA, instructed a new offshoot of X-2 counterintelligence within the Special Intelligence division of the OSS to uncover and collect evidence, particularly in neutral countries, concerning the transfers of Nazi loot and gold. However, this effort required the cooperation of OSS agents already on the ground, and in Switzerland this was problematical—since one of the suspects of Operation Safehaven was Allen Dulles himself, because of his extensive corporate connections and his links with various Nazi groups. Despite this difficulty, the investigation necessarily focused on the gold dealings undertaken by Swiss banks. This became of major concern to Swiss ambassador Bruggmann once he learned of

Operation Safehaven through his indiscreet brother-in-law, vice president Henry Wallace. The exposure of the explicit links between Swiss banks and Nazi Germany would be a major potential embarrassment to the Swiss government once the war was over; accordingly, the Swiss Secret Service alerted Allen Dulles about the Safehaven investigation into his affairs.

BY FALL OF 1944, ALLEN DULLES was increasingly frustrated by Washington's policy decisions that, in his opinion, were prolonging the war. His main concern now was to minimize the encroachment of the Red Army into Western Europe, and the best way to do that was to end the war as soon as possible by any likely means.

His volume of work remained high, and his latest coup in September 1944 was the acquisition of information about the Germans' creation of what was termed a "National Redoubt" in the Bavarian Alps, where the Nazi leadership would hide and its fanatical supporters would wage guerrilla warfare even after the military defeat of Germany. The information came from an Austrian SD officer, SS Maj. Wilhelm Höttl, via an Austrian lawyer who lived in Switzerland, Kurt Grimm. Through his law firm, Grimm had excellent contacts throughout occupied Europe; Dulles's firm, Sullivan & Cromwell, shared business clients with Grimm and now the two men even shared the same tailor. According to a senior British intelligence officer, Grimm was "one of the three major sources of Allen Dulles's rather remarkable operation in Bern." Of particular interest to Dulles was the fact that Höttl was on the staff of SS and Police Gen. Ernst Kaltenbrunner, chief of the RSHA and second only to Heinrich Himmler in the SS hierarchy; Höttl thus represented another conduit to the Nazi leadership.

Although doubtful about the notion of a National Redoubt, Dulles duly passed the information to Washington. By this time, OSS communications from Bern were far more effective, thanks to another canny deal. Dulles had struck a bargain with Gen. Roger Masson, head of the Swiss Secret Service. Allied aircrews who had been obliged to make forced landings in Switzerland were held in internment camps, which by the end of the war held some 1,500 American airmen. Now, each day, up to a dozen of these USAAF personnel were allowed to work at the U.S. legation while on parole, returning to their camps in the evening. They provided a useful pool of technical expertise to Dulles and the OSS; this contravened the rules of war, but then, so did the German employment of crewmen from the *Admiral Graf Spee* in neutral Argentina. Communications are vital to the rapid flow of intelligence back to the decision-makers, but there was always a disconnect between the intelligence services and the Roosevelt administration. Often, current and timely intelligence assessments were ignored in favor of preconceptions and policy, not the least of which was the continuing appeasement of Stalin. No matter how often Allen Dulles reiterated the growing threat of communist expansionism in Eastern Europe, his advice was ignored.

Dulles was also targeted by German intelligence, including an elite Luftwaffe code-breaking unit designated *Luftfahrtforschüngsamt* (Luftwaffe radio intercept unit). When Abwehr agents learned of Operation Safehaven through their agent Habakuk, they set about frustrating its efforts, particularly in Switzerland, where it was potentially most dangerous to the ongoing German capital transfers. The Abwehr agents passed the word to Dulles that both the British and the Americans were intercepting his communications—as they themselves had been, but would now no longer be able to, thanks to their revealing their hand in this way. They, too, told Dulles that he was a subject of investigation by the Treasury Department through Operation Safehaven. He immediately changed his encryption methods to the more secure "one-time pad" system and from then on his message traffic remained secure. Transcribing the messages from the Vernam cipher is a laborious handwritten process, hence Dulles's need for the services of interned USAAF personnel for encryption.

Dulles also exposed Henry Wallace as the source of the revelation of both the Morgenthau Plan and Operation Safehaven to Ambassador Bruggmann and ultimately to the Germans. President Roosevelt had no choice but to ditch Wallace and nominate the senator from Missouri, Harry S. Truman, as his candidate for vice president in the upcoming presidential election. As a committed opponent of communism, Truman was far more acceptable to Dulles. At the same time, in responding to the instructions for Safehaven dated December 6, 1944,

Dulles stated with casual insouciance:

> Work on this project requires careful planning as it might defeat direct intelligence activities and close important channels. . . . Today we must fish in troubled waters and maintain contacts with persons suspected of working with Nazis on such matters. . . . To deal effectively . . . would require special staff with new cover. . . . At present we do not have adequate personnel to do effective job in this field and meet other demands.

AMONG THE "OTHER DEMANDS" on Allen Dulles's time and personnel was the creation, as of November 21, 1944, of the OSS Art Looting Investigation Unit. This had a similar remit to the Monuments, Fine Art, and Archives (MFA&A) branch already working with the field forces, but, backed by the full apparatus of the OSS, it had far greater resources.

As well as their primary task of protection, the Monuments Men catalogued all artworks found in the territories that had been recaptured from the Germans, in order to identify their true ownership and return them in due course if they had been stolen. Capt. Walker Hancock of the MFA&A, a renowned sculptor in civilian life, was now attached to the U.S. First Army. On December 15, 1944, he arrived at the quiet farming village of La Gleize in eastern Belgium, close to the border with Luxembourg. It had escaped damage during the Allied advance and now lay peacefully under a weak winter sun, with the forbidding forests of the Ardennes dark in the distance. Walker was anxious to see a famous and revered fourteenth-century wooden statue, the Madonna of La Gleize, which stood in the nave of the village church. To Hancock, it was a sublime work of art that seemed to dominate its surroundings, and he was relieved to find it untouched by the war. After a pleasant meal in the local inn, he continued his tour of the area.

At 5:30 a.m. in the pre-dawn darkness of the following day, an artillery bombardment by 1,600 guns saturated the area with shells. Behind this curtain of fire came seven armored and nine infantry divisions of the Fifth and Sixth Panzer Armies, while further south formations from the Seventh Army also plunged westward. *Unternehmen Wacht am Rhein*—Operation Watch on the Rhine—was Hitler's last gamble for victory in the West. The strategy was to hurl his remaining armor through the Ardennes, across the Meuse River, and on to Antwerp, whose strategic port had finally become operational for the Allies on November 28. If he achieved this, he could drive a wedge between the American and the British-Canadian army groups; less realistically, he hoped that this attack would buy time for his new "wonder weapons"— jet aircraft and Type XXI "electro-drive" U-boats—to enter service in significant numbers. On December 11, the Führer had traveled from Berlin in his private train to the Adlerhorst (Eagle's Nest) field head-quarters near Bad Nauheim in south-central Germany, to exercise per-sonal command over the offensive.

The story of the Battle of the Bulge has been told at length else-where. In fog and snow that initially grounded the Allied tactical air forces, the Germans achieved complete surprise. The American divi-sions that they first encountered either were being rested in this quiet sector after the bitter fighting for the Hürtgen Forest or were fresh from the United States. But the difficult terrain and bad weather were also an obstacle for the panzers. In June 1940, when a dash along a similar axis of advance had successfully divided the bulk of the French armies from the British Expeditionary Force, it had been difficult enough to negotiate the narrow forest roads of the Ardennes in high summer with tanks weighing no more than twenty tons. Now the roads were coated with snow and ice and progress was immeasurably more difficult for tanks weighing twice as much or more.

Despite the shock of the assault and the collapse of many units, pockets of determined American resistance formed and combat engineers made heroic efforts to destroy bridges that lay in the line of the German advance—the availability of fuel and bridges would determine the very success or failure of the German offensive. With the destruction of the bridges, the leading German battle group was forced northward off its intended line of march toward the village of La Gleize. However, the skies were clearing and the long column of armor and trucks was strafed by U.S. fighter bombers, causing the advance to falter. As American reinforcements poured into the area, the German battle group was virtually surrounded by December 20.

After a fierce two-day battle, the group's remnants broke out on foot, leaving their wounded and a small band of Waffen-SS troops to cover the withdrawal. They made their last stand in the church of La Gleize under constant American bombardment until the building was pounded to destruction and finally overrun on the twenty-fourth. On the same day, Chief of the General Staff (Army) Gen. Heinz Guderian advised the Führer to halt the offensive since progress on the other routes was now minimal and to little avail.

The shock of the unexpected offensive had caused near panic in some Allied quarters. On January 4, even General Patton confided in his diary, "We can still lose this war." Despondency grew with distance from the battlefield, and in Washington, the U.S. Army chief of staff, Gen. Marshall, mused, "If Germany beats us, we will have to recast our view of the whole war. We will have to take a defensive position along the German frontier. The people of the United States would have to decide whether they wanted to continue the war enough to raise large new armies." By now a bitter joke circulated among the troops: "The war might still be over by Christmas . . . Christmas 1950." An aftershock struck at dawn on New Year's Day 1945, when the Luftwaffe launched its Operation Baseplate against numerous Allied airfields in Belgium, France, and Holland, destroying some 439 aircraft, mostly on the ground. While such material losses could quickly be made up and the many German fighter pilots shot down and killed were effectively irreplaceable, the Allied commanders took this attack as further evidence of the Wehrmacht's ability to prolong the war.

In total, beating off the Ardennes offensive cost the Americans 89,000 casualties, including 14,872 killed, making it the U.S. Army's bloodiest battle of the war. However, German casualties were 130,000 with 19,000 killed, as well as almost 400 irreplaceable tanks lost. Within weeks, nine fresh American divisions arrived in the European theater. Hitler's last gamble in the West had failed and the frontiers of Germany now lay open to invasion.

THE MONUMENTS MAN Capt. Walker Hancock returned to La Gleize on February 1, 1945. From a distance, the village appeared to be completely obliterated. The church where the Waffen-SS had made its stand was reduced to a shell; the roof had collapsed, broken beams lay all around, the nave was knee-deep in frozen snow, and an icy wind blew through gaping holes in the walls. The church pews were piled up to form bullet-riddled barricades, and bloody bandages, ammunition boxes, and ration cans littered the ground. But in the center of this desolation Walker found the Madonna of La Gleize totally undamaged:

> She stood just as he had seen her two months ago, in the middle of the nave, one hand on her heart, the other raised in benediction. She seemed hardly to notice her surroundings, focused as she was on the distant divine. But against that backdrop, she looked more miraculous and hopeful than ever, her beauty triumphant even in the midst of devastation and despair.

Chapter 11

RAIDERS OF THE REICH

THE ARDENNES OFFENSIVE CAME as a particularly rude shock to the Allied high command because it had relied for years upon Ultra intelligence for warnings of German capabilities and intentions. There were officers on the ground who had feared a major German assault against the U.S. VIII Corps' line in the Ardennes, such as Col. Oscar Koch, the Third Army G-2 intelligence chief, but his premonitions had been ignored. There was too much reliance on Ultra among the Allied commanders, and too little on human intelligence or battlefield reconnaissance.

The masterly German deception plan for *Unternehmen Wacht am Rhein* had been based on strict radio silence, so there had been no opportunity for intercepts by Bletchley Park. Other security measures had included forbidding any officers privy to the plan to fly in an aircraft west of the Rhine in case they were shot down or crash-landed, and all troop movements had been made at night. By day, Allied photoreconnaissance had been compromised by the awful weather, and as they closed up to the borders of Germany the Allied troops no longer received useful information from local Resistance fighters, as they had when further west.

The great majority of German communications were now made by the latest model teleprinter cipher machines, such as the Siemens & Halske T52d *Geheimfernschreiber* (secret teleprinter) and the Lorenz SZ42. The T52 series of machines and their traffic were code-named "Sturgeon" by Bletchley Park while the Lorenz was "Tunny." By the winter of 1944, the specialists at Bletchley Park were physically and intellectually exhausted after years of painstaking decryption work, and unraveling the secrets of the new Sturgeon and Tunny machines required yet another concerted effort. The situation was exacerbated when it was discovered that Enigma machines were now fitted with a more sophisticated version of the return cylinder that made decryption much more difficult, requiring further modifications to the room-sized protocomputer Colossus and the electromechanical decryption devices known as "bombes." Similarly, the Luftwaffe later employed a cipher system known as Enigma Hour that automatically generated a massive number of extra permutations on encryption. Fortunately, the repeated indiscipline of some German Enigma operators—particularly in the Luftwaffe—made the task easier for Bletchley Park to decipher messages, and a shortage of Sturgeon machines at this stage of the war meant that they never posed a dangerous problem for the Allies. Nevertheless, the latter quickly realized that such technology in the wrong hands would create a serious threat in the postwar era. It was essential to capture examples of these encryption devices intact and to deny them to potential adversaries.

In February 1945, an Anglo-American organization known as the Target Intelligence Committee (TICOM) was set up to hunt for German cryptographic equipment and its operators as the Allies advanced into Germany. The TICOM teams of British and American personnel divided up any spoils of war on a "one-for-me-and-one-for-you" basis. There was by now a tacit agreement that the United States and Britain must continue to cooperate in the field of signals intelligence that had served both countries so well during the war. Together, they had broken virtually every military and diplomatic code used by the Axis powers, giving the Allies an extraordinary advantage on the battlefield. Curiously, the one state that proved to be invulnerable to penetration of its codes or ciphers was the Vatican, but then the papacy was not supposed to be in league with the Fascists or the Nazis.

After a stupendous effort, Colossus was able to break the Tunny cipher and read significant amounts of Sturgeon traffic, but now there was a new sound coming over the radio speakers of the Hut 6 intercept room at Bletchley Park. It was the characteristic noise of yet another new German encryption device, code-named "Thrasher," and this one seemed to be impervious to penetration by Colossus. The Germans had devised an unbreakable code for their latest machine—the Siemens & Halske T43 *Schlüsselfernschreibmaschine*. It was all the more vital to capture such equipment in order to maintain the Allies' superiority in signals intelligence in the years to come.

A WHOLE RANGE OF SPECIALIST UNITS were by now poised on the borders of Germany, eager to advance and uncover the secrets of the Third Reich. In addition to the nuclear research hunters of the Alsos Mission; the MFA&A heritage protectors and art detectives; the heavily armed "Red Indians" of Ian Fleming's 30 Assault Unit, which was now named 30 Advance Unit; the scientists and technologists of the T-Forces; the gold-seekers of the Klondike teams; and the TICOM teams hunting for encryption technology, several other organizations had also been activated, each with its own tight focus. To reduce the risk of mutual confusion, the G-2 intelligence division at SHAEF created a Special Sections Subdivision in February 1945 to coordinate the activities of all these specialized teams with the fighting troops as they advanced into Germany.

With her cities and factories devastated by air attack and still being bombarded by V-2 missiles, Britain was anxious to acquire Germany's industrial machinery and manufacturing processes to rebuild an economy that was on the brink of bankruptcy. In booming America such considerations were not a factor; instead, the United States wanted German intellectual property and the personnel who had devised the weapons systems that were still impeding an early Allied victory. The role of the new Enemy Personnel Exploitation Section (EPES) was to prioritize the desirable fields of German technology and identify the scientists, engineers, and technicians involved in such projects.

The first task was relatively simple. Thanks to Ultra, the Allies knew many details of the technical and operational capabilities of the latest weapons and even their secret German designations. For instance, the Messerschmitt Me 262 jet fighter was code-named "Silver" and the Arado Ar 234—the world's first dedicated jet bomber—was "Tin." EPES's second task was more difficult, since intelligence was lacking as to the specific locations of research laboratories and their staff. All such facilities were now widely dispersed across the Reich to reduce the effects of Allied bombing; many were in Bavaria, Austria, and Czechoslovakia, so as to be at the extreme range of bombers flying from Britain or Italy.

The advanced German capabilities that justified the creation of EPES were brought into sharp focus after the Ludendorff Bridge over the Rhine at Remagen was captured intact by elements of the U.S. 9th Armored Division on March 7, 1945. After a doomed attack by three lumbering Stuka dive-bombers, all of which were shot down by the American antiaircraft defenses, the Germans committed some of Hitler's *Wunderwaffen*. On the following day the bridge was attacked by fighter-bomber Me 262s and then by Arado Ar 234s. Thereafter, the German's sophisticated rocket unit SS Werfer Abteilung 500 launched eleven V-2 ballistic missiles from the Eifel Forest area. The closest struck 300 yards from the target, killing three American soldiers; no damage was done to the bridge, but it was yet another demonstration of Germany's considerable lead in weapons technology. Subsequently, Gen. Hugh J. Knerr, deputy commander of the U.S. Army Air Forces in Europe, observed:

Occupation of German scientific and industrial establishments has revealed the fact that we been alarmingly backward in many fields of research. If we do not take the opportunity to seize the apparatus and the brains that developed it and put the combination back to work promptly, we will remain several years behind while we attempt to cover a field already exploited.

This incident led directly to Operation Lusty, which was set up by the U.S. Army Air Forces to capture German aeronautical secrets and equipment, and personnel involved in the design and development of jet- and rocket-powered aircraft. Significantly, in July 1945, two months after the German surrender, the British initiated Operation Surgeon specifically to deny such prizes to the Soviet Union, which many in the West now believed was fast becoming a serious threat to European unity. These schemes came under the overall supervision of Operation Overcast, an initiative of the Joint Chiefs of Staff, whose object was to recruit or persuade German scientists and technicians in selected fields that it was in their best interests and those of their families to seek protection and possible employment by the Western Allied powers. In particular, the Americans were anxious to exploit the expertise of German scientists involved in the development of ballistic missiles and atomic weapons. Some analysts had drawn the sensible conclusion that the future lay in a combination of the two weapons systems so it was all the more important to deny such technology to the Soviets.

In March 1945, the exploitation of German technology had assumed such importance at SHAEF that the Special Sections Subdivision and the EPES were now reporting directly to Gen. Eisenhower's chief of staff, Gen. Walter Bedell Smith. Similarly, at 21st Army Group, all exploitation teams, such as 30 Advance Unit and Target Force, were now responsible to SHAEF through Field Marshal Montgomery's chief of staff, Gen. Freddie de Guingand. The chain of command was specific, detailed, and coordinated. There was, however, a serious obstacle to the success of Operation Overcast. By special decree, President Roosevelt expressly forbade the employment in America of any German who had been a Nazi Party member or who was associated with any war crimes. Since advancement or even employment in any important field in Nazi Germany was often dependent on party membership, this ruling presented a major stumbling block. Similarly, since slave labor, which was used in the production of virtually all German weapons, constituted a war crime under international law, every weapons project was tainted.

THE YALTA CONFERENCE between "The Big Three"— Roosevelt, Churchill, and Stalin—was held in the Crimean city of Yalta between February 4 and 11, 1945. Code-named Operation Argonaut, its purpose was to discuss the structure of Europe once hostilities with Germany ceased. By now, President Roosevelt was gravely ill, but his policy of conciliation toward Stalin continued unabated. Poland—the original casus belli of World War II—was abandoned to its fate; the Balkans also became a Soviet sphere of influence and final boundaries were drawn up for the imminent linkup of Western Allied and Soviet armies in Germany. The country was to be divided into four zones of occupation administered by the Americans, British, French, and Soviets. Stalin demanded the reiteration of the insistence on unconditional German surrender; he still feared a separate peace between the Western Allies and Germany, whereby they would join forces and mount a grand capitalist crusade against the Soviet Union—a policy recommended by some Allied commanders, such as Gen. George S. Patton.

President Roosevelt was quick to concur and made yet more concessions to ensure that the Soviet Union would join in the war against Japan. He still did not know whether the atomic bomb would actually work, but he did know that any amphibious invasion of the Japanese home islands would be unspeakably costly in casualties, with estimates running as high as 1 million Allied troops. Stalin promised to attack Japan ninety days after the defeat of Germany. Publicly, the Grand Alliance stood firm in its resolve: "It is our inflexible purpose to destroy German militarism and Nazism and to ensure that Germany will never again be able to disturb the peace of the world." In private, Churchill's suspicion of Stalin's intentions was as sharp as ever: "The only bond of the victors is their common hate."

ON THE FINAL DAY OF THE YALTA CONFERENCE, the first enriched uranium U-235 arrived at Los Alamos from Oak Ridge—a vital step in the construction of the first atomic bomb. The emphasis of the Alsos Mission was now on preventing the Soviets from acquiring German research material and the scientists involved in the *Uranverein* or Uranium Club. From papers captured at the University of Strasbourg, Alsos discovered that there was an industrial facility producing high-purity uranium metal at the Auergesellschaft plant in Oranienburg. This was deep inside the proposed Soviet occupation zone of Germany and well beyond the reach of the Alsos Mission. Gen. Groves advised Gen. Marshall that the plant be attacked to prevent its falling into the hands of the Red Army intact. On March 15, 612 B-17 Flying Fortress heavy bombers dropped 1,506 tons of high explosives and 178 tons of incendiary bombs on Oranienburg; the plant was devastated.

Following the successful crossing of the Rhine by the Allied armies in March 1945, the Alsos Mission could begin its task of finding the *Uranverein* scientists and any uranium in Germany. Based on intelligence provided by the Special Sections Subdivision, the Alsos Task Force A was directed to undertake Operation Big. This required them to reach Haigerloch in southwest Germany without delay. Haigerloch was designated to be part of the French zone of occupation—and the Yalta Conference had determined that nothing could be removed from each nation's areas of responsibility—but SHAEF gave unequivocal orders that Col. Pash's men were to get there before Gen. Jean de Lattre de Tassigny's French First Army. Mounted in trucks and armored cars, Task Force A barreled into Haigerloch and found the B-VIII nuclear reactor in a cave. It was simply too small to ever go critical. The Germans were indeed years behind the Allies, since Fermi had achieved the first ever nuclear reaction in America as far back as December 1942. Close by, in Hechingen, the team found all the German scientists they sought except for Otto Hahn and Werner Heisenberg, and these two were apprehended within days. Everything and everybody associated with atomic research was safely spirited out of the future French zone.

In the closing months of the war, the leading Soviet atomic research facility designated Laboratory No. 2 possessed only seven tons of uranium oxide. The F-1 uranium reactor required forty-six tons to continue operation, whereas the plutonium-production Reactor A needed 150 tons. The Soviets were in desperate need of large quantities of uranium ore, and Gen. Groves was determined that they should not find it in Germany.

On April 12, 1945, Team 5 of 30 Advance Unit, commanded by Lt. James Lambie Jr., U.S. Navy Reserve, was deep inside Germany, investigating a factory at Stassfurt some eighty miles west of Berlin. Among other things, they found multiple barrels—several of them broken—containing an unidentified black substance. This news was immediately passed up the line to SHAEF, and the barrels' contents were subsequently identified as the missing Belgian uranium ore. But Stassfurt was in the designated Soviet zone of occupation. The second in command of the Alsos Mission, Lt. Col. John Lansdale Jr. (the former head of security for the Manhattan Project), consulted SHAEF with a proposal for organizing a strike force to remove the material. Landsdale noted in his report that the Twelfth Army's G-2, when shown the plan, "was very perturbed at our proposal and foresaw all kinds of difficulties with the Russians and political repercussions at home." Realizing the urgency of the situation, Lansdale approached Gen. Omar Bradley, commander of 12th Army Group, for permission to raid the facility against the rules laid down at Yalta. Bradley reportedly responded: "To hell with the Russians." On April 17, Lansdale and his team headed for Stassfurt and located the plant where the uranium ore was stored—a total of some 1,100 tons. When most of the barrels were found to be too unstable for transport, Lansdale's men purloined 10,000 heavy-duty bags from a nearby paper mill to use as containers. Within forty-eight hours, the vast bulk of Germany's hoard of uranium ore was safely in the American zone of occupation and beyond the reach of the Soviets. The Western Allies now controlled most of Germany's atomic scientists, its only functioning reactor, and virtually all its supplies of heavy water and uranium ore. The Uranium Club had been closed down. Although the Alsos Mission was highly successful in thwarting Soviet nuclear ambitions, Martin Bormann was still one step ahead in his plans to utilize Nazi high technology. Once he was safely ensconced in Argentina during the summer of 1948, his final down payment for continued safe haven under the Perón regime was the highly attractive inducement of the fruits of Nazi nuclear researches and advanced aviation designs that made Argentina the sixth country in the world to produce its own jet aircraft, after Britain, Germany, the Soviet Union, the United States and France.

ON THURSDAY, APRIL 12, 1945, the day that Lt. Lambie's team discovered the uranium at Stassfurt, President Franklin D. Roosevelt suffered a massive cerebral hemorrhage and died some hours later. His successor was Vice President Harry S. Truman. For the past few months Truman had chaired the Senate Special Committee to Investigate the National Defense Program, which had been probing massive discrepancies in military funds allocated to the War Department. Within days of becoming the thirty-third president of the United States, Truman was informed about the Manhattan Project; now he knew where the missing funds had gone. In August, President Truman made the painful decision to drop an atomic bomb on the Japanese city of Hiroshima and then a second bomb on Nagasaki. Within days the Japanese empire surrendered and the military invasion of Japan was no longer necessary. Thanks to the Alsos Mission, America for the time being had a monopoly of atomic weapons and was now capable of producing three bombs every month.

Chapter 12

Bormann, Dulles, and Operation Crossword

ADOLF HITLER LEFT HIS WOLF'S LAIR in East Prussia for the last time on November 20, 1944. During the war he had spent more time in this mosquito-infested pine forest than anywhere else. After a brief stay in Berlin, on December 10, he took up residence at his Eagle's Nest headquarters in south-central Germany to oversee the Ardennes offensive in person. As ever, Martin Bormann was with him, but the Reichsleiter was extremely unhappy with the accommodations assigned to him and his staff at Bad Nauheim. Above all, there were insufficient secure teleprinters to allow him safe and instant communication with his network of gauleiters, many of whom were now being tested as never before as the fighting fronts approached their regions.

Despite the worsening war situation, the German telephone system generally remained highly efficient. In January 1945, Gen. Alfred Jodl noted that the Armed Forces Supreme Command generated some 120,000 telephone calls and 33,000 telex messages to German military units every day. Day in and day out, the Führer stood hunched over the situation maps with his magnifying glass, spewing out an avalanche of orders for formations whose present equipment and capabilities he often wildly overestimated. As Albert Speer observed, "The more difficult the situation, all the more did modern technology widen the gap between reality and the fantasy being operated from that table."

Martin Bormann was not privy to the endless military conferences at the Adlerhorst, so he had plenty of time to further his schemes. For months past, he had been reducing the access of other Nazi leaders to the Führer, thereby increasing his own influence as the inner circle's numbers dwindled. By Christmas 1944, only a small remaining group had undeniable access to Hitler. Among these was Hermann Göring, but his star was waning fast; his Luftwaffe remained incapable of stemming the Allied bombing offensive against Germany and now proved unable to support the ground forces in the faltering Ardennes offensive. On December 26, Göring's stock plummeted further when he suggested that it was time to negotiate an armistice with the Allies, only to receive the full force of one of Hitler's raging tirades: "I forbid you to take any step in that direction! If, in spite of what I say, you do anything to defy my order, then I will have you shot." Bormann duly noted Göring's defeatism.

On New Year's Day 1945, Hitler made a radio broadcast to the nation, proclaiming that "Germany will rise like a phoenix from the ashes and rubble of her cities and . . . despite all setbacks, will go on to win final victory." On January 4, 1945, virtually the whole senior Nazi hierarchy was present at the Eagle's Nest, including Göring, Goebbels, von Ribbentrop, and Bormann. Also attending as a guest was Col. Hans-Ulrich Rudel of the Luftwaffe, a favorite of Hitler's and the most decorated man in the Wehrmacht. Only Heinrich Himmler was absent, due to his newfound role as a military commander, directing Operation North Wind in the Rhineland. Bormann had plans for all of them.

On January 12, some 3 million troops of the Red Army began their long-anticipated offensive along the Vistula riverfront in Poland, behind the largest artillery bombardment of the war thus far. Within twenty-four hours, the German defenses were broken and the Soviets had advanced ten miles. Gen. Guderian telephoned the Führer headquarters pleading for reinforcements. Hitler was only willing to release the Sixth Panzer Army for the Eastern Front. Although this formation had, on paper, an elite corps of SS armor, it had been worn down in the Ardennes. Despite the unfolding defeat on the Vistula, Hitler was disturbed by the discovery that there was no emergency exit from his command bunker at the Eagle's Nest. And when the Führer was unhappy, Bormann was invariably at hand to rectify the situation. On January 14, the bunker's architect, Franz Werr, was summoned to Hitler's presence; he was warned in advance that he could not hoodwink the Führer, since the latter's interest in architecture made him "the greatest master mason of all time." Werr explained that there was no need for an emergency exit from the bunker, because in the unlikely event of the main exits being blocked after an air raid, then hundreds of laborers were on hand to clear the rubble. Hitler insisted that another exit be installed immediately, but when Werr returned with a work party two days later, Hitler had left for Berlin.

BORMANN'S SCHEME TO MARGINALIZE Himmler was bearing fruit. His authority as overlord of the entire SS apparatus was still unchallengeable but, like most men, he had an exploitable weakness. In addition to his other titles, Himmler nursed a fervent wish to hold a high military appointment. Accordingly, in the aftermath of the July 1944 bomb attempt, when Hitler was seething with suspicion of the Wehrmacht officer class, Bormann had suggested to the Führer that Himmler should be made commander of the Ersatzheer or Replacement Army. Thereafter Himmler became, successively, the commander in chief of Army Group Upper Rhine, attempting to stem the advance of the U.S. Seventh and French First armies in Alsace, and then head of Army Group Vistula, which stood in the path of a Soviet advance on Berlin.

Needless to say, these command appointments were nominal rather than executive: Himmler was devoid of military insight or talent so actual day-to-day command was exercised by professional soldiers. However, since "Himmler's" army groups were doomed to failure by the strength of the opponents they faced, the Führer's faith in his "*treue Heinrich*" was shaken—just as Bormann had intended. Others in the Nazi hierarchy saw which way the wind was blowing, concluding that any hope of surviving the maelstrom of defeat was more likely to lie with Bormann rather than with the waning, faltering Himmler or the drug-addled Göring. Bormann now had a strong coterie of allies in his bid for power and exclusive access to the Führer. These included SS and Police Gen. Ernst Kaltenbrunner, Himmler's deputy as head of the RSHA; the enigmatic SS and Police Gen. Heinrich Müller, head of the Gestapo; and SS Gen. Hermann Fegelein, the brother-in-law of Eva Braun, who was Himmler's adjutant and representative of the SS at Hitler's headquarters. Fegelein's defection to Bormann's camp was crucial; like Bormann, he was a sensualist and the two became close drinking companions.

By the end of January 1945, the Red Army had created a vast westward salient reaching to the Oder River, only sixty miles from Berlin. A counterattack on the salient's northern flank from Pomerania failed, and on February 20, Bormann wrote to his wife, Gerda, in triumph: "Uncle Heinrich's offensive did not work out. He did not properly organize it and now his reserve divisions must be assigned somewhere else." Himmler retired to the military hospital at Hohenlychen and asked the Führer to be relieved of his command on "medical grounds," so as to be able to concentrate on all his other responsibilities. Meanwhile, Göring had retreated to Carinhall, his country residence, to try to save his vast art collection from the advancing Red Army.

Bormann now sought to eject from Hitler's inner circle even minor figures who were beyond his easy control. One of these was Heinrich Hoffmann, the Führer's personal photographer, art adviser, and long-time confidant, who had introduced Hitler to Eva Braun. Out of apparent concern for Hoffmann's health, Bormann suggested that Hoffmann needed a medical examination by Hitler's physician, Dr. Theodor Morell. After various tests, Hoffmann was informed that he was a carrier of the dangerous Type B paratyphoid bacterium; accordingly, he represented a threat to the health of the Führer and must be banished from his presence and from headquarters. Mystified, Hoffmann sought a second opinion. The tests proved negative but the medical report crossed Bormann's desk and Hoffmann remained in exile. Next Bormann turned on Hitler's personal surgeon, Dr. Karl Brandt, the originator of the Nazi Project T4 euthanasia program.

Bormann's purge continued with ruthless efficiency. Any Germans, from ordinary citizens to top party officials, were expendable if their removal would benefit Bormann and his plan for saving the lives and fortunes of a handful of the Nazi leadership.

With his grip on the Nazi court now increasingly assured, Bormann turned his attention to asserting his absolute authority over the gauleiters—the party chiefs who governed the forty-two regions of the Greater German Reich. In "Gestapo" Müller, Bormann had a powerful ally to enforce his will. As always, Bormann's technique was the carrot and the stick. Total loyalty to the Führer remained paramount, and the faithful execution of all orders emanating from the Führer's headquarters was vital for the well-being of the party. In the office of every gauleiter a torrent of instructions poured out of the teleprinters from the "Telex General." Invariably, these began: "National Socialists! Party comrades! By the Führer's command, I hereby direct . . . " Thanks to Müller's Gestapo spiderweb, Bormann's intelligence on activities across the shrinking Reich remained extensive. The Gestapo was a vast organization, embracing many sections and subsections responsible for a wide range of surveillance and executive functions in the Reich and beyond. When the gauleiter of Bayreuth had the temerity to consign Bormann's telexes to the trash bin, he was shot as a defeatist by Müller's men on Bormann's orders. That was the stick: the carrot was a new identity at the end of the war for those who toed the party line. The new identity papers were produced by the Jewish forgers at Sachsenhausen concentration camp through Operation Bernhard.

Following the failure of the Ardennes offensive, Hitler returned to Berlin and took up residence in the Old Reich Chancellery until repeated air raids forced him to seek permanent shelter in the Führerbunker, situated beneath the chancellery gardens, in mid-February. Thursday, April 12, 1945, was a day of rejoicing in the underground bunker. In the midnight hours, when Hitler was at his most energetic, the news arrived of President Roosevelt's death. To Hitler, this seemed like a salvation reminiscent of the death of Empress Elizabeth of Russia in 1762, which had saved Hitler's hero Frederick the Great of Prussia during the Seven Years' War. In his order of the day to the Wehrmacht on April 13, Hitler predicted that the fortunes of war had changed "now that destiny has removed the greatest war criminal in the world from the Earth." Bormann was equally exultant; immediately contacting all his gauleiters by telex, he prophesied "a total reversal in the attitude of the Western powers toward the Soviet offensive in Europe." Stalin's ultimate fear of a separate peace between the Western Allies and Germany, and Hitler's ultimate hope of an accommodation with the Allies, now appeared feasible, since the champion of unconditional surrender was dead and Nazi Germany was still not defeated. Bormann concluded his telex message with the claim that this was "the best news we have had in years. . . . Tell all the men, the most dangerous man of this war is dead." To Bormann, Roosevelt's death provided a golden opportunity to make the ultimate deal to secure the success of his Project Land of Fire.

IN BERN, THE OSS STATION CHIEF Allen Dulles had continued to cultivate his own web of contacts, despite the frustration of his hopes to support the German resistance movement prior to the July bomb plot. Both Britain and America still discouraged contact with any envoys extending peace feelers from the Nazi hierarchy, for fear of offending Joseph Stalin and compromising the agreement to demand unconditional surrender. However, with the death of Roosevelt and the very heavy casualties suffered by the Western Allies during the winter of 1944–45, opinion was beginning to soften slightly in some quarters. Similarly, perceptions of "Uncle Joe's" Russia as simply a stalwart ally against Nazi Germany were changing rapidly. To Dulles, the advance westward of the Red Army presented a clear and present danger to Europe and to American interests in the future.

Now that Allied forces had opened the Swiss borders from the west, communications with the outside world were much easier. Dulles was able to travel to Paris or London for conferences with his director, Gen. Donovan, and others in the intelligence community. At the same time, Dulles enjoyed far closer liaison with the U.S. Army Counter Intelligence Corps and the G-2 staffs at SHAEF and the U.S. 6th and 12th Army Groups, as well as with the U.S. Seventh Army as they advanced into Germany. In the winter of 1944–45, Dulles reached an agreement with Gen. Masson, head of the Swiss Secret Service, to allow the American legation in Bern to install a secure radio-teleprinter transmitter for direct communications with London, Paris, and Washington. The Swiss authorities were far more amenable to the clandestine activities of the Allies now that defeat was looming for Nazi Germany.

Nevertheless, in February 1945, the military situation both on the German border and in Italy remained problematic. The campaign in the Rhineland had become a protracted battle of attrition as the Allies fought their way up to the Rhine, the last physical barrier to Germany's industrial heartland in the Ruhr. In Italy, the Allies were stalled below the Gothic Line, which stretched from coast to coast across the Apennine Mountains. On both fronts, Allied casualties were depressingly high and German resistance remained dogged. The whole Italian campaign had been a grinding series of costly attacks against successive German hilltop defense lines, and now there was a prospect of the Wehrmacht's retreating in good order into the mountain reaches of the Alps. In SHAEF there were growing concerns about the existence of a National Redoubt in that region, where the last remnants of the Nazi regime and its diehard defenders could congregate for a final stand that might last for months or even years. The able German commander in chief of Army Group Southwest, Field Marshal Albert Kesselring, still had more than a million troops under arms in northern Italy and the Alpine regions. Worse still, the Soviet Union was now claiming hegemony over Austria and Yugoslavia. The latter would give the Soviets possession of warm-water ports on the Adriatic and immediate access to the Mediterranean Sea—a strategic nightmare for the West.

Despite the stern injunctions from London and Washington, Dulles did not ignore the increasing number of approaches he received from various parties and individuals representing members of the Nazi hierarchy—notably Heinrich Himmler—in search of a separate peace agreement with the West. The first came in November 1944 through the German consul in Lugano, Alexander von Neurath. He was followed in December by SS and Police Gen. Wilhelm Harster, the immediate subordinate to SS and Waffen-SS Gen. Karl Wolff, the supreme SS and police leader and de facto military governor of northern Italy. In January 1945, an emissary from Wolff reaffirmed the possibility of a separate agreement for the surrender of all German forces in Italy. To

Dulles this seemed too good an offer to refuse out of hand, so he initiated negotiations with Wolff under the designation of Operation Sunrise (also subsequently known as Operation Crossword).

The first face-to-face meeting between representatives of Dulles and Wolff took place on March 3, 1945, at Lugano. Paul Blum, the X-2 counterespionage chief for the Bern station, acted for the OSS, and SS Gen. Eugen Dollmann represented Wolff. As a gesture of good will, the Germans agreed to release two prominent Italian partisan leaders—one was Ferruccio Parri, who became prime minister of Italy in June. Five days later, Dulles and Wolff met in person at a safe house in Zurich. With Kesselring's departure for the Western Front on March 10, the negotiations faltered, but they resumed on March 19 when Wolff actually agreed to permit an OSS radio operator dressed in German uniform to be stationed in his own headquarters at Bolzano for better communications. This agent was a Czech known as "Little Wally," who had escaped from Dachau concentration camp. Significantly, Wolff also submitted a list of art treasures from the Uffizi Gallery in Florence that he was willing to return intact if the surrender talks prospered.

Throughout these delicate negotiations, Dulles kept Washington informed via Gen. Donovan at OSS headquarters, but from there, news of the contacts was quickly passed to the suspicious Soviets. There were several Soviet spies in the OSS, including Maj. Duncan Chaplin Lee, a counterintelligence officer and legal adviser to Donovan, and Halperin, head of research and analysis in the Latin America division. Fearing a separate peace, incensed Stalin cabled Roosevelt and Churchill:

> The Germans have on the Eastern Front 147 divisions. They could without harm to their cause take from the Eastern Front 15–20 divisions and shift them to the aid of their troops on the Western Front. However, the Germans did not do it and are not doing it. They continue to fight savagely for some unknown junction, Zemlianitsa in Czechoslovakia, which they need as much as a dead man needs poultices—but they surrender without resistance such important towns in Central Germany as Osnabrück, Mannheim, and Kassel. Don't you agree that such behavior by the Germans is more than strange, [it is] incomprehensible?

Both Roosevelt and Churchill angrily rejected the Soviet leader's implications, but the damage was done. Roosevelt finally recognized the threat posed by Stalin and the Soviet Union just two days before his death. This episode was, essentially, the beginning of the Cold War.

Stalin now refused to endorse the agreed separation pact of Austria and Germany to allow the former to become once again an independent state. The U.S. Joint Chiefs of Staff expressly forbade the continuation of the talks with Wolff. Intelligence about these contacts had reached Bormann, and SS and Police Gen. Kaltenbrunner also ordered that such negotiations cease immediately—he and Bormann did not wish to jeopardize their own agenda.

A FELLOW AUSTRIAN, ERNST KALTENBRUNNER had joined Hitler's inner circle following the July bomb attempt, when as chief of the Reich Main Security Office he took charge of the investigations leading to the arrest and execution of the plotters and the imprisonment of their families. The fearful retribution exacted by the tall, cadaverous, scar-faced Kaltenbrunner earned him much favor with the Führer. In December 1944, he was granted the parallel rank of General of the Waffen-SS (important in that it gave him military as well as police authority) and the Gold Party Badge. On April 18, 1945, he was appointed commander in chief of the German forces in southern Europe.

Kaltenbrunner's adjutant, the former SD intelligence officer Maj. Wilhelm Höttl, had already passed information to Allen Dulles concerning the creation of the National Redoubt (see Chapter 10, page 101). Höttl renewed the connection with the OSS in February 1945 through an Austrian friend of his, Friedrich Westen—a dubious businessman who had profited from expropriations of Jewish property and from slave labor. Both wished to ingratiate themselves with the Americans (though not at the expense of offending Kaltenbrunner and, by extension, Martin Bormann), and the stories they told soon became even more misleading and devious.

During early 1944, when Höttl was in Budapest organizing the transportation of Hungary's Jewish population to the extermination camps, he had become friendly with Col. Árpád Toldi, Hungary's commissioner for Jewish affairs. Now, a year later, Toldi was in charge of the "Gold Train." This was laden with Hungary's national treasures, including the crown jewels, precious metals, gems, paintings, and large quantities of currency, much of it stolen from Hungary's Jews. The train—whose value was put at $350 million (approximately $6 billion today)—was destined for Berlin and was moving westward to escape the advance of the Red Army. As it passed through Austria, Höttl advised Kaltenbrunner of its presence, whereupon the train was stopped near Schnann in the Tyrol and many especially valuable crates were offloaded onto trucks. The contents and the whereabouts of those crates remain unknown to this day. Ostensibly, Höttl was instructed to use the Gold Train as a bargaining chip with the OSS in an attempt to arrange a separate truce for Austria like the deal that was under discussion in Italy.

Yet again, Dulles sent an intermediary—this time a senior OSS officer named Edgeworth M. Leslie—for the first meetings with Höttl on the Swiss-Austrian border. In his debrief to Dulles, Leslie reported that Höttl "is of course dangerous":

> He is a fanatical anti-Russian and for this reason we cannot very well collaborate with him . . . without informing the Russians. . . . But I see no reason why we should not use him in the furtherance of [common] interests . . . namely the hastening of the end of the resistance in Austria by the disruption of the [Redoubt]. . . . To avoid any accusation that we are working with a Nazi reactionary . . . I believe that we should keep our contact with him as indirect as possible.

Believing that Höttl was a conduit to Kaltenbrunner, Dulles agreed: "This type requires utmost caution." Concurring, Gen. Donovan advised, "I am convinced [that Höttl] is the right hand of Kaltenbrunner and a key contact to develop."

During these early meetings, Höttl revealed more details about the National Redoubt. He also stated that a Nazi guerrilla movement known as *Wehrwolf* (Werewolf) had been organized over the past two years, with access to hidden arms dumps, explosives, and ample funds. They could muster some 100,000 committed SS soldiers and fanatical Hitler Youth under the command of another Austrian, SS Lt. Col. Otto Skorzeny—an old friend of Kaltenbrunner's and Hitler's favorite leader of Special Forces, whose impressive reputation was well known to the Allies. These "details" were actually disinformation created by Bormann, but they succeeded admirably in causing consternation at SHAEF, particularly to Gen. Eisenhower. As his chief of staff, Gen. Bedell Smith, stated, "We had every reason to believe the Nazis intended to make their last stand among the crags."

SINCE THE BREAKOUT FROM NORMANDY, Gen. Eisenhower had pursued a measured strategy whereby the disparate Allied armies, under their often fractious and competitive commanders, advanced on a broad front. Although ponderous, this plan was politically astute and in tune with the moderate capabilities of conscript armies. Massed firepower, inexhaustible logistics, and overwhelming air support were the answer to superior German tactical performance on the battlefield. Only once did Eisenhower deviate from this strategy, when a failure of Allied logistics halted the broad advance and he accepted the bold plan for Operation Market Garden—the attempted airborne thrust deep into Holland. If it had succeeded, then a rapid advance eastward across the north German plains would have brought Berlin within reach. The capture of the enemy's capital city and the triumphal parade through its streets following victory has always been the ultimate ambition of all great commanders. But Eisenhower's ambitions were maturing and he had every reason—both humanitarian and pragmatic—to shrink from the prospect of losing 100,000 GIs during a prolonged and bitter street battle for Berlin.

Over days of brooding, Eisenhower revised his strategy for the campaign in Europe. On the afternoon of March 28, 1945, he declared his intentions in three cables. One was a personal message to Joseph Stalin—the only occasion during the war when Eisenhower communicated directly with the Soviet leader. The second was to Gen. Marshall in Washington, and the third was to Field Marshal Montgomery, commander in chief of the British-Canadian 21st Army Group in northern Germany. Against vehement protests from some of his

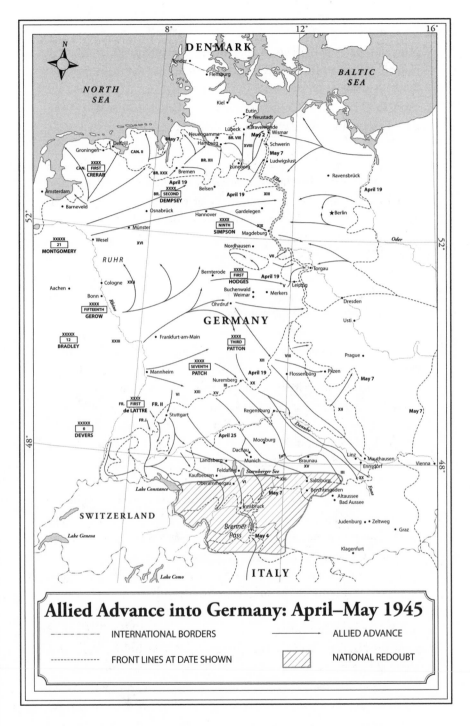

Allied Advance into Germany: April–May 1945

------------- INTERNATIONAL BORDERS   ⟶ ALLIED ADVANCE

------------- FRONT LINES AT DATE SHOWN   ⟦▨⟧ NATIONAL REDOUBT

THE GERMAN ARMY crumbled before the might of the Allies, who rushed to take not just the territory of the former Reich but its art, industrial secrets, and scientists.

generals—particularly Patton and Montgomery, who each wished to lead an assault on Berlin—Eisenhower stated that the main thrust of his armies was to be southeastward toward Bavaria, Austria, and the supposed National Redoubt. Berlin was to be left to the Red Army. Eisenhower was seeking valuable military plunder, not empty glory.

BY NOW, THE SWISS AUTHORITIES were becoming increasingly disconcerted by the number of Nazi emissaries and fugitives trying to cross into Switzerland, many of whom were being held by Swiss border guards. The Swiss indicated to Allen Dulles that it would be desirable if his talks could be conducted more discreetly and preferably not on their territory. They were not trying to be obstructive but they wished to maintain the facade of neutrality to the last. Their greatest fear remained a flood of refugees descending on Switzerland, so an early resolution to the war was their chief priority.

As always, Dulles had an elegant solution. Due to a historical anomaly on the maps dating back to 1798, the Italian enclave of Campione d'Italia on the shore of Lake Lugano was totally surrounded by Swiss territory, with only water access from Italy. During the dark night of January 28, 1945, about twenty OSS agents invaded Campione—at that date the sovereign territory of Mussolini's rump Italian Socialist Republic—and claimed it for the Allies. The six Carabinieri policemen defending the enclave offered no resistance. Thereafter, the Swiss authorities could turn a blind eye to OSS activities in Campione, so long as they were discreet. From the enclave OSS agents were infiltrated into Italy and, in March and April 1945, Campione became the venue for feverish negotiations during Operation Sunrise.

Meanwhile, other members of the Nazi hierarchy were trying to save their own skins by opening negotiations with the Western Allies. It remained the dearest dream of Heinrich Himmler to construct an anti-Soviet coalition or, at the least, a truce in the West that would allow the Nazis to continue the struggle against the Bolshevik hordes. This baffling delusion was shared by Foreign Minister Joachim von Ribbentrop and by Himmler's trusted subordinate, SS Gen. Walter Schellenberg, the chief of the SD foreign intelligence department. All three tried to seek peace through contacts in both Switzerland and Sweden. In January 1945, Schellenberg was in Switzerland trying to cut a deal with the former federal president of Switzerland, Jean-Marie Musy. While there, he passed word through Gen. Henri Guisan, chief of staff of the Swiss army, that he wished to contact Allen Dulles, but this came to nothing. In March, Ribbentrop was seeking a separate peace with the British through the Swedish banker Marcus Wallenberg, whose business interests had prospered so greatly through trading with the Nazis. Himmler sought a similar agreement through the Swedish diplomat Count Folke Bernadotte. As an inducement, some 17,000 mainly Scandinavian prisoners in Germany's concentration camps were returned to their homelands in convoys of "White Buses" in a Red Cross humanitarian mission. In return for a prompt peace in the West, Himmler was willing to spare and release the 400,000 Jews remaining in Germany and to this end he ordered the evacuation and destruction of the extermination camps in the east; in the aftermath, however, an estimated quarter million camp survivors lost their lives while being herded westward on freezing death marches. There were conditions to Himmler's proposals, not the least of which was a demand for an assurance that no black occupation troops would be allowed to enter Germany, in the interests of "racial hygiene."

The Western Allies were not interested in the deluded Himmler's grisly deals or in a separate peace. They wanted unconditional surrender and the spoils of war. In particular, they wanted Nazi weapons technology, gold, and loot. (It was Allied policy to restore gold to its rightful owners as well as looted art, but in fact this restitution took many years and some spoliated art has still not been returned to its rightful owners to this day; many museums across the world have artifacts of dubious origin from the Nazi era that do not bear too close a scrutiny as to their provenance.) Martin Bormann was willing to give the Western Allies what they wanted—in exchange for the survival of Adolf Hitler, himself, and a small coterie of the "mountain people."

THE HUNGARIAN GOLD TRAIN arrived on April 8, 1945, within the confines of the so-called National Redoubt at Werfen in the Salzach valley, where it was hidden from Allied aircraft in a tunnel.

SS Maj. Höttl, now code-named "Alperg" by the OSS, revealed the existence of the train during further discussions with Edgeworth M. Leslie. He also imparted information concerning the whereabouts of other repositories of Nazi treasure hidden across Germany and, just as importantly, reinforced the proposal of SS Gen. Wolff to return the treasures of the Uffizi Gallery in Florence—looted artworks were now an inducement in any deal. A radiotelephone link was established between the OSS in Bern and the Austrian SS faction under Gen. Kaltenbrunner centered on the Villa Kerry, his home at Altaussee in the heart of the Bavarian Alps. Bormann now had a direct line of communication to Allen Dulles via Ernst Kaltenbrunner and Operation Crossword.

During the second half of April 1945, events in this shadowy endgame of the European war accelerated day by day. On the fourteenth, Allen Dulles met Gen. Donovan at the Ritz Hotel in Paris to explain his conduct over the peace overtures from the Nazi hierarchy. "Wild Bill" Donovan was anxious to return to Washington in the wake of Roosevelt's death, to befriend the new president and cement the position of the OSS. The Joint Chiefs of Staff were furious with Dulles and the OSS following the acrimonious exchange of cables between Stalin, Roosevelt, and Churchill concerning Operation Sunrise/Crossword. William J. Casey (later director of the CIA from 1981 to 1987) was present at the Ritz meeting and observed that "Dulles fidgeted in his chair, alternately outraged and embarrassed. . . . Bluntly put, all hell broke loose." Dulles protested that as yet nothing concrete had emerged from his discussions with SS Gen. Wolff and that everything could still be plausibly denied as far as the Soviets were concerned. Even so, Donovan closed down Sunrise/Crossword negotiations for the time being, but allowed the negotiations with Ernst Kaltenbrunner to continue since the White House was not yet aware of them. As Dulles ruefully commented about the situation: "It is easy to start a war but difficult to stop one." Donovan and Dulles decided to keep knowledge of the Kaltenbrunner talks between themselves, as security had become inexcusably lax. Too many interested parties were aware of the various putative peace plans emanating from the Nazi hierarchy via Switzerland or Sweden—including the Soviet spy Kim Philby, who later recalled, "The air was opaque with mutual suspicions of separate peace feelers."

Chapter 13

"Wo bist Adolf Hitler?"

ON APRIL 20, 1945, HITLER'S ENTOURAGE dutifully celebrated his fifty-sixth birthday, but it was hardly an auspicious occasion. Himmler and Göring were present at the Führerbunker in Berlin to mark the event, but both quickly left the capital, never to return. Göring departed for Berchtesgaden in Bavaria to supervise the arrival of his art collection in eight railroad cars from Carinhall, though there were few suitable places left to hide it.

The Western Allies were now racing eastward across Germany toward their rendezvous with the Red Army on the Elbe and Mulde rivers. Montgomery's 21st Army Group had turned northeastward and was advancing toward Oldenburg, Bremen, and Hamburg. On their right, William H. Simpson's U.S. Ninth Army and Courtney Hodges's First Army had reached the Elbe at Magdeburg and the Mulde beyond Leipzig. Patton's Third Army had swung southeastward, forging ahead for the Czech border. Any defended village that surrendered promptly was spared; those that did not were utterly destroyed, to become "Third Army Memorials"—stark reminders that Patton's men had passed this way. To speed the advance, mayors of towns that had been captured or destroyed were often sent ahead with the leading U.S. reconnaissance units to persuade recalcitrant or dilatory officials that a display of white flags and sheets on every house was in the inhabitants' best interests. To Patton's south and inside his wheeling movement, Alexander Patch's Seventh Army had just reached Nuremberg. To the south again, Jean de Lattre's French First Army had reached the outskirts of Stuttgart and was heading for the Danube and Austria. The Obersalzberg, the top Nazis' retreat in the Bavarian Alps, would soon be cut off from northern Germany and from Berlin in particular.

For Bormann the situation was becoming critical, since the Soviets were about to surround Berlin, with Red Army troops extending pincers forward from the north and south. As yet, the Führer was refusing to leave the capital and Bormann's carefully laid plans for Aktion Feuerland were in danger of collapsing. Aircraft of the Fliegerstaffel (flying squadron) des Führers—Hitler's personal air transport unit—were standing by at the Berlin airports of Gatow and Tempelhof to fly him to Bavaria, Spain, or elsewhere. But they would soon be within range of Soviet artillery guns. Similarly, long-range flying boats of Kampfgeschwader 200—the Luftwaffe's special missions wing—were ready to fly the Führer even further, from a base at Travemünde on the Baltic coast. Seaplanes were even stationed by night on Lake Havel, ready to fly the Nazi hierarchy out of Berlin at a moment's notice. The Ost-West-Asche (East-West-Axis boulevard)—between the Brandenburg Gate and the Victory Monument, in the heart of the city—had been cleared as a makeshift runway.

On April 20, Bormann instituted Operation Seraglio or Harem, whereby many government staff and records, including Hitler's private papers, were dispatched to Bavaria. That night ten transport aircraft were assembled at Gatow for evacuation to Munich. Nine arrived safely but the tenth crashed into the Heidenholz Forest while flying at treetop level and disintegrated. Many of Hitler's personal papers were consumed in the burning wreckage. At that stage it was intended that the Führer and his entourage would fly south two days later, on April 22.

MEANWHILE, ALLEN DULLES RESUMED the Operation Sunrise negotiations with SS Gen. Wolff, despite Donovan's recent orders to cease the mission. On April 23, Karl Wolff indicated to Dulles that he now had full powers to order the surrender of all German troops in Italy after discussions in Berlin with Hitler and Bormann on April 18–19. On April 24, both Kaltenbrunner and SS Lt. Col. Hans Helmut von Hummel flew south to Austria to take over the negotiations of Crossword from Höttl. Helmut von Hummel was Bormann's adjutant responsible for maintaining the records of all the Führer's looted art holdings and the locations where they were hidden. The most important of these repositories was at Altaussee, close to Kaltenbrunner's home, where an old salt mine now contained the vast majority of Hitler's art collection; this hoard was to be a major factor in any deal with Dulles.

Events were now moving at such speed that the two originally separate sets of negotiations under Sunrise/Crossword—with Wolff and with Kaltenbrunner—were inextricably linked. On April 26, Höttl reported to Kaltenbrunner on the results of another visit to Switzerland, at which he had agreed with the OSS officer Edgeworth M. Leslie to arrange a personal meeting between Dulles and Kaltenbrunner at Feldkirch in Austria, close to the Swiss border. Dulles realized that Höttl was purely a stooge and that much of his information concerning the National Redoubt was highly suspect. Dulles knew that Austria could not surrender in the same manner as Italy had in September 1943. Despite the formation of a provisional government that month, the country remained an integral part of the German Reich. Whatever emerged from these talks, the sands were running out for Austria, since the Red Army tanks of the 3rd Ukrainian Front were advancing rapidly westward after the capture of Vienna. There had to be an ulterior motive for Kaltenbrunner to be negotiating—and that was explained by Martin Bormann's proposals.

(*Italics* are used in the following section to identify conclusions based on deductive research; see page 185 in Chapter 16 for further discussion.)

In Bormann's characteristic style—the carrot and the stick— *Kaltenbrunner and Hummel indicated to Dulles that Bormann was willing to provide the Allies, as an inducement or "carrot," with information as to the whereabouts of all the Nazis' looted art. It would be handed over intact, together with the remainder of the national treasure of Germany, including its gold deposits, currency reserves, bearer bonds, and industrial patents*—except, of course, for the substantial part of this treasure that Bormann had already secreted abroad. An additional and supremely attractive carrot was Bormann's undertaking to deliver to the Allies examples of the most modern weapons technology together with the whereabouts of the designers, such as Wernher von Braun and his V-2 team, and the nuclear scientists of the Uranium Club. Furthermore, the ceasefire in Italy would be ratified immediately. But what was the desired price for such treasures? *A blind eye turned to the escape of Adolf Hitler, Eva Braun, Martin Bormann, Heinrich "Gestapo" Müller, Hermann Fegelein, and Ernst Kaltenbrunner.* The rest of the Nazi hierarchy were to be abandoned to their fate.

The "stick" was simple. Germany now claimed to be capable of bombarding the eastern seaboard of the United States with weapons of mass destruction; considerable effort had been invested in selling this disinformation to U.S. intelligence agencies, with some success (see Chapter 16). These weapons incorporated warheads armed with the most toxic nerve agents ever devised, sarin and tabun. In addition, many repositories of artworks hidden in deep mine shafts would be destroyed with explosives and buried forever. A high proportion of the greatest works of art produced during centuries of Western civilization was now held hostage, and this threat was entirely credible following Hitler's "Nero Decree" of March 19. Officially titled "Demolitions on Reich Territory," this decree ordered the utter destruction of all German industrial infrastructure and technology; although not included in the official order, it also implied the destruction of cultural assets and the elimination of any key personnel who might be useful to the Allied powers.

The decision lay with the Allies, but the clock was ticking. On the previous day, April 25, the city of Berlin had been surrounded by the Red Army, and troops from Gen. Ivan Konev's army group had made contact with GIs from Hodges's U.S. First Army on the Elbe River. Germany was cut in half by a broad belt of Allied-occupied territory, with only the extreme north and south still under Nazi control.

THE LARGEST DAYLIGHT RAID ON BERLIN so far had been launched on February 3, 1945. In total, 937 Flying Fortresses dropped 2,298 tons of bombs, killing thousands of people and inflicting massive damage on the city, including the government quarter.

Among the other government buildings hit that day were the Reich Chancellery on the corner of Wilhelmstrasse and Voss-Strasse, where Bormann's office was badly damaged; the Gestapo headquarters on Prinz Albrechtstrasse and the Reichsbank on Hausvogteiplatz were virtually demolished by a string of bombs. In a letter to his wife on February 4, Bormann wrote:

> I have just taken refuge in my secretary's office which is the only room in the place that has some temporary windows. Yesterday's raid was very heavy. The Reich Chancellery garden is an amazing sight—deep craters, fallen trees, and the paths obliterated by a mass of rubble and rubbish. The Führer's residence [in the Old Reich Chancellery] was badly hit several times. The New Reich Chancellery was also hit several times, and is not usable for the time being. The Party Chancellery buildings [offices on the upper floor of the central block of the New Reich Chancellery], too, are a sorry sight. Telephone communications are still very inadequate and the Führer's residence and Party Chancellery still have no connection with the outside world.
>
> To crown everything, in this so-called Government Quarter, the light, power and water supply is still lacking! We have a water cart standing in front of the Reich Chancellery and that is our only water supply for cooking and washing up! And the worst thing of all is the water closets. These commando pigs [the SS bodyguards] use them constantly and not one of them even thinks of taking a bucket of water with him to flush the place. From this evening I am apparently to have a room in the bunker in which to work and sleep.

By the middle of February, Hitler and his entourage—including Bormann—had been forced to take up permanent residence in the Führerbunker.

The president of the Reichsbank, Dr. Walter Funk, decided to transfer the bulk of the bank's cash and gold reserves to safety outside of Berlin. The treasure was shipped to Merkers in Thuringia, two hundred miles southwest of the capital. There, bullion and currency with a value of about $238 million were deposited deep underground in the Kaiseroda potassium mine, alongside a huge cache of artworks. This was but one of 134 repositories dotted across the Third Reich under the control of Martin Bormann. In accordance with Hitler's Nero Decree of March 19, many of them were now rigged with high explosives to prevent their falling into the hands of the Allies. In the salt mines at Altaussee were the most valuable pieces in Hitler's collection, including Michelangelo's Bruges Madonna, Jan van Eyck's *Adoration of the Mystic Lamb* or Ghent Altarpiece, and many other priceless treasures. Among the innumerable crates were eight that were marked *Vorsicht—Marmor—nicht stürtzen* (Attention—Marble—Do Not Drop). Placed underground between April 10 and 13, these contained not statues but half-ton Luftwaffe aerial bombs. Also primed for destruction was the accumulation of most of the artworks looted from France and the Low Countries, now stored in the fairytale castle of Neuschwanstein in Bavaria. Nothing was intended to survive the coming Götterdämmerung of the Third Reich.

AMONG THE ALLIED TROOPS POISED to deny the Nazis the chance to destroy their secrets were Cdr. Fleming's Red Indians of 30 Advance Unit. Intelligence on where to search was now flooding in from the OSS office in Bern, thanks to the dialogue between Dulles and Bormann. The unit's Team 4, under Lt. Cdr. Patrick Dalzel-Job, began driving northward between Bremen on the Weser River and Hamburg on the Elbe. Their task was to capture the latest U-boat technology.

Surging ahead of 21st Army Group, Team 4 of 30 AU was the first Allied unit to enter the major port of Bremen. They accepted the surrender of the city by the mayor some twenty-four hours before the arrival of conventional forces, and a small detachment of Royal Marines captured sixteen U-boats. Further south, Lt. Cdr. Jim Glanville's Team 55 set off on April 14 for Schloss Tambach near Bad Sulza in Thuringia, where they captured the complete records of the Kriegsmarine from

1850 up to the end of 1944, including all the logs of U-boats and surface ships. These archives were of immense value to Allied naval authorities and were judged to be one of the most important intelligence hauls of the entire war. Meanwhile, after their success locating the uranium ore for the Alsos Mission, Team 5 under the command of Lt. James Lambie was searching the Harz Mountains for the underground V-2 assembly facility at Nordhausen, following instructions from SHAEF to capture documentation and personnel connected with the ballistic missile program. The Monuments Men were also hard on the heels of the combat troops, on their way to safeguard the major caches of artworks hidden across Germany, including the castle of Neuschwanstein in Bavaria, which was saved from destruction on May 4, 1945, and with it the treasures of France and the Low Countries.

THROUGHOUT APRIL 1945, BORMANN pursued his plans for Aktion Feuerland with ruthless efficiency. It was time to tie up loose ends, of which one of the most outstanding was Adm. Wilhelm Canaris, now held in Flossenbürg concentration camp. Canaris knew far too much about the site of the refuge that Bormann had prepared for Hitler in Argentina and about a major staging post for the Führer's journey between Europe and South America. On April 5, Ernst Kaltenbrunner presented Hitler with some highly incriminating evidence against Canaris. The Führer flew into a rage and signed the admiral's death warrant. He was hanged in humiliating circumstances on April 9 (see page 235).

In the detached netherworld of the Führerbunker—dubbed the "cement submarine" by many of the staff working there—Hitler was living the claustrophobic life of a U-boat captain on the ocean floor, with little sense of time or reality of actual events in the world above. The Führer had always been subject to mood swings, but his rages became more frequent as the military situation deteriorated inexorably and he was confronted with the self-deluding futility of the orders he had been issuing. At a military situation conference on Sunday, April 22, attended by Bormann, the Führer exploded in a fit of unrestrained fury. For the first time he declared openly that the war was lost and announced repeatedly that he would die in Berlin. Bormann insisted that this was the time to fly south to the Obersalzberg to finalize the Führer's personal affairs before fleeing in accordance with the preparations made for Aktion Feuerland, but Joseph Goebbels persuaded Hitler otherwise; Goebbels saw it as their duty to die among the ruins of their city. Gen. Jodl pointed out that Germany still had armies in the field theoretically within reach of Berlin— Field Marshal Ferdinand Schörner's remnant of Army Group Center and Gen. Walther Wenck's Twelfth Army. The Führer became vague about the military steps to be taken, but repeated that he was determined to remain in Berlin to the last.

Frustrated, Bormann nevertheless continued juggling the possibilities that remained open to him. That night, he sent a telex to Göring at the Obersalzberg indicating that the Führer was indisposed. It was a trap and Göring fell straight into it. On the following day he sent a telegram to the Führerbunker stating that if he did not hear instructions to the contrary, he would assume full command of the Reich from 10:00 p.m. that night, in accordance with his responsibility as designated successor to Hitler. Bormann immediately informed the Führer, urging the need to annul the decree of succession as Göring was obviously staging a coup. At first, Hitler demurred. Bormann then sent Göring a telex accusing him of treacherous behavior but also stating that no further action would be taken if he resigned from all his many offices of state. Within an hour, Göring's resignation was on the Führer's desk. This was seen as confirmation of his treachery, and the SS detachment at the Obersalzberg was ordered to place the Reichsmarschall under house arrest.

With Göring sidelined, Bormann turned his attention to ousting Himmler. It was time for him to use his ace in the hole. He had known from late March 1945 that Himmler had begun negotiations with the Allies in Stockholm. His close friend Gen. Fegelein, Himmler's representative in the bunker, had kept him well informed. The Reichsleiter had prepared a detailed dossier detailing Himmler's treachery, which he would present to Hitler. Bormann had achieved his ultimate ambition—to destroy all competing candidates for the power and influence of being the Führer's only unquestionably trusted deputy. It was something of a Pyrrhic victory, though, since on

April 25 the Red Army completed its encirclement of Berlin and the Obersalzberg was comprehensively bombed by the Lancasters of No. 617 Squadron RAF, thereby rendering it useless as a bolt-hole during any planned escape to the south. The rush for the shelters probably saved Göring's life, since his SS guards were on the point of executing him when the sirens sounded. The confirmation of Bormann's total victory in the intrigues of the Nazi court came on April 26, when Hitler promoted Gen. Robert Ritter von Greim to the rank of field marshal and appointed him commander in chief of the Luftwaffe. Bormann must have been ecstatic over Hitler's first order to Ritter von Greim: he was to fly to Karl Dönitz's headquarters at Plön and arrest Heinrich Himmler for treason. This was impossible, however, since Ritter von Greim had been badly wounded earlier that day by Red Army gunfire shortly before landing in Berlin in a plane piloted by the daredevil aviatrix Hanna Reitsch.

ALTHOUGH THE BULK OF THE REICHSBANK'S HOLDINGS had been transferred to the Kaiseroda mine at Merkers, much still remained in Berlin, ostensibly to pay the city's Wehrmacht defenders in cash. At a meeting between the Führer, Dr. Funk, and Bormann on April 9, it had been decided to transfer the remaining gold and currency reserves of the Reichsbank to Bavaria. They were to be transported to the so-called "Bormann Bunker" in Munich, by road in a convoy of six Opel Blitz trucks and by two special trains code-named *Adler* and *Dohle*—"Eagle" and "Jackdaw." The trains and trucks left Berlin on April 14 but took almost two weeks to arrive in Bavaria, due to the devastated road and rail networks and the chronic lack of gasoline.

Following the Operation Seraglio/Harem exodus of nonessential personnel from the Führerbunker on April 22, Bormann instructed SS Gen. Kaltenbrunner to fly south in order to pursue Allen Dulles's Operation Crossword. Kaltenbrunner decided that he should make his own arrangements for survival rather than relying solely upon Aktion Feuerland. In his capacity as head of the RSHA, he ordered SS Gen. Josef Spacil to take a party of SS troops to remove everything of value left in the vaults of the Reichsbank—securities, gems, and 23 million gold reichsmarks, worth $9.13 million (approximately $110 million in today's money). One of the last transport planes to get out of the city flew this loot to Salzburg in Austria. From there it was taken by truck to the high Tyrolean town of Rauris and buried on a wooded mountainside nearby.

This largest armed bank robbery in history soon came to the notice of Martin Bormann, who commented to his confederate, "Gestapo" Müller,

> Well, Ernst is still looking out for Ernst. It doesn't mean much to the big picture. But find out where he has it taken. When it's buried—and it will probably be in an Austrian lake close to his home—we might want one of our party Gauleiters to watch over it. Kaltenbrunner may never last the war out, and it would be useful to the party later.

In reality, by striking out on his own, Kaltenbrunner had signed his own death warrant, but he was still useful to Bormann as long as the talks with Dulles continued. The Allies recovered less than 10 percent of this enormous booty. The rest was used to finance the various escape networks for Nazi war criminals fleeing justice in the postwar years.

The final authorization for the implementation of Operation Crossword came in the form of three "highest priority signals" from Washington on the morning of April 27, 1945. It took two days for all the various representatives to meet and sign the actual surrender document for the German forces in Italy. In the meantime, Bormann had just barely enough time to activate the final option for Aktion Feuerland (see Chapter 15 and the escape to Tønder). At 2:00 p.m. on May 2, 1945, a simultaneous Allied and German ceasefire came into effect in northern Italy. Five minutes earlier, an eighteen-year-old radio announcer, Richard Beier, made the very last broadcast by Grossdeutscher Rundfunk (Greater German Broadcasting) from its underground studio on Masurenallee in Berlin: "The Führer is dead. Long live the Reich!" But where was Hitler's body?

THIS WAS THE QUESTION ASKED by the first Soviet troops to enter the Führerbunker at 9:00 that morning. A few days earlier, on April 29, a special detachment of the SMERSH (NKVD counterespionage) element serving with the headquarters of the 3rd Shock Army had been created at Stalin's insistence, specifically to discover the whereabouts of Adolf Hitler, dead or alive. The SMERSH team arrived at the Reich Chancellery moments after its capture by the Red Army. Despite intense pressure from Moscow, its searches proved fruitless. Although the charred bodies of Joseph and Magda Goebbels were quickly found in the shell-torn garden, no evidence for the deaths of Adolf Hitler or Eva Braun was found.

Close behind the assault troops and NKVD officers, a group of twelve women doctors and their assistants of the Red Army medical corps were the first to enter the bunker in the early afternoon of May 2. The leader of the group spoke fluent German and asked one of the four people then remaining in the bunker, the electrical machinist Johannes Hentschel, *"Wo bist Adolf Hitler? Wo sind die Klamotten?"* ("Where is Adolf Hitler? Where are the glad rags?"). She seemed more interested in Eva Braun's clothes than in the fate of the Führer of the Third Reich. The failure to find an identifiable corpse would vex the Soviet authorities for many months, if not years. That day, the Soviet official newspaper *Pravda* declared, "The announcement of Hitler's death was a fascist trick."

PART III

THE
ESCAPE

Chapter 14

THE BUNKER

THE FÜHRERBUNKER, under the rear and the garden of the Old Reich Chancellery building on Wilhelmstrasse in the government quarter of Berlin, was built in two phases. The contractor was the Hochtief AG construction company, through its subsidiary the Führerbunkerfensterputzer GmbH—which also built the Berghof, Hitler's Bavarian mountain retreat, as well as his Wolf's Lair in Rastenburg. The initial Führerbunker structure, which later became known as the Vorbunker (ante-bunker), was intended purely as an air raid shelter for Hitler and his staff in the Reichskanzlei (Reich Chancellery). Construction began in 1936 and was usefully obscured by the work on a new reception hall then being built onto the western, rear face of the Old Chancellery. The construction of Albert Speer's massive New Chancellery building, fronting onto the Voss-Strasse and adjoining the Old Chancellery in an L-shape to the south, was essentially complete by January 1939. This range of buildings, and the adjacent SS barrack blocks aligned north–south on Hermann-Göring-Strasse to the west, incorporated from the start two very large complexes of linked underground shelters, working quarters, garages, and tunnels.

On January 18, 1943, in response to the heavier bombs then being used by the Allied air forces, Hitler ordered Speer to extend the shelter under the Old Chancellery by constructing a deeper complex. Under the supervision of the architect Carl Piepenburg, an excavation for this Führerbunker or *Hauptbunker* (main bunker), codenamed "B207," was dug below and to the west of the Vorbunker. The major works were completed in 1943, at a cost of 1.35 million reichsmarks—five times the amount of the original shelter. However, it was not until October 23, 1944, that Dr. Hans Heinrich Lammers, the state secretary of the Reich Chancellery, was able to inform Hitler that the new facility was entirely ready for his use.

The new bunker lay twenty-six feet below the garden of the Old Chancellery and 131 yards north from the New Chancellery building. Two floors deeper than the Vorbunker, the Führerbunker adjoined its west side and was linked to it by a corridor, an airtight compartment, and a staircase down. The new complex had two main means of access: this route from the Vorbunker and another staircase from the far end leading up to the Chancellery garden. The ceiling of the Führerbunker was formed of reinforced concrete that was 11 feet, 3 inches thick; the external walls were up to 13 feet thick, and heavy steel doors closed off the various compartments and corridors. The bunker was built in Berlin's sandy soil below the level of the water table, so pumps were continuously at work to keep the damp at bay. The complex incorporated its own independent water supply and air-filtration plant, and it was lit and heated with electricity generated by a diesel engine of the type used on U-boats.

The general layout of the Führerbunker was a series of rooms leading off each side of a central corridor, divided into outer and inner ranges. The outer range, nearest to the access from the Vorbunker, contained the practical amenities such as machine rooms, stores, showers, and toilets. The inner half of the corridor functioned as a reception and conference space, and leading off it were telephone and telegraph rooms; a first aid station; quarters for orderlies, valets, and medical personnel; and the Führer's private quarters. Beyond a small refreshment room, these comprised a study, a living room, and Hitler's bedroom and bathroom; from the bathroom a second door led to Eva Braun's bedroom and dressing room. None of these rooms was larger than 140 square feet. Comfortably furnished with items brought down from the Chancellery and with paintings lining the walls, the bunker complex had a kitchen stockpiled with luxury foods and wines. It has been portrayed in movies as a drab, damp, concrete cellar, but while conditions certainly deteriorated in late April 1945, when leaking water and dust from the shelled streets above penetrated into the upper parts of the complex, some late visitors to the Führerbunker—such as the pilot Hanna Reitsch—described it as "luxurious."

The bunker's major weakness was that it had never been designed as a Führerhauptquartier, or command headquarters. After the intensity of Allied bombing forced Hitler and his staff to move underground permanently in mid-February 1945, the means of communication were woefully inadequate for keeping in touch with daily developments in the conduct of the war. The telephone exchange, more suited to the needs of a small hotel, was quite incapable of handling the necessary volume of traffic.

Apart from the Vorbunker's above-ground access to the Old Chancellery building, three tunnels provided the upper Vorbunker with underground links. One led north, to the Foreign Office; one crossed the Wilhelmstrasse eastward, to the Propaganda Ministry; and one ran south, linking up with the labyrinth of shelters under the New Chancellery. However, the Old Chancellery—a confusing maze of passages and staircases, much altered over the years—also had an underground emergency exit to a third, deeper, secret shelter, known to only a select few. Hitler maintained his private quarters in the Old Chancellery throughout the war until forced underground in February 1945. To get to the secret shelter, Hitler did not have to leave his private study: as part of Hochtief's extensive underground works, a tunnel had been built that connected Hitler's quarters directly with the shelter. The tunnel was accessible via a doorway covered by a thin concrete sliding panel hidden beside a bookcase in the study. This tunnel, in turn, was connected to the Berlin underground railway system by a five-hundred-yard passageway. The third shelter had been provided with its own water supply, toilet facilities, and storage for food and weapons for up to twelve people for two weeks. Bormann had never really planned

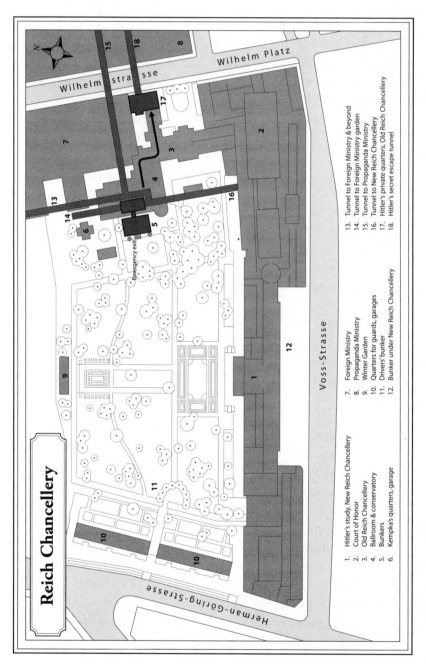

Reich Chancellery

1. Hitler's study, New Reich Chancellery
2. Court of Honor
3. Old Reich Chancellery
4. Ballroom & conservatory
5. Bunkers
6. Kempka's quarters, garage
7. Foreign Ministry
8. Propaganda Ministry
9. Winter Garden
10. Quarters for guards, garages
11. Drivers' bunker
12. Bunker under New Reich Chancellery
13. Tunnel to Foreign Ministry & beyond
14. Tunnel to Foreign Ministry garden
15. Tunnel to Propaganda Ministry
16. Tunnel to New Reich Chancellery
17. Hitler's private quarters, Old Reich Chancellery
18. Hitler's secret escape tunnel

Emergency exit

Herman-Göring-Strasse

Wilhelmstrasse

Wilhelm Platz

Voss-Strasse

DESIGNED BY HITLER'S favorite architect, Albert Speer, the New Reich Chancellery was to have been the seat of power of the Thousand-Year Reich. During the war as the Allied bomber offensive intensified, the Führerbunker was built to protect Hitler from the increasingly devastating aerial bombs employed by the RAF and USAAF.

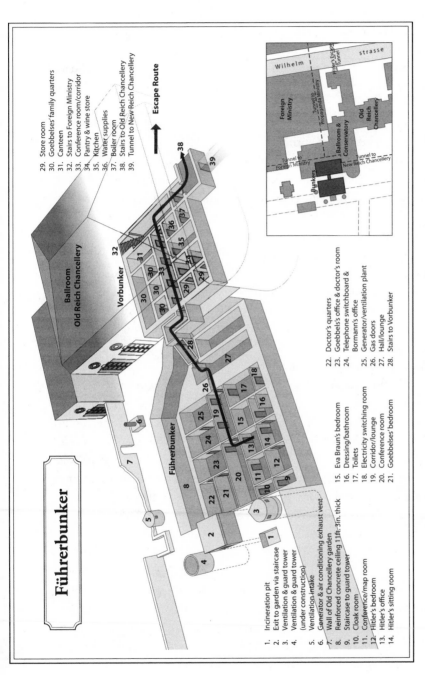

Führerbunker

Ballroom
Old Reich Chancellery

Vorbunker

Führerbunker

Escape Route

1. Incineration pit
2. Exit to garden via staircase
3. Ventilation & guard tower
4. Ventilation & guard tower (under construction)
5. Ventilation-intake
6. Generator & air conditioning exhaust vent
7. Wall of Old Chancellery garden
8. Reinforced concrete ceiling 11ft-3in. thick
9. Staircase to guard tower
10. Cloak room
11. Conference/map room
12. Hitler's bedroom
13. Hitler's office
14. Hitler's sitting room
15. Eva Braun's bedroom
16. Dressing/bathroom
17. Toilets
18. Electricity switching room
19. Corridor/lounge
20. Conference room
21. Goebbelses' bedroom
22. Doctor's quarters
23. Goebbels's office & doctor's room
24. Telephone switchboard & Bormann's office
25. Generator/ventilation plant
26. Gas doors
27. Hall/lounge
28. Stairs to Vorbunker
29. Store room
30. Goebbelses' family quarters
31. Canteen
32. Stairs to Foreign Ministry
33. Conference room/corridor
34. Pantry & wine store
35. Kitchen
36. Water supplies
37. Boiler room
38. Stairs to Old Reich Chancellery
39. Tunnel to New Reich Chancellery

Wilhelm strasse

Foreign Ministry

Tunnel to Foreign Ministry

Tunnel to Propaganda Ministry

Hitler's Escape Tunnel

Bunkers

Ballroom & Conservatory

Tunnel to New Reich Chancellery

Old Reich Chancellery

IN THE FINAL months of the war, Adolf Hitler retreated to the depths of the Führerbunker beneath the Old Reich Chancellery; Bormann had organized a secret tunnel that allowed the Führer and his select companions to escape via the Berlin subway system to an improvised airstrip and flee to Denmark and onward to Spain and Argentina.

for it to be used; it was simply one of the range of options available to get Hitler out of Berlin. But by Friday, April 27, 1945, it was the obvious means of escape to take the Führer away from the devastating shells that were raining down on the government quarter of Berlin as Soviet troops fought their way in from three directions.

ON THAT DAY, IN THE PRIVATE STUDY in the bunker, Eva Braun was seated at the table, writing; Hitler was fidgeting on the sofa. An SS bodyguard stood to attention at the open doorway. Hitler walked over to him and asked about casualties outside; the dull thud of artillery shells could be heard and felt even this far underground and through the thick walls. The SS officer recalled that Hitler then appeared to make a decision. Speaking as if to an assembled audience, the leader of the collapsing Third Reich said that as long as he lived there could never be a hope of conflict between the Western Allies and Russia. But his was a difficult decision: alive, he would be able to lead the German people to final victory—but unless he died, the conditions for that victory could never be achieved. "Germany," he said, "can hope for the future only if the whole world thinks I am dead. I must . . . "—his words tailed off.

The mesmerized SS man was brought sharply out of his riveted attention and saluted smartly as two of the half-dozen most powerful and dangerous men in the Nazi hierarchy entered the room: Reichsleiter Martin Bormann and SS and Police Gen. Heinrich "Gestapo" Müller, head of the Secret State Police. The guard was dismissed. Bormann and Müller brought news for Hitler alone, and it shook him to the core: Fegelein had divulged a thorough account of how Reichsführer-SS Heinrich Himmler—the Führer's "loyal Heinrich"—was negotiating with the Allies for the surrender of German forces in the West.

Hitler's fury over Himmler's betrayal left Bormann in an unchallengeable position of influence, but timing was now crucial. There had been opportunities aplenty from April 21 on, but Hitler's refusal to leave earlier had limited Bormann's carefully planned options. Nevertheless, on April 27 and 28 there were still potentially feasible land routes out of Berlin. The army commandant of the Berlin Defense

Area, Gen. Helmuth Weidling, offered to use the forty tanks still at his disposal to spearhead an attempted breakout to the west, across the Havel River bridge at Pichelsdorf, to secure Hitler's escape from the capital. But Bormann's planning required that the Führer be flown out, and he needed to be certain of getting Hitler and his party to some location where an aircraft capable of carrying them out of Allied-held Europe could pick them up.

BORMANN HAD RECOGNIZED the inadequacy of the communication system early on. A separate room in the bunker was in use as a telex center, manned by dedicated navy operators with seven machines, three of which were central to the Reichsleiter's plans. Bormann had already sent and signed the message "Agree proposed transfer overseas" to the key operatives along the Führer's planned escape route using the Nazis' still unbroken cipher, designated "Thrasher" by the British. This cipher was employed by Bormann's private communications network built around the top-secret Siemens & Halske encryption machine, the T43 *Schlüsselfernschreibmaschine* (see Chapter 11, page 109). Adm. Hans-Erich Voss, Hitler's Kriegsmarine liaison officer, had first brought the Siemens & Halske T43 to Bormann's attention when the latter approached him late in 1944. Bormann needed to establish a totally secure communications network, one that was capable of reaching U-boats at sea and ground stations in Spain and the Canary Islands and that could relay messages across the Atlantic to Buenos Aires. A modified version of the T43 machine was the answer to his needs.

By February 1945, Bormann had taken control of all these adapted machines, and on April 15, Adm. Voss's team had installed three of them with their naval operators in the Führerbunker, where they would continue transmitting until Bormann left the bunker on May 1. At least one machine was with the Abwehr operation in Spain, another at the secret outpost Villa Winter on Fuerteventura in the Canary Islands, and yet another in Buenos Aires. Eight of Adm. Karl Dönitz's U-boats also carried these top-secret machines. After April 20, Dönitz had six machines waiting for him at in Flensburg, where he moved his headquarters at the end of the war, thus enabling Bormann to relay the final movement and shipment orders to be carried out by remnants of the

U-boat fleet based at Kristiansand in Norway. With his communications network set up, Bormann could set about organizing how to get the Führer and his party out of Berlin.

FROM JANUARY TO APRIL 1945, Martin Bormann and his ally "Gestapo" Müller were the gatekeepers controlling all access to Hitler. In drawing up the final escape plans, they were assisted by Bormann's drinking companion, SS Gen. Hermann Fegelein. Since early 1943, Fegelein had been Reichsführer-SS Heinrich Himmler's liaison officer at the Führer's court and so was party to many secrets. Moreover, as the husband of Eva Braun's sister Gretl, and Eva's close personal friend, Fegelein was one of Hitler's most trusted "mountain people."

The first essential was to identify a practical location from which the Führer could be flown out and to decide how to get him there. The vast Soviet noose was tightening fast, and the defense of central Berlin was becoming increasingly desperate. In the city as a whole, Gen. Weidling had approximately 45,000 soldiers and 40,000 aging men of the Volkssturm (Home Guard), supplemented by the Berlin police force and boys from the Hitler Youth. On April 22, SS Gen. Wilhelm Mohnke—an ultraloyal veteran combat officer of the Waffen-SS—had been personally appointed by Hitler as commander of a battle group to defend the government quarter around the Reichstag building and Chancellery, operating independently of Weidling. This Kampfgruppe (Battle Group) Mohnke had fewer than 2,000 men: about 800 from the SS Guard Battalion "Leibstandarte Adolf Hitler"; 600 men from the Reichsführer-SS Escort Battalion (Himmler's bodyguard unit); the Führer Escort Company (a mixed army/air force unit); and various others swept up from replacement depots. In addition, there were supposed to be perhaps 2,000 men of the so-called Adolf Hitler Free Corps, comprising volunteers from all over Germany who had rallied to the Führer's defense, and even a number of secretaries and other female government staff who would also take up arms. With such meager resources, Weidling and Mohnke faced some 1.5 million Red Army troops of Marshal Koniev's 1st Ukrainian Front and Marshal Zhukov's 1st Byelorussian Front.

Although Tempelhof and Gatow airports were already either in Soviet hands or under the Soviet guns, there were still a number of temporary landing strips available. The East–West Axis along the Unter den Linden boulevard was still in use by light aircraft, but a last-minute troop landing there on April 25, by Junkers Ju 52 transports carrying naval troops to join the garrison, had wrecked several aircraft that had run into shell holes, damaging their landing gear and making further takeoffs impossible. The Ju 52 trimotor was the type most suitable for flying out the Führer and his party; the standard Luftwaffe transport aircraft throughout the war, it was elderly, slow, but extremely robust, could carry up to eighteen passengers, and needed a relatively short takeoff and landing run. Fegelein had reconnoitered the remaining viable areas for a pickup; the wide boulevard at Hohenzollerndamm was not perfect, but it was the best available. The underground railway system—the U-bahn—offered a safe route from the government quarter to Fehrbelliner Platz, and from there (so long as the area was still held by German troops) it was a short drive to the proposed landing strip.

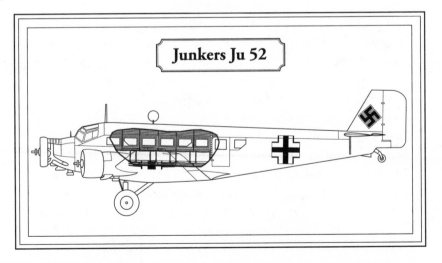

Junkers Ju 52

NEARLY 5,000 JUNKERS Ju 52s were built from 1932 to 1945 and the Tante Ju would serve on deep into the postwar years. It has a 13-mm (.50-inch) MG 131 machine gun in the dorsal position (not shown).

Crucial to the plan was the most up-to-date intelligence about the situation on the ground, and during his reconnaissance sorties Fegelein had identified an officer whom he trusted to supply it. The twenty-four-year-old SS Lt. Oskar Schäfer, a veteran of France and the Eastern Front as a Waffen-SS infantryman, had been wounded several times. Now commissioned as a Panzer officer, he was assigned to SS Heavy Tank Battalion 503, and his Tiger II ("King Tiger") was one of a handful of these 76.9-ton monsters from that unit that were still fighting in the heart of Berlin. Late on April 27, 1945, Schäfer and two comrades were summoned to the Reich Chancellery command bunker with orders to report directly to SS Gen. Mohnke for a thorough debriefing on the situation at Fehrbelliner Platz and the Hohenzollerndamm. Mohnke closely questioned Schäfer—who had been slightly wounded in action—about the disposition of his troops and the likelihood of a breakthrough by the "Ivans" attacking his positions. Schäfer gave as detailed a report as possible: it was his opinion that they could hold the area for no longer than two more days, and the other two officers agreed. After Schäfer had had a night's rest, Mohnke awarded him the coveted Knight's Cross, writing the citation into his *Soldaten Buch*.

"GESTAPO" MÜLLER COULD NOW PUT into effect his and Bormann's plans for spiriting the Führer out of Berlin—but first, those who had been chosen to escape had to "die." Fegelein was the first to disappear into the smokescreen of confusion, lies, and cover-ups that would mask the escape of all the main participants. There would be several versions of Fegelein's death. One stated that SS Lt. Col. Peter Högl captured him in his Berlin apartment wearing civilian clothes, ready to go on the run with his mistress, variously "identified" as a Hungarian, an Irishwoman married to a Hungarian diplomat, and an Allied secret agent. Fegelein was supposedly carrying quantities of cash, both German and foreign, and also jewelry, some of which allegedly belonged to Eva Braun (though that was also hearsay). Högl, a former policeman well known to Heinrich Müller, would be shot in the head while fleeing the bunker and died on May 2, 1945. One SS officer claimed to have shot Fegelein before he made it back to the bunker, while another supposed witness even alleged that Hitler "gunned him down" personally. Most stated that Fegelein had been shot, perhaps after interrogation by Müller, following a summary court-martial presided over by Wilhelm Mohnke—but Mohnke would later deny that the court-martial ever took place.

According to the book *Nazi Millionaires*, by Kenneth D. Alford and Theodore P. Savas, Walter Hirschfeld—a former SS officer working for the U.S. Counterintelligence Corps in Germany—interviewed Fegelein's father Hans in late September 1945. Hans Fegelein stated to Hirschfeld that "I think I can say with certainty that the Führer is alive. I have received word through a special messenger [an SS Sturmbannführer] . . . after his death had already been announced." The courier reportedly relayed the following message from Hermann Fegelein: "The Führer and I are safe and well. Don't worry about me; you will get further word from me, even if it is not for some time." The courier "also said that on the day when the Führer, Hermann, and Eva Braun left Berlin . . . there was a sharp counterattack in Berlin in order to win a flying strip where they could take off." Hirschfeld was said to have been dumbfounded: "Many SS officers claim the Führer is dead and his body was burned!" However, Hans Fegelein allegedly assured him that it was a smokescreen: "They are all trusted and true SS men who have been ordered to make these statements. Keep your eye on South America."

In actuality, Fegelein had flown into Berlin on April 25 on board a Ju 52 put at his disposal by Heinrich Himmler. He went to his apartment and then, while in communication with Bormann and Müller, reconnoitered the temporary landing strip at the Hohenzollerndamm. He would be waiting in the secret escape tunnel to the underground for his sister-in-law and Adolf Hitler. The Ju 52 then returned to its home base at Rechlin, the same airfield Capt. Peter Baumgart is believed to have flown into Berlin from. The same pilot flew the aircraft back into Berlin on April 28.

Hitler's personal pilot, SS Gruppenführer Hans Baur, confirmed that Eva Braun's brother-in-law always flew in a Ju 52, but Baur said he had not seen the landing on the twenty-eighth or had it reported to him. He had accompanied two old flying friends, Hanna Reitsch and Ritter Von Greim, to the temporary landing strip at the Brandenburg gate that same night but denied seeing any Ju 52 on the ground.

However, Reitsch, who flew out of Berlin on the twenty-eighth with the newly appointed head of the air force, Luftwaffe Chief Ritter Von Greim, said that she took off "around midnight" and that just as her Arado AR 96 trainer became airborne they both saw a Junkers-52 transport plane "near the runway. . . . A lone pilot was standing by in the shadows. He was obviously waiting for somebody." It is possible that Reitsch and Von Greim, flying at roof-height to avoid Soviet fighters, could have seen the escape aircraft on the ground at the Hohenzollerndamm, less than ninety seconds away by air from the Brandenburg Gate airstrip.

Creating the myth of Fegelein's execution was the first of Müller's perfect cover-ups, and it was soon followed by his masterstroke.

(*Italics* are used in the following section to identify conclusions based on deductive research; see page 185 in Chapter 16 for further discussion.)

JUST AFTER THE STROKE OF MIDNIGHT *as April 28, 1945, began, while the rest of the occupants of the Führerbunker were trying to get some sleep, Hitler's escape got under way. The Führer, his beloved dog Blondi, Eva Braun, Bormann, Fegelein, and six trusted soldiers from the SS Guard Battalion "Leibstandarte Adolf Hitler" slipped quietly away through the Vorbunker and up to his private quarters in the Old Reich Chancellery building. The light concrete panel was slid aside, revealing the secret escape tunnel. At the end of the electrically lit passageway, down a slight incline, they entered the wider space of the third-level bunker. When the party reached the chamber, they found waiting for them two people whom Müller had had brought there from up the tunnel via the underground railway: two doubles—a stand-in for Hitler (probably Gustav Weber) and one for Eva Braun.*

GUSTAV WEBER HAD BEEN STANDING IN FOR HITLER since July 20, 1944, when the Führer had been wounded in the bomb attempt on his life at his Wolf's Lair field headquarters near Rastenburg in East Prussia. Hitler had suffered recurrent aftereffects from his injuries; he tired easily, and he was plagued by infected wounds from splinters of the oak table that had protected him from the full force of the blast. (His use of penicillin, taken from Allied troops captured or killed in the D-Day landings, had probably saved his life.)

Weber had impersonated Hitler on his last officially photographed appearance, when he handed out medals to members of the Hitler Youth in the Chancellery garden on March 20, 1945. Weber's uncanny resemblance to Hitler deceived even those quite close to him, and on that occasion the Reichsjugendführer (Hitler Youth National Leader) Artur Axman was either taken in or warned to play along. The only thing liable to betray the imposture was that Weber's left hand suffered from occasional bouts of uncontrollable trembling. Bormann had taken Hitler's personal doctor into his confidence, and SS Lt. Col. Dr. Ludwig Stumpfegger had treated Weber with some success. Weber was often kept sedated, but his trembling became more noticeable when he was under extreme stress.

Eva Braun's double was simply perfect. Her name is unknown, but she had been trawled from the "stable" of young actresses that Propaganda Minister Joseph Goebbels, the self-appointed "patron of the German cinema," maintained for his own pleasure. The physical similarity was amazing, and after film makeup and hairdressing experts had done their work it was very difficult to tell the two young women apart.

Eva paused in the chamber to dash off a note to tell her parents not to worry if they did not hear from her for a long time. She handed it to Bormann, who pocketed it without a word (its charred remains would later be found on the floor—it was too much of a security risk for Bormann to allow it to be delivered). Bormann then saluted the group, shook Hitler's hand, and led the counterfeit Führer and his soon-to-be bogus bride back up the tunnel to the Führerbunker.

In the anteroom of the third-level chamber, the fugitives donned steel helmets and baggy SS camouflage smocks. Hitler carried slung from his shoulder a cylindrical metal gas mask case; this contained the painting of Frederick the Great that had hung above his desk. Like his dog, this portrait by Anton Graff went everywhere with Hitler, and his final act in the bunker had been to remove the 16 x 11-inch canvas from its oval frame, roll it widthwise, and slide it carefully into the long-model Wehrmacht gas mask canister. It fitted perfectly.

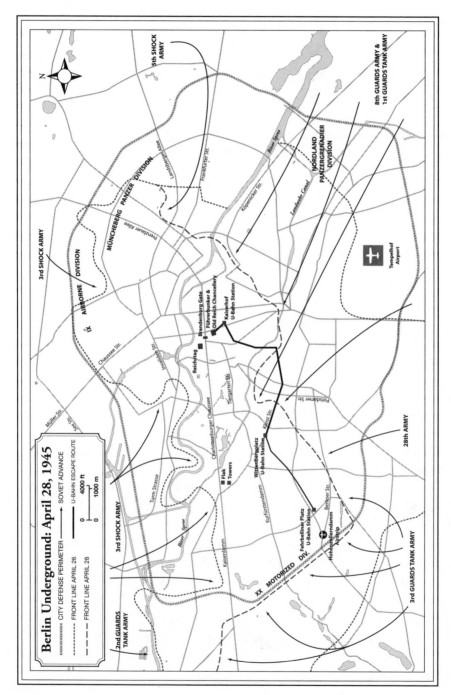

Berlin Underground: April 28, 1945

- ✕✕✕✕✕ CITY DEFENSE PERIMETER
- ⟶ SOVIET ADVANCE
- ▬▬▬ U-BAHN ESCAPE ROUTE
- ········ FRONT LINE APRIL 26
- – – – FRONT LINE APRIL 28

0 ——— 4000 ft
0 ——— 1000 m

N

5th SHOCK ARMY

8th GUARDS ARMY & 1st GUARDS TANK ARMY

MÜNCHEBERG PANZER DIVISION

NORDLAND PANZERGRENADIER DIVISION

3rd SHOCK ARMY

AIRBORNE DIVISION

IX

Landsberger Allee

Frankfurter Str.

Prenzlauer Allee

River Spree

Köpenicker Str.

Landwehr Canal

Tempelhof Airport

Chaussee Str.

Brandenburg Gate
Führerbunker & Old Reich Chancellery
Kaiserhof U-Bahn Station

Reichstag

Invalidenstr.

Tiergarten Str.

Charlottenburger Chaussee

Müller Str.

Tuxm Strasse

Turm Strasse

Flak Towers

Wittenbergplatz U-Bahn Station

Klest Str.

Potsdamer Str.

28th ARMY

3rd SHOCK ARMY

Kurfürstendamm

Kaiserdamm

Fehrbelliner Platz U-Bahn Station

Berliner Str.

Hohenzollerndamm Airstrip

XX MOTORIZED DIV.

2nd GUARDS TANK ARMY

3rd GUARDS TANK ARMY

River Spree

158

THE ESCAPEES USED the Berlin U-Bahn system to reach a makeshift airstrip on Hohenzollerndamm where they boarded a Ju 52 piloted by SS Capt. Peter Baumgart.

The party entered the U-bahn system near Kaiserhof (today, Mohrenstrasse) station. The walls were painted with a phosphor-based green luminous paint, so the flashlights hanging from the soldiers' chests bathed the fugitives in an eerie glow. The tunnel was wet, and in places they had to slosh along ankle-deep in water as they made their way to the junction at Wittenbergplatz and on toward Fehrbelliner Platz. The stumbling four-mile journey took three hours, and they were goaded along not only by the sound of bursting shells overhead, but also by echoing small-arms fire in the distance—elsewhere in the system, Soviet and German soldiers were fighting in the railway tunnels.

As the group emerged onto the station concourse at Fehrbelliner Platz they were met by Eva's other sister, Ilse, and by Fegelein's close friend SS Gen. Joachim Rumohr and his wife. In January 1945, Ilse had fled Breslau by train to Berlin to avoid the advancing Soviet forces. She had dined with Eva at the Hotel Adlon and—despite furious rows with her sister about the conduct of the war—had remained in the city until her brother-in-law Hermann Fegelein sent a detachment of "Leibstandarte" soldiers to fetch her. As for Joachim Rumohr, this was the second time in three months that he would escape from a ruined capital city just ahead of the Red Army. A former comrade of Fegelein's, Rumohr had been wounded in February 1945 during the bloody fall of Budapest. Erroneously reported to have committed suicide on February 11 to avoid capture by the Russians, he had managed to reach the wooded hills northwest of Budapest and from there escaped to Vienna. Now his friendship with Fegelein guaranteed him the chance of another escape, this time with his wife.

When the fugitives reached the main entrance to the Fehrbelliner Platz station, they found three Tiger II tanks and two SdKfz 251 half-track armored personnel carriers waiting to take them on the half-mile drive to the makeshift airstrip on the Hohenzollerndamm.

Chapter 15

THE FLIGHT

RED SIGNAL LAMPS WERE PLACED along an eight-hundred-yard stretch of the wide boulevard, where troops had been set to clearing away debris and filling shell holes. At 3:00 a.m. on April 28, 1945, the lamps were lit, revealing a Junkers Ju 52/3m less than a hundred yards from the parked vehicles. The aircraft, assigned to the Luftwaffe wing Kampfgeschwader 200, had taken off in rainy conditions from Rechlin airfield, sixty-three miles from Berlin, just forty minutes earlier. Rechlin had long been the Luftwaffe's main test airfield for new equipment designs, but in the closing weeks of the war it had reverted to more essential combat duties. It was one of several bases used by "Bomber Wing 200"—the deliberately deceptive title of a secret special-operations section of the air force commanded from November 15, 1944, by a highly decorated bomber pilot, Lt. Col. Werner Baumbach.

The Ju 52 that landed on the Hohenzollerndamm was flown by an experienced combat pilot and instructor named Peter Erich Baumgart, who now held the parallel SS rank of captain. More unusually, until 1935 Baumgart had been a South African, with British citizenship. In that year he had left his country, family, and friends and renounced his nationality to join the new Luftwaffe. In 1943 he had been transferred from conventional duties into a predecessor unit of KG 200; by April 1945 he was thoroughly accustomed to flying a variety of aircraft on clandestine missions, and his reliability had earned him the award of the Iron Cross 1st Class.

Baumgart prepared his aircraft for takeoff and his passengers boarded. Baumgart's orders were to fly to an airfield at Tønder in Denmark, forty-four miles from the Eider River, which runs through northern Germany just below the Danish border. Thankfully, the rain in which he had taken off from Rechlin had now stopped, at least for the time being. Baumgart pushed the throttles forward, and the old "Tante Ju"—"Auntie Judy"—rattled and shook its way down the patched length of roadway until it lifted its nose into the air. It would take seventeen minutes to climb to 10,000 feet, where Baumgart could level and settle the Junkers at its cruising speed of 132 miles per hour. It was not until he was airborne and the escape party had removed their helmets that he realized who his main passengers were. Knowing that as soon as the daylight brightened he would be in grave danger from enemy aircraft, Baumgart motioned his copilot to keep a sharp lookout. It was essential to fly as far as possible in darkness at treetop level, given sufficient moonlight, to avoid marauding night fighters protecting the Allied heavy bombers flying between 15,000 and 20,000 feet. At Rechlin he had been promised an escort of at least seven Messerschmitt Bf 109 fighters, but there was no sign of them.

Baumgart would say later that he followed an indirect flight plan, landing for some time at Magdeburg to the west of Berlin to avoid Allied fighters and then flying northward through what the pilot said was an Allied artillery barrage to the Baltic coast. His luck held, and he encountered no further Allied aircraft before finally touching down on April 29 at Tønder, a former Imperial German zeppelin base. It was strewn with wrecked machines; just four days earlier, this field and that at Flensburg had been strafed by RAF Tempest fighters (of No. 486 "New Zealand" Squadron) that had destroyed twenty-two aircraft on the ground. As Baumgart closed down the engines and waited for the ground crew to approach, he caught sight of at least six Bf 109s dispersed around the field—the promised escort. Baumgart unbuckled

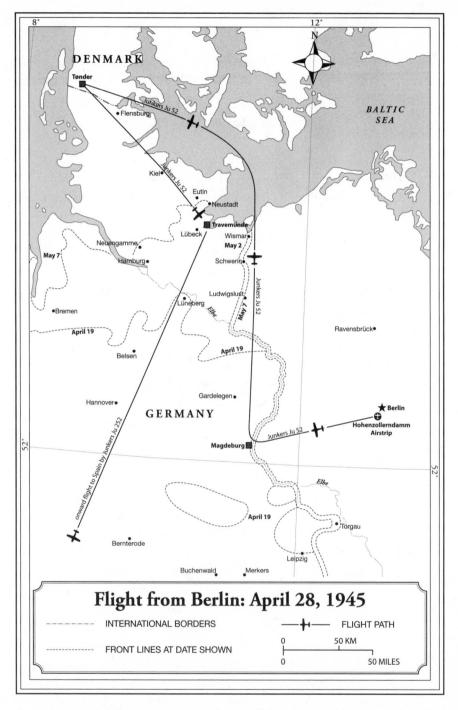

Flight from Berlin: April 28, 1945

----------- INTERNATIONAL BORDERS	——+—— FLIGHT PATH
------------- FRONT LINES AT DATE SHOWN	0 50 KM 0 50 MILES

LEAVING FROM HOHENZOLLERNDAMM, the Ju 52 detoured to Magdeburg to avoid an Allied bomber group. Baumgart flew the Ju 52 on to the former German Imperial Zeppelin Base at Tønder in Denmark. The party transferred to another Ju 52 to reach the long-range Luftwaffe base at Travemünde, where they boarded a Ju 252 for their flight to Reus, near Barcelona, in Spain.

himself and pulled the flying helmet from his head. In the rear he could hear his passengers getting ready to disembark; they had brought little luggage with them. He climbed out of his seat and walked back down the fuselage, coming to attention and saluting when he reached Hitler. The Führer took a step forward and shook his hand, and Baumgart was surprised to find that he was being slipped a piece of paper, which he put in his trouser pocket to look at later. He watched as the ground crew opened the door from the outside, and Hitler, Eva Braun, Ilse Braun, Hermann Fegelein, Joachim Rumohr, and Rumohr's wife disembarked.

ST. PETERSBURG TIMES, FRIDAY, DECEMBER 19, 1947

Flier Claims
Hitler Escaped

WARSAW — (P) — Capt. Peter Baumgart, 32-year-old former German air force pilot, told a district court Wednesday that he flew Adolph Hitler to Denmark shortly before the fall of Berlin.

The 6-foot flier claimed that Hitler was accompanied on the flight by German Gen. Roemer and his wife and a woman who he believed was Eva Braun. Baumgart said the party boarded an airplane at Hohenzollerndamm April 28, 1945, and that he landed them in Denmark about 40 miles from the Either river.

Upon landing, the flier said, Hitler shook hands with him and gave him a check for 20,000 marks drawn on a Berlin bank. Baumgart said he immediately was ordered to fly back to Berlin. After that, he said he did not know about Hitler and his party, but he said he thought they had boarded a submarine.

Baumgart was returned to Warsaw from the British zone in Germany and is on trial on a charge of having been an SS member.

Baumgart, who claimed to have shot down 128 Allied planes in combat over Crete, Italy, North Africa and the eastern front, was quoted by the Warsaw evening newspaper, Weiczor, two weeks ago as saying that Hitler and Miss Braun had fled to the United States two days before Berlin fell. He was quoted in similar fashion by the same paper last October but he did not say at that time that Hitler and Miss Braun had boarded a submarine.

CAPT. BAUMGART HAD been sent for psychiatric tests when he first made these claims which the Associated Press and other news outlets reported in contemporary newspapers. Declared sane, he repeated his story in detail in court in Warsaw. Released in 1951, he was never heard of again.

Friedrich von Angelotty-Mackensen, a twenty-four-year-old SS lieutenant of the "Leibstandarte Adolf Hitler," would claim to have seen Hitler on Tønder airfield. Wounded in the fighting around the government quarter on April 27, he and three comrades, including his superior, SS Lt. Julius Toussaint, had been lucky enough to be put aboard one of the last medical evacuation flights out of Berlin. Mackensen—running a fever and slipping in and out of delirium—was unable to remember the place from which he had left. He described lying on a stretcher in the dimly lit interior of the plane and asking for water. At Tønder, where he would have to wait for several days, he was carried out of the plane by his comrades and laid on the ground. At some point he heard somebody say, "The Führer wants to speak once more." Mackensen was moved nearer and laid down again with a knapsack to pillow his head. Hitler spoke for about a quarter of an hour. He said that Adm. Karl Dönitz was now in supreme command of the German forces and would surrender unconditionally to the Western powers; he was not authorized to surrender to the Soviet Union. When Hitler finished speaking, the assembled crowd—estimated by Mackensen at about a hundred strong—saluted, and Hitler then moved among the wounded, shaking hands; he shook Mackensen's, but no words were exchanged. Eva Braun was standing near an aircraft, which Hitler then boarded, and it took off.

For this next leg, on April 29, the Junkers was not flown by Capt. Baumgart, who was ordered to fly another aircraft back to Berlin for further evacuation flights. The piece of paper in his pocket turned out to be a personal check from Adolf Hitler for 20,000 reichsmarks, drawn on a Berlin bank. The Führer's aircraft returned to the field at Tønder, flying over it about an hour later, and a message canister was thrown down onto the airfield; it held a brief note to the effect that Hitler's party had landed at the coast. Hitler's flight from Tønder to Travemünde on the German coast northeast of Lübeck had taken the Ju 52 just forty-five minutes. Waiting there was Lt. Col. Werner Baumbach of the Luftwaffe, the commander of KG 200.

Baumbach had been assessing his diminishing options. At the start of that month, three huge six-engined Blohm & Voss Bv 222 flying boats, with a range of at least 3,300 miles, had been made ready to take

Q Who had command of the plane?

A Well, of course, I have no idea. I only know that in one of the planes in which Hitler was, that this plane was being flown or piloted by a certain Capt. Baumgart.

Q How many were there in the plane--how many motors were there in the plane in which you were riding?

A I was lying in the grass and then I was being picked up again. I was carried to some certain place around the plane. Then somebody set me down. All the others were standing there already. Somebody put a knapsack under my head and then Hitler was standing there and - one moment now. Now, now, at the crucial point! Hitler has said that General, Admiral Doenitz is now in supreme command of the German army and Admiral Doenitz-- will enter into unconditional surrender with the Western powers. He is not authorized to surrender to the Eastern powers. Oh goodness! The combat against Bolshevism will go on. Maybe we shall see each other again in different circumstances. Something to that effect.

A Yes, then we saluted--not I--Hitler said farewell. In particular, he said farewell to the wounded people. I remember very well that he shook hands with me. Hè didn't say anything and I didn't say anything. The others didn't say anything. It was complete calmness.

Q He came over and shook hands with you as you were lying on the ground?

A Yes, when I was lying on the ground several others were lying beside me. I don't know who they were.

Q Well--when he finished his speech and they gave him the salute, did they also say Heil Hitler?

A Yes, of course.

Q All right, and then he shook hands with you?

A Yes.

Q And what did he do then?

A Then he entered the plane.

PART OF A lengthy March 15, 1948 U.S. interrogation of Friedrich von Argelotty-Mackensen, a wounded SS officer who had seen Hitler and Eva Braun at Tønder airfield after their flight from Berlin. He watched as they flew away to destinations unknown to him.

senior Nazis to safety. To provide another possibility, a four-engined Junkers Ju 290 land aircraft with a similar range had also been ordered to Travemünde. Two of the flying boats were now at the bottom of the inlet, destroyed by Allied air attack. The Ju 290 had also been caught by strafing RAF pilots just as it landed on a specially lengthened concrete strip beside the shore; it was hit several times, forcing the pilot to overshoot, and had pitched over to one side, ripping off a wingtip. Baumbach had one Bv 222 flying boat left in the hangar, but he had never liked the type; its great size made it unwieldy, and although heavily armed it would be no match for an Allied fighter.

MARTIN BORMANN HAD FINALLY RECEIVED confirmation from the Abwehr in Spain, through the modified T43 communications system, that an airfield had been made ready for the Führer's arrival. Hitler would be flown to Reus in Catalonia, a region in which Generalissimo Franco's fascists maintained an iron grip following their defeat of Catalan Republicans during the Spanish Civil War. Lt. Col. Baumbach personally drew up the flight plan. With the Ju 290 out of action, the mission would be entrusted to a trimotor Ju 252—a plane Baumbach knew well, having flown them during his time with KG 200's 1st Group. While a descendant of the old "Tante Ju," the Ju 252 was a vast improvement; its top speed was still only 272 miles per hour, but it had a range of just under 2,500 miles, a pressurized cabin, and a ceiling of 22,500 feet. It could reach the Spanish airfield at Reus, just over 1,370 miles away, with fuel to spare.

As the passengers disembarked from the Ju 52 at Travemünde after its short flight from Tønder, the Ju 252 was waiting on the tarmac with its engines already turning. Eva Braun now bade her sister Ilse a fond farewell—Ilse had decided to take her chances in Germany. Hermann Fegelein also embraced her. His own wife—Eva and Ilse's sister Gretl—was heavily pregnant with their first child, and it had been considered too dangerous for her to flee with her husband. Bormann had assured his colleague that there would be plenty of time later to bring his wife and child to join him in exile. Joachim Rumohr and his wife had also decided to stay in Germany. Born in Hamburg, the cavalryman knew the countryside of Schleswig-Holstein well, and he felt

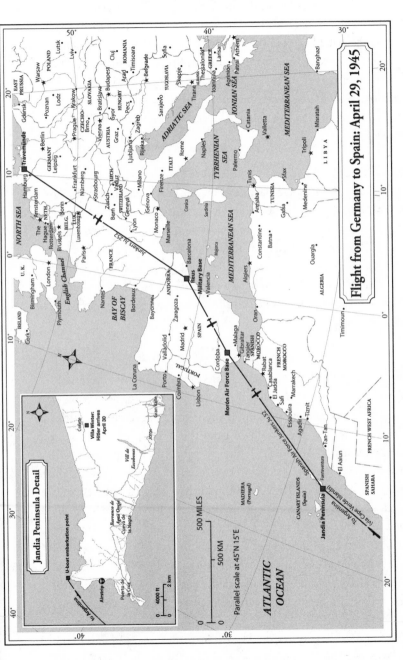

THE FINAL ESCAPE party—Hitler, Eva, Fegelein, and Blondi—flew to Reus in a long-range Ju 252 of KG 200. On arrival at Reus, a Spanish air force Ju 52 picked the party up for the flight to the Canary Islands. To eliminate evidence, the KG 200 aircraft was dismantled. Hitler and his party flew from Reus to Fuerteventura, stopping to refuel at the airbase at Morón, before arriving at the Nazi base at Villa Winter to rendezvous with the U-boats of Operation Seawolf.

sure he and his wife could find sanctuary there. (The overwhelming motive for Hitler's hangers-on had been to escape the threat of Russian captivity; the Allied forces now advancing fast to the coasts north of Lübeck and Hamburg were from the British Second Army.)

The remaining members of the escape party then boarded the Ju 252, *and Baumbach saluted his Führer for the last time on German soil. As the aircraft rolled down the runway and took off, he felt great relief:*

> Thank God that's over. I would rather leave some things unsaid, but it occurs to me that these diary notes may one day shed a little light on the strains, the desperate situation and maddening hurry of the last few days. At that time I had almost decided to make my own escape. The aircraft stood ready to take off. We were supplied with everything we needed for six months. And then I found I could not do it. Could I bolt at the last moment, deserting Germany and leaving in the lurch men who had always stood by me? I must stay with my men.

THE SPANISH MILITARY AIRBASE at Reus, eighty miles south of Barcelona, dated back to 1935. (During the Civil War there were three military airfields near Reus, the other two being at Maspujol and Salou.) After perhaps a six-hour flight from Travemünde, Hitler and his companions stepped down from the Ju 252. The crew lined up on the tarmac to salute; the Führer returned the compliment, and his party was taken away quickly in two staff cars to a low building on the edge of the airfield. The KG 200 pilot had been in radio contact with the military commander at Reus during his approach to the airfield, and that officer in turn had called the military governor of Barcelona. Fifteen minutes later a Spanish air force Ju 52 in national markings landed at the far edge of the field. The Ju 252 in which the party had arrived would be dismantled; there was to be no physical evidence that the flight had ever taken place, thus allowing Franco complete deniability.

The fugitives' next stop would be the Spanish Canary Islands in the Atlantic, where Villa Winter, a top-secret facility, had been established on the island of Fuerteventura. From there they would embark on the next leg of their journey to a distant place of safety. For a number of other Nazis, however, Spain would be the final destination of choice.

On May 8, 1945—the day victory in Europe was celebrated—the wounded SS Lt. Friedrich von Angelotty-Mackensen was at last about to leave Tønder airfield in Denmark, destination Malaga. He would report that before his plane took off he saw another recognizable figure there: the Belgian SS Col. Leon Degrelle, the leader of the fascist Rexist Party and, as the highly decorated commander of the Belgian Waffen-SS contingent, a much-photographed personality. Degrelle had fled from Oslo that day in a Heinkel He 111H-23 bomber stripped out for passenger transport, flown by Albert Duhinger (who later lived in Argentina flying commercial aircraft). As a fighting soldier on the Eastern Front, Degrelle had earned Hitler's respect; the Führer had once told him, "If I had a son, I would want him to be like you." The Heinkel made it as far as Donostia-San Sebastián in northern Spain, right at the limit of its range, and Degrelle would survive the injuries he suffered when it crash-landed off a beach. On May 25, Degrelle was quoted as "expressing his belief that Adolf Hitler is alive and is in hiding." A Spaniard who saw him in the hospital said Degrelle had spoken of visiting Hitler in Berlin the day before the Russians entered the city; the Führer had been preparing to escape and was in no mood for either suicide or a fight to the death.

Among other European collaborators to be offered a way out was Norway's puppet leader, Vidkun Quisling. At his trial in Oslo in September 1945, he related how Josef Terboven, the Nazi Reichskommissar of Norway, had offered him passage in an aircraft or a U-boat to get to Spain or some other foreign country. Quisling said that as a "true patriot" he had refused the offer and stayed to face his countrymen; he would soon pay for this decision in front of a firing squad. At the beginning of May, Pierre Laval, the former Vichy French prime minister, was flown to Spain aboard a Ju 88. (Franco would expel him, and he too would be executed by his countrymen in autumn 1945.) It was reported that the Berlin ambassador of Italy's rump Fascist republic, Filippo Anfuso, had also escaped late in April 1945, apparently aboard a "Croat plane."

As early as April 26, 1945, Moscow Radio had charged that Spain was receiving Nazi refugees at an airfield on the Balearic island of Minorca. Quoting Swiss sources, the Soviets said, "To supervise the business, Gen. José Moscardo, an intimate of Franco . . . visited Minorca last month. Recent arrivals at the airdrome are the family of [Robert] Ley and several Gauleiters." Robert Ley, the head of the German Labor Front since 1933, committed suicide while awaiting trial for war crimes at Nuremberg in October 1945. During his interrogation, however, Ley stated that when he last met Hitler in the bunker during April, the Führer had told him to "Go south, and he would follow." Albert Speer, Hitler's armaments minister, said much the same about a meeting in the bunker on Hitler's birthday, April 20: "At that meeting, to the surprise of nearly everyone present, Hitler announced that he would stay in Berlin until the last minute, and then 'fly south.'" SS Staff Sgt. Rochus Misch, the telephone operator in the Führerbunker, said, "There were two planes waiting to the north of Berlin. One of them was a Ju 390 [sic], and [the other] a Blohm & Voss that could fly the same distance. So Hitler could have escaped if he had wanted to."

The feasibility of Hitler making a last-minute escape from Berlin was apparently accepted by the most senior Soviet officers. On June 10, 1945, the commander of the Soviet Zone in Germany, Marshal Georgi K. Zhukov, stated that Hitler "could have taken off at the very last moment, for there was an airfield at his disposal." The Soviet commandant of Berlin, Col. Gen. Nikolai E. Berzarin, said, "My personal opinion is that he has disappeared somewhere into Europe—perhaps he is in Spain with Franco. He had the possibility of taking off and getting away."

Whatever the popular image of total Allied air superiority over Western Europe in the last days of the war, in reality it was unnecessary to maintain total surveillance of thousands of cubic miles of sky; the remnants of the Luftwaffe were encircled in an ever-decreasing area. For Allied fighter pilots it was a "target-poor environment"; the very fact that air-to-air encounters were at this point so rare argues that single machines flown by intrepid, experienced, and lucky German airmen could slip across it unnoticed. Since it is established that Leon Degrelle was flown all the way from Norway—and according to Mackensen, via Tønder in southern Denmark—to northern Spain as late as May 8, there is certainly nothing inherently impossible about Hitler having beaten him to it on April 29.

IN BERLIN, BORMAN AND MÜLLER were meanwhile "tidying up" with ruthless efficiency. During April 28–29, the two actors in the private quarters of the Führerbunker played out a ghastly panto-mime orchestrated by the Nazi Party's grand puppet-master, Martin Bormann. It ended on April 30 in a fatal finale that would have been executed by "Gestapo" Müller. At some time that afternoon Eva Braun's double was poisoned, and Hitler's double, probably Gustav Weber, was shot at close range by Müller in person. Shrouded in blankets, the two bodies were carried upstairs to be burned in the shell-torn Chancellery garden, as described by Erich Kempka, the head of the Chancellery motor pool. Although accounts by witnesses are confused and some-times contradictory, this iconic scene has become an accepted historical fact. Indeed, everything about it may be correct—apart from the true identities of the two burning corpses. A picture of an unburnt Hitler "corpse" with a gunshot wound to the forehead circulated extensively after the war. It is now believed to be possibly that of a cook in the bunker who bore a vague resemblance to Adolf Hitler. It was just one of at least six "Hitler" bodies, none of them showing any signs of having been burnt, that were delivered to the Soviets in the days after the fall of Berlin. A third impersonator would also die: Dr. Werner Haase, one of Hitler's physicians, used a cyanide capsule on Blondi's double. Her recently born pups—which the Goebbels children loved to play with in the bunker—as well as Eva's Scottish terriers Negus and Stasi, and Haase's own dachshund, were killed by Sgt. Fritz Tornow, who served as Hitler's personal veterinarian.

Bormann communicated the news of "Hitler's" death to Adm. Karl Dönitz, appointed as the new Reich president in Hitler's will. Before Bormann and Müller could finish their "cleaning," there was one more potential witness to be silenced. SS Lt. Col. Peter Högl, the last person to have seen Hermann Fegelein, was also shot in the head, as the final groups of would-be escapers left the bunker on the night of May 1–2 (see Chapter 14, page 154) At this point, SS and Police Gen. Heinrich Müller, Bormann's principal co-conspirator and hit man, disappeared from the "official" history record without a trace. A few days later his family would bury a body in a Berlin cemetery; the casket bore the touching inscription "To Our Daddy," but it would later be determined that it contained body parts from three unknown victims.

In the early hours of May 2, Bormann made his own escape from the Führerbunker along with Werner Naumann, Goebbels's nominated successor as propaganda minister, who later in 1945 would turn up in Argentina; Artur Axmann, the leader of the Hitler Youth; Hitler's doctor, Ludwig Stumpfegger; and Waffen-SS Capt. Joachim Tiburtius. This party clambered aboard two Tiger II tanks, which tried to make their way up Friedrichstrasse, but the attempt was short-lived. One of the tanks took a direct hit from a Soviet antitank weapon, and the wreck blocked the other Tiger's path. Bormann and Tiburtius made it on foot separately to the Hotel Atlas; Bormann had already stashed escape clothes, new identity papers, and cash there (as he had at various other points around the city.) Tiburtius and the Reichsleiter pushed on together toward the Schiffbauerdamm, a long road running beside the Spree River in Berlin's Mitte district; then the SS captain lost sight of Bormann.

The following day Bormann was in the town of Königs Wusterhausen, about twelve miles southeast of the Chancellery. He had been wounded; a shell fragment had injured his foot. He managed to commandeer a vehicle that took him to a German military first aid station for medical treatment. A young, slightly wounded SS sergeant found himself seated alongside a familiar-looking, short, heavyset man wearing a leather overcoat over a uniform stripped of insignia. The young NCO said that he was on his way to the house of his uncle, a Luftwaffe pilot who had been killed in Russia, and invited Bormann to go with him. Joined by another officer, they later walked through the dark streets to the house at Fontanestrasse 9 in the Berlin Dahme-Spreewald neighborhood.

Bormann later made it safely through the British lines by following the autobahn to the outskirts of Flensburg, where he had planned to make contact with Dönitz. Waiting for him at a safe house just outside the town was "Gestapo" Müller, who had also managed to slip through the British lines. Müller told Bormann that it would be impossible to meet Dönitz, who had by now carried out unconditional surrenders in both Reims and Berlin. The plans had to be changed; Martin Bormann headed south, for the Bavarian mountains.

Chapter 16

GRUPPE SEEWOLF

THERE WAS LITTLE OPTION but to choose a submarine as the means to carry Hitler across the Atlantic to Argentina, but it was still a high-risk plan. Since the tipping point in the Battle of the Atlantic in May 1943, the balance of power in the sea war had shifted. The Kriegsmarine had lost its French U-boat bases in the summer of 1944, making the approach voyages to possible patrol areas much longer, more difficult, and more dangerous. Allied antisubmarine naval and air forces with greatly improved equipment now dominated the North Atlantic sea-lanes and the waters around most of Europe, so Allied shipping losses were a small fraction of what they had been. In 1944, U-boat loss rates had outstripped the numbers of new boats being commissioned; consequently, the remaining crews and most of their commanders were much less experienced. From January through April 1945 alone, no fewer than 139 U-boats and their crews were lost. The chances of a successful submarine escape directly from northwest Europe to South America would have been slim; however, the odds improved significantly with Spain as the point of departure.

The only available U-boat class that had the range and capacity to carry passengers to Argentina in anything approaching comfort was the Type IXC. In March 1945, nine Type IX boats sailed for the Atlantic; this was the last major U-boat operation of the war, and the first such operation since the scattering of the failed Gruppe Preussen a year previously. Two of the boats, U-530 and U-548, were directed to operate in Canadian waters, to "annoy and defy the United States." The other seven, designated Gruppe Seewolf—U-518, U-546, U-805, U-858, U-880, U-881 and U-1235—were to form a patrol line code-named Harke ("Rake"). It is believed, however, that in mid-April three of these boats opened sealed orders that would divert them southward on a special mission.

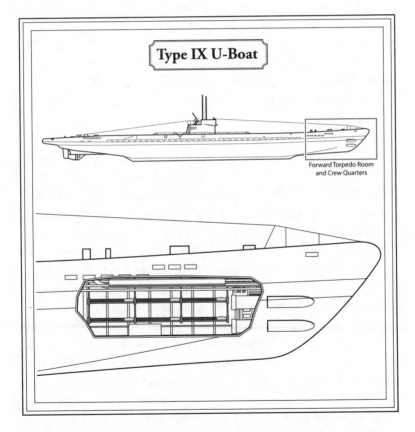

Type IX U-Boat

Forward Torpedo Room and Crew Quarters

THIS U-BOAT TYPE was designed to be able to operate far from home support facilities. As an example of their endurance, the Type IX boats briefly patrolled off the eastern United States. Some 283 were built from 1937–44.

IT WAS NOT BY CHANCE that the word "Wolf" was used in the operation's designation. From early in his career and throughout his life Hitler used the pseudonym Wolf. Among the most successful German operational techniques during the war were the "wolf-pack tactics" (known as *Rudeltaktik*, literally "pack tactics") by which the U-boats preyed on Atlantic shipping, and the submarines themselves were lauded by the Propaganda Ministry as "Grey Wolves."

It was typical of Bormann's meticulous planning that three separate U-boats of Gruppe Seewolf were assigned to the escape mission to provide alternatives if needed and that the mission was concealed within a conventional Atlantic operation so as not to attract Allied curiosity. The planning for this phase of the escape had begun in 1944, when Aktion Feuerland had already been under way for more than a year. On Bormann's instructions, navy and air force assets across the Reich had been allocated to play contingent parts in the complex and developing escape plan. One such part was a misinformation phase.

IN JULY 1944, NEWS AGENCIES REPORTED that Hitler had approved a plan for an imminent attack on New York, with "robot bombs" launched from submarines in the Atlantic. On August 20, the Type IXC boat U-1229 (Cdr. Armin Zinke) was attacked and forced to surface off Newfoundland on the Canadian east coast, and among the captured survivors was a German agent, Oskar Mantel. Under interrogation by the FBI, he revealed that a wave of U-boats equipped with V-1 flying bombs was being readied to attack the United States. In November 1944, U-1230 landed two agents off the Maine coast; they were spotted coming ashore and arrested. During their interrogation, Erich Gimpel and William Colepaugh (an American defector) corroborated Mantel's story. This also seemed to be supported by the prediction in a radio broadcast by the Reich armaments minister, Albert Speer, that V-missiles "would fall on New York by February 1, 1945."

On December 10, 1944, New York's mayor Fiorello La Guardia broke the story to an astonished American public. On January 8, 1945, Adm. Jonas H. Ingram, commander of the U.S. Atlantic Fleet, announced that a new wave of U-boats approaching the United States might be fitted with V-1 rockets to attack the eastern seaboard. The Nazis might launch "robots from submarine, airplane or surface ship" against targets ranging from Maine to Florida, but the U.S. Navy was fully prepared to meet the threat. Many Americans took this V-1 scare seriously. The British dismissed it as propaganda, and—with the grim experience of four years' bombardment and some 60,000 civilian deaths behind them, about 10 percent caused by V-1s—believed that even if such attacks occurred they would not cause a great deal of damage. After all, Hitler's Operation Polar Bear had succeeded in hitting London with 2,515 V-1s (about one-quarter of those launched), so the handful that might be fired by a few U-boats seemed negligible. On February 16, 1945, a British Admiralty cable to the U.S. Navy chief of operations, Adm. Ernest J. King, played down the threat, while conceding that it was possible for U-boats to store and launch V-1 flying bombs. (The Germans had indeed tested a submarine-towed launch platform with some success, but were nowhere near any operational capability. There was even an embryo project, Prüfstand XII, to launch the much larger V-2 ballistic missile at sea from a sealed container, which would be flooded at the base to swing it upright.) However, the planted misinformation achieved its purpose. It would focus American attention toward any detected pack of U-boats, such as the majority of Gruppe Seewolf, thus drawing USN and USAAF assets in the Atlantic eastward and northward—away from the latitudes between Spain's southern territories and Argentina.

CENTRAL TO THE ESCAPE PLAN was the use of the *Schnorkel*, a combination of air intake and exhaust pipe for a submarine's diesel engines, which became widely available from spring 1944. This allowed a U-boat to cruise (very slowly) on diesel power a few feet below the surface, while simultaneously recharging the batteries for the electric motors that had to be used for cruising at any depth. Using the Schnorkel limited a boat's range to about 100 miles per day; it was normally raised at night, and in daylight hours the boat cruised submerged (again, very slowly) on electric power. While the theoretical ability to remain underwater twenty-four hours a day was a lifesaver for many U-boats, using the Schnorkel was noisy, difficult, and sometimes dangerous, especially in choppy seas. The low speed it imposed robbed the boats of their tactical flexibility on patrol, and remaining submerged made navigation difficult. While no transits to Argentina could have been contemplated without the concealment offered by the Schnorkel, it also worsened the U-boats' communication problems.

Remaining submerged almost permanently made the reception of radio messages a hit-or-miss affair. Neither U-boat Command nor the British eavesdroppers at Bletchley Park near London could ever be certain when, or even if, a specific U-boat had received the orders transmitted to it. In order to receive and send anything other than long-wave signals, a U-boat had to bring its aerials above the surface, exposing the conning tower and risking radar detection. In theory, long-wave messages were detectable while submerged if the conditions were perfect, but Schnorkel boats had a poor record of picking up long-wave transmissions.

THANKS TO THE DECRYPTION EXPERTS at Bletchley Park, the Allies were well aware of the dispatch of Gruppe Seewolf in March 1945, and the relatively slow speed of Schnorkel boats—whether or not they were the rumored "V-1 boats"—gave the U.S. Navy time to orga- nize a massive response, code-named Operation Teardrop. Convoys were rerouted further south with limited escorts, leaving most of the U.S. Navy assets free to concentrate on hunting down Gruppe Seewolf and the two associated boats. The U.S. Navy supposedly achieved dev- astating results, claiming seven sunk and two surrendered; however, until this day there remains uncertainty as to the extent of the attacks, and while the Kriegsmarine remained relatively ignorant about the extent of Allied naval radar capabilities—one of the best-kept secrets of World War II—the U-boat commanders were well aware of the dan- gers of radio location and recognized that maintaining radio silence was central to a U-boat's chances of survival.

High-frequency direction finding—HF/DF, or "Huff-Duff," intro- duced by the British Royal Navy—was a means of locating U-boats by taking cross bearings on the high-frequency radio transmissions they employed. Numerous long-range listening stations were built on many of the Atlantic's coasts, and "Huff-Duff" was also installed on the warships of Allied escort and hunter-killer groups. Any transmission from a U-boat risked betraying its rough position, allowing the hunters to close in for more sensitive searches by radar and sonar. It was not necessary to understand what the U-boat commander was saying—figuring that out was a lengthier task for Bletchley Park; for the hunters, it was enough that the commander was making himself "visible" by transmitting.

In obedience to their orders, none of the Gruppe Seewolf boats transmitted any traffic after April 2, 1945. While U-boat Command sent occasional orders to the boats of patrol-line Harke, there is no actual evidence that any of them picked up these messages and acted on them. After that date, the Royal Navy's submarine-trackers at Bletchley Park, and Western Approaches Command in the northwestern English port of Liverpool, were unable to verify the actual positions of the U-boats by using any form of direction-finding. All they had to work on was the information decrypted from U-boat Command's transmissions to the boats, filtered through past experience and gut instinct, and as a result they had only a vague idea where the boats might be. The Admiralty situation report for the week ending April 2 stated that the U-boats were "*likely* to operate against convoys in mid-Atlantic but *may* tend to move along the estimated convoy routes in the general direction of the U.S. departure ports" (italics added).

THE U.S. NAVY OFFICIAL HISTORY claims that of the nine U-boats that sailed for the Atlantic in March and April 1945—seven of them forming Gruppe Seewolf—two surrendered at sea and seven were claimed as having been sunk. However, there was no real evidence to support the destruction of four of these boats. These four were some of the last unconfirmed U-boat sinkings at sea; the few losses of Type IX boats that sailed subsequently are well documented and correct. From December 1944, the U.S. Navy would employ four escort-carrier groups in Operation Teardrop—the carriers USS *Mission*, *Croatan*, *Bogue*, and *Core*, with no fewer than forty-two destroyers. This largest Allied hunter-killer operation of the whole Atlantic war was undertaken in the North Atlantic's worst weather in forty years, with high winds and mountainous seas.

Of the seven Gruppe Seewolf submarines facing this overwhelming force, only one was a confirmed kill. U-546 (Lt. Cdr. Paul Just) left Kiel, Germany, on March 11, 1945, and joined the Harke patrol line on April 14. On April 23, aircraft from USS *Bogue* spotted her; the next day the Edsall-class destroyer escort USS *Frederick C. Davis* made contact, but Paul Just got his torpedoes off first, sinking the destroyer with the loss of 115 lives. A subsequent ten-hour hunt ended with the U-boat being hit and forced to the surface; Just and thirty-two survivors were rescued and shipped to Newfoundland. It has been confirmed that both there and after being transferred to Washington, Lt. Cdr. Just, two of his officers, and five seamen were treated with great and repeated brutality. The reason seems to have been American fears about submarine-launched V-1 attacks—grim confirmation of the success of the misinformation plan.

Lt. Cdr. Richard Bernadelli's U-805 sailed from Bergen, Norway, on March 17 and also joined patrol line Harke on April 14, later surviving several attacks from aircraft and warships. After the breakup of Gruppe Seewolf, U-805 operated off Halifax, Nova Scotia, eventually surrendering at sea on May 9—five days after Adm. Dönitz transmitted his surrender order to all U-boats still on patrol. This crew were also interrogated about the supposed V-1 boats, but apparently were not roughly treated—after all, the war with Germany was now over.

Lt. Cdr. Thilo Bode's U-858 left Horten in Norway on March 11 and was judged by the Royal Navy's Submarine Tracking Room to have joined the patrol line on April 14. It seems not to have been detected before Bode surrendered at sea on May 14. Bode's crew were also questioned about the alleged V-1 launchers.

U-881, helmed by Lt. Cdr. Dr. Karl Heinz Frischke, was late joining the line. It left Bergen belatedly on April 7 after problems with its Schnorkel. Frischke clearly did not pick up Dönitz's surrender order of May 4, and U-881 was detected and claimed to be destroyed by the destroyer escort USS *Farquar* as it approached the carrier USS *Mission Bay* on May 6. However, no physical evidence of its destruction ever came to light.

Nor was there any proof of the destruction of U-1235, U-880, and U-518, all claimed as sunk during Operation Teardrop. In reality, they were nowhere near where the Submarine Tracking Room thought them "likely" to be.

U-1235 (First Lt. Franz Barsch) left Bergen on March 19 and was judged by the Submarine Tracking Room to have joined patrol line Harke on April 14. Officially, this boat was lost during the night of April 15–16 to an attack by the destroyers USS *Stanton* and *Frost*, which assumed from a violent underwater explosion that U-1235 had been destroyed—and that it had, indeed, been carrying V-weapons. No wreckage came to the surface, and no other evidence was produced to confirm this kill. In conformity with the orders of April 2 to all Gruppe Seewolf boats, U-1235 sent no radio messages at all during its last patrol. U-boat Command certainly had no idea that the submarine was "lost," continuing to send it orders as late as April 22.

Lt. Cdr. Gerhard Schötzau's U-880 had left Bergen on March 14, and the British tracking room plotted its arrival on the line exactly a month later. The U.S. Navy claimed that this boat, too, was "killed" in a joint attack by the destroyers *Stanton* and *Frost* on April 15–16, within an hour of the destruction of U-1235. "Several underwater explosions" were assumed to have destroyed the boat, but no wreckage came to the surface or was recovered. Again, U-boat Command kept transmitting messages to U-880 until April 22.

Finally, the veteran U-518, commanded by First Lt. Hans-Werner Offermann, left Kristiansand on March 12. U-518 was judged by the Admiralty to have joined the Harke patrol line on April 14. The official U.S. Navy description of the loss of this boat was similar to the descriptions of U-1235 and U-880. The Cannon-class destroyers USS *Carter* and *Neal A. Scott* claimed the kill on April 22, but again no wreckage came to the surface.

The Royal Navy's brilliant Capt. Rodger Winn, head of the Submarine Tracking Room, highlighted the shaky nature of these claims. In a memorandum of May 20, 1945, he noted, with classic British understatement, that the outcome of these actions had been

> reconsidered in an optimistic light, and as a result it is thought that possibly as many as 14 U-boats were sunk. . . . On this assumption it would follow since the identities of the boats in Norway

are now well established that 11 remain to be accounted for. So far as is known these 11 boats are at sea but the Americans claim, possibly rightly, to have sunk 2 of them. . . . What the remaining boats are doing or intend to do is a fruitful and intriguing subject for speculation.

The same memorandum implicitly cast some doubt on the U.S. Navy's claim to have sunk U-530, commanded by First Lt. Otto Wermuth. For a confirmed kill, that boat did indeed look surprisingly intact when it surfaced off Mar del Plata, Argentina, and surrendered to the authorities on July 10, 1945.

SEALED ORDERS MUST HAVE BEEN DELIVERED to the commanders of U-1235, U-880, and U-518 before they sailed in March 1945, with instructions for them to be opened at a specified longitude. Drafted in Berlin on Bormann's instructions, the contents of these orders would be known only to a select few.

The specified longitude was reached before the formation of the Harke patrol line on April 14; the orders instructed the three commanders to break away from Gruppe Seewolf at a time that would allow them to rendezvous on April 28 at Fuerteventura in Spain's Canary Islands, off the Atlantic coast of Morocco. They were to maintain complete radio silence, while monitoring reception in the Thrasher cipher over their Siemens & Halske T43 encryption machines, and were to ignore all orders destined for the Gruppe as a whole. The British Admiralty's daily war diary for April 15 stated that an independent Liberty-class merchant ship, SS *Samoland*, saw a surfaced U-boat in the approximate position where U-518 could have been. It was steering a course of 101 degrees, back across the Atlantic in the direction of the Canary Islands—1,300 miles away, and thirteen days' submerged cruising with Schnorkel assistance.

THE STORY OF THE CODE-BREAKERS and computer pioneers of Bletchley Park, the sixty-acre facility fifty miles northwest of London where the British government's Code and Cypher School— Station X—was installed in August 1939, has been told at length elsewhere. The bare essentials are that in January 1940, British specialists, building upon invaluable prewar Polish research, managed to crack the encrypted German Army transmissions generated by the Enigma machine (see Chapter 1). Decryption of the Luftwaffe's transmissions soon followed; however, the Kriegsmarine's encryptions for message traffic between Adm. Dönitz's U-boat Command and his boats at sea remained unbroken.

The huge toll of Allied and neutral shipping that the U-boats were taking in 1940 made solving this mystery a priority. It became even more urgent from September 1940, when Dönitz successfully pioneered his wolf-pack tactics, using encrypted communications to vector multiple boats into the path of a sighted convoy. Lt. Cdr. Ian Fleming of British naval intelligence concocted a scheme to crash-land a captured German aircraft in the English Channel, wait for rescue by a German patrol boat, overpower its crew, and capture an Enigma machine. The men and the aircraft for this Operation Ruthless got as far as Dover before the plan was canceled, on the sensible grounds that none of the vessels operated by the Germans in the Channel at night was a suitable target (and that there was no guarantee that the ditched plane would float long enough for its crew to be rescued).

On May 9, 1941, U-110 was attacking convoy CB318 in the North Atlantic, south of Iceland, when Royal Navy escorts forced it to the surface by a depth-charge attack. The U-boat crew abandoned ship after setting scuttling charges, but these failed to detonate; the British apparently shot the submarine's captain, the U-boat ace Lt. Cdr. Fritz Julius Lemp, when he tried to return to the vessel to finish the job. Royal Navy sublieutenant David Balme of HMS *Bulldog* led a boarding party across, risked going down the hatch, and recovered the Enigma machine and its priceless accompanying instruction books—a success that the British went to great lengths to conceal from the captured crew. Constant radio intercepts and ceaseless work to keep up with the changing settings of the naval Enigma machines were still necessary to maintain the flow of Ultra intelligence, and (as mentioned in Chapter 1) the introduction of the Schlüssel M four-rotor Enigma machine defeated Bletchley Park from February to December 1942 and continued to hamper the decrypters until September 1943. Nevertheless, Ultra gave the Allies a massive intelligence-gathering advantage; concealing the Allies' knowledge of Enigma transmissions—their greatest secret "weapon"—from the Germans was a matter of life and death.

THE GERMANS NEVER DID DISCOVER that the Enigma codes had been broken, but in February 1945, a new sort of traffic was coming over the radio speakers in Hut 6 at Bletchley Park—traffic that nobody had ever encountered before and that nobody had the slightest idea how to break (see Chapter 11). The British gave the names "Tunny" and "Thrasher" to these two latest weapons in Germany's cryptographic arsenal; neither seemed to be generated using the now relatively familiar Enigma systems. In time, a stupendous effort and the use of the Colossus computer would allow Tunny, produced by the Lorenz SZ42 machine, to be read (at least intermittently), but Bormann's communications network based on the Siemens & Halske T43 machine remained secure. On April 23, 1945, Adm. Karl-Jesco von Puttkamer, Hitler's navy adjutant (and another survivor of the July 20, 1944, bomb attempt), was sent to the Berghof in Bavaria to destroy Hitler's private papers there. Puttkamer had three T43 machines in mobile radio trucks in an underground garage at Berchtesgaden, guarded by forty SS troops, and on April 25 the machines began transmitting. They continued to communicate with a variety of stations until May 1, and many of the messages were for German agents in South America.

Hut 3 at Bletchley Park housed a team headed by Prof. (RAF Wing Cdr.) Oscar Oeser, a South African–born physicist; this group sifted incoming traffic for deciphering by Colossus. In late April 1945, Oeser received a visit from Ian Fleming, whose latest target was Thrasher and the Siemens & Halske T43 machine; this was still defying all efforts at decryption, and Thrasher was being used with increasing frequency. Fleming said that he had located at least two of the latest machines, and he asked if Oeser would join a commando mission into Germany to capture and evaluate them. Oeser was unique in holding degrees in both physics and psychology, and he had studied in Germany. Despite the forty-one-year-old academic's unwarlike and sedentary background, his work at Bletchley Park, his breadth of expertise, and his fluency in German made him the perfect candidate for the task of both evaluating equipment and interrogating its operators. Oeser was immediately interested. A week later he was on the ground near Berchtesgaden as part of TICOM (Target Intelligence Committee) Team 5.

On May 2, 1945, the TICOM team targeted Adm. von Puttkamer's group, met with no resistance from the SS guards, and captured the three T43 machines. (Oeser later handed two of the machines over to the Americans under Operation Paperclip.) Prof. Oeser was amazed at what he found, which he described as "a digital computer system . . . decades ahead" of anything the Allies had. Bletchley Park never did break the Thrasher cipher. However, the TICOM team also captured the premier signals-intelligence unit and almost eight tons of its most secret equipment. With this apparatus the decrypters were able to break the cipher of the latest Soviet military teleprinter that was known by Bletchley Park as "Russian Fish" and subsequently "Caviar." The TICOM team was in awe of the Nazis' advanced technology, which gained many German operators comfortable employment in Britain for the next few years decoding Soviet military traffic.

HITLER'S ESCAPE FROM BERLIN IS, as can be seen from preceding chapters, remarkably well documented. The Führer's trail led us as far as Reus near Barcelona, where his trimotor escape plane was dismantled and he boarded a Spanish aircraft. His next documented sighting would be deep in Argentina in the Southern Hemisphere, at the San Ramón estate near Bariloche in Río Negro province, in June 1945.

It has not been possible to establish precisely how Hitler and his party reached Argentina, but taking into account the "pieces on the board"—to use a chess axiom—it is likely it happened in the following way. By using logic, deduction, and research on what vessels, aircraft, locations, and people were available to the Nazis and how they could be used, we believe Hitler would join with the three missing boats from Seewolf and some six weeks later arrive at Necochea on the coast of Argentina.

The deductive pieces of our reasoning have been italicized to separate them from what we know are the established facts. As when you are hunting an animal, you do not always see your quarry, but you can see traces of where it has been and where it is going. The hunt for Grey Wolf is no different.

ON APRIL 28, 1945, THE THREE DESIGNATED U-BOATS *from Gruppe Seewolf—U-518, U-880, and U-1235—arrived one-half nautical mile off Fuerteventura at Punta Pesebre, at latitude 28°07'00" N and longitude 14°28'30" E. Their crews had no knowledge of what their mission was to be; they had simply been ordered to this position and told to wait for further orders for up to ten days if necessary. A signal lamp from shore had been flashed at a specific time for the previous two nights. When the submarines arrived, a single, brief message was sent to Berlin from Villa Winter, confirming their presence. Bormann's reply was equally brief: "Agree proposed transfer overseas." While they awaited further orders, the U-boat crews took the welcome opportunity to relax in the warm sunshine.*

THE VILLA WINTER BASE on the deserted Jandía peninsula of Fuerteventura had been built in 1943 under the supervision of the senior Abwehr agent in the Canary Islands and had then been manned by personnel of the SS intelligence service. The base had deliberately been excluded from utilization during the Nazi war effort. Bormann intended this facility to serve one purpose only: to act as a key link in the escape route from Berlin. It was the perfect place for the Führer to be picked up by the "last wolf-pack."

The Nazis had first begun their search for a base in the Canary Islands when Hermann Göring financed a "fishing expedition" to the islands between July 14 and August 14, 1938. Leading the search was Gustav Winter, a German engineer and senior Abwehr agent, "in the Canary Islands in charge of observation posts equipped with radio, and of the supplying of German submarines."

It was Winter who had conceived the idea of developing the uninhabited Jandía peninsula as a base for Nazi operations. Born at Zastler, near Freiburg, on May 10, 1893, Winter studied in Hamburg before deciding to travel to the new German frontier in Patagonia in 1913. After the outbreak of World War I the following year he sailed for home, but his ship was stopped, and he was interned by the British on a prison ship in Portsmouth. He first came to the attention of British intelligence in 1915, when he escaped by swimming to a Dutch ship, the *Hollandia*, and making his way to Spain. Winter spoke English

fluently; upon his arrival in Spain he went to the British consulate, persuaded the consul that he was a British citizen in dire economic straits,
and received a cash payment that enabled him to return to Germany.
Between 1921 and 1937 he lived in Spain, traveling back to Germany
regularly "to continue his studies."

Winter had been on the verge of buying Isla de Lobos ("Wolf's
Island"), a small barren rock to the north of Fuerteventura, but Göring's
funded "fishing trip" in 1938 and Winter's own travels aboard his yacht
Argon led him to a much better site for a clandestine operations base.
The desert-like southern peninsula of Jandía comprised nearly 44,500
acres of uninhabited land, and in 1941, Gustav Winter purchased the
whole area through a Spanish front company, Dehesa de Jandía SA.
The ostensible intention was to develop this barren area for agriculture,
and tens of thousands of trees were planted to support this story.

Construction started in 1943. Franco's dictatorship provided a
ready supply of disposable labor among its political prisoners; the road
to Villa Winter is still known as the "Way of the Prisoners." Details are
unknown, since the story of the concentration camps at Tefía on the
island has yet to be written—as have many other dark tales from the
Spanish Civil War and its aftermath.

Gustav Winter himself spent much of his time between 1940
and 1944 at the U-boat base near Bordeaux, returning to Spain only
in August 1944 as the Allies overran the French Atlantic coast. In
his absence, roads, tunnels into the mountains, defensive positions,
and a strange castle-like structure—the "villa" itself—were all built
between 1943 and 1945. Villa Winter had an extensive, sophisticated
military telecommunications system that was probably centered on
the Siemens & Haske T43 machine, giving it constant contact with
Germany, Argentina, and the U-boats that were hungry for resupply
from other bases on Spain's supposedly neutral Canary Islands. The
villa itself was equipped with tiled medical treatment rooms and a
range of attics fitted out for the accommodation of troops and senior
personnel. By late 1944, with the movement of funds out of Germany
in top gear after the Hotel Maison Rouge meeting of that August
(see Chapter 9), the Germans had built a runway at the end of the
peninsula; 1,650 yards long by 66 yards wide, this could easily handle

four-engined aircraft like the Junkers Ju 290 or the Focke-Wulf Fw 200 Condor. Bormann was covering all the bases, providing his escape plan with built-in redundancies.

Between late 1943 and February 1944, at least 250 Nazi agents made their way into the Canary Islands and the Spanish Saharan colony of Rio del Oro, via the Spanish port of Cádiz. The Spanish authorities did not hinder them in any way. At least four months before the long-awaited Allied invasion of France, Bormann was moving key personnel involved in Aktion Feuerland to new bases, and these relocations to the Canaries rapidly increased later in 1944.

In October 1944, German activities in Spain were increasingly annoying the influential U.S. broadcaster and columnist Walter Winchell—a close friend of FBI director J. Edgar Hoover and usually well informed by both U.S. and British intelligence services. Winchell reported, "Hitler had been building air bases in Spain since 1939. . . . Work was supervised by German Army engineers, done by Franco's political prisoners who worked at bayonet point." He went on to state that "Spanish islands off the coast of Villa Garcia were cleared of their civilian population last year. Landing fields, advance Luftwaffe, and three whole regiments of Nazi flyers took over the islands. All civilian travel has been suspended between the Spanish mainland and the Balearics and the Canaries." Civilian travel to the islands was indeed banned. Winchell said that there were two major Nazi bases on Gran Canaria: Gando airfield and a nearby submarine base. If civilians had been able to travel to the islands, Winchell said, they "would see the great storage tanks for submarine fuel, in Las Palmas they would see German officers marching with the Falangists and ten times as many soldiers as in normal times. They would also see the great Nazi seaplane base in Baleares [on the Mediterranean island of Mallorca]."

HITLER'S CHANGE OF AIRCRAFT ON APRIL 29 at the Spanish military base at Reus, from the Luftwaffe Ju 252 to a Ju 52 with Ejército del Aire markings, was carried out quickly and in secrecy. The Führer's party was then flown to Villa Winter on Fuerteventura. During this leg of the journey, the sense of relief on the aircraft must have been palpable. The refugees were flying through neutral Spanish airspace while Allied eyes were still focused on Berlin and, in the case of U.S. intelligence, Bavaria. In the back of the plane Blondi slept peacefully, sedated with drugs supplied by Dr. Haase. Stopping briefly to refuel at the Spanish air force base at Morón in southern Spain and guided by the extensive communications network from the Villa Winter, the aircraft was on the ground in the Canary Islands by late on April 29 or early on the thirtieth. Its passengers were driven along dirt roads from the airstrip to the luxurious villa, to receive a good meal and to sleep— for the first time in months—free from the ominous rumble of bombing and artillery.

Willi Koehn—a regular U-boat passenger to Buenos Aires and the man responsible for the Aktion Feuerland shipments from Spain—had flown in the day before from Cádiz, Spain. Koehn was the chief of the Latin American division of the German Foreign Ministry and a close confidant of Gen. Wilhelm von Faupel, who ran the Nazi Ibero-American Institute—the headquarters for German espionage in the Western Hemisphere. Koehn's last two shipments had preceded him by sea and were waiting to be loaded aboard two of the U-boats.

Hitler and Eva Braun were apparently ferried out to U-518 aboard one of the eleven fishing boats at the disposal of the base. Although Franz Barsch of U-1235 was, at thirty-three, the oldest and most experienced commander, his crew had made their first patrol only in May 1944—as had the sailors of Gerhard Schötzau's U-880. Twenty-five-year-old Hans-Werner Offermann, although the youngest of the three commanders, was a seasoned submariner with personal experience in South American waters, and his crew had been sailing on war patrols since May 1942. By 1945—when the average life expectancy of U-boat men was one and a half patrols—that longevity set them apart as unusually lucky and skillful veterans, and this combination of experience made U-518 a sensible choice for Hitler's boat.

When the passengers had been made as comfortable as possible in the cramped conditions of a fighting U-boat, it departed the island for its voyage of 5,300 miles. The trip would take fifty-nine days, during which the time must have hung as heavily as it had in the "concrete submarine" of the Führerbunker. Meanwhile, U-880—with Hermann Fegelein and Willi Koehn aboard—and U-1235 continued to shelter safely on the seabed off Punta Pesebre. Both submarines would have disposed of their torpedoes, firing them into the deep waters off the island to make way for one final cargo. Over the next two days, boxes of loot transferred from Cádiz were stored in the torpedo compartments.

CONDITIONS ABOARD U-518 must have been normal for an operational boat: it stank. U-boat crewmen were allowed only the clothes on their backs and a single change of underwear and socks, a wardrobe that tended to be augmented by nonregulation items of the crew's own choosing. *The usually relaxed atmosphere among U-boat officers and men must have changed immediately after the Führer came on board, even though Hitler would have asked for formality to be kept to a minimum, recognizing that constant saluting in the cramped confines of a U-boat would be ridiculous. First Lt. Offermann informed the crew of the passengers' identities and the new destination using the boat's internal speaker system. Some space for the couple, their luggage, and a cargo of small but heavy chests had been made by stripping U-518 of almost all its munitions and transferring a number of its seamen. Torpedoes and extra ammunition for the deck antiaircraft guns were off-loaded, and twelve crew members who were considered inessential for a noncombat patrol were transferred to the other two U-boats. For a sting in the tail in case of emergencies, however, Offermann did keep his stern torpedo tubes loaded, with two T5 Zaunkönig acoustic homing torpedoes—"destroyer-busters."*

On combat patrol, the forward torpedo room was also crew quarters. With the stowed torpedoes removed and the normal crew of forty-four reduced to thirty-two, the compartment now provided a bare degree of comfort for Hitler, Eva, and Blondi, but the passengers' privacy must often have been disturbed by sailors carrying out routine maintenance on essential equipment. Most of the crew of a U-boat, apart from specialists such as the radio operators, worked in eight-hour shifts. Crew space was always at a premium, privacy was nonexistent, and even with twelve of their shipmates transferred out the men of U-518 must have been unusually cramped during this voyage. They must also have felt constrained by the presence of the passengers—or of two of them, anyway. To have a dog on board a submarine was not absolutely unknown; Blondi was given the free run of the boat and became a firm favorite with the crew. She quickly got used to the tray provided for her toilet needs, but for humans using the toilet in a submarine was something of a trial.

On U-518, the toilets were equipped with a flushing supply from the sea, which emptied into a sanitary tank that was "blown into the sea periodically." Normally there was only one toilet available until the food stored in the other two had been eaten. For this voyage the toilet in the forward torpedo room was kept for the exclusive use of the Führer and Eva Braun; it also had a metal cabinet with a mirrored front, which housed two fold-up washbasins. Fresh water was limited and strictly rationed, but water for washing was made available to the passengers—a privilege unknown to U-boat crews, for whom laundry had to wait, and liberal use of the standard-issue "Kolibri" cologne was ordered.

Food consisted mainly of canned goods supplemented by a bland soy-based filler called Bratlingspulver; the crew called it "diesel food," due to its constant exposure to engine fumes. A major problem caused by running submerged for an entire patrol was the disposal of the garbage that inevitably accumulated on board, in humid and fetid conditions. Garbage could be dumped in small quantities from the ejector for the BOLD sonar decoy, but the usual practice was to store it in an empty forward torpedo tube for firing into the sea when safe to do so. After dark on May 4, 1945—two days after the "official" announcement of Hitler's death, which caused some wry smiles aboard U-518—the boat anchored for four hours off the southwestern side of the uninhabited island of Branco, in the Cape Verde Islands off the coast of West Africa. Taking the opportunity to "air" the boat, Offermann allowed Eva Braun in particular to come up onto the bridge to smoke—she was finding the conditions aboard the submarine almost intolerable. For a fleeting moment four days later, at approximately 30°W, Offermann considered surfacing for the customary equator ceremony of "crossing the line," but he quickly dismissed the idea. He had a rendezvous.

SS GEN. HERMANN FEGELEIN arrived off the Argentine coast aboard U-880 on the night of July 22–23, some five days ahead of the Führer's boat. The boat had maintained maximum speed throughout its journey to enable Eva's brother-in-law to organize preparations for the Führer's arrival. He transferred into a tugboat of the Delfino SA line *about thirty miles off Mar del Plata in the early hours of July 23. Sailors from U-880 off-loaded forty small but heavy boxes, the size of ammunition chests, from the submarine onto the Delfino tug. U-880's final service to the Reich had now been performed. The crew transferred to the tugboat, the last men opened the seacocks and scrambled to safety, and as they watched quietly their U-boat flooded with seawater and sank for the last time into the South Atlantic depths.*

Meanwhile, in the tugboat captain's cabin, Fegelein showered and shaved for the first time in fifty-four days. Fifteen minutes later, Fegelein was dressed in a sharp grey double-breasted suit, courtesy of Buenos Aires's finest tailor. This had been brought aboard for him by Col. Juan Perón's personal representative Rodolfo Freude, the son of the Nazi "ambassador" in Argentina, the wealthy businessman Ludwig Freude. For the trip to the shore the two men were joined in the wheelhouse by U-880's other passenger, Willi Koehn, the chief of the Latin American division of the German Foreign Ministry and former head of the Nazi Party in Chile.

Koehn had last been in Buenos Aires in January 1944, when he had also made use of the regular U-boat run from Rota in Spain to Mar del Plata to bring in forty heavy boxes. Koehn was well known to the anti-Nazis in Argentina; three weeks after his arrival with Fegelein, democratic Argentine exiles in Montevideo, Uruguay, confirmed that Koehn was back in Argentina. This time he was in Patagonia, with "the knowledge of the Buenos Aires government." He was not alone.

When Fegelein and Freude landed on the quay at Mar del Plata, a black Argentine navy staff car was waiting for them. A short while later the SS general and the Argentine Nazi boarded a Curtiss Condor II biplane—freshly painted in the colors of the Fuerza Aérea Argentina, established less than six months before—and took off. This Curtiss was one of four originally ordered by the Argentine navy in 1938; the type was renowned for its short take-off and heavy payload capability. It touched down again just half an hour later, on the grass airstrip at a German-owned ranch four miles from the coast near Necochea.

IN THE LAST days of the Nazi regime, Ernst Kaltenbrunner conducted the largest armed robbery in history against the wishes of Martin Bormann. Accordingly, he was denied an escape route and was left to face justice. Here, along with other Nazi leaders he stands trial in September 1946 at the Nuremberg International Tribunal for crimes against humanity. Seated in the middle row, from left to right: Hermann Göring, Rudolf Hess, Joachim von Ribbentrop, Wilhelm Keitel, and Kaltenbrunner. He was condemned to death and hanged on October 16, 1946.

WITH THE BOMB-DAMAGED Old Reich Chancellery looming in the background of this photograph taken some time after 1945, the bodies of the Hitler and Braun doubles were soaked in gasoline and burned in the small depression visible halfway between the tree and the conical ventilation tower. The blockhouse and doorway were above the stairway and emergency exit of the Führerbunker. To the right of the ventilation tower is the ballroom of the Old Reich Chancellery, below which the Vorbunker was situated. Hitler used to walk his dog Blondi in this area of the Reich Chancellery gardens every day up until their escape.

NAZI MINISTER OF Propaganda Joseph Goebbels poses with his wife Magda, three of their six children, and the Führer at the Obersalzberg, 1938. The entire Goebbels family died in the Führerbunker on May 1, 1945, with the six children poisoned and their parents committing suicide. The bodies were burned in a funeral pyre in the Reich Chancellery garden—the same fate that befell the body doubles of Adolf Hitler and Eva Braun. The little boy is Helmut Goebbels, who was reputedly the bastard son of Magda Goebbels and Adolf Hitler following a passionate affair during a vacation on the Baltic Sea in the summer of 1934.

IN "HITLER'S" LAST official appearance, he left the safety of his bunker to hand out medals to members of the Hitler Youth in the Chancellery garden on March 20, 1945. In actuality this was the unfortunate Gustav Weber, whose uncanny resemblance to Hitler deceived even those quite close to him; on this occasion the National Leader of the Hitler Youth, Artur Axmann, was either taken in or warned to play along.

THE NAZI-FINANCED Gran Hotel Viena built on the isolated shores of Argentina's inland sea, Mar Chiquita, now in ruins. Hitler and Eva visited the hotel's hospital and health spa in 1946.

A MODERN-DAY aerial view of the town center of San Carlos de Bariloche, with its German-influenced architecture. In the background are Lake Nahuel Huapí and the Andes in the far distance, below which was situated "Adolf Hitler's Valley."

A VIEW OF the front of the Berghof (left), Adolf Hitler's estate in Obersalzberg, Berchtesgaden, Upper Bavaria, Germany, c. 1938. Note the similarity in design to Inalco (below), Hitler's main residence in Patagonia between 1947 and 1955. Built in 1943, parts of Inalco are modeled on the Berghof.

BUILT BY THE same architect as Inalco, the Saracen Tower on Lake Nahuel Huapí guarded the air and water routes to Hitler's home. While the Saracen Tower overlooked the lake itself, there was a series of *refugio* [literally "refuges"] situated in the mountain passes from Chile and in the hills above San Carlos de Bariloche. These mountain chalets controlled every avenue of approach to "Adolf Hitler's Valley." One *refugio* above Bariloche was named the Berghof after Hitler's home in the Bavarian Alps, and it was there that Juan Domingo Perón often came to ski with the Nazi members of the Club Andino Bariloche.

THE "ARCHITECT OF the Holocaust," Adolf Eichmann, escaped from American custody early in 1946 and, with the help of Bishop Alois Hudal, sailed for Argentina on a Red Cross passport on July 14, 1950. For the next ten years, he lived openly as Ricardo Klement (see identity card, above) and ultimately worked as a foreman at the Mercedes Benz factory in Buenos Aires. On May 11, 1960, Israeli secret agents kidnapped him in a suburb of Buenos Aires and took him to Jerusalem, where he was tried in 1961 (left). On May 31, 1962, Eichmann was hanged and cremated, and his ashes discarded outside Israeli territorial waters.

KNOWN AS "The Angel of Death" for his vile medical experiments on prisoners, particularly on twins and dwarves, at Auschwitz-Birkenau, Josef Mengele was one of thousands of Nazis who escaped justice after the war and settled in South America. There he acted as an illegal abortionist, living in San Carlos de Bariloche in Patagonia (where he failed his driving test twice) and Buenos Aires, before fleeing to Paraguay after Eichmann's kidnapping. Using various names from José Mengele to Wolfgang Gehard, he subsequently lived in Brazil where he died on February 7, 1979, while swimming in the sea. He is shown here during the 1970s in Brazil eating with an unidentified woman (on left), sitting across from an unidentified man and his maid Elza Gulpian de Oliveira. De Oliveira, who worked for Mengele for several years, testified that she knew him as "Mister Pedro."

PRESIDENT JUAN PERÓN and his wife Eva are seen here with Rodolfo Freude, Perón's private secretary and intelligence coordinator, in October 1946, several months after Perón took office. Freude's father, Ludwig, was the de facto Nazi ambassador in Argentina and in control of the massive fortune sent by Bormann, much of which was acquired by the Peróns for their own use. The Peróns also made large amounts of money from the indiscriminate sale of immigration visas that allowed many wanted Nazi war criminals to escape justice in Europe and make a new life in Argentina after the war.

Shown here in 1994, Catalina Gomero was the housemaid—and virtual adopted daughter—of the Eichhorn family. She waited on Hitler at their home in La Falda, in Cordoba Province in 1949. She said that his visit was "kept very, very secret." She also saw Hitler with the Eichhorns at their mountain retreat, El Castillo, that same year.

Hernán Ancin, Croatian dictator Ante Pavelić's carpenter, shown in 1995. He met the Hitlers five times in Mar del Plata between September 1953 and October 1954. He described Hitler as "very polite" and said Eva Hitler seemed to have "suffered a great deal."

Retired policeman Jorge Colotto, Juan Domingo Perón's personal bodyguard, in a 2009 photograph. He saw Bormann in 1954 when the Brown Eminence met with Perón. Colotto was entrusted with the task of taking an envelope of cash from Perón every month to the Hotel Plaza in central Buenos Aires, to pay for Bormann's expenses.

Chapter 17

Argentina—
Land of Silver

IN 1536, SPANISH CONQUISTADORES established a settlement on the Río de la Plata (River Plate) that was to become the cosmopolitan city of Buenos Aires. It lay on the edge of the vast pampas or plains that stretched hundreds of miles to the Andes Mountains on the western edge of South America. The conquistadores came in search of gold and silver. Such was their lust for precious metals that they called the newfound territory Argentina, or Land of Silver, after the Latin *argentum*. There was little gold or silver to be had from the nomadic Native American hunter-gatherers living on the pampas, but the Spaniards brought with them something far more valuable: the horse and the steer. The pampas were ideal for the raising of cattle. The legendary gauchos (cowboys) tended immense herds, spending months at a time in the boundless countryside. The end product was leather, which was exported in huge quantities to Europe. It was a wasteful process, as the only monetary value lay in the hides and the meat was mostly discarded. And then in 1879, with the advent of refrigerated shipping, whole carcasses of beef, lamb, and mutton were dispatched by the millions across the seas from specially constructed ports—Buenos Aires in Argentina, Fray Bentos in Uruguay, São Paulo in Brazil—to feed the workers of the industrial revolution and generate great wealth in South America.

With burgeoning populations in the Old World, many Europeans sought a new life in the Americas. Between 1850 and 1930, over six million immigrants flocked to Argentina: mostly Italians, but many Spaniards, British, and French as well. This medley of races gave rise to the quixotic nature of the Argentines, who have been described as "Italians who speak Spanish and think they are British living in Paris." The southern Europeans provided the labor while the Anglo-Saxons supplied the capital for the country's growing infrastructure of railroads and ports. The English also purchased vast tracts of the pampas for their cattle farms, or estancias, and encouraged the widespread cultivation of wheat for export. After the unification of Germany in 1871, German immigrants began to arrive in Argentina in significant numbers, but the best lands of the pampas were in the hands of the English or the old, established Spanish families. The Germans were obliged to look elsewhere. Their eyes fell on the desolate hinterland of Patagonia that straddled the borders of Argentina and Chile to the south.

It is difficult to comprehend the scale of Patagonia: one and a half times the size of Texas or nearly four times that of Great Britain. Most tellingly, its population in 1945 was minimal. By comparison, if New York City had the same population density there would be just thirty-five people living in Manhattan. On one side, Patagonia is bordered by the magnificent Andes Mountains and on the other by the cold and forbidding waters of the South Atlantic. Although Imperial Germany had been stripped of all its colonial possessions by the Treaty of Versailles in 1919, Patagonia, which remained in Argentine and Chilean sovereign territory, was a de facto German colony. When war broke out in 1939, there were 60,000 members of the overseas Nazi Party living in Argentina, the largest group of National Socialists outside of Germany. The total German population of approximately 237,000—not including German Jews—represented a small, but economically and politically important section of Argentine society. Its influence at the government level far exceeded its numerical size.

IN GERMANY, STRATEGIC DREAMS for the Americas had predated Hitler's rise to power by at least three decades. As early as 1904, Ernst Hasse, president of the Pan-German League in Berlin, had even been moved to predict that "the Argentine and Brazilian republics and all the other seedy South American states will accept our advice and listen to reason, voluntarily or under coercion. In a hundred years, both South and North America will be conquered by the German Geist [philosophical mind-set], and the German Emperor will perhaps transfer his residence to New York."

During the Nazi era, the two key figures in German penetration of Latin America were Adm. Wilhelm Canaris, from 1935 the head of the Abwehr, and Gen. Wilhelm von Faupel, head of the Ibero-American Institute, the headquarters for German espionage and conspiracy in the Western Hemisphere.

Canaris knew Argentina and Chile well. He had joined the German Imperial Navy in 1905, and by the outbreak of World War I he was serving as an intelligence officer on board the SMS *Dresden*. The *Dresden* was the only German cruiser to escape destruction by the British at the Battle of the Falkland Islands in December 1914. The Royal Navy finally caught up with the *Dresden* in March 1915, at Robinson Crusoe Island off the coast of Chile. After a short battle against overwhelming odds, the German crew scuttled their ship and spent the rest of the war interned in Chile. Canaris escaped in August 1915; he was already fluent in Spanish, and during an early stage of his long journey back to Germany he was helped by German settlers in Patagonia, in particular at the Estancia San Ramón outside San Carlos de Bariloche, in the foothills of the Andes. Canaris even evaded capture in England during his sea voyages home (he also spoke good English). He then served as an undercover agent in Italy and Spain before ending World War I as a U-boat commander in the Mediterranean. His brilliant talents and unusual firsthand knowledge of the Patagonian region would be invaluable during the development of the Nazi intelligence network in southern Argentina.

The preexisting basis and principal cover for this activity was the Lahusen company, a major enterprise with offices and shops throughout Patagonia since before World War I (now defunct). Central to its early profitability was the wool trade, supplied by the German sheep ranches of Patagonia; before refrigeration made meat shipments to Europe possible, wool was Argentina's largest export and its trade fueled the country's vibrant economy. The Lahusen organization facilitated the German espionage system throughout Argentina, Chile, Uruguay, and Paraguay in both world wars. It employed over a thousand people and owned nearly a quarter of a million acres of land in the territory; its headquarters in the Montserrat district of Buenos Aires took up seven floors of a modern office building. Every town and village in Patagonia had its Lahusen store and agent, and it was a standing joke in Buenos Aires's diplomatic circles that Hitler knew more about Patagonia than the Argentine government did.

Wilhelm von Faupel, the German General Staff's primary expert on Argentina, also had experience in Argentine affairs that predated World War I. From 1911 to 1913 he was a professor at the military academy in Buenos Aires. At the outbreak of war, he was relocated to Spain, where he ran German espionage and sabotage activities in the Mediterranean. Following Germany's defeat, he returned to Argentina as chief adviser to the Argentine General Staff. From 1927, Faupel supported the rise of the Nazis in Germany; he recruited important German émigrés— such as Walter and Ida Eichhorn—to help fund the National Socialist Party; the Eichhorns in particular would, for decades to come, play a central part in Nazi plans for Argentina. From 1938, from a mansion on Fuerenstrasse in Berlin, Faupel organized the training of German and South American agents and saboteurs. He had contacts with the Falange Española—the Spanish fascist political party that underpinned the Nationalist uprising by rebel army officers in July 1936—and was instrumental in the creation of the Condor Legion soon afterward. This force combined cadres of German military instructors and squadrons of combat airmen that assisted the Nationalist forces—and acquired useful experience themselves—during the Spanish Civil War. Wilhelm von Faupel's activities over three decades would bring him huge influence in Spain after the Nationalist leader, Gen. Francisco Franco, established his military dictatorship in 1939. In time, this influence would enable Martin Bormann's plans for a "Fourth Reich in the South" to move toward reality.

TODAY, IF YOU VISIT VILLA GENERAL BELGRANO, San Carlos de Bariloche, Villa La Angostura, Santa Rosa de Calamuchita, or any of a hundred other German settlements in Argentina, it is still difficult to believe that you are in Latin America. The architecture and the almost exclusively Caucasian population are very obviously Central European. Each of the larger towns has always had its own German school, cultural institute, beer hall, and restaurants. Even at the time of this writing in 2010, Argentines of German descent account for more than three million of the country's population of forty-two million, and many of these families arrived in the country decades before National Socialism was born. Of course, not all German-Argentines were Nazi sympathizers, but it is a common phenomenon for overseas settler communities to remain frozen in the conservatism of previous generations—and in the 1930s, a proportion of German-Argentines were fiercely nationalistic *Volksdeutsche*. When the Allies captured the Nazi Party's master membership files, they were found to contain nearly eight million names. Among the cards of the Ausland-Organisation ("Overseas Organization"), Nazis were particularly numerous in Argentina. Estimates vary for the membership of the Nazi Party and its affiliated organizations in that country, but the combined membership of both the official German NSDAP (Nationalsozialistische Deutsche Arbeiterpartei) and the home-grown equivalent stood at close to 100,000.

The Nazi sympathizers in Argentina advertised and sought to extend their already widespread support of the party with brash displays on a grand scale. In the spring of 1938, more than 20,000 of them gathered for a "Day of Unity" rally at the Luna Park stadium in Buenos Aires to celebrate the Anschluss—the annexation of Austria into the Third Reich on March 12. German Nazi banners flew alongside the Argentine flag while uniformed children marched past and gave the Hitler salute. The rally spurred citywide anti-German protests. The Argentine Nazi Party was officially dissolved by presidential decree on May 15, 1939, but this ban had little practical effect. In 1941, a report submitted to the Argentine congress by Deputy Raúl Damonte Taborda, chair of a congressional committee investigating Axis activities, stated:

Do not believe that we are shouting in the dark. 22,000 perfectly disciplined men are ready, plus 8,000 Germans from the Nazi Party, 14,000 members of the German Workers Front, 3,000 Italian Fascists, 15,000 Falangists, many others from the Juventud Germano Argentina [Argentina's Hitler Youth organization], and many thousands of others affiliated with the Argentine Nationalist Alliance—all are ready to strike.

In 1943, the American author Allan Chase produced a detailed picture of the groups of Nazi sympathizers across Latin America, centered in the external organization of the Spanish Falange. He summed up:

Wherever you turn in Latin America, whether in small but strategic Panama or in large and powerful Argentina, the Falange Exterior hits you between the eyes. Upward of a million Falangistas and their dupes—acting on orders dictated by Nazi General Wilhelm von Faupel in Madrid—are actively engaged in warfare against the United Nations, for the Axis. Hitler is not fooling—and the Falanges in Latin America are Hitler's.

In 1943, when Germany's disastrous defeats in Russia and North Africa and the collapse of Fascist Italy convinced the more clear-sighted of the Nazis that ultimate defeat was inevitable, Argentina offered their last best hope for a postwar refuge. Martin Bormann, as always, was entirely clear-sighted, and during that year he put in hand his plan to prepare and fund that refuge—Aktion Feuerland. The Nazi sympathizers in Argentina enjoyed a virtually free rein, continuing to operate schools with Nazi symbols and ideology and meeting regularly (although by 1943 not as publicly as before), but the key conspirators were few—a group limited to people Bormann had reason to trust. These included a clique of powerful, venal bankers and industrialists such as Ludwig Freude; a charismatic, ambitious army officer, Juan Domingo Perón; and a beautiful, intelligent actress, Eva Duarté.

THE NAZIS' PENETRATION OF ARGENTINA can be considered in two parts (though they were intimately linked): first, the creation of Bormann's human network, and second, the infusion of assets, which included the funding of capital projects such as "Hitler's Valley" and the Hotel Viena, and investment and banking deposits.

Ludwig Freude, labeled Argentina's number one Nazi by the U.S. State Department, was to be the power behind the military strongman Juan Perón. From October 1942, the year before Aktion Feuerland moved into gear, he was also the de facto Nazi ambassador in Buenos Aires. Freude had gone to Argentina from Germany in 1913 and built up a construction company that would eventually make him one of Latin America's ten wealthiest men. (His son Rodolfo, appointed as Juan Perón's private secretary, was a key Nazi liaison after the spring of 1945.)

Juan Domingo Perón, born in 1895, was brought up to ride and shoot in the cold, windswept south—"Argentina's Wild West." He was not a son of the aristocratic *estanciero* class—the rancher oligarchy that dominated Argentine politics and society—so he was fired by ambition rather than a sense of entitlement. After joining the army in 1911, Perón excelled in physical activities, but also earned approval as a student of military history (he would go on to publish five books on Napoleonic subjects), and by 1915 this "unusually intelligent, alert professional soldier" was one of the youngest full lieutenants in the service. In 1936, he was sent to Chile as a military attaché, but was expelled for espionage. In 1938, before the outbreak of World War II, Perón was posted overseas to Mussolini's Fascist Italy, where—already an expert skier—he was attached to the Italian Alpini mountain troops. On June 10, 1940, as Wehrmacht armor threatened the French capital of Paris, Mussolini finally decided that it was safe for Italy to enter the war on Germany's side, and Perón was soon in Paris to watch the Germans' ceremonial parade through the surrendered capital. On his return to Argentina, Perón was to use his firsthand experience of Italian Fascism and German Nazism to build his own political model for a "New Argentina." By summer 1941, both he and his friend Eva Duarté (an opportunistic twenty-two-year-old actress whose film career had been limited to bit parts but who was becoming very popular on Argentine radio) would be among those Argentine citizens in the direct pay of Berlin—or more precisely, of Reichsleiter Martin Bormann.

Mr. E. A. Tamm
Mr. Clegg
Mr. Glavin
Mr. Ladd
Mr. Nichols
Mr. Rosen
Mr. Tracy
Mr. Carson
Mr. Coffey
Mr. Harbo
Mr. Hendon
Mr. Kramer
Mr. McGuire
Mr. Piper
Mr. Quinn Tamm
Tele. Room
Mr. Nease
Miss Beahm
Miss Gandy

Federal Bureau of Investigation
United States Department of Justice
Washington, D. C.

September 4, 1944

CAG:FOS

MEMORANDUM FOR THE DIRECTOR

Re: Possible Flight of Adolph Hitler to
Argentina

Many political observers have expressed the opinion that
Adolph Hitler may seek refuge in Argentina after the collapse of Germany.

Political ramifications lend credence to this possibility
when it is recalled that the duly appointed Argentine Consul Hellmuth,
ostensibly assigned to a Consular post in Spain, had plans which included clandestine
meetings with Hitler and Himmler for the arranging of importing arms and technicians
into Argentina. Hellmuth, intercepted by the British at Trinidad, never completed
his mission.

Argentina remains a mysterious maze of questionable characters.
who will be recalled for her notorious affair with the German diplomatic
representative in New York, is presently residing in Buenos Aires. , former
Austrian munitions king and ex-husband of recently converted his bicycle
factories into an Argentine plant for the manufacturing of munitions. Arnulfo Arias,
pro-Axis ousted President of Panama, conducts a long range political campaign from
Buenos Aires. well known as the sweetheart of the American
industrialist Vivian Fellers, still claims to be in Argentina as the postwar planner
for the German cartel Metallgesellschaft.

A large wealthy German colony in Argentina affords tremendous possibilities
for the providing of a refuge for Hitler and his henchmen. One of the members, Count
Luxburg, has been mentioned as operating a ranch which would serve in providing a haven.

By the very nature of any plans formulated for the abandoning of Germany in
its collapse, it is virtually impossible to substantiate any allegations with regard
to Argentina's serving the Nazis after defeat; however some significance may be
attached to the fact that Argentina remains silent despite all the accusations that
she will serve as a terminus for Hitler after a non-stop flight of 7,376 miles from
Berlin to Buenos Aires in an especially constructed plane or as a passenger in a long
range submarine.

This matter continues to be the subject of a coordinated investigation by
the Bureau representatives throughout the world. Information developed to date has,
of course, been furnished to other interested governmental agencies.

Respectfully,

D. M. Ladd

AN FBI DOCUMENT from 1944 details where Hitler would find refuge in
Argentina if he lost the war.

MUCH OF THE CREDIT FOR EXPOSING Nazi links with leading Argentine figures belongs to the one-time Radical Party deputy for the province of Entre Ríos, Silvano Santander. This dedicated anti-Nazi had worked with Raúl Damonte Taborda since 1939, and in 1944 their refusal to be silenced led to a warrant for their arrest, obliging them both to flee the country. Santander went only as far as Montevideo in Uruguay, just across the Río del Plata from Buenos Aires, where he continued to work tirelessly in exile. In November 1952, he and his team traveled to West Germany, following a tip-off about a mass of documentation uncovered by the war crimes commission in Berlin during its hunt for Nazi links with Argentina. Santander subsequently published two books about the background of the Peróns' rise to become Argentina's first couple; his work was based on the documents he had studied in Berlin, which had been authenticated by U.S. Department of State foreign service investigator William Sidney and Herbert Sorter, chief of the External Assets Investigation Branch in the U.S. High Commissioner's Office.

Among the documents were confidential reports about diplomats and Nazi agents, sent from South America to Bormann, Foreign Minister Joachim von Ribbentrop, and the spymaster Gen. von Faupel. Among them were handwritten memos that had passed between Bormann and the German ambassador in Buenos Aires, Baron Edmund von Thermann (who, unsurprisingly, held the rank of SS major). In one such memo, Ambassador von Thermann praised the Buenos Aires government as loyal supporters of Nazism and pointed out that the Buenos Aires provincial governor from 1936 to 1940, Dr. Manuel A. Fresco, had installed on his ranch, Estancia Monasterio, "a powerful radio transceiver by which they had a permanent communication system" between Argentina and Germany. This would be a crucial link in Bormann's plans for Hitler's escape, allowing for the likely use by Ludwig Freude of a Siemens & Haske T43 encryption machine that would have been delivered to Buenos Aires in 1944.

AS EARLY AS MAY 1940, many of the Nazis' Argentine supporters would gather regularly for friendly games of poker at the German embassy in Buenos Aires. The German players included

Ambassador von Thermann; Prince Stephan zu Schaumburg-Lippe, a consular officer based in Chile; the naval attaché Capt. Dietrich Niebuhr; the press attaché Gottfried Sandstede; Ricardo von Leute, the general manager of Lahusen; and the multimillionaire banker Ludwig Freude. On the other side of the dealer, the Argentine players included various military and naval officers: Generals von der Becke, Pertiné, Ramírez, and Farrell, and Colonels Perón, Brickman, Heblin, Mittelbach, Tauber, Gilbert, and Gonzalez (the number of German family names is striking). Occasionally Carlos Ibarguren, head of the legal department of the Banco de la Nación, and Miguel Viancarlos, chief of investigations for the Argentine police, would also sit in. The Nazis were "useless" at poker and lost heavily. Allied intelligence reported that the Argentines would leave with smiles on their faces, remarking how innocent their German opponents were, but Thermann would later tell the Allied war crimes commission, "We wanted to make our friends happy—we always let them win."

Press attaché Gottfried Sandstede had two other roles: he was also an employee of the Delfino shipping line and Gen. von Faupel's personal representative. The FBI suspected that Delfino SA was heavily involved in Bormann's shipments of loot from Europe, at first by surface vessel and aircraft and later by submarine. On September 8, 1941, *Time* magazine reported:

> In the three months since thirty-two-year-old Deputy Raúl Damonte Taborda began a [congressional] investigation of anti-Argentine activities he has stealthily and steadily crept closer to Argentina's cuckoo nest: the German Embassy. Last week Deputy Damonte thought he had his hands on the biggest cuckoo in the nest.

The bird he was after was not Ambassador von Thermann, but Gottfried Sandstede. Damonte believed that Sandstede was the senior Nazi spy in Argentina and that Thermann actually took instructions from him—a suspicion that Thermann would later verify.

When Damonte came after him, Sandstede claimed diplomatic immunity, but, as an employee of Delfino, he was denied this status by the Argentine Foreign Ministry. Somebody tipped off the German embassy about Sandstede's imminent arrest, giving him time to arrange his urgent departure. Police were posted outside his house and the German embassy and at checkpoints along the roads leading from the city to the airport. One of these pickets stopped a suspicious-looking car that tried to pass through the cordon, and arrested Karl Sandstede, the fugitive's brother. Believing they had the wanted man, the police relaxed the cordon, and early the next morning Gottfried Sandstede boarded a plane for Brazil at Buenos Aires airport. Upon Sandstede's arrival in Rio de Janeiro, Ambassador von Thermann "announced blandly that Herr Sandstede had been recalled to Berlin to report on anti-German activities in Argentina."

The truth was more interesting. On the morning of the escape, the Kriegsmarine attaché, Capt. Niebuhr, wrote to Gen. von Faupel, "We had to send our press attaché Gottfried Sandstede from the country in haste. We received information from our Miss Eva Duarté, an Argentinean who is always excellently informed." The actress was more than simply an informant, however; she had played an active part in the escape by turning up at the German embassy in Col. Perón's War Ministry staff car with an Argentine military uniform complete with greatcoat and cap: a disguise for Sandstede. Thus disguised as a senior Argentine military officer, with a stunning blonde beside him, Sandstede was simply waved through the police cordon. Three days after Sandstede's flight, Deputy Damonte submitted to the Argentine congress a report by his investigative committee. Among its major conclusions, the report stated that, despite its official dissolution in May 1939, the Argentine Nazi Party continued to operate cells throughout the country, organized on military lines, and that the German embassy participated directly in the party's activities.

The papers studied by Santander in 1952 revealed that Eva Duarté would soon enjoy the trust of the Nazi agents to a remarkable degree. When Niebuhr himself had to leave the country after being "outed" for espionage activities, he wrote to von Faupel, "Luckily, with some exceptions, they did not have news of our most important staff or of our contacts." Niebuhr reported that he was actually passing over responsibility for parts of the Nazi network in the "Brazil and South Pacific [southern Chile] sections" to Duarté, whom he described as "a devilishly beautiful, intelligent, charming, ambitious, and unscrupulous woman, who has already caught the eye of Colonel Perón."

Three months after the flight of Gottfried Sandstede, the Japanese attack on Pearl Harbor brought the United States into World War II. In January 1942, President Franklin D. Roosevelt's government summoned a conference of all the nations of the Americas to meet in Rio de Janeiro. The State Department exerted pressure on all Western Hemisphere countries to cut diplomatic relations with Japan, Germany, and Italy. Within two weeks, on January 28, all but two of the twenty-one republics announced their agreement; those that refused were Chile and Argentina. Despite the revelations of the Damonte report, it would be October 23, 1942, before Ambassador von Thermann left Buenos Aires for good. His practical functions passed, unofficially but unequivocally, to the banker and industrialist Ludwig Freude.

IN APRIL 1943, WHEN THE TIDE OF WAR was obviously beginning to turn in the Allies' favor, von Faupel traveled to Buenos Aires in person by U-boat. He was accompanied by Sandstede, who had not returned to the country since he had been spirited out with Eva Duarté's help in September 1941. When they arrived on May 2, they were received by Argentina's outspokenly pro-fascist and anti-American navy minister, Adm. Leon Scasso. Von Faupel stayed in the German evangelist church on Calle Esmeralda in Buenos Aires. Before they departed on May 8, they held meetings with—among others—Ludwig Freude, Ricardo von Leute of the Lahusen company, and Col. Perón and Eva Duarté. Thermann would later tell the war crimes commission that "the real motive for Faupel's visit was to make Argentina a safe place for the future, in the certainty of defeat."

Von Faupel told Perón that it was now possible that Germany would lose the war. In that case, he warned, Perón and his friends were going to end up facing charges of high treason. The Nazi spymaster told his Argentine contacts that there was only one way to avoid this: they had to seize power and "maintain it at all costs." It would take less than a month for them to act on his advice.

On June 4, 1943, Gen. Arturo Rawson and the Grupo de Oficiales Unidos (United Officer's Group, or GOU)—a secret clique of senior military officers in which Col. Perón played a significant part—launched a coup d'état. It took about half a day to overthrow the three-year-old regime of Argentina's conservative president, Ramón S. Castillo; Rawson himself would preside for less than two days, however, before being replaced by Gen. Pedro Pablo Ramírez. Germany, Italy, and the U.S. State Department immediately recognized the new regime; the United States hoped that Argentina would finally give up its neutrality and join the fight against the Axis. The precedent of the authoritarian Getúlio Vargas regime in Brazil, which had joined the Allies in August 1942, was encouraging. However, the new Argentine government proved even less cooperative than the old one. Ramírez was president in name only; the real power lay with the GOU, known simply as "the Colonels," and well placed among them was Juan Domingo Perón. (One of the GOU's early acts was to close down Deputy Damonte's committee of enquiry into Nazi activities.) Perón became an assistant to the secretary of war and, a short time later, the head of the Department of Labor. This then-insignificant ministry would provide him with an unsuspected power base.

At the German embassy, Capt. Niebuhr's replacement in the Nazi network was Erich Otto Meynen (another of the poker players), and he could hardly contain his triumph when he wrote to his predecessor: "I have spent day and night traveling or receiving Party members; they come from all parts of the country to see me. My efforts have not been in vain. The success of our friends' revolution has been complete." Eva Duarté had shown Meynen a letter that outlined Perón's political philosophy: "The Argentine workers were born animals of the herd, and they will die as such. To rule them it is enough to give them food, work, and laws to follow, which will keep them in line." Niebuhr thought Perón followed "the good school."

AMERICAN ANGER AT ARGENTINA'S REFUSAL to curb Nazi activities, and at the Ramírez government's stubborn maintenance of an ostensible neutrality in the war, came to a head with the publication of a blistering exchange of letters between Argentine foreign minister Adm. Segundo Storni and U.S. secretary of state Cordell Hull in September 1943. The row was deliberately made public by the

United States, causing a storm in Buenos Aires; Storni resigned, and anti-American feeling blossomed in Argentina. The press reported one typical young "hothead" as declaring, "To hell with the U.S. We're looking toward Europe, for now and after the war."

Continuing American pressure only made the Colonels more popular, but then Great Britain and the United States threatened to go public with detailed information on the Nazis' links with members of the Argentine government—which would lead to global ostracization of Argentina. In January 1944, President Ramírez, folding under this threat, suspended diplomatic relations with Germany and Japan. (Italy had already surrendered to the Allies on September 8, 1943.)

The GOU immediately replaced Ramírez with his fellow poker player Gen. Edelmiro J. Farrell. Perón became vice president and secretary of war, while retaining his labor portfolio. His work in this ministry helped him to forge an alliance with the Argentine labor unions; together they put forward laws that strengthened the unions and improved workers' rights. Against intuition, the military conspirator Perón increasingly became the voice of the working people, and now he was just one step from the presidency.

PERÓN'S PUBLIC RELATIONS BREAKTHROUGH followed the devastating earthquake that hit San Juan on January 15, 1944, which claimed over 10,000 lives and leveled the central-western Argentine city. Vice President Perón moved into overdrive; he was entrusted with fundraising efforts and enlisted media celebrities to help. His work made a real difference in the region's recovery and gained him great popular support. This was also the perfect time for his relationship with Eva Duarté to be revealed to the public. Accepted history tells us that Perón met the young radio star at one of his fund-raising events in May 1944; in reality, as we have seen, their working and romantic relationship went back considerably further. It was at this time that Eva's public profile was created—as a girl from humble beginnings who used her achievement of stardom and social connections to work for the interests of the poor among whom she had grown up. It was a perception that fit neatly alongside Col. Perón's pose as a defender of workers' rights. This image of a beautiful, glittering champion of the poor—*los descamisados* (the "shirtless ones")—would earn "Evita" unparalleled public affection, and indeed a sort of secular sainthood, which would endure in the hearts of many Argentines for generations after her death.

IN MARCH 1944, JOSEPH GOEBBELS made clear his vision for a new world order in Latin America. The German propaganda minister foresaw that

Argentina will one day be at the head of a tariff union comprising the nations in the southern half of South America. Such a focus of opposition against the United States of America will—together with Bolivia, Chile, Paraguay and Uruguay—form a powerful economic bloc; and eventually, by way of Peru, it will spread northward to place the dollar colony of Brazil in a difficult position.

The following month, Vice President Perón echoed this expansive prediction:

In South America it is our mission to make the leadership of Argentina not only possible but indisputable. Hitler's fight in peace and war will guide us. Alliances will be the next step. We will get Bolivia and Chile. Then it will be easy to exert pressure on Uruguay. These five nations will attract Brazil and its important group of Germans [Brazilian-German immigrant communities]. Once Brazil has fallen the South American continent will be ours. Following the German example, we will instill the masses with the necessary military spirit.

On June 22, 1944, the United States broke off diplomatic relations with Argentina; Great Britain followed suit, and shortly afterward so did much of Latin America. Argentina found herself in diplomatic quarantine, recognized only by Nazi Germany and by fascist-leaning Chile, Bolivia, Paraguay, and Ecuador. Seeing this apparent setback as an opportunity, Perón rallied the extreme nationalists in the army and the labor movement behind him to defend their nation's honor. However, the diplomatic freeze was followed by the threat of an Allied trade embargo (although such a move by Britain—which depended on Argentina's huge meat exports at a time when the British population was suffering severe food rationing—would have caused Winston Churchill's government extraordinary difficulties).

Despite the bellicosity of Argentine nationalists, the threat of a trade embargo and continued U.S. diplomatic rumblings did have some effect. In apparent moves to appease the U.S. State Department, the increasingly powerful vice president ostensibly clamped down on Nazi activities and closed down some German-language newspapers. Behind this front, Ludwig Freude continued to further Bormann's plans with Perón's help, but he was advised by his friend to lower his profile.

On November 22, 1944, Freude wrote to Gen. von Faupel:

> In order to provide the smallest target possible and so as to facilitate the defense of our interests, I have resigned from all my duties in the German institutions, as well as in the industrial and commercial companies, and I have adopted Argentine citizenship. Let the Allied diplomats waste their time now faced with my position, which is as unshakable as that of Perón himself.

Freude also explained to von Faupel how he would manage to maintain Nazi assets in Argentina if—as by then seemed inevitable—Germany lost the war: "We have agreed to invent . . . Argentine [reparation] demands to the Reich, and to guarantee they are fulfilled [by] impound[ing] all the German wealth in Argentina."

Freude made it clear that he reported directly to Bormann, and he asked von Faupel to smooth his way. He refused to have anything to do with either the Ausland Abwehr—the Office for Espionage, Counterespionage, Sabotage, and Foreign Information—or with von Ribbentrop's Foreign Office. Von Faupel was in complete agreement; he had never trusted Adm. Canaris of the Abwehr (who had in fact already been removed from his post in February 1944 under suspicion of anti-Nazi activities), and he considered von Ribbentrop a fool.

Gen. von Faupel knew how to keep his collaborators happy. Freude wrote that "the diamond necklace arrived with the last shipment, destined for our friend Eva from you. I have already handed it over, and have the duty to convey to you her warm and grateful greetings." Freude was also lavish with his presents; when the widowed Perón finally married Eva in October 1945, Freude gave her a house in the Buenos Aires suburb of Belgrano as a wedding present. She never lived there, but Juan Perón used it for "quiet meetings"; in 1953 he would meet Martin Bormann there.

IT WAS THE LOOT OF CONQUERED EUROPE that provided not merely Evita's diamond necklace, but the whole funding for the structure of Bormann's influence in Argentina and the preparation of the future Nazi refuge. Apart from shipments from Italy and Spain by means of Bormann's front-company shipping and airlines, a U-boat run began in August 1942, continuing at six- to eight-week intervals during 1943 and 1944. A single submarine made the trip each time, from Rota near Cádiz. A former officer of the scuttled *Admiral Graf Spee*, Capt. Paul Ascher, arranged the unloading in Argentina.

Among the many deposits made in Argentine banks, Reichsmarschall Hermann Göring had $20 million in an account transferred via Swiss banks in Geneva. Göring collected a whole range of high-paying government posts, but had also amassed a huge personal fortune from criminal activities. He had seized Jewish properties, taken bribes for allowing others to do the same, and—as detailed in Chapter 4—amassed an incredible collection of art looted from Nazi-occupied territories. As part of his role as director of the Four-Year Plan—the Nazi's economic strategy to rearm and to reduce unemployment—he took huge bribes from industrialists bidding for contracts. He had even made money from supplying weapons to Spanish Republicans fighting Franco's Nationalists. A plot to ship at least $10 million of Göring's loot by U-boat to Buenos Aires was uncovered in 1943 by British intelligence, but the British dismissed it because they were dubious about the trustworthiness of their source, Ernesto Hoppe. Propaganda Minister Joseph Goebbels had $1.8 million in a safety deposit box at another bank, where Foreign Minister Joachim von Ribbentrop also had a box containing a more modest half million U.S. dollars. None of these three Nazis, of course, would reach Argentina to enjoy his loot, but before von Ribbentrop's execution he told one of his confidants, Otto Reinebeck, former German minister to the Central American Republics, "Argentina is the last German bridgehead in the Western Hemisphere, the maintenance and development of which are of the greatest significance for later on."

These personal sums are tiny, however—nothing but loose change when compared to the real scale of Bormann's Aktion Feuerland shipments. The gold alone came to $1.12 billion at 1948 prices—the equivalent of at least $50 billion today—before one even considers the platinum, precious stones, coinage, art works, stocks, and bonds.

Ludwig Freude's and Eva Duarté's involvement in the smuggling operation was made clear in an Argentine police document of April 18, 1945. This detailed the operations of Freude, "agent of the Third Reich," and his dealings with an Argentine agent, "Natalio." This informant reported that Freude had made very substantial deposits in various Buenos Aires banks in the name of the "well-known radio-theatrical actress María Eva Duarté." Freude told Natalio that on February 7, 1945, a U-boat had brought huge funds to help in the reconstruction of the Nazi empire. Subsequent police investigations revealed that cases from the U-boat, with the words *Geheime Reichssache* ("Reich Top Secret") stenciled on them, had been taken to a Lahusen ranch run by two "Nazi brothers, just outside Buenos Aires." Deposits of gold and various currencies were later made in Eva's name at the Banco Alemán Transatlántico, Banco Germánico, and Banco Tornquist.

Ludwig Freude was the central figure in the Nazis' financial survival plan. His original operation had been relatively low-key; as president of the committee of the Argentine Nazi Party he had set up local fund-raising, taking monthly dues from all party members and supporters. He kept offices at the Banco Alemán Transatlántico and was also president of many other Nazi front companies. Most of these were set up during 1942 and 1943; they extended through every aspect of Argentine industry and owned huge tracts of land in Patagonia. More than two hundred German companies established major offices in Argentina between 1942 and 1944. Specialists were sent out from Berlin to assist Freude, among them Heinrich Doerge, a senior official at both the Reichsbank and the Ministry of Economics.

Doerge was Perón's economics adviser and the man behind the transformation of the Argentine banking system; the Allies had him marked down as a "Nazi considered dangerous for the security of the hemisphere." (Later he would also prove dangerous to the Bormann "Organization" and would be among the trail of corpses left behind as Bormann tried to regain control of the Nazis' looted fortune in 1952, see Chapter 21, page 259.) Between them, Freude and Doerge managed to hide hundreds of millions of dollars of funds, shares, patents, and convertible bonds in a complex web of Argentine companies.

Eva Duarté's original recruiting officer at the German embassy, Capt. Niebuhr's colleague Gerda von Arenstorff, would tell war crime investigators in October 1945 that in February 1944 the German embassy had 47 million pesos in banks in Buenos Aires and that these funds were made to disappear by transfers to "trusted people." In February 1944, the German embassy also had seven safety deposit boxes in the Banco Germánico, holding gold and silver coins with a value of 115 million pesos. Ludwig Freude, in a 1944 memo to von Faupel found after the war, noted that other deposits to the value of $37.66 million had been made in a bank in Buenos Aires in the names of German and Argentine Nazis. Keys to the deposit boxes were held by two of the original poker players, Erich Otto Meynen and Ricardo von Leute, who had countersigned the deposit documents. (These men would also join the body count left by the purging of the "Organization" in December 1952; the coins simply disappeared.)

Share certificates were just as transferable as bullion, jewels, and cash. When the Germans had invaded Holland in 1940, they found shares of Compañia Argentina de Electricidad (CADE), Buenos Aires's electrical supplier, to the value of $48.67 million, which were confiscated and sent to Argentina. Many major German companies were implicated in the transfer of assets to Argentina, including Siemens, Krupp, Mannesman, Thyssen, IG Farben, and Schröder's Bank, dealing through local or Swiss holding companies.

THE HUGE SUMS AT THE DISPOSAL of Bormann's and Ludwig Freude's "Organization" had bought influence, blind eyes, protection, financial hiding-places, and cooperation in Aktion Feuerland to create safe refuges for important fugitives from the final collapse of the Third Reich. In the years to come, Perón's regime would extend to thousands of Nazis—many of them wanted war criminals—a discreet welcome and continuing concealment and protection. But Juan Perón had personal plans for his own and his country's future, and whatever his other faults he was a patriotic Argentinean. If for nothing else, the world may at least be grateful that he would prove entirely unwilling to allow his state to be hollowed out as the nest for any insane "Fourth Reich in the South."

Juan Domingo Perón was a dictator, whose ruthlessness toward those who opposed him abused and alienated large sections of Argentine society. The "state of siege" that had been enforced by Argentina's late president Ramon S. Castillo since shortly after the attack on Pearl Harbor—including the muffling of the press and the banning of oppositional political activity or public assembly—was "retained . . . and improved on" by Perón. He briefly lifted the siege on August 20, 1945, ahead of promises of an election, but fifty-two days later he reimposed it. On October 8, 1945, *Time* magazine reported, "Argentina was back to normal. Anybody who was anybody was in jail. After fifty-two days of abnormal freedom, Vice President Juan Domingo Perón had again imposed the repressive 'state of siege' under which Argentines had suffered for almost four years." Perón also smashed what was left of Argentina's free press. He was desperate that the Argentine public should never learn of the revelations about his— and especially Evita's—wartime payments from the Nazis, divulged to the war crimes investigators by the former diplomats Prince Stephan zu Schaumburg-Lippe and Edmund von Thermann.

Perón was a fascist, in the true sense of that term. He had been greatly impressed by Benito Mussolini's regime, and he openly supported the Axis. But like Mussolini, he did not have the character to become an ideological mass murderer. He recognized—as his successors in the juntas of the 1970s and 1980s would not—that despite the reactionary instincts of many Argentines, they would never tolerate for long a regime of actual concentration camps. Neither was Perón anti-Semitic; he had many Jewish friends and placed them in positions of authority in his postwar government. We might imagine that the ghastly revelations that followed the liberation of Hitler's death camps by Allied troops in April and May 1945 shocked even Juan Perón. They did not prevent him honoring his undertaking to provide refuge for some of the men responsible for those horrors, but we may imagine that they made him watchful.

BY THE TIME THAT HITLER was on the ground at Villa Winter on Fuerteventura in the Canary Islands, preparing for his long and comfortless journey by submarine, the refuge organized and financed for him by Bormann's Aktion Feuerland was built, decorated, and ready. Two months later, on the windswept coast of Argentina, the last U-boat of Gruppe Seewolf would land its passengers.

PART IV

THE GREY WOLF OF PATAGONIA

Chapter 18

THE U-BOAT LANDINGS

THE AIRFIELD AT SAN CARLOS DE BARILOCHE, a lakeside town in Patagonia's Río Negro province, was opened in 1921 as part of the global boom in aviation following World War I. For the wealthy German estancia owners of Patagonia it opened up the region to commerce; the British-built railway did not arrive in the area until 1934.

The U.S. journalist Drew Pearson reported on December 15, 1943, that "Hitler's gang has been working to build up a place of exile in Argentina in case of defeat. After the fall of Stalingrad and then Tunisia, they began to see defeat staring them in the face. That was their cue to move into Argentina." The airfield had been extended and modernized during 1943 as part of the Aktion Feuerland program. This improvement made it capable of handling long-range four-engined aircraft such as the Focke-Wulf Fw 200 Condor and Junkers Ju 290, several of the options that Bormann included in his contingency planning for Hitler's escape. The airfield was situated on the extensive lands of the Estancia San Ramón, a little over twelve miles from San Carlos de Bariloche. A dirt road led from the airfield to a large timber-built house about three miles away from the airfield, where the young

Lt. Wilhelm Canaris of the German Imperial Navy had been sheltered thirty years earlier during his escape from Chile (see Chapter 6, page 59, and Chapter 17, page 195). On July 26, 1945, German sailors—a handpicked party from among the stranded crew of the *Admiral Graf Spee*—were protecting the house in expectation of important visitors.

About 650 miles to the northeast, a smaller group of *Admiral Graf Spee* men were being mustered by Capt. Walter Kay on another airfield, this one on the Estancia Moromar near Necochea on the Argentine coast. Carlos Idaho Gesell had bought the property, covering more than 3,200 acres, in 1932. He developed the nearby town of Villa Gesell, which he named after his father; the family was wealthy and undoubtedly had close links to the Lahusen organization. The former first officer of the *Admiral Graf Spee*, Kay normally ran his operation out of offices on the seventh floor of the Banco Germánico on Avenida Leandro in Buenos Aires. Kay was central to facilitating the employment—by the Nazi intelligence service in Argentina—of his supposedly "interned" sailors. The men of the *Admiral Graf Spee* had been interned by the Argentine authorities when they sought refuge after their humiliating defeat by the British Royal Navy in the Battle of the River Plate in 1939. However, the internment was at best loose, with many men simply disappearing from "captivity." Kay—despite his interned status—had helped more than two hundred of the ship's gunnery, communications, and other specialists to return to Germany on ships sailing under neutral flags, but he had opted to stay on in the south, where he believed he could be of more use. Kay had motivated the remaining crew, many of them committed Nazis, to regain some self-respect. Six years had been a long time to wait, but even now that the Reich had been defeated they would have a real chance to salvage something from the flames.

On July 28, 1945, three *Admiral Graf Spee* petty officers named Alfred Schultz, Walter Dettelmann, and Willi Brennecke were at the Estancia Moromar, equidistant between Necochea and Mar del Sur on the Argentine coast. With submachine guns slung from their shoulders, the sailors were organizing eight trucks to drive to the beach. The vehicles all carried Lahusen markings; five of them had been brought in by a potato farmer from his Lahusen-run property thirty-eight miles north of the Estancia Moromar, at Balcarce.

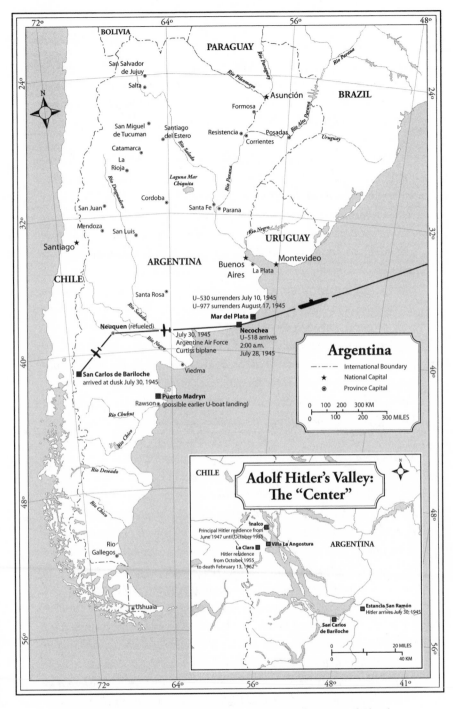

AFTER FIFTY-THREE DAYS at sea, U-518—carrying Hitler, Eva, and Blondi—
arrives at Necochea on the Argentine coast. Fegelein is there to meet them.
The next day the party flies to the Estancia San Ramón on the outskirts of
San Carlos de Bariloche to begin their exile.

AT I:OO A.M. ON JULY 28, 1945, *SS Gen. Hermann Fegelein, wrapped in a borrowed greatcoat to protect him from the Argentine winter's night, was waiting under a starlit sky on the beach at Necochea for his sister-in-law and his Führer. U-518 arrived off the coast an hour later.*

Hans Offermann brought his submerged boat as close to the shore as he could, moving dead slow and with a tense hydrophone operator straining for the sounds of surface vessels; the commander had little detailed or recent information about the coastline he was approaching. Eventually he ordered the boat to periscope depth and cautiously raised the observation periscope; a careful 360-degree sweep satisfied him that no vessels or aircraft were nearby and that the light signals from shore coincided with those in his orders. Still taking no chances, he ordered his gun crews to prepare to man the 37mm and 20mm antiaircraft cannons as soon as the boat surfaced, although they had little ammunition in the lockers.

Fegelein sent out a small motorboat belonging to the ranch to meet the submarine. For the middle of the Southern Hemisphere winter, the water was surprisingly calm. As the launch approached the beach, lit by sailors' flashlights, Fegelein raised his arm in the classic Nazi salute. The Admiral Graf Spee *men splashed into the small breakers on the beach and helped pull the craft up onto the sand, and Fegelein moved forward to help Eva Braun from the boat. Hitler was helped down by the boat crew, returned Fegelein's salute, and shook him by the hand.*

The one-time ruler of the Thousand-Year Reich was almost unrecognizable. He was pasty-faced from the long voyage, the trademark moustache had been shaved off, and his hair was lank and uncut. Eva had made an effort to look good throughout the trip, but the prison-house pallor of her skin was highlighted by the lipstick and rouge she had applied before leaving the submarine. Of the three arrivals, Blondi probably looked the best; her excitement at being in the open air at last was controlled with the familiar red leather lead, gripped firmly in Hitler's right hand as the party walked up the beach to a waiting car. No doubt Fegelein took the opportunity of the short drive to brief Hitler on the immediate arrangements. An avenue lined with tamarisk trees led to the main house of the Estancia Moromar, where they would spend the first night. Security at the ranch house was surprisingly light: the fewer people who knew about the visitors, the better.

The petty officers Shultz, Dettelmann, and Brennecke helped in the subsequent unloading of many heavy boxes, which were ferried ashore from the U-boat on repeated trips by the motorboat and the submarine's rubber boats. The boxes were loaded onto the farm trucks and driven to outbuildings on the Estancia Moromar; repacked in new boxes, the contents would be taken to Buenos Aires and deposited in Nazi-controlled banks. *At the end of the unloading, most of the crew from U-518 came ashore in the rubber dinghies and marched in column in civilian clothes, their kitbags slung over their shoulders, to quarters on the estancia. Meanwhile, an eight-man skeleton crew took U-518 out on its final voyage, to be scuttled further from shore. They would return in the motorboat, to join their shipmates for their first fresh meal in two months.* They did not know that their operation had almost been compromised.

DON LUIS MARIOTTI, THE POLICE COMMISSIONER at Necochea, had called his off-duty men in from their homes on the evening of the previous day, July 27, 1945, and ordered them to investigate unusual activity reported on the coast. The officers arrived at the beach to see an unidentified vessel offshore making Morse code signals, and they found and arrested a German who was signaling back. Interrogated through the night, he eventually admitted that the signaling vessel was a German submarine that wanted to put ashore at a safe place on the coast to unload.

The next morning a six-man police squad led by a senior corporal decided to comb several miles of beach north and south of the place where they had caught the signaler. After some hours, they found a stretch of sand bearing many signs of launches and dinghies being beached; heavy boxes had also been dragged toward the tire tracks of trucks. The police squad followed the tire tracks along the dirt road that led to the entrance of the Estancia Moromar. The corporal sent one of his men back to the station with his report, and then, without waiting for orders, he decided to enter the farm. The five police officers had walked a couple of miles in along the tree-lined drive when they came to some low hills, which hid the main buildings. Four Germans carrying submachine guns challenged them. The corporal had no search warrant and was seriously outgunned; he decided to withdraw and report back to his superior.

Commissioner Mariotti telephoned the chief of police at La Plata. The call was taken by the latter's secretary, who told him to do nothing and remain by the telephone. Two hours later Don Luis was ordered to forget the matter and release the arrested German. The following month an FBI message from Buenos Aires stated: "Local Press reports indicate provincial police department raided German colony located Villa Gesell . . . looking for individuals who possibly entered Argentina clandestinely via submarine and during search a short-wave . . . [illegible] receiving and transmitting set found. Other premises along beach near same area searched by authorities but no arrests made."

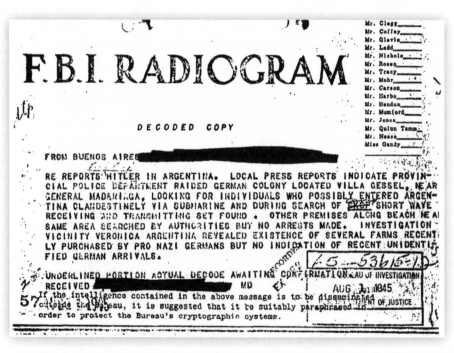

FBI REPORT RECORDED in August 1945, substantiated in Argentine police files, of the landings at Necochea and the support system awaiting Hitler.

ANOTHER SAILOR from the *Admiral Graf Spee* also had recollections of the landing. Petty Officer Heinrich Bethe, whose later role in Hitler's life is discussed at length in Chapter 23, was interviewed by one Capt. Manuel Monasterio in 1977, when Bethe was living in the Patagonian coastal town of Caleta Olivia under the pseudonym Pablo Glocknick (he was also known as Juan Paulovsky). Bethe had repaired Monasterio's car one day after it had broken down. The captain and the former Kriegsmarine petty officer immediately hit it off, and on a number of occasions over bottles of wine and local seafood, the former sailor recounted his time as Hitler's companion in exile. Bethe said he had escaped the clutches of the Bormann organization after Hitler's death in Argentina and had lived in obscurity on the coast, working as an occasional mechanic, his trade aboard the *Admiral Graf Spee*.

Petty Officer Bethe's recollections of the U-boat landings are essentially similar to those of Schultz, Dettelmann, and Brennecke, but his description of the location of the landing site differs substantially (see map on page 219). Bethe spoke of a landing area "several hours" of driving over rough roads from the city of Puerto Madryn, which is much further south than Necochea. Bethe recalled that on the evening of July 28, he directed trucks to a determined point on the coast and from there proceeded to load a large number of boxes that came ashore on rubber dinghies from two submarines. The trucks carried the boxes to two large depositories where they were carefully unloaded. Later, about seventy people disembarked from the U-boat. In Bethe's opinion, "the cargo was very valuable, and the people that arrived were not common sailors like [himself], but presumably hierarchy of the Third Reich."

The two accounts may seem to describe the same landing, but there were in fact two such missions: one at Necochea that delivered Hitler, and one further south that unloaded the loot to finance his future. Ingeborg Schaeffer, the wife of First Lt. Heinz Schaeffer, commander of U-977, which surrendered at Mar del Plata on August 17, 1945, was asked in 2008 if her husband had brought Hitler to Argentina. Mrs. Schaeffer replied, "If he did not bring him, there were another two U-boats that could have brought him, and [my husband] could have given them food and so forth, because the others went on to Puerto Madryn." Although her comments are somewhat cryptic, she was obviously aware of other Nazi submarines in Argentine waters at the same time as U-977, information she could have got only from her husband. Schaeffer's U-977 was a Type VIIC from U-Flotille 31. The Allies had believed that Argentina was beyond the range of this smaller class of U-boat, but the fact remains that Schaeffer reached Mar del Plata. However, Puerto Madryn was indeed beyond his range unless he stopped to refuel, as it was more than 500 miles away as the crow flies and much more following the coastline. Ingeborg Schaeffer's testimony, and other evidence from Argentine navy documents, clearly point to two separate groups of U-boats.

One pair was U-880, which likely passed Fegelein over to a tug off Mar del Plata on July 23, and U-518, which is believed to have landed Hitler at Necochea on July 28. Both of these were Type IXC boats from U-Flotille 33, large enough to carry passengers and cargo (as also were U-530 and U-1235).

A separate group included U-530, which First Lt. Otto Wermuth surrendered at Mar del Plata on July 10—two weeks ahead of the boat that brought Hitler. This boat was in terrible condition and contained nothing of value; it may already have offloaded cargo at Necochea for Estancia Moromar. Wermuth's interrogation report—translated from German into Spanish, and finally into English by the U.S. Navy—says that he considered landing at "Miromar" before deciding to surrender at Mar del Plata. He said that he had left Kristiansand on March 3, 1945, and proceeded to Horten in Oslo Fjord, Norway, where for some reason "not stated" he remained for two days (possibly to load cargo). U-530 had no torpedoes, weapons, or ammunition on board; by contrast, U-977 was carrying its full complement of weapons and torpedoes when it surrendered on August 17—a full five weeks after U-530. Wermuth's mention of "Miromar," and the fact that getting rid of the torpedoes would have provided space for clandestine cargo, suggest that he may have had something to hide from his interrogators. He refused to say whether or not U-530 was alone, but he did say that he operated under direct orders from Berlin and that the last direct contact he had was on April 26. Wermuth said that he did not know of any other submarines headed for Argentina, but that if any more were coming, they would arrive within a week of his own arrival.

F.B.I. RADIOGRAM

DECODED COPY

Mr. E. A. Tamm
Mr. Clegg
Mr. Coffey
Mr. Glavin
Mr. Ladd
Mr. Nichols
Mr. Rosen
Mr. Tracy
Mr. Carson
Mr. Egan
Mr. Hendon
Mr. Pennington
Mr. Quinn Tamm
Mr. Nease
Miss Gandy

FROM BUENOS AIRES   NR 134

REPORT HITLER IN ARGENTINA. DATA AVAILABLE THIS OFFICE CONTAINED
IN REPORT OF SPECIAL AGENT   JULY 18 ENTITLED SURRENDER
OF GERMAN SUB U 530, MAR DEL PLATA. CONCERNING RUMOR RE LANDING
SAN JULIAN, ARGENTINA,   THERE NOW REPORTS HE
DISCOVERED TWO SETS FOOT PRINTS LEADING IN ONE DIRECTION ONLY
FROM HIGH WATER MARK THEN ACROSS MUD FLATS TO SHORE PROPER NEAR
SAN JULIAN. AT POINT WHERE FOOT PRINTS ENDED TIRE MARKS FOUND
INDICATING CAR HAD BEEN TURNED AT RIGHT ANGLE TO SHORE. FOOT
PRINTS MUST HAVE BEEN MADE ABOUT JUNE 25 WHILE FLATS COVERED WITH
FLOOD WATERS AS AREA FROZEN THIS TIME OF YEAR. EFFORTS BEING
MADE TO TRACE CAR. INQUIRIES CONTINUING AT VERONICA.

RECEIVED

RECORDED 65-53615-7X

FEDERAL BUREAU OF INVESTIGATION
AUG 1 1945
U.S. DEPARTMENT OF JUSTICE

EX-22

ORIGINAL COPY FILED IN

If the intelligence contained in the above message is to be disseminated
outside the Bureau, it is suggested that it be suitably paraphrased in
order to protect the Bureau's cryptographic systems.

REPORT FROM FBI in Buenos Aires recorded in August 1945, concerning
arrivals in Argentina by U-boat.

INGEBORG SCHAEFFER'S TESTIMONY suggests that a second group of boats, responsible for the landings near Puerto Madryn described by Heinrich Bethe, might have been escorted by her husband's fully armed U-977, which left Kristiansand on May 2, 1945—the day before U-530 sailed. Both U-530, and U-1235 from Gruppe Seewolf, had the range for the southernmost landings. The presence of a second group of three boats is also suggested in two separate television interviews conducted in Buenos Aires with Wilfred von Oven. Oven was the personal press adjutant to Propaganda Minister Joseph Goebbels between 1943 and 1945. He had accompanied the Condor Legion in Spain as a war correspondent and was acquainted with Gen. Wilhelm von Faupel of the Ibero-American Institute. Oven went into hiding in 1945 under an assumed name and fled to Argentina in 1951; a committed Nazi, he was declared persona non grata by the Federal German Embassy in Buenos Aires. Before he died in 2008, Oven was asked about a "fleet" of Nazi submarines coming to Argentina in 1945. On two occasions—once to an Argentine author, and again to a British TV crew—he replied, in what appeared to be almost a conversational slip, "No, there were only three, just three." His interviews are rambling and given in an arch manner suggesting that he knew more than he was willing to tell, but on the matter of the three U-boats he seemed quite lucid.

An Argentine government memorandum of October 14, 1952, stated:

> I bring to your attention that our agents [names deleted] have detected at Ascochinga, in the mountainous region of Córdoba province, a farm located on the Cerro Negro, which has been acquired by a former officer who disembarked from U-235 [sic] at the Mar del Plata naval base. This boat, together with other German submarines, came to Patagonia from Germany after the conclusion of hostilities.

The Canadian author William Stevenson also mentions a U-235:

> It was reported that members of the brotherhood began to quarrel over money during the 1960s, and this seemed probably true.

The leader of the rebellion against Bormann was described as the commander of U-235. He was said to have brought his vessel to Argentine waters, discharged a cargo of stolen Nazi treasures, scuttled the U-boat, converted the cargo to money and bought a large estate.

Confusion in these sources between the numbers U-235 and U-1235 seems quite plausible. It is certain that the real U-235, a Type VIIC, was lost with all hands in the Kattegat Bay area off the Danish coast on April 14, 1945, to a depth-charge attack in error by German S-boat T-17. There is no official record of a third boat in addition to U-530 and U-977—which might have been U-1235—surrendering to the Argentine authorities at Mar del Plata. However, on July 19, 1945, the Buenos Aires daily newspaper *Critica* reported that yet another U-boat had been "surrounded by Argentine Navy vessels thirty miles off the coast of Mar del Ajo" just north of Mar del Plata. Nothing more is ever heard of this boat.

The question of what happened to the crews that landed from those U-boats that were scuttled rather than surrendering—potentially, U-518, U-880, and U-1235—naturally arises. Despite the story that the commander of what was probably U-1235 (Lt. Cdr. Franz Barsch) survived to buy a farm in Córdoba, where he was still living in 1952, there are no reports of any of the other submariners surfacing in Argentina after the war. The three boats together had a total of about 152 crewmen. The simplest answer is that it would have been perfectly possible to disperse these sailors among the hundreds of German communities scattered across Patagonia. It is possible to imagine that numbers of them might have preferred this prospect over a return to ruined, starving, occupied Germany, especially if their families had perished in the air raids or were now lost somewhere in the Soviet zone. A much more sinister alternative explanation is that they may have been disposed of shortly after their arrival. Nobody was looking for them in Argentina, after all, just as nobody was looking for Hitler, Eva Braun, Hermann Fegelein, or the masterminds of the entire escape plan, Martin Bormann and Heinrich "Gestapo" Müller. Bormann's and Müller's utter ruthlessness is beyond question; and Fegelein's service in Russia had been spent commanding SS units employed in "antipartisan" warfare behind the fighting front.

IN 1945 THERE WAS NOTHING CONTROVERSIAL about the idea that German submarines were operating clandestinely along the coast of Argentina. The possibilities were outlined in a letter dated as early as August 7, 1939, from Capt. Dietrich Niebuhr, the naval attaché at the Buenos Aires embassy, to his Berlin espionage controller Gen. von Faupel: "The strategic situation of the Patagonian and Tierra del Fuego coast lends itself marvelously to the installation of supply bases for [surface] raiders and submarines." The Nazi-hunting Argentine congressman Silvano Santander had no doubts that such plans were carried out: "These [contact points] were established, and served to supply fuel to the German submarines and raiders. The Argentine government's tolerance of this provoked numerous protests from the Allied governments. Later on, after the Nazi defeat, these bases were also used so that mysterious submarines could arrive, bringing both people and numerous valuables." Allied intelligence services were aware of such possibilities from at least 1943, when the Americans began actively seeking a secret U-boat refueling and resupply base near the San Antonio lighthouse.

On May 22, 1945, after the end of the war with Germany, the Argentine foreign ministry informed the navy of "the presence of German submarine warships in the waters of the South Atlantic, trying to reach Japanese waters"; and on May 29, the Argentine navy carried out antisubmarine operations in the Strait of Magellan to prevent submarines passing from the Atlantic to the Pacific. This did not stop the traffic. The federal police reported that on July 1, 1945, two persons landed from a submarine near San Julián, on the Atlantic coast near the southern tip of Argentina and the Strait of Magellan. The two Germans paddled ashore in a rubber boat and were met by "a person who owned a sailboat." The police said that the submarine was refueled from "drums hidden along the coast." Such stories were nothing new. In January 1945, Stanley Ross, who had been a correspondent in Buenos Aires for the Overseas News Agency, reported that Nazi submarines had intensified their activities, bringing "millions of dollars in German war loot to this hemisphere to be cached here until the Nazi leaders could claim it." Ross went on to write,

A Nazi submarine surfaced near the Argentine coast at Mar del Plata. It was seen to transfer to a tugboat of the Axis-owned Delfino line of Buenos Aires some forty boxes, and the person of Willi Koehn, chief of the Latin American Division of the German Foreign Ministry. While the submarine waited to take him back, Koehn, the former head of the Nazi Party in Chile, conferred in Buenos Aires with key Nazi agents and collaborationists.

By July 1945, Koehn was already back in Argentina, having joined Fegelein for U-880's last voyage from Fuerteventura.

COL. RÓMULO BUSTOS COMMANDED an Argentine coastal antiaircraft unit at Mar del Plata in the southern winter of 1945. In early June he was ordered by his superiors to cover a broad section of the coast between Mar del Plata and Mar Chiquita, to oppose any attempts by German U-boats to land and disembark; if anybody did disembark, he was to take as many prisoners as possible. "My group had to cover the area near Laguna Mar Chiquita, a few miles to the north of the naval base. We had nine cannons; we were ready to open fire. One dark night I saw light flashes from the sea to the coast, [directed] at a spot near the place where we were. I contacted the leader of our group. When he arrived at our position, the flashes had stopped," but when the commander was about to leave, the flashes started again.

As there were no more light signals on the following nights, the whole operation was reduced to observation, and a file classified "secret," reporting these events, was sent to the admiral in command. Bustos remembered a second incident at the end of June:

One of my soldiers found a cave almost three meters deep. We found that somebody had put three wooden shelves in the inside of the cave, ten or twenty centimeters above the high tide mark. On the shelves there were cans, the size of a beer can, without any type of identification except for one letter. The first we opened contained bread, and the next one chocolate bars. I thought the others would also have food and drinks. I then thought that this was a place to resupply either submarines or clandestine crew members who disembarked in the area. We took photos and wrote a detailed report. We took away the cans and the wood. I do not know what happened afterward to this evidence.

With hindsight, the retired colonel thought it was strange that the local press did not mention what happened, since "everybody in the area was talking about it."

Col. Bustos was present a couple of weeks later when U-530 arrived in Mar del Plata on July 10, 1945. "When I went on board, two things caught my attention: the nasty smell in the boat (although all doors were open), and finding cans identical to the ones we had seen on the beach."

THE GERMAN CAPABILITY TO SHIP OUT personnel and cargo by submarines, on an ambitious scale and over long distances, certainly survived into the final weeks of the war. Intriguing proof of this was provided by U-234, which sailed from Kiel on March 25, 1945. This was originally built as a Type XB mine-laying boat; at 2,710 tons displacement when submerged and fully loaded, this small class of eight were the largest U-boats ever built. After suffering bomb damage during construction, U-234 was reoutfitted as a long-range cargo transporter. On this occasion—U-234's first and only mission—its destination was Japan, and it was carrying not mines, but a dozen special passengers and 240 tons of special cargo, plus enough diesel fuel and provisions for a six- to nine-month voyage. The cargo included a crated Messerschmitt Me 262 jet fighter, a Henschel Hs 293 guided glider bomb, examples of the newest electrical torpedo guidance systems, many technical drawings, and over half a ton of uranium oxide. The passengers included Luftwaffe Gen. Ulrich Kessler, two Japanese naval officers, and civilian engineers and scientists; among the latter were Dr. Heinz Schlicke, a specialist in radar, infrared, and countermeasures who was the director of the Kriegsmarine test facility at Kiel (later recruited by the United States in Operation Paperclip), and August Bringewalde, who was in charge of Me 262 production at Messerschmitt.

The fate of U-234 would be decided by another of Martin Bormann's "carrot and stick" deals with U.S. intelligence. *On May 1, 1945, Lt. Cdr. Johann-Heinrich Fehler opened sealed orders that instructed him to head for the east coast of the United States. He was to deliver his cargo to the U.S. Navy, but was ordered not to let some things fall into U.S. hands.* Bormann would have needed to maintain his secure communications links, so the U-boat commander threw overboard his Kurier and T43 encryption equipment and all Enigma-related documents. On May 14 the USS *Sutton* took command of U-234 and led her to the Portsmouth Navy Yard.

DOZENS OF U-BOAT SIGHTINGS off Argentina are faithfully recorded in police and naval documents. Many of them took place within the crucial period between July 10, 1945, when the Type IXC boat U-530 surrendered at Mar del Plata, and August 17, when the Type VIIC boat U-977 surrendered at the same Argentine navy base. (U-977 allegedly took sixty-six days to cross the Atlantic, submerged all the way, and U-530 made it in sixty-three days.)

On July 21, just a week before the landing at Necochea that delivered Hitler, the Argentine navy's chief of staff, Adm. Hector Lima, issued orders to "Call off all coastal patrols." This order, from the highest echelon of the military government, effectively opened up the coast of Argentina to the landings described by the *Admiral Graf Spee* men. But despite the chase being called off by the navy, the reports of submarines off the coast kept coming in. There was a determined cover-up by highly placed members of the military government to ensure that U-530 and U-977 were the only "real" Nazi submarines seen to have made it across the Atlantic. Columnist Drew Pearson of the Bell Syndicate wrote on July 24, 1945,

> Along the coast of Patagonia, many Germans own land, which contains harbors deep enough for submarine landings. And if submarines could get to Argentine-Uruguayan waters from Germany, as they definitely did, there is no reason why they could not go a little further south to Patagonia. Also there is no reason to believe why Hitler couldn't have been on one of them.

Speaking from exile in Rio de Janeiro in October 1945, Raúl Damonte Taborda—the former chair of the Argentine congressional committee on Nazi activities, and a close colleague of Silvano Santander—said that he believed it was possible Adolf Hitler was in Argentina. Damonte said that it was "indicated" that submarines other than U-530 and U-977 had been sunk by their crews after reaching the Argentine coast; these "undoubtedly" carried politicians, technicians, or even "possibly Adolf Hitler."

GOV'T PROBES RUMOR HITLER IN ARGENTINA

State Dep't Asks Embassy There to Launch Inquiry Into It

WASHINGTON, July 17-Æ-The State Department is going to check u· on a report that Adolf Hitler and Eva Braun are hiding out in Argentina.

It directed the U. S. Embassy in Buenos Aires to follow up a Chicago Times story from Montevideo which said Hitler and his alleged wife have found haven in Patagonia.

Argentina has assured other allied governments that it would not harbor Axis war criminals.

The Chicago Times story was from correspondent Vincent DePascal. He said he was virtually certain that Hitler and the woman he is supposed to have married in Berlin's last days "are on an immense, German-owned estate in Patagonia."

"The pair reportedly landed on a lonely shore from a German submarine which supposedly returned to surrender to the allies," DePascal wrote.

Other stories have had Hitler put to death on his own orders. Some Germans claimed to have seen his and Eva Braun's burning bodies in Berlin. Allied sources have not agreed definitely on what happened to them.

AN AP ARTICLE published in the *Lewiston Daily Sun*, July 18, 1945: One of many newspaper reports taken seriously by U.S. authorities that Hitler and Eva Braun had been landed by submarine on the Argentine coast and were living in the depths of Patagonia.

Che Guevara's father, Ernesto Guevara Lynch, who was an active anti-Nazi "commando" in Argentina throughout the 1930s and '40s, was also convinced: "Not long after the German army was defeated in Europe, many of the top Nazis arrived in our country and entered through the seaside resort of Villa Gessell, located south of Buenos Aires. They came in several German submarines."

When asked by the authors about the submarines as recently as 2008, the Argentine justice minister, Aníbal Fernández, said simply, "In Argentina in 1945, anything was possible."

Chapter 19

To Patagonia

THE EXILES STAYED JUST ONE NIGHT *at the Estancia Moromar. The first thing the couple would have done was bathe in an attempt to wash away the lingering stench of the U-boat. Fegelein had provided a selection of traveling outfits and now arranged for their old clothes to be burned. Hitler and Eva stayed in separate rooms. On the dressing table in Eva's bedroom was her favorite perfume, Chanel No. 5; a bottle of Canadian Club whisky with an ice bucket and a tumbler; a pack of Lucky Strike cigarettes and a silver cigarette case—which Fegelein had not had time to get engraved with her distinctive "EB" monogram; and a gold Dunhill "Unique" lighter.*

The grass airfield at the ranch had been laid out in 1933, shortly after Carlos Idaho Gesell had bought the property. The next morning, July 30, 1945, Hitler, Eva, and Fegelein, accompanied by Blondi, boarded the same Argentine air force Curtiss biplane that had picked Fegelein up at Mar del Plata. They would travel the last leg of the months-long journey that had brought them nearly one-third of the way around the globe, from the rubble-strewn battlefield of Berlin to a world of huge, silent horizons.

Although Hitler had been thoroughly briefed about the vastness of Patagonia, such knowledge was theoretical, and during the daytime flight westward he was amazed at the physical spectacle unrolling below him. After what would have been a three-and-a-half-hour flight, the Curtiss Condor landed at another grass strip just outside the town of Neuquén in the north of Patagonia. None of the passengers bothered to leave the aircraft as a small tanker truck drew up, and the pilot supervised a group of men in air force uniforms while they refueled it. Topped up, the Condor was soon back in the air and heading southwest, while from the right-hand windows the three passengers watched the majestic, snow-capped Andes Mountains unrolling under the afternoon sun. Two hours later, with the waters of Lake Nahuel Huapí glinting below as dusk approached on July 30, the biplane came in to land again, bumped over the grass, and taxied to a halt on the airfield at San Ramón.

In this region, the Estancia San Ramón was the first officially delineated estate to be fenced in. The ranch is isolated, approached only via an unsurfaced road past San Carlos de Bariloche's first airfield. The family of Prince Stephan zu Schaumburg-Lippe—who had been, with his ardently patriotic princess, one of the regular poker players at the German Embassy in Buenos Aires—had bought the estate as long ago as 1910 and still owned it in 1945. In 1943 Prince Stephan and Wilhelm von Schön, respectively the Nazi government's consul and ambassador in Chile, had been called back to Germany as part of the planning for Aktion Feuerland. They left South America through Buenos Aires, where they held lengthy discussions with the de facto ambassador, the local millionaire Ludwig Freude.

A MAJOR VULNERABILITY IN THE PLAN had been the fact that it was Adm. Wilhelm Canaris of the Abwehr who had first spotted the Estancia San Ramón, when he had used it himself as a bolt-hole during his escape across Patagonia in 1915. In 1944, when Bormann was finalizing plans for the Führer's escape, Canaris's knowledge of the estate, and of Villa Winter on Fuerteventura—which had been set up by his Abwehr agent Gustav Winter—was more than dangerous. Canaris—as mentioned in Chapter 2—was a long-time and effective conspirator against Hitler. Although Canaris had covered his tracks for years, he had still attracted suspicion from Himmler and the SS hierarchy, who, on general principles, had long wished to absorb Canaris's military intelligence network under the Reich Main Security Office (RSHA). Canaris finally lost his ability to stay one step ahead of the SS and the Gestapo in February 1944, when two of his Abwehr agents in Turkey defected to the British just before the Gestapo could arrest them for links to an anti-Nazi group. Canaris failed to account for the Abwehr's activities satisfactorily to Hitler, who had had enough of the lack of reporting to the Nazi hierarchy and instructed SS Gen. Hermann Fegelein to oversee the incorporation of the Abwehr into the RSHA. The admiral was dismissed from his post and parked in a pointless job as head of the Office for Commercial and Economic Warfare.

The involvement of Abwehr personnel in the July 20, 1944, bomb plot finally led to Canaris being placed under house arrest; the noose tightened slowly, but eventually he was being kept in chains in a cellar under Gestapo headquarters on Prinz-Albrechtstrasse in Berlin. On February 7, 1945, he was sent to Flossenbürg concentration camp, but even then he was kept alive for some time—there have been suggestions that even at this late date Himmler thought that Canaris might be useful as an intermediary with the Allies.

Bormann could not take the risk that such a potentially credible witness to the refuge in Argentina and the staging post between Europe and South America would survive to fall into Allied hands. In the Führerbunker on April 5, 1945, Bormann's ally SS Gen. Kaltenbrunner presented Hitler with some highly incriminating evidence—supposedly, the "diaries" of Wilhelm Canaris. After reading a few pages marked for him by Kaltenbrunner, the Führer flew into a rage and signed the proffered death warrant. On the direct orders of Heinrich "Gestapo" Müller, SS Lt. Col. Walter Huppenkothen and SS Maj. Otto Thorbeck were sent to Flossenbürg to tie off this loose end. On the morning of April 9, stripped naked in a final ignominy, Adm. Canaris was hanged from a wooden beam. Although reports of his death vary, his end was not a quick one. At 4:33 that afternoon, Huppenkothen sent a secret Enigma-encoded message to Müller via Müller's subordinate, SS Gen. Richard Glücks. The latter was "kindly requested" to inform SS Gen. Müller immediately, by telephone, telex, or messenger, that Huppenkothen's mission had been completed as ordered. The only major figure who could have pieced together the details of Hitler's escape and refuge in Argentina was dead.

IN 1945, THE GERMANS HAD COMPLETE CONTROL over access to San Carlos de Bariloche and the Estancia San Ramón. No one got in or out of the area without express permission from the senior Nazis in the area. On July 24, Drew Pearson had written in his syndicated column,

> It may take a long time to find out whether Hitler and his bride Eva Braun escaped to Patagonia. The country is a series of vast Nazi-owned ranches where German is spoken almost exclusively and where Hitler could be hidden easily, and successfully for years. The ranches in this southern part of Argentina cover thousands of acres and have been under Nazi [note: there were Germans in the area long before the Nazis dominated] management for generations. It would have been impossible for any non-German to penetrate the area to make a thorough investigation as to Hitler's whereabouts.

The staff at the isolated San Ramón estate had been busy for days since being given advance warning of the impending arrival of important guests. The arrival of a security team of *Admiral Graf Spee* sailors a week before had already added to the staff's workload, and two new faces had joined the weekly shopping trip into San Carlos de Bariloche to ensure that no gossip betrayed the guests' presence. The cook at San Ramón, Carmen Torrentuigi, would have been thoroughly briefed on her guests' dietary requirements. Her rightly famed "Cordero Patagónico," Patagonian lamb, was off the menu for the time being, as were many of the other meats from the traditional Argentine "asado" or barbecue. The menu was to be heavy on vegetables, but with classic German dishes like liver dumplings and squab (baby pigeon). *She was to find out later that that was "his favorite" of the many meals she would prepare for him and the woman who was soon to be his wife.* The Germans on the estate had taken the official news of Hitler's "death" with an air of calm disbelief; it was with little surprise that Carmen, dressed in a clean starched apron over her homespun clothes, was introduced to the guests before supper.

Hitler and Eva Braun stayed in the main house at San Ramón for nine months. Contact with Martin Bormann, who was still on the move in Europe, was infrequent, but his "Organization" in Argentina was finalizing security plans for the couple's permanent residence. This more private and secure refuge was nearing completion; named Inalco, it was fifty-six miles from San Ramón, on the Chilean border near Villa Angostura.

URSULA, EVA'S DAUGHTER BY HITLER, *arrived at the Estancia San Ramón in September 1945. The six-year-old Ursula, nicknamed "Uschi," had sailed first-class from Spain; her uncle Hermann Fegelein met her off the ship in Buenos Aires and brought her to join her parents, flying into the airstrip on the hillside above the ranch on the same Curtiss Condor they had used.* Uschi's existence had been kept strictly secret from the German people, as indeed had her parents' relationship, although the rest of the world knew about Hitler and Eva as early as May 15, 1939, when *Time* magazine gave details of how "dark-haired, buxom Eva Braun, 28, had her apartment rent paid, as usual, by her old friend in Berlin. . . . To her friends Eva Braun confided that she expected her friend [Adolf Hitler] to marry her within a year." It was not to be. Hitler believed that his grip on the public mind depended upon his being seen as wholly dedicated to Germany's destiny. The child was said to have been born in San Remo, Italy, on New Year's Eve 1938. Her parents had not seen her since April 11, 1945, the last day of a secret three-day trip to Bavaria to visit Uschi for what they had both thought might be the last time. Hitler's double Gustav Weber would have covered for the Führer while the couple slipped away. Brought up largely by distant relatives of Eva's mother, the blonde-haired little girl had spent many happy hours at Berchtesgaden playing with Gitta, the daughter of Eva's childhood friend Herta Schneider, and was photographed and filmed extensively. After the war, she was variously described as Gitta Schneider's sister or Hermann Fegelein and Gretl Braun Fegelein's daughter—yet their only child, Eva, was born after the war ended. Uschi was neither. In 1945, she may have already spoken basic Spanish; *in 1943, Bormann would have arranged for both her and her caregivers (her "family") to be issued with Spanish documents, and on his instructions the "family" had spent much of 1944 learning the language.*

When Uschi arrived in Argentina in September 1945, Eva Braun was again pregnant—"as a last mission for Hitler"—having conceived in Munich in March 1945. The couple was still unmarried, and rumors of her pregnancy had been rife among the people in the bunker. (It was in fact her third pregnancy; she had had a stillborn child in 1943. August Schullten, gynecologist and chief physician of the Krankenhausen Links, a hospital in Munich, attended. He died in a car crash later that same year.) With the family now safe in Argentina, and with Eva's brother-in-law Hermann Fegelein on hand to give her away, the private Catholic chapel at San Ramón would have made a perfect place for the couple's real marriage. (The doubles allegedly "married" in the bunker on April 29, 1945—over twenty-four hours after the real couple fled from Berlin. There were no surviving witnesses to the ceremony except for Bormann.)

In March 1946, the San Ramón estate employees were called to a meeting and told that their guests had been tragically killed in a car crash close to the property. They were warned never to discuss the matter again. The trail in Patagonia was to go cold; not only were Hitler and Braun "dead" in the Berlin bunker, but now they were "dead" again in Argentina. If anyone managed to follow the Hitlers to Argentina, all they would find were more stories of corpses burned beyond recognition, this time in an automobile accident.

THE BRITISH AND U.S. GOVERNMENTS had put intense pressure on the Argentine authorities to repatriate to Germany all remaining members of the *Admiral Graf Spee* crew—those who had not escaped or disappeared—whether or not they had married local women. On February 16, 1946, the British troopship RML *Highland Monarch*, escorted by HMS *Ajax* (one of the Royal Navy cruisers that had driven the *Admiral Graf Spee* into Uruguayan waters in December 1939), arrived first in Buenos Aires, and then in Montevideo, to ship the German sailors home. The Argentine authorities turned over about nine hundred identity books (military identification papers) in a couple of mailbags. The boarding was chaotic, the *Highland Monarch* was ordered to sea as soon as possible, and no one had the time to check the papers against the individuals who had embarked. Despite the Allies' insistence, many officers and men of the "pocket battleship" had simply disappeared into Argentina. It was only on the long voyage to Germany that the documents and men were cross-referenced. Rumor had it that among them were eighty-six U-boat crewmen, whose presence in Argentina the Argentine, U.S., and British authorities were supposedly at a loss to explain, since the crews of the surrendered U-530 and U-977 had already been repatriated via the United States. In fact, documents in the British National Archives prove that the British identified everyone on the *Highland Monarch*, and none of them were submariners—so the fate of the men from the other three boats, U-880, U-1235 and U-518, remains undocumented.

THE "STAUFFENBERG BOMB" of July 20, 1944, had injured Hitler more extensively than the Nazi propaganda machine had made public. The deep cold of the Patagonian winter now contributed to his "rheumatism" and he suffered from inflamed joints and stiffness in his right hand, but more distressing was the fact that the surgeons had been unable to remove all the oak splinters that had sprayed from the table that saved his life. The constant pressure from an oak fragment lodged deep in the nasal bones between his eyes caused him acute neuralgic pain during the stay at Estancia San Ramón. Hitler needed surgery.

Since it was judged too much of a security risk for him to attend a hospital in Buenos Aires, he and Eva traveled north to the province of Córdoba and the Nazi hospital and health spa at the Gran Hotel Viena, at Miramar on the Mar Chiquita lake. The Gran Hotel Viena was built by an Abwehr agent, an early Nazi Party member named Max Pahlke, between 1943 and 1945—the same period as the construction of Villa Winter on Fuerteventura and the extension of the airfield at San Carlos de Bariloche. Pahlke, the capable manager of the Argentine branch of the German multinational Mannesmann, had acquired

Argentine citizenship in the 1930s, but was well known to the Allies for his espionage work in South America.

The building contained eighty-four rooms, a medical facility staffed by doctors, nurses, and massage therapists, a large swimming pool, a library, and a dining room that seated two hundred. Every room had air conditioning and heating, granite floors, walls lined with imported Carrara marble, and bronze chandeliers. The facilities included a bank, a wine cellar, a food warehouse, a bakery, a slaughterhouse, an electricity generating plant, and garages with their own fuel supply. Of the seventy hotel employees, only twelve were locals from Miramar, all of whom worked outside the facility and had no contact with hotel guests. The remaining fifty-eight employees were either from Buenos Aires or from Germany, and all spoke German. In addition to a modern telephone system that connected guests with the rest of the world, the Gran Hotel Viena also had a tall telecommunications antenna on the seventy-foot-high water tower. This vantage point, and a further tower just down the coast, enabled watchful guards to spot any approach to the hotel by land, water, or air.

The tiny market town of Miramar was a strange location for a huge, state-of-the-art hotel and spa complex, miles away from any major roads or other commercial routes. Pahlke, known for his business sense, had built Mannesmann Argentina into a massively profitable business. Pahlke supervised the opening of the hotel from December 1945 to March 1946; he then left. A former German army colonel named Carl Martin Krueger, the Viena's "chief of security," was put in charge. An immaculate figure known locally as "The Engineer," Krueger had arrived in Miramar in 1943. He did everything to make the Hitlers' stay at the medical facility as comfortable as possible; they had an exclusive suite complete with AH-monogrammed blankets, sheets, towels, and dishes.

With many local supporters, Hitler and his wife often took day-trips to Balnearia, a town some three miles from Mar Chiquita, to take tea. He had his photograph taken with other senior Nazis and would sign copies of *Mein Kampf* for well-wishers. One witness to these mundane encounters said that Hitler was often "lost in thought" and would say, "Now, I am far from here." The Hitlers enjoyed their stay at the exclusive, luxurious waterside hotel. One of his bodyguards recalled that the couple would regularly walk along the shore, Hitler commenting on the wonderful sunsets. The operation to remove the splinters at first seemed to be successful, but the pain in Hitler's face would return to plague him in later life.

In February 1946, Juan Domingo Perón was finally voted into untrammeled power as president of Argentina, which must have eased any latent fears of pursuit on the part of some of the fugitive Nazis. During the late 1940s, Hitler himself would move fairly freely between strategic points in Argentina, around a triangle based on San Carlos de Bariloche; the home of his friends and early financial backers, the Eichhorns, at La Falda; and Mar Chiquita. He owned huge tracts of land in all three areas.

MEANWHILE, MARTIN BORMANN WAS STILL IN EUROPE, controlling the network in Argentina from afar. He was in regular contact with Ludwig Freude through the portable T43 encryption system. He also made good use of his wide-ranging contacts, most importantly inside the Vatican, to advance his own plans for exile. After his abortive trip to Flensburg in May 1945 (see end of Chapter 15), Bormann had hidden in the Bavarian hills for five months before risking a visit to the old Nazi heartland of Munich, the Bavarian capital. J. A. Friedl, a former Nazi Party member and senior sergeant of Munich police who had known Bormann since the early days, saw him there in October 1945. Friedl recollected that Bormann had been "with some other men in a car, parked in front of the Spanish Consulate." When Friedl approached the car and greeted his old comrade, they chatted briefly; Bormann told Friedl that he was trying to arrange a visa to enter Spain.

Bormann stayed in Munich until July 1946, when he was spotted again, this time by a man who held no love for him. Jakob Glas, a disgruntled former chauffeur of Bormann's—who had been fired in a disagreement over stolen garden vegetables from the Führer's personal Berchtesgaden plot—also saw his old boss in a car, riding in the front seat next to the driver. The car was moving slowly, and Glas got a good look at Bormann; he was dressed in ordinary, rather shabby civilian clothes. According to the associated press, Glas said, "There were some other men with him, but I didn't get a close look at them. I was too busy staring after Bormann." Glas's report prompted the U.S. Army to mount a house-to-house search for Bormann, but without success. He returned to his personal "Alpine Redoubt," where he was protected by two hundred former members of the Waffen-SS (see Chapter 21, page 261). Toward the end of the summer of 1947, it was time for Bormann to get on the move again.

DURING THIS PERIOD, THE FBI was taking reports of Hitler being in Latin America very seriously. Thousands of documents pertaining to Hitler from these years are still classified as Top Secret on both sides of the Atlantic; nevertheless, and despite the very heavy censorship of the few files released into the public domain, some information can be gleaned.

A report from the Bureau's Los Angeles office to Director Hoover on June 5, 1947, details material that reached the office on May 16 of that year. The origin of the information was rather naively located near either Buenos Aires or Rio de Janeiro (thousands of miles apart), but it apparently came from a familiar and trusted contact. The contact knew a former French Resistance man, who had visited Casino, near Rio Grande, a town on the southeast coast of Brazil just above the Uruguayan border. The Frenchman claimed to have seen Eva Braun and Adolf Hitler sitting at a table in a crowded hotel dining room. This was enough to prompt Hoover to ask for more detail. He received it via secret air courier on August 6, 1947, in a seven-pager from his Rio de Janeiro office entitled "Adolph Hitler and Eva Braun Information Concerning." The former member of the French Resistance—who was traveling commercially in the Americas and had ambitions to move into journalism—had been told, through a number of contacts in Latin America, that the town of Casino in the Brazilian state of Rio Grande de Sol might provide something of interest. (The FBI was thorough in checking the provenance of their informant, whose name has unfortunately been lost to the censor's pen.)

The Rio office of the FBI described Casino as consisting "of approximately two hundred scattered residences. The majority of the inhabitants are German nationalists or are of German descent." The field

June 5, 1947

Re: ADO⬛PH HITLER AND EVA BRAUN
     INFORMATION CONCE⬛⬛⬛⬛⬛

        Near the middle of the table ⬛ observed a woman whom ⬛
immediately felt ⬛ had seen before. In refreshing ⬛ memory ⬛ suddenly
arrived at the conclusion that she was EVA BRAUN of whom ⬛ had observed
many photographs but had never seen in person. Upon recognizing this
woman ⬛ felt that HITLER might be nearby and examined more closely the
other members of the group sitting at the large table. There was one man
in particular having numerous characteristics of HITLER. This man was
described as having the same general build and age of HITLER, was clean-
shaven, and had a very short German crew haircut. This man was rather
emaciated and ⬛ felt that this party was definitely HITLER, but ⬛
was not as sure as ⬛ was that the woman described above was EVA BRAUN.
The HITLER suspect appeared to be friendly with everyone at the table.

        After the performance, which was well received, dancing was
held and a number of people including guests at the hotel and those at
the large table remained for dancing. It was noticed that the young girl
stayed with an elderly woman most of the time. However, ⬛ was introduced
to the young girl and ⬛ She was very talkative in
German, gay, and rather proud. She seemed to want to impress ⬛ This
girl had, during one of the intermissions, given ⬛ a bank note as a
sort of gratuity for a fine performance and stated that she hoped ⬛ would
keep it for a souvenir.

        ⬛ learned the name of the young girl was ⬛ABAVA (phonetic) and
she claimed to be a German but was now a Chilian and resided in Chile.
⬛ mentioned that these people who claimed to be Chilian spoke German
entirely and there was no evidence of the Spanish or Portuguese language
being used, which made ⬛ doubt that they had not resided in that section
of the country very long.

        During the next day ⬛ and ⬛ further circulated
in the village and ⬛ took a trip out to the aforementioned manufacturing
plant near Rio Grande. ⬛ further noticed that everyone spoke German.

        During the performance of the second evening at the hotel,
the same table was set up but on this evening the table contained an extra
chair and as of the previous evening the occupants of the table came in late ⬛
⬛ again observed the girl whom ⬛ thought to be EVA BRAUN and the young
girl but did not observe the man whom ⬛ judged to be HITLER on the
previous evening. ⬛ did notice a very large man of approximately fifty

                              - 7 -

INITIAL REPORT TO J. Edgar Hoover of Hitler's presence in Casino, Brazil,
June 5, 1947. Hoover immediately asked for more details.

Rio de Janeiro, Brazil
August 6, 1947

SECRET - AIR COURIER

Director, FBI

Re: ADOLPH HITLER AND EVA BRAUN
     INFORMATION CONCERNING

Dear Sir:

Reference is made to Bureau letter dated July 9, 1947
bearing the above-captioned title.

in the State of Rio Grande Do Sul, advised that the
town referred to as Casino is a suburb of the city of Rio
Grande. This suburb commonly is referred to as Casino, although it is a part of the municipality of Rio Grande.
advised that Casino was located in a summer resort
area and that it consisted of approximately two hundred scattered
residences. The majority of the inhabitants are German nationals
or are of German descent.

According to   it could be expected that
a Nazi refugee would seek asylum or assistance in the Casino
area because of the existence of the predominantly German
element. The center of activity in Casino is a large hotel
which includes a gambling casino. Since gambling has been pro-
hibited, the hotel manager from time to time has endeavored to
arrange some form of entertainment for guests and visitors from
nearby Rio Grande. It may be pointed out that the Casino section
is on the coast and that the beach which borders the suburb
regularly is frequented by residents of the city of Rio Grande.

With regard to the alleged necessity for passes to
travel in the area of Casino, it is believed that the allegation
is without specific foundation. For the information of the
Bureau, foreign nationals in Brazil are required by law to
possess "carteiras de identidade", which are identification
cards issued officially by the Brazilian Government. Often
when traveling from one city to another by automobile police
may request drivers and passengers to exhibit their identification cards or their passports. Such a request may be

ENCLOSURE ATTACHED   RECORDE

An FBI REPORT to Hoover, dated August 6, 1947, giving further details of
Hitler and Braun's time in Casino, Brazil.

officer also reported that "no one could live in Casino except persons who had homes there prior to the time it became a military area and blocked off from the rest of the surrounding community. This area allegedly became restricted three to four months before the end of the war in Europe." It is no coincidence that this was the time when Aktion Feuerland was getting into top gear and Bormann was moving people and matériel around. The Resistance veteran's account continued: "This was an unusual community in as much as it was necessary to secure a pass to enter the vicinity of the town, and furthermore it was practically of one hundred percent German population. This area lacked commercial establishments and consisted of villas or homes and a large hotel, which had been remodeled and was very modern. It appeared in size out of proportion to the size of the community." Hotel Casino had one other feature in common with Villa Winter on Fuerteventura and Gran Hotel Viena at Miramar: a very large radio antenna, in this case parallel to the ground and fenced off.

The Resistance man had booked at the hotel in advance (and simultaneously arranged passes to the area) as part of a group, with another Frenchman, a Russian, a Nicaraguan, an Australian, and an American. Their reason was ostensibly to attend three nights of entertainment, including a performance of *Les Sylphides*, the famous ballet in one act set to Chopin's music. With the exception of the Russian—a man well known in Brazil, at whom the management apparently looked somewhat askance—the party were welcomed courteously, both at the hotel and when invited into local homes.

The first hint of something a little strange came when the Frenchman observed one of the hotel maids speaking to an attractive teenage girl with chestnut hair, who caught his eye when she gave the servant a "Heil Hitler" salute. For the first evening's ballet performance, a large ballroom was filled to capacity by several hundred people, described by a stage manager as "rich South Americans," but the Frenchman noticed that they all spoke German. In the course of the evening, spotlights played extensively over the audience, and at one champagne-filled table the Frenchman suddenly recognized a distinctively scarred face. He identified him as a former Nazi officer named Weismann—a man who he feared might remember his own face, from occupied Paris. The former Resistance man had been trained in the old Bertillon or *portrait parlé* system of identification, and he was sure of his powers of recognition.

Now alerted, the Frenchman claimed also to have recognized—from her many photographs—a woman whom he identified as Eva Hitler, née Braun. When he realized who she was he scanned the table more closely, and sure enough, "There was one man . . . having numerous characteristics of Hitler." Though thinner, he had the same general build and age as Hitler, was clean-shaven (as described by almost all of the witnesses in Argentina), and had very short-cropped hair. He appeared to be friendly with everyone at his table.

Later that same evening, the Frenchman was introduced to the young girl he had seen earlier. She gave her name as Abava, a recent German immigrant who was now a Chilean citizen. He learned that she was a "niece" of the woman he had recognized as Eva Braun and that most of the group was from Viña del Mar in central Chile, close to Villa Alemana (literally, German Town), a small city founded by immigrants in 1896. The Frenchman did not believe her; he had the distinct impression that "this young girl as well as the persons believed to be Hitler and Eva Braun actually lived in Casino." (However, the couple was simply vacationing there.) His general curiosity about the town, expressed under the cover of planning to write a travelogue describing this delightful and uncommercialized location, prompted the girl's immediate advice that it would not be a "fit subject" to write on—the people of Casino did not like tourists. Subsequent brushes with the hotel management and Casino chamber of commerce verified her opinion, and an hour after his meeting with the latter his party were asked abruptly to vacate their rooms, as "the hotel was full."

The next day, as the Frenchman was waiting, bags packed, for his car to pick him up, he saw the girl's "aunt" and two other people leave the hotel and walk toward the sea. The woman was wearing a short beach skirt, and in the daylight he was even more positive that she was Eva Braun.

Chapter 20

ADOLF HITLER'S VALLEY

IN 1943 ADM. KARL DÖNITZ had declared, "The German U-boat fleet is proud to have made an earthly paradise, an impregnable fortress for the Führer, somewhere in the world." The following year Dönitz told a graduating class of naval cadets in Kiel, "The German Navy has still a great role to play in the future. The German Navy knows all hiding places for the Navy to take the Führer to, should the need arise. There he can prepare his last measures in complete quiet."

Of all such possible locations, few fit the bill better than somewhere in Patagonia. The region extends over 386,000 square miles of Argentina and Chile—one and a half times the size of Texas. Its scenery is dramatically varied, from the windswept, barren coastal plains around San Matías Gulf to the alpine foothills of the Andes, from the lush pastures in the north to the glacier fields in the south. Philip Hamburger, writing for the *New Yorker* in 1948, was wrong when he dismissed it simply as "barren, wind-swept and rainy, a dreary, remote stretch of rock, thorn and sand, of black lava and volcanic ash. Only its western part is irrigated and under cultivation." However, he could not be faulted when he went on, "Scattered about are lonely sheep ranches, many of them owned by settlers of German descent. To an ex-Führer ... Patagonia would presumably be an attractive refuge."

Hamburger continued:

The way the Patagonian part of the stories goes, shortly after the arrival of the U-boats with their mysterious human cargo, travelers through this vast region began to hear tales of a huge estancia remote almost beyond imagination and surrounded by an electric fence. Behind the fence fierce dogs bark continuously. The Führer is naturally behind the fence. He never leaves the estate. He is unable to do so. Drugs, defeat and the shattering of his nervous system have left him monumentally wrecked and insane. He looks like a man over seventy. Eva Braun stays with him, for there is no other place to go.

Hamburger based his account on numerous tales that he heard while visiting Argentina—"this strange country, so different from the rest of the world, so far removed and other-planetary."

SOME DETAILS OF THE NAZIS' LIFE IN PATAGONIA, and of the refuge that Hamburger had imagined, were given to the Polish press in 1995 by a man who identified himself only as "Herr Schmidt." He said that his father had "worked in the Reich Main Security Office at Prinz Albrechtstrasse in Berlin . . . in the Gestapo center." Schmidt explained that his father was a high-ranking SS official who during the war often traveled around Europe; where, and what crimes his father had committed, Schmidt didn't know. In 1945, Schmidt was twelve years old and living with his mother and younger sister in Munich. His father had not come back from the war. Then, in 1948, his mother received extraordinary news: her husband was alive, living in Argentina, and his family was to join him. A few weeks later they went to Italy and from there sailed for Argentina on a Spanish ship. Ferdinand Eiffler, a senior Argentine Nazi organizer and close associate of Ludwig Freude, met them as they disembarked in Buenos Aires. The family was taken to a safe house in the suburb of Vicente López, where they were given new identity papers. A week later Schmidt's father came to the house, and, after an ecstatic family reunion, Eiffler took them in his car on a two-day trip.

They drove through towns with "exotic" names until they saw the Andes on the horizon. On a rough rural road, which Schmidt said was "barely visible" at times, they drove through San Carlos de Bariloche and around Lake Nahuel Huapí, then through the village of Villa La Angostura. They arrived at a set of gates; Eiffler showed papers to an armed guard, the gates were opened, and the car drove in.

"Schmidt's" description of his destination fits with similar accounts of the location of a Nazi colony called "the Center." The Center in "Adolf Hitler's Valley" (see map on page 219), was located around Inalco, the mansion owned by Hitler. The property surrounding Inalco—1.75 square miles—is known as Estancia Inalco. The Center was described by Heinrich Bethe, the former petty officer from the *Admiral Graf Spee*, who had met a second U-boat landing (the one not carrying Hitler) on the evening of July 28, 1945 (see Chapter 18, page 223). When Bethe's party was being driven to the Center in 1947 from his temporary base in the city of Neuquén, "There were valleys at first, but then they began to see mountains on whose summits they could see perpetual snow." After more than nine hours' driving, they finally arrived at what was apparently one of the classic ranches in the skirts of the Andes. After passing the first gate, they kept going for about three miles until they began to see some people; after that they saw a house in the distance, then some sheds and the main building. This also mirrors the mention in Paul Manning's book of Martin Bormann's hideout in Patagonia, where he lived until 1955, when President Juan Perón was forced from power: "A mountain retreat in the Argentinean Andes, a 5,000-acre cattle and sheep ranch about 60 miles south of San Carlos de Bariloche."

"Schmidt's" childhood memory was of three small neighborhoods widely spread out in a big, beautiful valley. In a solemn voice, his father told them that the place they had arrived at was called "Adolf Hitler's Valley" and that the neighborhoods were called respectively Deutschland (Germany), Heimat (loosely, Homeland), and Vaterland (Fatherland). Schmidt recalled his father telling him that German submarines had come to Argentina carrying the immense treasures of the Third Reich and that other treasures captured by the SS during the conquests of Europe had come by various different means. The family moved into a big, attractive house with a garden in the Heimat community. After the hunger of postwar Germany, they led an "almost luxurious life"—the family even had a servant, an old SS subordinate of his father's who took care of all the work in the garden and the house.

Heinrich Bethe also lived in the Center and described his more modest dwelling as "a small typical local cabin, it had one big room which served as a bedroom and living room, a small hearth, and all that was apparently needed to live comfortably in that area. On the left side was a bathroom and on the right a small room designed for keeping personal belongings." Bethe was allocated one of several offices off a corridor in one of the larger houses. The "quartermaster general" had his center of operations in the Center's main building, where sixteen people worked looking after the facilities and the grounds; nine Germans, three Chileans, and four Argentines.

"Schmidt" was sent to the German school in San Carlos de Bariloche. On the classroom walls there were portraits of Hitler, swastikas, and other decorations; it reminded the boy of his old school in Munich during the time of the Third Reich. All the students, regardless of age, had to join a youth organization. Although it was not called the Hitler Youth, it seemed very much like that paramilitary group to the young Schmidt. He recalled that he enjoyed the meetings, the marches, the drums, the military instruction, the war games, and the training with different firearms, all of which were pursued with an almost religious fervor. The discipline was severe, and youngsters were beaten for breaking the rules, poor grades, or a lazy attitude. There were lessons about the Third Reich and Hitler's activities, and everything was illustrated with films, slides, and photographs. The school had a "splendid" library that contained many copies of *Mein Kampf*, Hitler's and Goebbels's speeches, Rosenberg's books, annuals, old copies of the weekly Nazi propaganda newspaper *Das Reich*, and other Nazi books published during Hitler's time or secretly in West Germany after the war. The children were told that the Center was a small piece of the Third Reich, a haven where one day the struggle for a new and great Germany would begin, where the survivors would·begin to seek vengeance for the lost war. "We were educated as the avengers who would continue the work of our fathers." His schoolmates secretly told him that their fathers had also been in the SS or Gestapo or had held other important positions in the Third Reich, but they were not allowed to reveal their true surnames or ask others about theirs.

Nobody lived outside the valley; the members of the community grew most of their own food, and anything else they needed was brought in from the outside, from the nearby towns of San Carlos de Bariloche and San Martín de los Andes. Philip Hamburger told a similar tale in the *New Yorker*:

> Once a month the gates of the estancia swing open and a large black truck races down the driveway, careens onto the main road and heads for the main hamlet many miles distant, where a dozen stalwart blond men hop down and wander through the streets for ten or fifteen minutes, purchasing a bite to eat here and a trinket there. Then they hop into the truck and race back to the estancia.

IN 1946, "ADOLF HITLER'S VALLEY" was controlled by a mass murderer and wanted war criminal, SS and Police Gen. Ludolf von Alvensleben, known to his friends as "Bubi" (Little Boy). Born in 1901, Alvensleben came from the Prussian officer class and fought as a hussar at the end of World War I. After he became a Nazi Party member of the Reichstag in 1933, his rise was rapid: he commanded the 46th SS Regiment in Dresden the following year and became senior adjutant to Reichsführer-SS Himmler. During the war, he commanded SS and police units in the Crimea, and as commander of the Selbstschutz paramilitary forces in occupied western Poland he presided over mass executions and other atrocities. Married with four children, Alvensleben also fathered at least one illegitimate child as part of Himmler's "Lebensborn" program to breed a master race—Himmler was the "godfather" to Alvensleben's illegitimate son. Captured by the British in April 1945, Alvensleben walked out of his prison later that year while the guards at Neuengamme internment camp in Hamburg were celebrating Christmas. He fled with his family down the Vatican-organized ratlines through Italy (see Chapter 21, page 257), arriving in Argentina early in 1946. President

Perón and his "Blessed Evita" would welcome many such mass murderers to the Nazi home away from home among the lakes and mountains of Patagonia.

THE HITLERS MOVED INTO INALCO, THEIR NEW MANSION, after returning from holiday at Casino in Brazil in June 1947. Inalco Mansion is located in what had been plot number eight of the Nahuel Huapí agricultural colony, planned at the beginning of the twentieth century. The area was almost inaccessible until the 1960s, when the road that crosses the Andes into Chile was built. The area between San Carlos de Bariloche and Villa La Angostura in Río Negro province looks and feels distinctly European—specifically, Bavarian. It is an area of outstanding natural beauty, with snow-capped mountains and several lakes set amid mile after mile of untouched forest.

A short distance from the international border with Chile, at the very furthest end of Lake Nahuel Huapí, Inalco is almost hidden from view from the lake by two small islands. The offshoot of the lake where the house was built is called Última Esperanza or "Last Hope," since it was believed by early explorers to be the last hope of finding a water-borne route through to Chile. In the 1940s and '50s, Inalco was easily accessible only by boat or seaplane. One regular visitor, who was said to take Hitler on regular trips to meetings in the area, was a pilot coincidentally named Frederico Fuhrer, whose Grumman Goose seaplane was often tied up at the concrete jetty to the left of the main house's lawn. In the boathouse next to the jetty was Hitler's personal motorboat.

A ten-bedroom mansion, Inalco is a typical example of the style of famed Argentine architect Alejandro Bustillo, who openly acknowledged the influence of Albert Speer's work. Known colloquially as "Perón's favorite architect," Bustillo had designed the Llao Llao Hotel complex in San Carlos de Bariloche in 1939, and in mid- or late 1943 he was commissioned, almost certainly by Ludwig Freude, to work on a future home for Hitler. The mansion looks out on Lake Nahuel Huapí and the Andes—a stunning panorama of water, forest, and snow-capped mountains that rivals Obersalzberg. It is difficult to imagine a more beautiful alpine setting nor one that was so far beyond the reach of any but the most determined intruder. At the time, the house was accessible by motor vehicle only after an arduous journey along unmade roads and tracks from the nearest township, Villa La Angostura (as described by both "Schmidt" and Bethe). Lookout points were dotted around the neighboring forested hills, guarding the air and water approaches to the property. One puzzling aspect—considering how expensive the mansion must have been to build in the 1940s, and what a major task it must have been to bring the building materials to such an isolated location—was that its position, surrounded by hills and native towering trees, left it in constant shadow, never in direct sunlight.

Behind the house was a huge underground fuel tank that powered the electrical generators for the valley, and to one side a mound, now covered with trees, shows evidence of underground chambers and ventilation shafts. Heinrich Bethe's account of the Center described underground steel-lined chambers beneath the offices, where the "most important and sinister documents of that century" were kept. In 2008, the caretaker on the property warned that the mound was dangerous and kept collapsing in on itself. He said that when he first took over the job at Estancia Inalco he had to attend an interview at a local house where the property manager lived, and he remembered two massive bronze plaques decorated with swastikas on the wall of the main hall.

As well as the main house, Bustillo also designed and built a pastiche of a medieval-style watchtower at Peninsula San Pedro called the "Saracen tower" by locals; invisible from the main road, it can be seen only from the waters of Lake Nahuel Huapí or from the air. From the top of the tower a watchful observer could see virtually the whole lake and any aircraft or boats approaching Inalco from the Argentine side. Omar Contreras, a former journalist who is now the minister of tourism for Río Negro province, remembered visiting this tower as a young boy with his father at the end of the 1960s; Contreras senior worked for SS Col. Friedrich "Fritz" Lantschner's construction company. Contreras remembered being surprised when he saw the tower; he thought it was a castle, and beyond it he could see Lake Nahuel Huapí. A tall, fair-haired German chatted with his father and took them into the tower; Contreras thought he was Friedrich Lantschner. The hall had a double wooden door leading to a big room. Being a curious boy, Contreras walked through, and he remembered being surprised at seeing a number of Nazi flags inside—he recognized them from war comics. Back in the main room, he saw a group of about ten people talking in what he thought was German. In the car on the way home, he asked his father about the flags, but his father replied, "We do not talk about that."

INALCO WAS HITLER'S MAIN RESIDENCE from June 1947 until October 1955, and it was here that the former Kriegsmarine petty officer, Heinrich Bethe, was to become his closest servant. For Eva and her young daughters, living at Inalco was at first idyllic; during the summers they swam in the ice-cold waters of the lake, and in the winter enjoyed the skiing at the nearby mountain resort Cerro Catedral. In the early years, President Perón would visit too, skiing and climbing in the mountains with his Nazi friends from the Club Andino Bariloche, a mountaineering association set up in 1931 by Otto Meiling.

Hitler was in congenial company at the Center and on his regular trips to San Carlos de Bariloche; the town was home to hundreds of Nazis after World War II. A small yellow-brick building in the town center housed a delicatessen once owned by SS Capt. Erich Priebke, who was also chairman of the board of governors of the city's most prestigious German private school, Primo Capraro. (In 1996, after intense international pressure, Argentina finally extradited him. At the time of this writing in 2010, Priebke was serving a life sentence in Italy for his role in the massacre of 335 Italians at the Ardeatine caves in Rome on March 24, 1944.) Across the road from Priebke's delicatessen was the Club Andino Bariloche. Its membership from the late 1940s included the famous Stuka pilot Col. Hans-Ulrich Rudel, the Luftwaffe's most highly decorated ace and a close confidant of Hitler, as well as Friedrich Lantschner and his brother Gustav.

The town was also home for many years to an Austrian SS sergeant named Josef Schwammberger, a noted sadist who was eventually convicted of killing thirty-four victims personally and being directly responsible for the deaths of 274 others in the Polish ghetto and camp at Przemyśl. (Argentina finally agreed to his extradition in 1987; found guilty of murder by a West German court in 1992, he died in prison in 2004.) At the town hall, the "Angel of Death" Dr. Josef Mengele, the SS captain notorious for his medical experiments at Auschwitz, had to take his driving test twice in the 1940s. Others who lived in or visited the area at various dates included SS Lt. Col. Adolf Eichmann, the functionary who made Reinhard Heydrich's "Final Solution" a reality; SS Capt. Eduard Roschmann, christened "the Butcher of Riga"; SS Capt. Aribert Heim, Mauthausen concentration camp's own "Dr. Death"; and Martin Bormann himself. None of them except Eichmann were ever caught, and he only when he returned to live in the Argentine capital and became more accessible to his hunters.

President Juan Perón explained: "When the war was over, some useful Germans helped us build our factories and make the best use of what we had, and in time they were able to help themselves too."

IN 1947, WITH HITLER AND HIS FAMILY SECURE under the watchful eyes of senior SS officers and with Perón newly sworn in as president, Martin Bormann began to conclude his clandestine work in Europe. He was ready for his own final move to the south. One last meeting in Europe would seal his pact with the Peróns.

Chapter 21

GREEDY ALLIES, LOYAL FRIENDS

ON JUNE 6, 1947, ARGENTINA'S FIRST LADY left for a "rainbow" tour of Europe aboard a Douglas DC-4 Skymaster lent by the Spanish government. The metaphor came from a July 14 *Time* magazine cover: "Eva Perón: Between two worlds, an Argentine rainbow." President Perón, most of his government, and thousands of well-wishers saw her off. A second plane followed, carrying the first lady's wardrobe, the party's luggage, and numerous boxes (with their contents making a second clandestine trip across the Atlantic)—the "Rainbow" was prudently carrying her pot of gold with her. Evita was accompanied by her brother Juan Duarté, her personal hairdresser Julio Alcaraz (who also guarded her extensive collection of jewelry), and two Spanish diplomats sent by Franco to accompany her to her first destination, Madrid. Also on the aircraft was Alberto Dodero, a billionaire shipping-line owner who financed the trip. Dodero was a "flashy free-spending tycoon who dazzled even the free-spending Argentines." His ships would bring thousands of Nazis and other European fascists to Argentina.

Traveling ahead of Eva's party was Father Hernán Benítez, a Jesuit priest and an old friend of her husband's. Benítez had been briefed by Cardinal Antonio Caggiano, the archbishop of the Argentine city of Rosario, who was a strong link in the chain that led escaping Nazis to their new lives in Argentina. Caggiano had visited Pope Pius XII in Rome in March 1946 to collect his red hat. At a meeting with Cardinal Eugène Tisserant, Caggiano, in the name of the "Government of the Argentine Republic," had offered his country as a refuge for French war criminals in hiding in Rome, "whose political attitude during the recent war would expose them, should they return to France, to harsh measures and private revenge." Now it was the turn of the Germans. Bishop Alois Hudal was Bormann's main contact in the Vatican. A committed anticommunist, the Austrian-born, Jesuit-trained Hudal had been a "clerofascist" (clerical supporter of Mussolini) and an honorary holder of the Nazis' Gold Party Badge. Bishop Hudal was the Commissioner of the Episcopate for German-speaking Catholics in Italy, as well as father confessor to Rome's German community. In 1944, he had taken control of the Austrian division of the Papal Commission of Assistance (PCA), set up to help displaced persons. The PCA, with the help of Bormann's money, was to form the backbone of the ratlines organized to help escaping Nazi war criminals. (Note: *ratline*, a term often used in reference to Nazi escape routes, is formally defined by the U.S. Department of Defense dictionary of military terms as an organized effort for moving personnel and/or matériel by clandestine means across a denied area or border.)

Among the thousands of men Hudal helped to escape justice were the commandants of both Sobibor and Treblinka extermination camps, SS lieutenants Franz Stangl and Gustav Wagner. After escaping American captivity in Austria, Stangl reached Rome, where Hudal found a safe house for him, gave him money, and arranged a Red Cross passport with a Syrian visa. Erich Priebke, Josef Mengele, and Eichmann's assistant Alois Brunner were just a few of the infamous murderers who also passed safely through the Nazi bishop's hands on the way to Alberto Dodero's ships.

In 1947, Hudal's activities were exposed for the first time when a German-language Catholic newspaper, *Passauer Neue Presse*, accused him of running a Nazi escape organization, but this did not stop him. On August 31, 1948, Bishop Hudal wrote to President Perón requesting 5,000 Argentine visas—3,000 for German and 2,000 for Austrian "soldiers . . . whose wartime sacrifice" had saved Western Europe from Soviet domination.

WITH A LARGE ESCORT OF SPANISH FIGHTER PLANES, Evita's airliner took off on June 7 from the town of Villa Cisneros (present-day Dakhla) in the Spanish Sahara, destination Madrid. A crowd of three million Madrileños awaited her at the airport, which was decked with flowers, flags, and tapestries. Like visiting royalty, her arrival was marked by a twenty-one-gun salute, and she rode with El Caudillo—"the Leader"—Franco to the El Prado palace in an open-topped limousine, through adoring crowds chanting her name. Awaiting her was a cornucopia of expensive gifts. She was adored in every city she visited; the dazzling first lady behaved like a queen, and Spaniards—after years of civil war and the drab authoritarianism of the Franco regime—took the beautiful Argentinean to their hearts.

The all-conquering Evita left Spain for Rome on June 25, 1947. Father Benítez would smooth her way in the Vatican with the aid of Bishop Hudal. Two days after she arrived she was given an audience with Pope Pius XII, spending twenty minutes with the Holy Father—"a time usually allotted by Vatican protocol to queens." However, there was a more sinister side to the Rome trip. Using Bishop Hudal as an intermediary, she arranged to meet Bormann in an Italian villa at Rapallo provided for her use by Dodero. The shipowner was also present at the meeting, as was Eva's brother Juan. There, she and her former paymaster cut the deal that guaranteed that his Führer's safe haven would continue to remain safe, and allowed Bormann to leave Europe at last for a new life in South America. However, she and her team had one shocking disappointment for Bormann.

PROVING THAT THERE IS NO HONOR AMONG THIEVES, the Peróns presented Bormann with a radical renegotiation of their earlier understanding. Evita had brought with her to Europe some

$800 million worth of the treasure that he had placed in supposed safekeeping in Argentina, and she would deposit this vast sum in Swiss banks for the Peróns' own use. As her husband Juan Domingo reportedly said, "Switzerland is the country . . . where all the bandits come together [and] hide everything they rob from the others." This treasure—comprising gold, jewels, and bearer bonds—likely went straight to Eva's trusted contacts in Switzerland, who were awaiting her arrival later in her European tour to set up the secret accounts. The Argentines were leaving Bormann with just one-quarter of his looted nest egg in Argentina. This swindle had been accomplished with the connivance of Bormann's most trusted Argentine contacts—Ludwig Freude, Ricardo von Leute, Ricardo Staudt, and Heinrich Doerge—all of whom had been signatories of the Aktion Feuerland bank accounts set up in Buenos Aires.

The remaining share was still huge, and Bormann had no option but to accept this brutal unilateral increase in the premium for his insurance policy. He had been planning his bolt-hole for four years; everything was in place. Hitler was already in Patagonia and with the crimes of the Nazi regime now finally exposed for the world to see, there was nowhere else to go. Within the next nine months both Bormann and SS and Police Gen. Heinrich "Gestapo" Müller planned to settle in Argentina themselves, and they would need their reception arrangements to function smoothly. Bormann knew that Evita was a tough, experienced negotiator, whom he would later describe as far more intelligent than her husband.

However, the Bormann "Organization" had a keen memory. After the spring of 1948, when Müller based himself in Córdoba and became directly responsible for the security of the Organization, the bankers who had betrayed Bormann would begin to suffer a string of untimely deaths. Heinrich Doerge died mysteriously in 1949; in December 1950, Ricardo von Leute was found dead in a Buenos Aires street, and Ricardo Staudt would survive him by only a few months. Ludwig Freude himself, the kingpin of Aktion Feuerland in Argentina, died in 1952 from drinking a poisoned cup of coffee, and Evita's younger brother Juan Duarté met his end in 1954 with a gunshot to the head. Officially he was said to have committed suicide.

AFTER ECSTATIC RECEPTIONS IN LISBON AND PARIS, Evita took a break at the Hotel de Paris in Monte Carlo, where Dodero introduced her to his friend, the Greek shipping magnate Aristotle Onassis. The predatory millionaire would later boast that he slept with her there and in the morning gave her a substantial check for one of her many charity organizations.

After her short layover, the "Rainbow" went to join her pot of gold in Switzerland. When she arrived in Geneva on August 4, 1947, she was met by the chief of protocol of the Swiss Foreign Service. He was an old friend; Jacques-Albert Cuttat had worked at the Swiss Legation in Buenos Aires from 1938 to 1946. He was deeply involved in the transfer of Nazi assets to Argentina and had been one of the account holders of the many gold deposits in the city's banks. After meeting Swiss president Philipp Etter and foreign minister Max Petitpierre, Evita dropped out of sight. She joined Dodero and other friends at the mountain resort of St. Moritz, but there was more business to take care of in Zurich, the banking capital of Switzerland's German-speaking cantons. One meeting took place in a closed session at the Hotel Baur au Lac, where Evita was a guest of the Instituto Suizo-Argentino. The president of the institute, Professor William Dunkel, introduced her to an audience of more than two hundred Swiss bankers and businessmen, briefing them on the many opportunities in the "New Argentina." Many of these opportunities would be under the control of familiar friends and clients.

BORMANN RETURNED BRIEFLY TO HIS HIDEOUT in the Austrian mountains—by now a slimmer, fitter, and poorer man than he had been for years. Although believed by some to be dead, he had been tried in absentia by the International Military Tribunal at Nuremberg in October 1946 and sentenced to death. In late 1947, the British Army had broken up a clandestine Nazi radio network that had mentioned Bormann twice by name in May 1947, information the FBI took seriously (see document on opposite page). On August 16, 1947, a guide led him and his bodyguards over a secret route through the Alps to a base just north of Udine in Italy. In December he was ready for the

Office Memorandum • UNITED STATES GOVERNMENT

TO : The Director   **TOP SECRET**   DATE: May 15, 1948

FROM : D. M. Ladd

SUBJECT: MARTIN BORMANN
War Criminal

Further reference is made to my memorandum of May 14, 1948,
discussing the two intercepts received from Bureau Source Two in March of
1947, indicating that Martin Bormann is, in fact, still alive. SA S. W.
Reynolds made inquiry at the War Department and ascertained the following:

The release of the two messages discussing Martin Bormann, as
regular Source Two messages, caused a great flurry of excitement in
British circles. It appeared that the British were intercepting and
decoding traffic over a clandestine network, a survivor of the German
defeat, with ramifications in Europe and Germany. The existence of this
network was said to be a closely kept secret and the traffic intercepted
was handled on an "eyes only" basis (i.e. for the use only of the officer
to whom addressed) instead of the customary "top secret" basis on which
Source Two material is handled. On the day these particular messages,
dealing with Bormann, were received, the Army officer handling the "eyes
only" traffic was away and the Navy got hold of the two messages. They
were published as regular diplomatic traffic by the Navy. The State
Department caused a number of photographs and descriptions of Bormann to
be printed up and circulated among various embassies. State got considerable
publicity for the allegation that Bormann was still alive. The British
were, as usual, horrified at the lack of security. Their circuit apparently
was broken up and the rumbling from the incident is still going on in the
Army. (TS)

These intercepts, unless some very pointless deception was being engaged in,
are a very close indication that Bormann is still alive. The British, apparently,
are the only ones who have precise information about the network over which the
clandestine traffic was moving. The furor caused by the above-mentioned incident
apparently restrained the Army from inquiring into Bormann's whereabouts; CIA was not
well set up at the time and the State Department's investigation was probably
perfunctory. It would thus seem that the British are the only ones who have any
real information about the possible whereabouts of Bormann, as well as about the
clandestine traffic concerning him. Because of the security consideration involved,
it is necessary that the Bureau assume the posture that it has no information from
Source Two on Bormann. However, inquiry should be made of the British, and
probably could be made with some degree of success on the basis that persistent rumors
are being received concerning Bormann. (TS)

There is attached a proposed memorandum to the Legal Attache of the American
Embassy in London, containing a request that he contact available sources for any
information which will throw light on the question whether Bormann is still alive,
and also specific identifying data including physical description, handwriting,
fingerprints and photographs. U

RECOMMENDATION: If you approve, it is suggested that the attached memorandum
be forwarded to our representative in London.

TOP SECRET

A MAY 15, 1948 memo to FBI director Hoover on a postwar Nazi radio
network that had mentioned Bormann by name twice in 1947 before being
broken up by the British.

next leg of his journey, but it would not pass unnoticed. Capt. Ian Bell, a war crimes investigator based in Italy from the British Army's Judge Advocate General's office, had been tipped off about Bormann's presence. Bell, who had captured a number of wanted Italian war criminals, ordered a spotter plane to fly over the area where he had been told that Bormann and his two-hundred-man bodyguard were gathered. Two days later Bell called in an air strike; an American aircraft flew over and dropped a bomb, a number of the SS men made a break for it and were arrested, and under interrogation they admitted that they were shielding Martin Bormann. The SS told the British that Bormann was planning to flee, and provided details of the route and timing.

Bell and two of his sergeants lay in wait at a spot where they had been told Bormann would pass, reversing their jeep and trailer into a farm driveway. A short while later they saw a small convoy on the road below them—a large black car and two trucks with trailers. Capt. Bell estimated there were sixteen men in total, six in each truck and another three with Bormann in the staff car—too many for him and his two lightly armed NCOs to take on. They followed the convoy until Bell had the chance to use a telephone in a roadside inn to contact his headquarters. He was shocked by what his commanding officer told him: "Follow, but do not apprehend, now I repeat, do not apprehend." Over the next two days the British officer followed his quarry for more than 670 miles.

The German convoy passed through police and military roadblocks without any trouble, arriving at the docks in the Italian port of Bari in the early hours of a December morning in 1947. From cover, Bell and his men watched the vehicles being hoisted aboard a freighter by cranes and Martin Bormann walking up the gangway. The moment the last vehicle was put into the hold, the cranes swung away, the mooring cables were thrown off, and the ship moved away from the quayside. When Bell checked the ship's destination with the port authorities later that morning, he was told it was Argentina.

As Bell explained during an interview in a documentary aired on British television in 1999, he "very much" regretted not arresting Bormann:

We were absolutely devastated and it took us a little while to get over the trauma of seeing him get away, one of the biggest; Hitler's right-hand man to just be at liberty to board a ship and go to freedom. After all the trouble and the journey we had and the strain of having to restrain ourselves from doing something was very hard on us. And just to see that, just go away like that and not be able to do anything about it, yes, I was very upset about, I was very disheartened. But that was life, we had to get on with it, and go back to headquarters and take on another role, another brief.

Bell was asked how Bormann could have been allowed to go free and who he thought was responsible.

We were sure that the Vatican had a lot to do with Martin Bormann's escape, because nowhere down the whole line was he ever stopped by the Carabinieri [the military force charged with police duties among civilian populations in Italy] or any army personnel; he was allowed through with complete liberty. It had been well organized. Who else could do that but the cooperation [sic] between the Vatican and the Italian government?

Martin Borman arrived in Buenos Aires on May 17, 1948, on the ship *Giovanna C* from Genoa. (Although it is not evident when or where Bormann changed ship, the *Giovanna C* was almost definitely not the same vessel that Bormann and his vehicles had boarded in Bari.)

He was dressed as a Jesuit priest, and he entered the country on a Vatican passport identifying him as the Reverend Juan Gómez. A few weeks later he registered at the Apostolic Nunciature in Buenos Aires as a stateless person and was given Identity Certificate No. 073, 909. On October 12, 1948, he was given the coveted "blue stamp" granting him permission to remain in Argentina permanently. With dreadful irony, Martin Bormann was now known, among other pseudonyms, by the Jewish name Eliezer Goldstein.

Bormann and the Peróns met in Buenos Aires shortly after the Reichsleiter arrived. The final negotiations over the Nazi treasure would have been heated and protracted. Documents made public in 1955 after the fall of Perón, and later in 1970, showed that the Peróns handed Bormann his promised 25 percent. The physical aspect of the treasure—outside of investments carefully structured by Ludwig Freude on behalf of his Nazi paymaster, which the Peróns had left untouched—was impressive:

187,692,400 gold marks
17,576,386 U.S. dollars
4,632,500 pounds sterling
24,976,442 Swiss francs
8,370,000 Dutch florins
54,968,000 French francs
192 pounds of platinum
2.77 tons of gold
4,638 carats of diamonds and other precious stones

Bormann's quarter of these physical assets was still a massive fortune. Coupled with investments in over three hundred companies across the whole economic spectrum of Latin America—banks, industry, and agriculture—with Lahusen alone getting 80 million pesos—this money became "a major factor in the economic life of South America."

The sailor Heinrich Bethe was present when Bormann once again met with his Führer at Inalco later the same year. Bormann, now disguised as "Father Augustin," arrived wearing priest's clothing. He was there for just over a week. On the final day of his stay, Hitler and Bormann had a private meeting that lasted almost three hours, after which he left the Center.

By the time Bormann arrived in Argentina in 1948, the world was a very different place from the one in which Col. Perón had first got involved in Aktion Feuerland with the agents of the Third Reich. The time for swastikas and defiant rallies was long over; Bormann, ever the realist, recognized that, and he would be content (once he had settled certain scores) to oversee the substantial remaining part of the looted wealth. He would be a regular visitor to the Center, but, confident of the close protection he had bought from the Peróns, he spent most of his time in Buenos Aires, where he could oil the wheels of the Organization and plan for a secure financial future.

TWO OF THE MOST IMPORTANT PLAYERS in the Nazis' attempted seduction of Argentina were the millionaire La Falda hoteliers Walter and Ida Eichhorn. They had been supporters and friends of the Nazi Party and Hitler since at least 1925, and Hitler would visit them—without Eva—in 1949 at La Falda.

The Eichhorns first came to the attention of FBI director J. Edgar Hoover in a couriered document from the American embassy in London in September 1945. After reporting what was known of the Eichhorns' relationship with Hitler, the document ends with a paraphrased quote from Ida Eichhorn: "if Hitler should at any time get into difficulty wherein it was necessary for him to find a safe retreat, he would find such safe retreat at her hotel (La Falda), where they had already made the necessary preparations." Hoover wrote to the American Embassy in Buenos Aires several weeks later, apprising them of the situation (see reproduction of both documents on pages 266 and 267).

The relationship between Ida Eichhorn and her "cousin," as she always called Hitler, went back much further than 1944, though there is some dispute over the date the Eichhorns actually joined the Nazi Party. On May 11, 1935, Walter and Ida were awarded the "honor version" of the Gold Party Badge; fewer than half a dozen of the 905 such badges awarded were given to non-Reich citizens. The Führer sent the Eichhorns a personal congratulatory letter dated May 15, an unusual extra compliment accompanying the award. In the letter, which thanked Walter Eichhorn for his services, the Führer used the words "since joining in 1924 with your wife," which seems to indicate that the Eichhorns were among the earliest members of the party. They were also personally given No. 110 of the limited edition of 500 copies of *Mein Kampf* when they first met Hitler at his apartment in 1925—the year the book was published.

The Eichhorns saw him again in 1927 and 1929, and thereafter they began to travel more regularly to Germany. At least one letter of

JOHN EDGAR HOOVER
DIRECTOR

Federal Bureau of Investigation
United States Department of Justice
Washington 25, D. C.

IN REPLY, PLEASE REFER TO
FILE NO.

American Embassy, London, England
September 17, 1945

ATTENTION: SIS EUROPEAN DESK   VIA US ARMY COURIER SERVICE

Director, FBI
Washington, D. C.

Dear Sir:

Re: HITLER HIDEOUT IN ARGENTINA
Security Matter - G

The following information was obtained from the War Room through ▮▮▮▮▮▮ of OSS regarding the above-captioned matter, which in turn was obtained by OSS from ▮▮▮▮▮

"A certain Mrs. EICHHORN, an allegedly reputable member of Argentine society and proprietress of the largest spa hotel in LA FALDA (Argentina) made, at an intimate party some time ago, (precisely when or where is not stated) the following observations:-

a. Her family have been enthusiastic supporters of HITLER since the Nazi Party was founded.

b. Even before the Nazis came into power she placed immediately by cable her entire bank account, amounting to 30,000 Marks, at GOEBBEL's disposal. This was done in response to the latter's request to her for 3-4,000 Marks for propaganda purposes.

c. HITLER never forgot this act and during the years after he came into power their (meaning presumably her and her husband's) friendship with him became so close that they used to live together (sic) in the same hotel on the occasion of their annual stay in Germany on the PARTEITAG. They were then permitted to enter the private rooms of the Fuehrer at any time without being previously announced.

d. If the Fuehrer should at any time get into difficulties he could always find a safe retreat at LA FALDA where they had already made the necessary preparations."

The above is being furnished the Bureau merely for its information.

Very truly yours,

JAC:FML   Legal Attache

SIS Co...

~ ~ ~ ?.../5-48

~~~~ - AIR C........

Date: November 13, 1945

To: Mr. ~~~~~~~~
The American Embassy
Buenos Aires, Argentina

From: John Edgar Hoover - Director, Federal Bureau of Investigation

Subject: Hitler Hideout in Argentina
Security Matter - G

The Bureau is in receipt of a report from the Strategic Services Unit of the War Department dated October 23, 1945 concerning the possibility of a "Hitler Hideout" in Argentina. This report is as follows:

"One Mrs. Eichhorn, reported to be a reputable member of Argentine society and the proprietor of the largest spa hotel in La Falda, Argentina, recently made the following observations:

"a. that even before the Nazi Party was founded she made available to Goebbels her entire bank account which, at the time, amounted approximately to thirty thousand marks, which money was to be used for propaganda purposes;

"b. that she and her family have been enthusiastic supporters of Adolf Hitler since the Nazi Party was founded;

"c. that this voluntary support of the Nazi Party was never forgotten by Hitler and that during the years after he came into power her friendship with Hitler became so close that she and members of her family lived with Hitler in the same hotel on the occasion of their annual visit to Germany;

"d. that if Hitler should at any time get into difficulty wherein it was necessary for him to find a safe retreat, he would find such safe retreat at her hotel (La Falda) where they had already made the necessary preparations."

This is being furnished only for your information and for the completion of your files.

COMMUNICATIONS SECTION

MAILED 8

NOV 1 ... P.M.

50 NOV 30 1945

FEDERAL BUREAU OF INVESTIGATION
U.S. DEPARTMENT OF JUSTICE

DECLASSIFIED BY 60 69
ON 11/4/22

A November 13, 1945 FBI report sent to the American embassy in Buenos Aires, recapping the September FBI report detailing the Eichhorns' relationship with Hitler.

Hitler's from 1935–36 directly thanks them for a generous personal money donation. The couple were described by their grandniece Verena Ceschi as "big idealists who were really enthused by the ideas of the Führer, like all Germany at that time, [and] they became great friends." At their luxurious Hotel Eden at La Falda, when Ida Eichhorn was asked if something could be accomplished, she would say anything was possible, "Adolf willing." On her office wall there was a large photo of Hitler personally dedicated to her. There was also a room in the hotel set up as a shrine to the Führer and always decorated with freshly cut flowers. The Eden's crockery, cutlery, and linen were stamped with the swastika, and there were many other pictures of Hitler throughout the hotel. Hitler's speeches were captured by a shortwave antenna on the roof of the Eden and broadcast on speakers both inside and outside the hotel. The hotel had more than one hundred rooms with thirty-eight bathrooms, central heating, a huge dining and ballroom, an eighteen-hole golf course, tennis courts, a swimming pool, and many other amenities. Even today, the now semi-derelict Eden shows signs of its former magnificence, which attracted many international celebrities in the 1930s, including celebrated Jewish physicist Albert Einstein and the Prince of Wales. (The prince was crowned Edward VIII in January 1936, but abdicated eleven months later to marry American divorcée Wallis Simpson; as the Duke and Duchess of Windsor, both suspected Nazi sympathizers, the couple visited Hitler in 1937). It appears that Einstein may have stayed at the hotel when the anti-Semitic Eichhorns were not present.

The Eden was the meeting place for many of the Nazi organizations of Córdoba province, and military training was carried out in a camp called "Kit-Ut" on land owned by the Eichhorns. Ida also founded the German School in La Falda in 1940. Its primary teachers had to swear an oath of allegiance to Hitler at the German Embassy in Buenos Aires, secondary teachers had to join the National Socialist League of Teachers, and the school provided a complete program of Nazi indoctrination. This devotion to Nazism, which by 1940 applied in almost two hundred German schools in Argentina, persisted—especially in the countryside—despite a 1938 decree by President Roberto Ortiz prohibiting the exhibition of foreign flags or symbols in schools.

The schoolchildren were present at a commemorative ceremony held at the Eden on December 17, 1940, the first anniversary of the scuttling of the *Admiral Graf Spee*. Most of the supposedly "interned" crew marched in full uniform and paraded the Nazi flag under the eyes of dozens of Argentine dignitaries and senior members of the military. The parade ended on the hotel's esplanade, where the Nazi Party marching song, the "Horst-Wessel-Lied," was sung, and there were impassioned pro-German speeches. However, despite the protection of the Argentine police and armed German sailors who were billeted nearby, the Nazi presence in La Falda did not go completely unchallenged. When the Eichhorns decided to raise money by showing Nazi propaganda films to a large audience, members of an anti-Nazi, pro-Allies group called Acción Argentina punctured the tires of the parked cars of the film attendees. Among the attackers was Ernesto Guevara Lynch, father of Ernesto "Che" Guevara—the Argentine Marxist leader and Fidel Castro's chief lieutenant of the Cuban Revolution.

THE EICHHORNS CONTINUED TO ORGANIZE COLLECTIONS for the Nazi cause, and as late as 1944 they were still transferring tens of thousands of Swiss francs to the Buenos Aires account of Joseph Goebbels. However, in March 1945, under intense pressure from the United States, Argentina finally declared war on the Axis powers— the last of the Latin American nations to do so. After this declaration, the Hotel Eden was seized as "property of the enemy" and—now surrounded by barbed wire and guards to keep people in rather than out—used for eleven months to intern the Japanese embassy staff and their families. Shortly after the Japanese were repatriated, anti-Nazis in La Falda broke in, pulled down the eagle from the facade of the hotel, and destroyed anything with the swastika on it.

In May 1945, Ida Eichhorn told her closest circle that her "cousin" Adolf Hitler was "traveling." The Eichhorns, shutting themselves away in their chalet a short distance from the hotel, created a network of distribution centers that sent thousands of clothing and food parcels to a devastated Germany. They also helped the network for Nazis who fled to Argentina, and Adolf Eichmann would often visit La Falda with his family. One of his sons, Horst Eichmann—who led Argentina's Frente Nacional Socialista Argentino (FNSA) Nazi party in the 1960s—married Elvira Pummer, the daughter of one of the Hotel Eden's gardeners.

The Eichhorns maintained close contact with the Gran Hotel Viena on the shores of Mar Chiquita; they owned a property just 150 yards from the hotel. They would have met Hitler and Eva there while he was convalescing in 1946. (Whatever the Nazis' long-term plans were for the Gran Hotel Viena, they never came to much. After the Hitlers' second visit in early 1948, the property was virtually abandoned. In March of that year the head of security, Col. Krueger, was found "poisoned" in a room off the hotel garage—the same fate that befell Ludwig Freude four years later.)

CATALINA GOMERO WAS FIFTEEN YEARS OLD when she went to live with the Eichhorns in 1945. She suffered from asthma and came from a poor family who believed she would have a better life at the Hotel Eden than they could offer her. Although a servant, Catalina was treated by the Eichhorns almost as a daughter. She said that Hitler arrived at their house in La Falda one night in 1949 and stayed for three days; she recognized him right away. "The driver must have brought him. He was put up on the third floor. We were told to take his breakfast upstairs and . . . knock at the door and leave the tray on the floor. He ate very well, the trays were always empty. Most of the meals were German." He had shaved his moustache off. There were usually people in the house all day, but for those three days, the third floor was private. "Mrs. Ida told me, 'Whatever you saw, pretend you didn't.' One of the drivers and I used to joke, 'I saw nothing and you saw nothing.' It was as if it had never happened. It was kept very, very secret." Hitler left his clothes, including green canvas trousers and a black collared shirt, outside the room, and Catalina would clean and iron them. She took him three breakfasts, three lunches, and three complete teas. On the fourth day she was told he had left.

Eight days after the "important visitor" left La Falda, Mrs. Eichhorn told Catalina to pack a picnic lunch. With the chauffeur driving the Mercedes-Benz and Walter Eichhorn seated next to him, the four drove to the Eichhorns' house on Pan de Azucar Mountain. This brick-and-timber construction had a large radio antenna and was part of the network of Nazi safe houses across the country. Hitler stayed for fifteen days at what the family called "El Castillo," but after that Catalina never saw him again. However, she remembered taking telephone calls from him at the Eichhorn home through operators in La Rioja and Mendoza; she recognized his voice. The calls continued until 1962.

John Walsh, an FBI agent stationed in Buenos Aires at this time, admitted the difficulties he and his operatives encountered in doing any undercover work in Argentina. Of the Hotel Eden and the Eichhorns, Walsh said, "We personally did not do surveillance work there. We would have sources that were outside the embassy that would do that. You just can't walk in and say, you know, that you are looking for something." Walsh said that he and his colleagues came under surveillance by the local police. A number of times when he was out with other agents they would see people who were obviously following and watching them.

DESPITE HIS DIRECT PROTECTION by the "Organization" and the more indirect but essential collaboration of the Perón government, the fact that Hitler moved around during the late 1940s and early 1950s rather than remaining buried at the Center made sightings almost inevitable. In time, Catalina Gomero would not be the only person willing to tell stories of meeting the former Führer in Argentina after the war.

Jorge Batinic, a bank manager from the city of Comodoro Rivadavia in the southern Patagonian province of Chubut, vividly remembered the story told to him by his Spanish-born mother, Mafalda Batinic. In summer 1940, she had been in France working for the International Red Cross, and on several occasions she had seen Hitler at close quarters when he was visiting wounded Wehrmacht soldiers. In later years she would often say, "Once seen, the face of Hitler was never forgotten." After the war Mafalda moved to Argentina, and by the beginning of 1951 she was working as a nurse in the Arustiza y Varando private hospital.

KEY SIGHTINGS OF Adolf Hitler and Eva Braun in Argentina post-World War II.

One day, a German rancher was brought in for treatment for a gun-shot wound, and a few days later three other Germans arrived to visit the patient. It was noticeable that two of them treated the third one as "the boss." Mafalda had to choke back an involuntary cry of amazement when she recognized him as Hitler. He had no moustache and was somewhat graying, but she had no doubt that it was him. Shocked, Mrs. Batinic told the owners of the clinic, Drs. Arustiza and Varando; they watched him and were surprised, but did nothing. Apart from greeting the patient, Hitler hardly said a word. When the three Germans left, Mrs. Batinic asked the patient the identity of his important visitor. Realizing that she had already recognized the Führer, the injured rancher told his nurse, "Look, it's Hitler, but don't say anything. You know they're looking for him, it's better not to say anything."

Chapter 22

DEPARTURES

THE GERMAN NAZIS WERE NOT THE ONLY FASCISTS
to escape to Argentina after the war. One of their most bloodthirsty
allies had been Ante Pavelić, the leader of the Ustaše regime in the
short-lived puppet state established by the Germans in Croatia. Styling
himself the *Poglavnik* (equivalent to Führer), Pavelić had been responsible for the murders of hundreds of thousands of men, women, and
children of Serbian, Jewish, and other origins in the ethnic jigsaw
puzzle of wartime Yugoslavia; even some members of the Gestapo had
thought Ustaše methods "bestial." Croatia was historically a Roman
Catholic region, and contacts in the Vatican enabled Pavelić and his
whole cabinet, followed later by his wife, Mara, and their children, to
travel along the ratlines to Argentina. The Perón government issued
34,000 visas to Croats in the years after the war. Indirectly, Pavelić's
escape from justice led to some of the clearest eyewitness testimony to
Hitler's presence in Argentina in 1953–54.

A carpenter named Hernán Ancin met the Hitlers on several occasions in the 1950s, while he was working for Pavelić as a carpenter in
the Argentine coastal city of Mar del Plata. The Croatian former dictator had a property development business there. Pavelić was known as

"Don Lorenzo," but one of his bodyguards said he had been president of Croatia. (Unsurprisingly, Hernán Ancin had never heard of him before—Pavelić was living under an assumed name and heavily protected, but he was not well known in Argentina for his crimes.) Ancin worked for Pavelić's company from the middle of 1953 to September or October 1954. In the southern summer of 1953, the Hitlers were regular visitors to the building site where Ancin was working. On the first occasion when the carpenter saw the two former dictators together, Hitler arrived with his wife and three bodyguards.

Hitler was clearly not well; he could barely walk unaided, and his bodyguards practically carried him. These meetings were held in private, but both leaders' security men were constantly present. Ancin said Hitler seemed dependent on his bodyguards, who set his schedule. He and Pavelić would converse until one of the guards said words to the effect of "that's enough," and then they would leave.

Like most other people who gave descriptions of Hitler after the war, Ancin said that while the Führer's appearance had changed, he was "basically the same. He had white, short hair, cut military style. No moustache." One particular moment stuck out in Ancin's memory. "When Hitler [arrived] he raised the closed fist of his right hand with his arm extended. Pavelić went to him and put his hand on Hitler's fist, enclosing it. Afterward, they smiled, and Pavelić shook hands with Hitler. This was always the greeting."

Ancin saw Hitler with Pavelić on five or six occasions. Pavelić's Argentine mistress (a woman from Córdoba named Maria Rosa Gel) practically never intervened in their conversations, simply serving the coffee. Hitler's wife also kept silent; Eva had not aged well, and she was unable to lose the weight she had gained when her second daughter was born late in 1945. Ancin said:

> Hitler's wife was a little heavy. She seemed to be just over forty years old. She was large, well-fed you could say. She wore work clothes, very cheap, beige, just like his. She was a woman who gave you the feeling that she had suffered a great deal, or at least that she was suffering from something, because it was reflected in her face. She always seemed worried, and almost never smiled.

From Ancin's testimony it seems that the conversation was carried out for the most part in Spanish. "Hitler's wife, I don't remember—I assume she spoke a bit of Spanish, because she always said 'thank you for the coffee.' . . . Hitler spoke Spanish with difficulty, and had a strong German accent." At one of these meetings, Pavelić introduced Hernán Ancin to Hitler as the carpenter who was working on the building, and invited him to join them for coffee. Hitler smiled at Ancin and made a gesture of greeting with his head, but did not offer his hand or speak. Ancin was "totally convinced" that the man was Hitler.

He also saw Hitler elsewhere in Mar del Plata, at an old colonial-style house behind the San Martin Park. He saw Hitler's car enter, and the guards at the door; he was not sure if Hitler lived there or was simply visiting (the house was in fact a Lahusen property). While in the city Hitler always traveled by car, but on one occasion the carpenter saw him near the shore; he had gotten out of the car and was sitting on a bench contemplating the sea. Ancin thought Hitler had problems with his circulation and could not walk far; he dragged his feet, and Eva held his arm when he walked. In contrast to Pavelić, whom the retired carpenter remembered as rude and hard-eyed, Ancin recalled Hitler as having "light eyes, a friendly gaze—[he was] quiet and very polite."

Both Hitler and Pavelić disappeared from Mar del Plata in August or September 1954.

HITLER'S DETERIORATING HEALTH, and the fading of any fanatical dream of expanding a "Fourth Reich in the South" that had never really existed, led to a steady running down of activity at the Center during the early 1950s. Naturally, as time passed and reality sank in, many of the formerly committed Nazis became preoccupied with their new lives and jobs, and the appeal of working for a defeated leader and ideology simply dissipated. Even SS Gen. Ludolf von Alvensleben, who had become a firm friend of Juan Perón during their skiing trips together at San Carlos de Bariloche, resigned from his post as "governor" of the valley community in October 1952. He took up a post in Buenos Aires as President Perón's "Head of the Department for Fishing, Hunting and Yachting for Area R10111," and Perón also granted him a new identity in the name of Carlos Luecke.

Prominent among the few still keeping the flame alive was a man who was not a wanted war criminal, but a famous combat airman. Hans-Ulrich Rudel, the Stuka dive-bomber and tank-buster ace who had lost a leg when he was shot down late in the war, was Nazi Germany's most decorated pilot. Even so, he had moved to Argentina in 1948 and become a confidant of both Hitler and President Perón. Still nurturing dreams of a sort of "Fascist Internationale," Rudel was in touch with Sir Oswald Mosley, prewar leader of the British Union of Fascists, and with the Paraguayan dictator Alfredo Stroessner. Mosley and Rudel met in Buenos Aires in 1950, and in Britain two years later Mosley published Rudel's wartime memoir, *Stuka Pilot*, under the imprint of Euphorion Books—a company that he had set up with his aristocratic wife, née Diana Mitford. The book included fulsome praise for the principles of National Socialism; one must suspect that the legless British fighter ace Douglas Bader, who contributed a foreword, was manipulated into doing so on the pretext that this was simply the flying memoir of a one-legged airman. Rudel was an unrepentant Nazi whose only regret was that Germany had lost the war. During his time in Argentina he met regularly with Heinrich "Gestapo" Müller, whom he used as a reference and contact point, and would have also met with Hitler. In 1953, Rudel returned to West Germany, where he made a failed attempt to launch the belligerently named Deutsche Reichspartei.

IF ANCIN HAD THOUGHT EVA HITLER LOOKED SAD, it was hardly surprising. She had been a high-spirited, shallow-minded young woman who loved lively company and parties, and her life on the sprawling, isolated estate at Inalco was not what she had hoped for. Her formerly beloved "Mr. Wolf," once so impressive at the center of his fawning court, was now constantly ill or busy in mundane meetings, and the shine had quickly worn off a remote rural life spent caring for two young children. It is widely documented that despite the demonic energy and conviction that Hitler could display, both publicly and within his close circle, when his emotions were engaged, he was a fundamentally lazy man, easily distracted from practical work by resentments and abstract preoccupations. Without even the illusion of controlling great events, or a circle of toadies to play up to his pretensions, he must have been wretched company indeed for a woman who could feel her youth fading. Since her "death" in the Führerbunker, nobody had been looking for a young mother with two children, so Eva's relocation under another false identity would not present any great difficulty. Probably in 1954, after their return from the dismal holiday at the Lahusen-owned house in Mar del Plata (during which Hitler's meetings with Pavelić had been observed by Hernán Ancin), Eva finally left Inalco and Hitler. She and her daughters moved to Neuquén, a quiet but growing town about 230 miles northeast of San Carlos de Bariloche. The "Organization" would, as always, continue to look after them.

MARTIN BORMANN STAYED OUT OF POLITICS. His interest now lay purely in protecting and multiplying the Organization's funds. His trips to the valley became less and less frequent, as he distanced himself and his network from the ailing Hitler. He spent much of his time in Buenos Aires; his front was a company that manufactured refrigerators, behind which he extended his financial dealings across the world. His regular meetings with President Perón were detailed by Jorge Silvio Adeodato Colotto, the head of Perón's personal police bodyguard from 1951 until the coup against him in September 1955. Now eighty-seven, well over six feet tall, dressed smartly, and carrying a pocket Derringer pistol, Colotto remains an impressive figure, lucid and happy to talk to us about his time as the head of the former Argentine president's personal security detail.

Colotto explained that while he was with Peron he wrote down every interesting episode about the president, including many one-liners, on small pieces of paper—and he had stored them all in a can! From this unusual archive of 6,200 papers, which Colotto had itemized and translated into an as-yet unpublished English-language book, came his recollection of a key encounter.

Colotto was present on one occasion in the spring of 1953 at Perón's house on Teodoro Garcia Street in Belgrano, an exclusive suburb of Buenos Aires. This was the house that the Nazi "ambassador" Ludwig Freude had given to Evita as a wedding present in 1945. The twice-widowed president, who now used it for private meetings and romantic liaisons, would arrive wearing a hat and glasses as a disguise. (Another frequent visitor was the shipping magnate Alberto Dodero. He had fallen out with Perón in 1949 when the president nationalized his shipping interests at a fraction of their true value, but the rift did not last long.)

On this occasion, Colotto was on duty at the house when Perón told him, "Bormann is coming at 8:00 p.m. Be careful—he is German, not Argentine, and they are punctual." At 8:00 sharp, Colotto was waiting at the door when Bormann arrived in a taxi. They shook hands, and the bodyguard showed him through to the president's living room. Colotto remembers the Reichsleiter as "all German." Bormann had grown a moustache and was wearing a jacket and tie. He spoke very little Spanish, but could make himself understood. Perón was in his office, and the bodyguard went to tell him his guest had arrived. When they met in the living room they greeted each other with a tight hug, like old friends; then they went to the office, where they stayed until 10:00 p.m. As the house was used mainly for clandestine meetings, Colotto said security was minimal. "There were two agents outside during the day when Perón was not there. But when Perón was there, the agents were dismissed. I was the only guard in the house when Perón was there." Perón's butler Romano and cook Fransisca were also in the house; the president was going to invite Bormann to stay for dinner, but the visitor said he had other commitments. When the two of them came out of the office, Perón told Colotto to "walk with Mr. Bormann" to Cabildo, an avenue three hundreds yards from the house, to get him a taxi. When Colotto returned, President Perón said, "Bormann gave me an undeserved present." He did not say what it was, but Colotto guessed that it could have only been something small and valuable.

Colotto saw Bormann at the house on a second occasion during the weeks that followed, and the German's presence in the capital became part of his working life. Bormann kept a suite at the luxurious Plaza Hotel, facing the Plaza San Martin at the end of Calle Florida, the world-famous shopping avenue in Buenos Aires. Colotto would go to the Plaza Hotel every month to pay Bormann's expenses and accommodation with money that Perón gave him in a brown envelope.

Bormann's mistress, a German-Brazilian named Alicia Magnus, stayed there with him. Located across the plaza from the hotel are the impressive buildings of the Círculo Militar (a military club founded in 1881) and the Argentine Foreign Ministry, in an area that is also close to the banking district. Colotto thought Bormann held regular business meetings at the Círculo Militar.

ANOTHER WOMAN IN BUENOS AIRES who was convinced she knew Martin Bormann well was Araceli Méndez, who had arrived in Argentina from Spain in 1947 when she was twenty-four. She met him in 1952 at a café in Buenos Aires; when he needed someone to write letters and documents in good Spanish, she introduced him to her brother. Araceli said that the relationship deepened; they became good friends, and she went to work for him. He told her that he was a senior Nazi and that the Curia (the Vatican papal court) had helped him to reach Argentina—he had been very specific about this phrasing. He also said that he had been in the hospital and had work done to alter his hairline.

Bormann apparently had four or five different passports; Araceli knew him as Ricardo Bauer, but he would also use the name Daniel Teófilo Guillermo Deprez, from Belgium. Under that name he was the owner of a factory that produced "Apis" refrigerators, on Ministro Brin Street in Lanús, Buenos Aires. Araceli Méndez ended up doing bookkeeping work for him in an office at Pasaje Barolo, and she claimed that he then began to woo her (his greed for sex seems to have been as great as his personal financial avarice). She witnessed many of his financial dealings; he once received a bank transfer for US $400,000 from Europe. He told her that he had shares in a factory in Belgium and another in Holland and that this transfer and many others were part of his profits. Bormann had also brought many precious stones from Europe, including one diamond that he sold in Buenos Aires for US $120,000.

THE RELEASED FBI FILES on sightings of Hitler in South America, sparse as they are, are relatively extensive when compared to the mere dribble of information that has come out of the Central

Intelligence Agency, but one report from the agency's Los Angeles office does stand out. This allegedly placed the Führer in Colombia in January 1955. While ultimately unconvincing, it is unusual in that it contains a very poor quality photostat of a photograph, alleged by the CIA informant's contact (a former SS man named as Phillip Citroen) to show Hitler, using the identity of one Adolf Schüttelmayer (on the written report, shown on page 282, it is spelled "Schrittelmayor"). In the photo "Hitler"—who at this date would have been sixty-five—still has dark hair and the classic moustache, and it is thus at odds with other, apparently better-founded testimonies. The picture is marked "Colombia, Tunga, America del Sur, 1954." There is a town of Tunja in central Colombia, but it has no known Nazi affiliations; indeed, after World War II it became home to many Jewish refugees from Europe.

The "secret" CIA report bears a disclaimer that neither the unnamed informant nor the Los Angeles station is "in a position to give an intelligent evaluation of the information and it is being forwarded as of possible interest." Even so, the fact that the CIA's Los Angeles office thought it worthwhile to do so is significant. Neither the FBI nor the CIA seems to have been convinced by the declaration, made with absolute confidence nearly ten years earlier by the British historian and former intelligence officer Hugh Trevor-Roper, that Hitler had died in the bunker—an assertion made despite a complete lack of forensic evidence.

UNDER THE PROTECTION OF PRESIDENT PERÓN, Argentina had become a haven for German, French, Belgian, and Croatian fascists. They would meet Perón in his official residence, the Casa Rosada, facing the square at the eastern end of the Plaza de Mayo. Rodolfo Freude, son of Ludwig and friend of Evita's brother Juan Duarté, managed the secret network of former Nazis' contacts with the regime. He had risen to become Perón's chief of presidential intelligence and had an office in the Casa Rosada.

Juan Perón was reelected president in June 1952 by a margin of over 30 percent (this was the first time that Argentine women had been able to vote). A month later, on July 26, 1952, his charismatic wife Evita died of cancer at the young age of thirty-three. By the time of her death she had spent much of the stolen money that she, in her

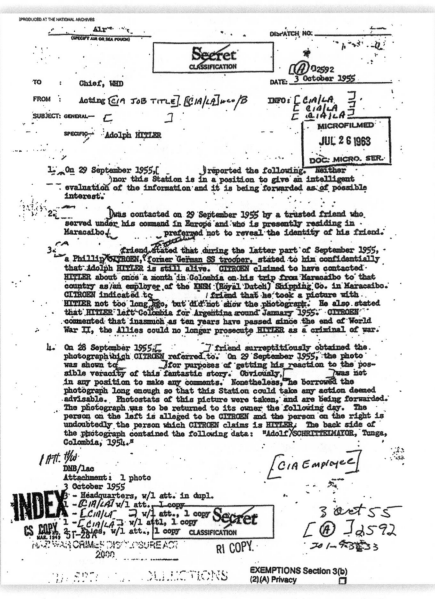

A CIA DOCUMENT from 1955, detailing a report that Hitler was in Colombia.

turn, had stolen from Bormann, mostly to finance philanthropic work for the Argentine poor—her *descamisados* (literally, "shirtless"). The country went into mourning. Crowds kept vigil throughout the night in front of the presidential palace and later in front of the Ministry of Labor, where she was taken to lie in state. Carrying candles, people knelt in prayer in the wet streets, and women cried openly. On July 27, the whole country came to a standstill.

"Little Eva" had been Juan Perón's lucky charm and his main hold on public affection. By 1955, much of the money the couple had taken had run out, and without her by his side his luck ran out with it. His economic reforms had divided the country, and a number of terrorist attacks and consequent reprisals were moving Argentine politics rapidly in the direction of yet another revolution. Ironically, the last straw was not some new oppressive measure, but Perón's liberalizing plan to legalize divorce and prostitution. The leaders of the Roman Catholic Church, whose support for the president had been dwindling, now began to call him "The Tyrant."

A serious blow to Perón's popularity with those who worshipped the memory of Evita was a scandal, aired in the gossip pages of the press, concerning the fifty-nine-year-old president's relationship with a thirteen-year-old girl named Nelly Rivas. He misjudged the public mood when he replied to reporters' questioning about his girlfriend's age, "So what? I'm not superstitious." But his sense of humor soon failed him, and in response to what he perceived as the church's support for the opposition he expelled two Catholic priests from the country. Pope Pius XII retaliated by excommunicating Juan Perón on June 15, 1955.

The following day, navy jet fighters flown by rebel officers bombed a pro-Perón rally in the Plaza de Mayo opposite the Casa Rosada, reportedly killing no fewer than 364 people. Maddened Perónist crowds went on a rampage, burning the Metropolitan Cathedral and ten other churches in Buenos Aires. Exactly three months later, on September 16, 1955, a Catholic group from the army and navy led by Generals Eduardo Lonardi and Pedro Aramburu, and Adm. Isaac Rojas, launched a coup from Argentina's second city of Córdoba. It took them only three days to seize power.

Perón—who had himself come to power through the military coup of 1943—had never been blind to the danger of revolution. On Martin Bormann's advice he had built his very own "Führerbunker." On the ground floor of the Alas building at Avenida Leandro N. Alem in San Nicolas, Buenos Aires, a secret passage led to an underground vault lined with rosewood. A bedroom there had silk pajamas, an emergency supply of oxygen, and a walk-in wall safe. At the back of the safe was a plaster wall, concealing a long underground passage leading to a secret exit in the docks of Puerto Madero. It is not known if Perón used the bunker to escape through the cordon of troops closing in on him. It is known that he made it to Puerto Madero. Waiting there for Perón was a gunboat sent by Paraguayan dictator Alfredo Stroessner. Without bothering to collect his teenage lover, the once-and-future president fled the country.

THE "REVOLUCIÓN LIBERTADORA" sent shockwaves through the Nazi community in Argentina. Bormann issued instructions to close the operations in the Estancia Inalco valley and arranged for Hitler to move to a smaller house where he could live in complete obscurity. Now accompanied only by his two closest aides—his personal physician, Dr. Otto Lehmann, and the former *Admiral Graf Spee* petty officer Heinrich Bethe—Hitler moved to a property called La Clara, even deeper within the Patagonian countryside. Bormann was the only one within the Organization who knew its location, and he told everyone else that this was necessary for the Führer's security. Once again, he completely controlled access to Hitler. The frail, rapidly aging Hitler was now nothing more than a distracting problem for the international businessman Martin Bormann—a problem that time would solve, as the Führer faded away into an exile within an exile.

Chapter 23

Ghosts in
the Shadows

LITTLE IS KNOWN ABOUT HITLER'S PERSONAL PHYSICIAN,
Dr. Otto Lehmann. "Lehmann" may or may not have been his true
name. From what can be gleaned from the little documentation that
exists, he had been a Nazi Party member from the early years, but had
not held a senior military position in the Reich. During the last years of
the war he had apparently been involved in a review of the Wehrmacht
medical corps. He said he had been captured by the Allies immediately after the war, but after an arrest warrant was issued for him by
the Soviets, he managed to escape. He arrived at Estancia Inalco in
1947, via the Vatican-controlled escape route, and was immediately
appointed as the medical officer for "Adolf Hitler's Valley." A man of
few words, Lehmann avoided political discussions at the Center, pre-
ferring to spend his leisure time reading and writing.

Otto Lehmann's supposed memoir detailing his life as Hitler's
physician was preserved by the *Admiral Graf Spee* sailor Heinrich
Bethe, with whom Lehmann shared the care of the sick and aging
Hitler. Bethe is believed to have handed over the "Lehmann papers"
to Capt. Manuel Monasterio, who befriended Bethe in the late 1970s

(the captain said the papers were unfortunately lost during many house moves over a long life). Monasterio's 1987 book, *Hitler murió en la Argentina*, incorporates both the Lehmann papers and Bethe's recollections, which he shared with Monasterio (see Chapter 18, pages 223)

The Lehmann papers, as recounted in the Monasterio book, are not a straightforward narrative; they are full of references to mysticism, the occult, and the radical thinkers behind the growth of National Socialism in Germany in the 1920s. Lehmann appears to have known many of these figures well. His strange ramblings, which make Hitler out to be some sort of medium for occult powers determined to destroy the earth, come across simply as an absurd apologia for the all-too-human evil of the Holocaust. (At one stage Lehmann even suggested that there was some sort of "magical battle" between Hitler and occultists in Great Britain who managed to save the country from invasion in 1940.)

Hitler murió en la Argentina also relates Lehmann's observations of Hitler's decline; Lehmann laid much blame at the door of Dr. Theodor Morrell, the society "pox doctor" (a practitioner who treats sexually transmitted diseases) who had been introduced to the Führer by the photographer Heinrich Hoffmann and his assistant Eva Braun in 1936. Lehmann accused Morrell of "the dangerous administration of drugs and other substances of dubious effect." He gave his fellow medical man some credit for apparently resolving some of Hitler's gastric problems, but said that the treatments had left Hitler's already delicate nervous system "chronically affected" and that Morrell had "severely poisoned tissue that could not easily recover." Lehmann also accused Morrell of having administered "hallucinogenic substances" to increase his control over his patient.

IN MONASTERIO'S BOOK, Lehmann's notes on Hitler's condition grow more detailed after the move to La Clara in 1955. Adolf Hitler had turned sixty-six, and his health, which had improved when he first arrived in Argentina, now began to decline. Numerous medical historians have theorized that Parkinson's disease had affected Hitler since perhaps the 1930s; after 1950 his symptoms worsened, and he now spent a large part of his time resting or brooding. Politics were becoming less and less important. Bormann, whom he still trusted, had told him that the fall of Perón threatened great danger to the Organization, but, due to his growing depression, the aging dictator was no longer in a condition or a position to do anything about it. Deprived of contact with the outside world and no longer at the head of any sort of effective network, he was left in solitary retirement.

The captain writes that, according to Dr. Lehmann, Hitler's days were mundane. Normally he would appear on the scene a little before noon. After greeting Lehmann and Bethe, he would take a walk with his dog—the second in the line of Blondis. For the rest of the day he alternated between resting, chatting with his two companions, or taking more walks. After dinner he maintained rambling "work" meetings with Bethe, which often kept the sailor up until three or four in the morning. Lehmann said that Hitler's spirits would sometimes "bloom again," but only briefly. His nervous system had been damaged permanently, and as the years dragged by, "melancholy" became his most common state.

The three men talked a lot. Lehmann described the little group as "strange," "banished," and removed from all external events. From his notes, the doctor's feelings about Hitler seem to have been complex. He expressed the normal concern of any doctor for his patient, but at other times he reviled Hitler as a "monstrous dictator who has now lost his mask and his uniform." He was also dismissive about Heinrich Bethe, "a man who appears to have died years ago." His own plight prompted Lehmann to outbursts of self-pity—he was "an old, forgotten doctor who has found himself, in the final stage of his life, in circumstances that inevitably are just too much for him."

ON HIS SIXTY-SEVENTH BIRTHDAY, April 20, 1956, Hitler was expecting to receive four important guests (Lehmann did not mention who they were). Hitler had been informed that he would be given a thorough briefing on the Nazi Party's situation—but in any event, no one arrived. It was then, for the first time, that Hitler began to suspect that Bormann had finally betrayed him. In September of that year he had to take to his bed due to a heart complaint. Dr. Lehmann forbade him to indulge in any kind of worry, and he abandoned thoughts of politics for good.

Lehmann recalled that at the start of November 1956, Bormann, who had been visiting Chile, arrived at La Clara. At first, he was received coolly by Hitler. They talked for more than three hours, and at the end of the meeting Hitler once again appeared optimistic; his old deputy had assured him that the Organization was once more moving ahead solidly. Bormann stayed for two days, and on the morning of his departure he took Bethe aside. After thanking the sailor for his invaluable services to the cause, he begged him not to worry Hitler with questions of any sort, and to try to make him live as quietly as possible. Bormann said that the day would arrive when Hitler would speak to the world once again, but for now the most important thing was his health.

Hitler's optimism did not last; he was beset many times by the idea of suicide, from which he was dissuaded by Lehmann and Bethe—by now his closest companions. Unlike eyewitnesses in the bunker, who suggested that up until April 28, 1945, Hitler was tired but otherwise in complete control, Lehmann believed that Hitler had thought of suicide before: "An identical suicidal mania attacked him in the bunker in 1945, but at that stage Bormann still considered Hitler key to his post-war plans, and prevented what would have meant a severe setback for the ambitions of organized Nazism to become reality." However, we must recall that Lehmann had not been in the bunker himself.

IN THIS WEIRD LIMBO IN WHICH HE WAS TRAPPED with two such ill-assorted companions, Hitler also had some surprising confessions to make. He told Bethe of a love affair he had had with a "true representative of the Aryan race," the athlete Tilly Fleischer. This Nazi Olympian had won gold for her javelin-throwing at the infamous Berlin games of 1936, and Joseph Goebbels had introduced her to the Führer. Immediately smitten, Hitler installed her in a country house on the outskirts of Berlin. The romantic interlude lasted eight months, but when Hitler found out that Tilly was expecting a baby, he asked his friend Dr. Fritz Heuser to marry her. Heuser obliged, and when Tilly was five months pregnant he was amply compensated for his "patriotic" assistance by being appointed chief supervisor of the medical service throughout the Frankfurt area. When the Third Reich collapsed in 1945, Dr. Heuser obtained a divorce, packed his bags, and left Germany. Hitler had only once seen the child, who was named Gisela.

Bethe, who revered Hitler as a god and had dedicated his life to the Nazi cause, was shocked by this revelation. He remembered another story that had appeared in October 1946. The wife of Hitler's former secretary of state, Otto Meissner, astonished the world with a claim that Magda Goebbels had had a son by Hitler in 1935, the result of a passionate affair while both were vacationing on the Baltic Sea in the summer of 1934. Frau Meissner claimed that Magda herself had told her that Hitler was Helmut Goebbels's true father. Magda killed Hitler's son in the bunker along with her five daughters before she and her husband committed suicide.

HITLER TRIED TO REVISIT HIS OLD PASSION for painting, but Parkinson's disease made holding a brush almost impossible. The doctor described him as in a state of near collapse, complaining of "sharp neuralgic pains in his face" caused by a botched operation to remove the splinters driven into it by Stauffenberg's bomb. Hitler also suffered from migraines that became stronger and more prolonged with time. According to Monasterio, Lehmann, who had an old-fashioned turn of phrase, admitted, "Oh God, help me! At times I have felt a strange pleasure in the face of the terrible sufferings of this man. It has seemed to me that all the incalculable blood spilt clamors from the arteries of the Earth for vengeance on Hitler's person."

The years between 1957 and 1961 passed with dreary monotony while Lehmann detailed a steady decline in Hitler's physical and mental state. One night, just before dawn in late January 1962, he and Bethe heard "horrifying moans" and went to Hitler's bedroom. He was sitting on the edge of his bed in "a deplorable state of nervous depression." Scattered on the bed next to him were photos of the aftermath of the war. Lehmann claimed that one of them showed "a group of massacred Jewish children." Hitler was crying rhythmically, rocking back and forth on the edge of his bed, and did not even notice their presence.

Nowhere in Lehmann's memoirs was there any suggestion that Hitler either did not know of the Holocaust or had not been central to its planning. The doctor's diary made many references to Hitler's complete and total hatred of the Jewish race—a point of view, incidentally, that Dr. Lehmann shared, although he wrapped it up in esoteric pseudo-intellectual language.

As January 1962 progressed, Hitler's mental and physical condition deteriorated more rapidly, and his face became partially paralyzed. He spent hours sitting watching the horizon of lake and mountain, like "a person possessed." Lehmann felt that there was nothing to do but wait, until "the ghosts of Auschwitz, Buchenwald, Treblinka and so many others end up dragging him from this life. It won't be long now." For several nights Hitler suffered hallucinations of "mutilated faces, fields blanketed with cadavers rising up to accuse him with trembling gestures." He could hardly sleep; despite the efforts of both Lehmann and Bethe, he refused to eat, and he spent his time "between sobs remembering the days of his infancy."

On February 12, 1962, at midday, the seventy-two-year-old Hitler collapsed as his two caregivers were helping him to the bathroom. Three hours later he suffered a stroke that paralyzed the left side of his body. After spending a restless night, the dictator slipped into a coma. On February 13, 1962, at 3:00 p.m., Dr. Lehmann verified that all signs of life were absent.

WITH HITLER'S DEATH, Otto Lehmann and Heinrich Bethe were no longer useful to the Organization; they had become nothing more than mouths to be silenced. Knowing this, Lehmann warned Bethe to escape. Taking with him Lehmann's papers and some other minor documents, Bethe managed to elude Müller and Bormann's network of killers and spies. Having changed his name to Juan Paulovsky, he died on the outskirts of the small Patagonian coastal town of Caleta Olivia in 1977. It seems that Dr. Lehmann was not so lucky; he disappeared shortly after Hitler's death, probably murdered on Bormann's orders. It was the final act in the life and death of Adolf Hitler in Argentina.

Bormann's and Müller's trail ran out later. In 1971, the *Boston Globe* of Monday July 26 quoted Zwy Aldouby, a former Israeli Intelligence officer and co-author of a 1960 book on Adolf Eichmann entitled

Minister of Death, as saying that Martin Bormann lived on a ranch in Paraguay. The author Ladislas Farago said he had seen Bormann personally—seemingly senile and having lost the will to live—in a remote part of Bolivia the same year. With Juan Domingo's Perón's return to power on June 20, 1973, Farago said Bormann moved back to Argentina and lived in a house north of the affluent San Isidro district in Buenos Aires. The Reichsleiter was still there when Farago wrote his book in June 1974.

Paul Manning wrote that Bormann, born in 1900, was still alive in 1980 in Argentina, as was Heinrich "Gestapo" Mueller who had been born in the same year as his boss. There are no reliable reports of the ultimate end of either of these senior Nazis.

IN HIS MEMOIRS, ALBERT SPEER recalled a conversation he had with Adolf Hitler in November 1936 concerning the Thousand-Year Reich. Hitler was standing before the massive picture window of his Berghof retreat and staring at his beloved Bavarian Alpine mountainscape, a landscape eerily similar to the view from his Patagonian home at Inalco. Hitler stated, "There are two possibilities for me. To win through with all my plans or to fail. If I win, I shall be one of the greatest men in history. If I fail, I shall be condemned, despised, and damned." To this day, the world condemns, despises, and damns Adolf Hitler and his utterly evil regime.

Yet, as the failed and faded Führer died in Argentina, tormented, demented, and betrayed, seventeen years after fleeing from the bunker in which the world believed he had committed suicide, the words that he and Joseph Goebbels had made famous had come true: "Make the lie big, make it simple, keep saying it, and eventually they will believe it." The world believes that Hitler died in Berlin.

Winston Churchill, Hitler's British nemesis, once famously said, "History will be kind to me for I intend to write it." But his archenemy had foreseen that possibility, and before Churchill wrote his history, Adolf Hitler, one of the most evil men in civilized history, pre-empted him by saying, "The victor will never be asked if he told the truth."

At the end of World War II the victors were never asked. We are asking them now. ■

ACKNOWLEDGMENTS

To all the authorities and individuals in Argentina who gave their indispensable support in the realization of this project, we extend our heartfelt thanks. Their conviction that the truth should finally be told—now that Argentina has become a mature democracy—allowed us to unravel this extraordinary story.

May we also take this opportunity to thank the following people: Maria Eugenia Faveret, a translator par excellence and an organizer without peer: muchas gracias, amiga; historian and U-boat expert Innes McCartney for his extensive researches at The National Archives, Kew, London, and elsewhere; Nahuel Coca, Argentine researcher and journalist extraordinaire, for all his help in Buenos Aires; aviation and Luftwaffe expert Tony Holmes; Philip Brace and the staff of the Ministry of Defence main library for obtaining a host of obscure and esoteric books and documents from a variety of sources; the staff of The National Archives in Kew for their unfailing assistance; Carolina Varasavsky for all her invaluable support; Capt. Manuel Monasterio for his courage in publishing Dr. Otto Lehmann's and Heinrich Bethe's stories at his own expense even when his life was threatened; Jorge Elbaum of the Delegación de Asociaciones Israelitas Argentinas for opening the organization's files and for its offers of security; noted Argentine television host Adrian Korol and his delightful life partner Silvina Shina for their help, introductions, and some of the best steaks we have ever eaten; and casting director, acting coach, and great friend Mariana "La China" Shina for everything.

Our thanks to the team at Greene Media, who had the vision to embrace this extraordinary story. At Sterling Publishing we would like to thank Marcus Leaver, president; Jason Prince, publisher; Michael Fragnito, editorial director; Elizabeth Mihaltse, art director, trade covers; and Blanca Oliviery, publicist. We would also like to acknowledge the packaging team at Buoy Point Media: Lary Rosenblatt, Fabia Wargin, and Laurie Lieb; and Amy King, for the striking cover design.

And finally, but not least, thanks to our brilliant editor at Sterling, Barbara Berger, who checked and re-checked our findings and made the whole thing readable.

— SIMON DUNSTAN AND GERRARD WILLIAMS

I am grateful to the Argentine cast and crew on the film *Grey Wolf*—too many to mention individually, but to all, my gratitude for your professionalism and friendship; Robert Stubbs and Ian Hall for all their help; Simon Goldberg, my lawyer in London, for his help and patience; Russell Tenzer for his long friendship, help, and advice; Eduardo Martín Boneo Villegas; Cuini Amelio Ortiz, filmmaker and chronicler of the Eichhorns' activities; James Rainbird, assistant director, composer, and great friend; and the Norris family for such unfailing friendship and support.

Let me thank, too, my father, ex-Sgt. Maj. Len Williams, and my mother, Mary, who both fought fascism in World War II and who would be disgusted at the truth. To them and all the others who took up arms from around the world, we should all be grateful.

To the memory of three wonderful people who were there at the beginning but did not live to see it happen: Bill Stout, a great cameraman, brother, and companion on more adventures than I care to remember; J.J. Swart, another great cameraman, chef, and friend; and one of the best women in the world, Tina Murdoch. I miss them all.

Above all I wish to acknowledge the extraordinary fortitude of my beautiful wife, Ginny, and my children Nick and Bex. Without their faith and support, none of this could ever have happened. And to Magnus Peterson—my benefactor, supporter, and convivial companion throughout the trials and tribulations of this project—go my thanks, best wishes, and undying friendship.

— GERRARD WILLIAMS

Notes

Preface

xix "facilitated the flight of hundreds of erstwhile Nazis": *The Office of Special Investigations: Striving for Accountability in the Aftermath of the Holocaust*, Department of Justice, Criminal Division, 2006. See http://documents.nytimes.com/confidential-report-provides-new-evidence-of-notorious-nazi-cases?ref=us#p=1; see also http://www.archives.gov/iwg/declassified-records/rg-330-defense-secretary/. See also Mark Aarons, *Sanctuary: Nazi Fugitives in Australia* (Melbourne: William Heinemann Australia, 1989), and Stephen Tyas, "British Intelligence and the Nazi Recruit," *History Today* 54, 2004, http://www.historytoday.com/stephen-tyas/british-intelligence-and-nazi-recruit.

xix **John Demjanjuk:** *New York Times*, "Demjanjuk Convicted for Role in Nazi Death Camp," May 12, 2011, http://www.nytimes.com/2011/05/13/world/europe/13nazi.html?_r=1&scp=2&sq=Demjanjuk&st=cse.

xxi "**Hitler's chauffeur, Erich Kempka**": James P. O'Donnell, *The Bunker: The History of the Reich Chancellery Group* (Boston: Houghton Mifflin, 1978).

xxii "**We found no corpse that could be Hitler's**": Marshal Georgi Zhukov, quoted on June 6, 1945, by United Press Berlin, *Miami Daily News*, "Hitler May Have Fled with Bride Before Fall of Berlin," June 10, 1945, http://news.google.com/newspapers?id=qE8yAAAAIBAJ&sjid=yecFAAAAIBAJ&pg=2861,2346002&dq=hitler+fled+berlin+zhukov&hl=en.

xxii "**There is *every assumption* that Hitler is dead**": Dwight D. Eisenhower, quoted on October 12, 1945, by The Associated Press, *Indian Express*, "Is Hitler Alive?," October 14, 1945, http://news.google.com/newspapers?id=orI-AAAAIBAJ&sjid=SEwMAAAAIBAJ&pg=4222,1007385&dq=eisenhower+hitler+alive&hl=en.

xxv "**Allied Powers employed numerous Nazi war criminals**": *New York Times*, "Nazis Were Given Safe Haven in U.S., Report Says," November 13, 2010, http://www.nytimes.com/2010/11/14/us/14nazis.html?scp=2&sq=nazis&st=cse. See also *The Office of Special Investigations: Striving for Accountability in the Aftermath of the Holocaust*, Department of Justice, Criminal Division, 2006, Report: "Klaus Barbie: The Butcher of Lyon."

xxv **Israeli government and Nazi hunting:** Ian Black and Benny Morris, *Israel's Secret Wars: A History of Israel's Intelligence Services* (New York: Grove Press, 1991).

xxv **Lothar Hermann:** http://www.holocaustresearchproject.org/trials/eichmanntrialcapture.html.

xxv "**It has now been proved**": *Daily Telegraph*, "Germany and US 'Knew Where Eichmann Was in 1952,'" January 9, 2011, http://www.telegraph.co.uk/news/worldnews/europe/germany/8248965/Germany-and-US-knew-where-Eichmann-was-in-1952.html.

xxvi **Gehlen Organization and the BND:** Klaus Wiegrefe, "The Nazi Criminals Who Became German Spooks," *Der Spiegel*, February 16, 2011, www.spiegel.de/international/germany/0,1518,745640,00.html.

Introduction

xxviii "**When Adolf Hitler returned from the Western Front**": Cris Whetton, *Hitler's Fortune* (Barnsley, UK: Pen and Sword Books, 2004).

xxvii "**Money does not bring happiness**": Paul Manning, *Martin Bormann: Nazi in Exile* (Secaucus, NY: Lyle Stuart, 1981).

xxxi "**Uncle Wolf**": Guido Knopp, *Hitler's Women* (New York: Routledge, 2003).

Chapter 1: Fueling the Beast

3 "**zenith of its success**": There are innumerable general histories of World War II, but for a single-volume treatment including the aspects relevant to this book the authors can recommend Norman Davies, *Europe at War 1939–1945: No Simple Victory* (London: Macmillan, 2006).

4 **"modification of the Enigma"**: Ronald Lewin, *Ultra Goes to War* (Barnsley, UK: Pen and Sword Books, 2008). The addition of a fourth rotor to the naval Enigma machines (Schlüssel M) virtually stopped British decryption of U-boat signals traffic for nine months.

4 **convoy SC-107**: *Wolf Packs* (The Third Reich series) (Alexandria, VA: Time-Life Books, 1989). See "Treatment of Military Ranks" on page xiv for translations of German ranks.

5 **U-boats of Gruppe Veilchen**: Further details of this battle are to be found on http://www. uboat.net.

5 **"730,000 tons of Allied shipping"**: Gordon Williamson, *Wolf Pack: The Story of the U-Boat in World War II* (Oxford: Osprey, 2005).

5 **"from 91 to 212 boats"**: Gordon Williamson, *U-Boat Tactics in World War II* (Oxford: Osprey, 2010).

5 **"only thing that ever really frightened me"**: Winston S. Churchill, *The Second World War*, vol. 2, *Their Finest Hour* (London: Cassell, 1949).

5 **"terms imposed on Germany"**: David Sinclair, *Hall of Mirrors* (London: Century, 2001).

6 **"enviable background experience"**: James Srodes, *Allen Dulles: Master of Spies* (Washington, DC: Regency, 1999). On one occasion during Dulles's service in Bern in World War 1, a man by the name of Vladimir Ilyich Ulyanov knocked on the door of his residence, requesting an audience and a visa for America. Anxious to meet a young lady at the tennis club, Dulles refused, dismissing his visitor as "not very important." This would be a matter of acute regret to him; V. I. Ulyanov would become better known as Lenin.

6 **"Uncle Bert" Lansing**: Ibid.

7 **"powerful and influential conglomerates"**: Diarmuid Jeffreys, *Hell's Cartel: IG Farben and the Making of Hitler's War Machine* (London: Bloomsbury, 2008).

8 **Dulles's meeting with Martin Bormann**: Manning, *Martin Bormann*.

8 **"enabling act"**: Michael Burleigh, *The Third Reich: A New History* (London: Macmillan, 2000).

9 **"happy to fill the gap"**: Edwin Black, *Nazi Nexus: America's Corporate Connections to Hitler's Holocaust* (Washington, DC: Dialog Press, 2009).

9 **"Order of the German Eagle"**: Agostino von Hassell and Sigrid MacRae with Simone Ameskamp, *Alliance of Enemies: The Untold Story of the Secret American and German Collaboration to End World War II* (New York: Thomas Dunne Books, 2006).

9 **Opel AG of Russelsheim**: Ibid.

10 **"Achilles' heel"**: Charles Higham, *Trading with the Enemy: The Nazi-American Money Plot 1933– 1949* (New York: Delacorte Press, 1983).

10 **"As Britain fought for her life"**: Glen Yeadon and John Hawkins, *The Nazi Hydra in America* (Joshua Tree, CA: Progressive Press, 2008). Yeadon and Hawkins provide (p. 92) a striking example of the duplicity of German-influenced U.S. business corporations: "An agreement between DuPont and Dynamit in 1929 controlled the production of tetrazine, a substance that greatly improved ammunition primers. When WW II began in 1939, Remington Arms (controlled by DuPont) received huge British ammunition orders. Because of a clause in the agreement with IG Farben, the British received an inferior cartridge lacking tetrazine."

11 **"personal representative of President Roosevelt"**: Srodes, *Allen Dulles*.

11 **"gentlemen do not read each other's mail"**: von Hassel et al., *Alliance of Enemies*.

11 **"Japanese diplomatic cipher"**: For a fuller account of the interservice rivalry that bedeviled U.S. code-breaking before World War II, see Thomas Parrish, *The Ultra Americans: The U.S. Role in Breaking the Nazi Codes* (New York: Stein and Day, 1986). Purple was the Japanese equivalent of the German Enigma encoding machine, and the decrypted intelligence provided was code-named "Magic." American cryptanalysts broke the Japanese diplomatic code some fifteen months before Pearl Harbor, but the failure in liaison between the various services and governmental agencies meant that the warnings of Japanese military intentions were either ignored or discounted in the days leading up to December 7, 1941—"a date which will live in infamy." Fortunately, the Japanese continued to use Purple and much vital intelligence concerning Nazi war plans was gleaned from intercepting the cables of the Japanese ambassador in Berlin, Hiroshi Oshima, following his frequent, lengthy meetings with Adolf Hitler throughout the war.

12 **"with war looming"**: Allen W. Dulles, *The Secret Surrender* (Guildford, CT: Lyons Press, 2006).

13 **"Oh So Social"**: *The Secret War* (The World War II series) (Alexandria, VA: Time-Life Books, 1998).

13 **U-559**: http://www.uboat.net. Lt. Tony Fasson and AB Colin Glazier were posthumously awarded the George Cross, and canteen assistant Tommy Brown lived to receive the George Medal—though he did not survive the war. Tragically, he died in 1945 trying to save his sister from a fire at their home.

Chapter 2: THE TURNING TIDE

14 **"all sorts of outlandish people"**: Srodes, *Allen Dulles*.

15 **"big window"**: Christof Mauch, *The Shadow War Against Hitler: The Covert Operations of America's Wartime Secret Intelligence Service* (New York: Columbia University Press, 2002).

15 **"bringing to my door purveyors of information"**: Srodes, Allen Dulles.

15 **"putting one over the Brits"**: Gordon Thomas, *Inside British Intelligence: 100 Years of MI5 and MI6* (London: JR Books, 2009).

16 **"George Wood"**: Lucas Delattre, *Betraying Hitler: The Story of Fritz Kolbe, the Most Important Spy of the Second World War* (London: Atlantic Books, 2005).

17 **Wilhelm Canaris**: Charles Whiting, *Hitler's Secret War: The Nazi Espionage Campaign Against the Allies* (Barnsley, UK: Leo Cooper, 2000).

18 **"pillow talk"**: von Hassell et al., *Alliance of Enemies*.

18 **"these east German Junkers"**: Ibid.

18 **"Yankee Doodle Dandy"**: Thomas, *Inside British Intelligence*.

18 **"all news from Berne"**: Delattre, *Betraying Hitler*.

19 **"All ammunition spent"**: *The World at Arms: The Reader's Digest Illustrated History of World War II* (London: Reader's Digest Association, 1989).

20 **"small hunk of horse meat"**: *The Illustrated History of the World: The World in Flames 1939–45* (London: Reader's Digest Association, 2007).

20 **"genuinely pivotal victory"**: Davies, *Europe at War 1939–1945*.

21 **Casablanca Conference and Operation Pointblank**: H. P. Wilmott, Charles Messenger, and Robin Cross, *World War II* (London: Dorling Kindersley, 2004).

21 **"Unconditional Surrender Grant"**: von Hassell et al., *Alliance of Enemies*.

22 **"We rendered impossible internal revolution"**: Letter to Chester Wilmot, January 3, 1949, Allen W. Dulles papers, Seeley G. Mudd Manuscript Library, Princeton, New Jersey, as cited in Lucas Delattre, *Betraying Hitler: The Story of Fritz Kolbe, the Most Important Spy of the Second World War* (London: Atlantic Books, 2005).

Chapter 3: THE BROWN EMINENCE

23 **"imbalance of resources"**: A mass of statistics is available, but the following snapshot figures for 1943 may suffice. Total Allied coal production was 928 million tons and Axis production 545 million. Total Allied production of iron ore was 145 million tons and Axis production 77 million. Total Allied crude steel production was 118 million tons and Axis production 47 million. Total Allied crude oil production was 259 million tons and Axis production just 18 million. As for manufacturing output, in 1943 the Allied nations built 61,062 battle tanks and self-propelled guns, the Axis nations 12,957. From John Ellis, *The World War II Data Book* (London: Aurum Press, 1993).

24 **"der totaler Krieg"**: Richard Bessel, *Nazism and War* (London: Phoenix, 2004).

25 **"greatest confusion that has ever existed"**: *The Center of the Web* (The Third Reich series) (Alexandria, VA: Time-Life Books, 1990).

25 **"Hitler exercised his absolute power"**: Burleigh, *Third Reich*.

26 **"state machinery defied all logical explanation"**: Brian L. Davis, *The German Home Front 1939–45* (Oxford: Osprey, 2007).

27 **"Telex General"**: Jochen von Lang, *Bormann: The Man Who Manipulated Hitler* (London: Weidenfeld & Nicolson, 1979).

28 **"Hitler's personal treasure chest"**: Whetton, *Hitler's Fortune*.

28 **"Bormann's proposals are so precisely worked out"**: Joachim C. Fest, *The Face of the Third Reich* (New York: Da Capo Press, 1999).

29 **"clung to Hitler like ivy"**: Patrick Delaforce, *The Hitler File* (London: Michael O'Mara Books, 2007). Bormann's power stemmed less from his party rank—there were seventeen different NSDAP departmental Reichsleitern—than from his appointment to particular duties close to Hitler.

29 **"I need Bormann"**: Guido Knopp, *Hitler's Hitmen* (Stroud, UK: Sutton, 2002).

29 **"my own private existence"**: Whetton, *Hitler's Fortune*.

30 **"financed from the AH Fund"**: Ibid.

30 **"household of the Führer"**: *Center of the Web*.

30 **"his brilliant business acumen"**: von Lang, *Bormann*.

Chapter 4: THE RAPE OF EUROPE

32 **Hitler's early life:** Michael Fitzgerald, *Adolf Hitler: A Portrait* (Stroud, UK: Spellmount Books, 2006).

32 **"racial purity":** Burleigh, *Third Reich.*

33 **"eliminating political opponents":** Bessel, *Nazism and War.*

33 **"'Aryanization' of all aspects of German society":** Mark Mazower, *Hitler's Empire: Nazi Rule in Occupied Europe* (London: Allen Lane, 2008).

34 **Kristallnacht:** James Pool, *Hitler and His Secret Partners: Contributions, Loot and Rewards 1933–1945* (New York: Pocket Books, 1997).

35 **"bureaucracy of murder":** John Cornwell, *Hitler's Scientists: Science, War and the Devil's Pact* (London: Penguin Books, 2004).

35 **"safekeeping of works of art":** Richard Z. Chesnoff, *Pack of Thieves: How Hitler and Europe Plundered the Jews and Committed the Greatest Theft in History* (London: Weidenfeld & Nicolson, 2000).

36 **"painter of idyllic landscapes":** Ronald Pawly, *Hitler's Chancellery: A Palace to Last a Thousand Years* (Ramsbury, UK: Crowood Press, 2009).

36 **"Look at those details":** Delaforce, *The Hitler File.*

36 **Rosenberg and "the character Wilhelm Furtwängler":** Jonathan Petropoulos, *The Faustian Bargain: The Art World in Nazi Germany* (London: Allen Lane, 2000). Museums were also required to provide some of their acceptable masterpieces for the decoration of the New Reich Chancellery. For instance, in 1938–39 Speer requisitioned "on loan" many works from the Art Historical Museum in Vienna, including twenty-one enormous seventeenth-century Dutch and Belgian tapestries; see Pawly, *Hitler's Chancellery.*

37 **Committee for the Exploitation of Degenerate Art:** Lynn H. Nicholas, *The Rape of Europa: The Fate of Europe's Treasures in the Third Reich and the Second World War* (New York: Alfred A. Knopf, 1994).

38 **"extraordinary bargains":** Ibid.

38 **"triumphal progress through Vienna":** Saul Friedländer, *Nazi Germany and the Jews* (London: Phoenix, 2009).

38 **Rothschilds:** Hitler reserved a special loathing for this famous Jewish family of financiers and art collectors whose collections in Vienna and Paris he plundered for his planned Führermuseum at Linz. His grandmother had once worked as a maid for the Vienna branch of the family, and rumors persisted that her bastard son, Hitler's father Alois Schicklgruber, had been sired by a Rothschild—which would have made Hitler one-quarter Jewish.

39 **"his eyes glittering" and "It was the dream of my life":** Albert Speer, *Inside the Third Reich* (London: Weidenfeld & Nicolson, 1970).

40 **"Jewish-owned works of degenerate art":** Nicholas, *Rape of Europa.*

40 **Jeu du Paume:** Hector Feliciano, *The Lost Museum: The Nazi Conspiracy to Steal the World's Greatest Works of Art* (New York: Basic Books, 1997).

41 **Aktion-M:** Chesnoff, *Pack of Thieves.*

41 **"Soviet Union lost 1.148 million artworks":** See footnotes of http://en.wikipedia.org/wiki/Nazi_plunder.

41 **"cultural center of the Thousand-Year Reich":** Mazower, *Hitler's Empire.*

42 **"Bormann knew the location":** Whetton, *Hitler's Fortune.*

42 **"bogus art dealerships in Latin American locations":** Stanley G. Payne, *Franco and Hitler: Spain, Germany and World War II* (New Haven: Yale University Press, 2008).

42 **"flow of confiscated art":** Nicholas, *Rape of Europa.*

43 **"involving 137 freight cars":** Shoah Resource Center, www.yadvashem.org, "Einsatzstab Rosenberg."

Chapter 5: NAZI GOLD

44 **German gold reserves:** John Weitz, *Hitler's Banker: Hjalmar Horace Greely Schacht* (London: Little, Brown, 1999).

45 **"abundance of gold":** Chesnoff, *Pack of Thieves.*

45 **plunder of European gold reserves:** Arthur L. Smith, *Hitler's Gold: The Story of the Nazi War Loot* (Dulles, VA: Berg, 1996).

46 **"Eventually the French agreed to hand over the Belgian gold":** Ibid.

46 **"saga of the Belgian gold"**: Ibid.
47 **"gold items taken from the victims"**: Yeadon and Hawkins, *Nazi Hydra in America*. The scale of Aktion Reinhardt—the theft of prisoners' possessions prior to their extermination in the death camps—was staggering, involving the expropriation of 53,013,133 reichsmarks in cash; foreign currency in bank notes to a value of 1,452,904 reichsmarks; foreign currency in gold coins to a value of 843,802 reichsmarks; precious metals to a value of 5,353,943 reichsmarks; other valuables, such as jewelry, watches, and spectacles, to a value of 26,089,800 reichsmarks; and clothing and textiles to a value of 13,294,400 reichsmarks, to give a grand total of 100,047,983 reichsmarks. The obscene exactitude of the Nazi accounting of the Holocaust utterly beggars belief.
48 **"favored the Bank for International Settlements"**: von Hassell et al., *Alliance of Enemies*.
50 **"In 1939 the Banco Nacional de Portugal held 63 tons of gold"**: Antonio Louça and Ansgar Schäfer, "Portugal and the Nazi Gold: The 'Lisbon Connection' in the Sales of Looted Gold by the Third Reich"; see online PDF at www.yadvashem.org.
52 **"$890 million in gold"**: John Loftus and Mark Aarons, *The Secret War Against the Jews* (New York: St. Martin's Press, 1994). It was not until May 1997 that the BIS admitted to accepting shipments of Nazi gold that had been melted down and stamped with prewar German markings to disguise the fact that it was looted from other countries.
52 **François-René de Chateaubriand**: von Hassell et al., *Alliance of Enemies*.

Chapter 6: EAGLE FLIGHT AND LAND OF FIRE

53 **Operation Citadel**: Davies, *Europe at War 1939–45*.
54 **"sales of 'degenerate art'"**: Nicholas, *Rape of Europa*.
55 **"290,000 carats of diamonds"**: Chesnoff, *Pack of Thieves*.
55 **"high-value minerals"**: Ladislas Farago, *Aftermath: Martin Bormann and the Fourth Reich* (New York: Avon Books, 1974).
56 **Operation Andreas/Bernhard**: Yeadon and Hawkins, *Nazi Hydra in America*. The forgeries were so good that the Bank of England could do little to call them in after the war without destroying faith in British paper money; as a result, nothing was said or done and they remained in circulation until 1954, when a new design of the five-pound note replaced the old white "bedsheet." The scale of the operation was considerable: 3,945,867 five-pound notes, 2,398,981 ten-pound notes, and 1,337,325 twenty-pound notes were produced, in addition to a quantity of fifty-pound notes. Work on counterfeit U.S. dollar notes began in the spring of 1944, and the first examples together with real bills were presented to Heinrich Himmler in January 1945. He was unable to tell the difference between the true and fake notes, but serious production of counterfeit dollars was never undertaken in quantity. For a fuller account of Operation Andreas/Bernhard, see "Report on Forgery in Sachsenhausen Concentration Camp," dated December 15, 1945, compiled by the Central Criminal Office of the Czechoslovak Ministry of the Interior.
56 **Project Eagle Flight**: Manning, *Martin Bormann*.
57 **"heavy water"**: Chesnoff, *Pack of Thieves*.
57 **"create some 980 front companies"**: Yeadon and Hawkins, *Nazi Hydra in America*.
58 **"every known device"**: Manning, *Martin Bormann*.
58 **"Bury your treasure deep"**: Ibid.
59 **"self-contained refuge for Hitler"**: Jim Marrs, *The Rise of the Fourth Reich* (New York: William Morrow, 2008).

Chapter 7: RED INDIANS AND PRIVATE ARMIES

63 **"Naval Intelligence Commando Unit"**: The National Archives, Kew, London; Enclosure 1 to File ADM 223/500.
63 **"Abwehrkommando"**: Steven Kippax, "Hitler's Special Forces," *Military Illustrated* 155 (2001).
64 **"Fleming's 'Red Indians'"**: This section is drawn from *The History of 30 Assault Unit 1942–1946* (London: King's College Library Military Archives, Ref GB99). Lt. Cdr. Fleming's room number was 39; Admiral Godfrey, in Room 38, was the role model for "M" in the James Bond novels. See also http://www.30AU.co.uk.
65 **"Maj. Wurmann"**: Richard Breitman, *U.S. Intelligence and the Nazis* (Cambridge, UK: Cambridge University Press, 2005).
66 **30 CU's jeeps**: David Nutting and Jim Glanville, eds., *Attain by Surprise: The Story of 30 Assault*

Unit Royal Navy/ Royal Marine Commando and of Intelligence by Capture (London: David Glover, 1997).

66 **Tiger tank:** David Fletcher, historian, Royal Armoured Corps Tank Museum, Bovington, Dorset, UK, in interview with Simon Dunstan, August 2010. This Tiger tank—turret number 131 of Panzer Abteilung 504—now resides at Bovington. It is the only remaining Tiger I in the world that can still motor on its own tracks. Very heavily armored and mounting an 88mm main gun, the Tiger was twice the weight and possessed twice the firepower of the M4 Sherman medium tank that was the mainstay of both the American and British armored forces in 1943–45.

67 **30 Assault Unit:** Nutting and Glanville, *Attain by Surprise.*

67 **"Monuments Men":** Robert M. Edsel, *Monuments Men: Allied Heroes, Nazi Thieves and the Greatest Treasure Hunt in History* (London: Arrow Books, 2009).

68 **"Prior to this war":** Nicola Lambourne, *War Damage in Western Europe: The Destruction of Historic Monuments during the Second World War* (Edinburgh: Edinburgh University Press, 2001).

68 **"Second Punic War":** National Archives and Records Administration (NARA), College Park, Maryland; RG 239/ 47.

69 **"Benedictine abbey of Monte Cassino":** *Report of the American Commission for the Protection and Salvage of Artistic and Historic Monuments in War Areas* (Washington, DC: U.S. Government Printing Office, 1946). Arguably, the destruction by Allied bombing of the Mantegna frescoes in the Ovetari chapel, Church of the Eremitani, Padua, on March 11, 1944, was a comparable artistic tragedy.

69 **"Tutti questi vaffunculi quadri!":** David Tutaev, *The Consul of Florence* (London: Secker & Warburg, 1966).

69 **"immense hoard of artistic plunder":** Edsel, *Monuments Men.*

70 **Uranium Committee and Manhattan Project:** Jim Baggott, *Atomic: The First War of Physics and the Secret War of the Atom Bomb 1939–1949* (London: Icon Books, 2009).

71 **"Jewish physics":** Richard Rhodes, *The Making of the Atomic Bomb* (London: Penguin Books, 1986).

72 **"Unless and until we had positive knowledge":** Cynthia C. Kelly, ed, *The Manhattan Project: The Birth of the Atomic Bomb in the Words of Its Creators, Eyewitnesses, and Historians* (New York: Atomic Heritage Foundation, 2007).

72 **Alsos Mission:** Baggott, *Atomic.*

73 **"bearer of this card":** Patrick Dalzel-Job, *Arctic Snow to Dust of Normandy: The Extraordinary Wartime Exploits of a Naval Special Agent* (Barnsley, UK: Pen and Sword, 2005).

73 **"targets of military or scientific importance":** Sean Longden, *T-Force: The Race for Nazi War Secrets 1945* (London: Constable, 2009).

73 **"Gold Rush" teams:** See Bernard Bernstein Papers at http://www.trumanlibrary.org/hstpaper/bernstein/htm.

Chapter 8: THE HUNTING TRAIL TO PARIS

74 **"peculiar fluttering noise in the air":** Dalzel-Job, *Arctic Snow.*

75 **"V-1 Vengeance Weapon":** Steven J. Zaloga, *V-1 Flying Bomb 1942–52: Hitler's Infamous "Doodlebug"* (Oxford: Osprey, 2005).

75 **"Operation Crossbow":** George S. Patton, *War, As I Knew It* (Cambridge, MA: Riverside Press, 1947). Between August 1943 and March 1945, Allied air forces flew 68,913 sorties and dropped 122,133 tons of bombs on V-1 and V-2 installations; this represented some 14 percent of all heavy bomber missions during that period.

76 **"fifteen miles beyond the American beachhead':** The National Archives, Kew, London; File ADM 223/214, History of 30 Commando Unit (later 30 Assault Unit and 30 Advance Unit).

76 **"high-speed fighters":** Zaloga, *V-1 Flying Bomb.*

76 **"greatest single technical capture of the war":** The National Archives, Kew, London; File ADM 223/214.

77 **V-1s:** Zaloga, *V-1 Flying Bomb.* A total of 8,617 V-1s were fired, of which 1,052 crashed on takeoff. Of the 5,913 that reached Britain, 3,852 were destroyed by the air defenses, including 1,651 by antiaircraft guns; only 2,515 hit their target areas. The others missed their targets and landed in the countryside. The very last (air-launched) V-1 struck the village of Datchworth, Hertfordshire, on March 29, 1945.

77 **"20,000 tons of bombs":** Adam Tooze, *The Wages of Destruction: The Making and Breaking of the Nazi Economy* (London: Allen Lane, 2006).

77 **"pulverized from the air":** Mazower, *Hitler's Empire.*
78 **"hanged like cattle":** Toby Thacker, *The End of the Third Reich* (Stroud, UK: Tempus, 2008).
79 **maskirovka:** The Red Army were past masters in their ability to hide whole military formations from enemy observation by a host of means that collectively was known as *maskirovka.* For Operation Bagration the deception was so effective that the Germans believed the main Soviet summer offensive in 1944 would be in the Ukraine when in fact it was in a completely different country, Byelorussia. Similarly, the Western Allies created false armies prior to D-Day to deceive the Germans as to where the actual amphibious landings would happen through Operation Fortitude. The phantom "First U.S. Army Group" commanded by Gen. George S. Patton was "formed" in southeast England—in much the same manner as *maskirovka*—with such success that the Germans believed the main Allied offensive was to be in the Pas de Calais region of France even after the D-Day landings in Normandy. It is interesting to note that the German army military intelligence unit on the Eastern Front (Fremde Heere Ost or FHO), which was comprehensively deceived by *maskirovka* prior to Operation Bagration, was commanded by one Col. Reinhard Gehlen. After the war he sold his "expertise" on the Red Army to the CIA, which funded the creation of the "Gehlen Organization" that was staffed by many former SS personnel. Riddled with Soviet agents throughout its existence, the Gehlen Organization was just as ineffective in its provision of military intelligence to the Western Allies as the FHO had been to the German army in 1944.
79 **"Operation Bagration":** Jonathan W. Jordan, "Operation Bagration: Soviet Offensive of 1944," *World War II* magazine (July–August 2006).
79 **"most calamitous defeat":** Steven J. Zaloga, *Bagration 1944: The Destruction of Army Group Center* (Oxford: Osprey, 1996).
80 **"Team 4 from 30 AU":** Dalzel-Job, *Arctic Snow.*
80 **S.Sgt. Bramah:** For an account of S.Sgt. Bramah's extraordinary exploits in Normandy, see http://www.nasenoviny.com/GPREN.html.
80 **"Woolforce":** The National Archives, Kew, London; File ADM 1/15798, Operation Woolforce: activities of No.30 Assault Unit in Paris 1944.
80 **"I had blown over 80 safes":** Nutting and Glanville, *Attain by Surprise.*
81 **30 AU:** The National Archives, Kew, London; File ADM 223/214.
81 **"first American vehicle":** Steven J. Zaloga, *The Liberation of Paris 1944* (Oxford: Osprey, 2008).
81 **"celebratory bottle of champagne":** Baggott, *Atomic.*
81 **"T-Force activities":** Longden, *T-Force.*
82 **"long, empty galleries":** Edsel, *Monuments Men.*
82 **"148 crates of looted paintings":** Ibid.
83 **"art train was trapped":** Ibid. These exploits were dramatized in the 1964 movie *The Train*, directed by John Frankenheimer and starring Burt Lancaster, Paul Scofield, Jeanne Moreau, and Suzanne Flon as "Mlle. Villard"—Rose Valland.

Chapter 9: CASH, ROCKETS, AND URANIUM

84 **"steps to be taken":** Manning, *Martin Bormann.*
85 **Fritz Thyssen and his wife detained:** Yeadon and Hawkins, *Nazi Hydra.*
85 **"Thyssen family's private bank":** Office of the Director of Intelligence, Field Information Agency/Technical, Report No. EF/ME/ 1, September 4, 1945; Examination of Dr. Fritz Thyssen, U.S. Group Control Council Germany.
85 **"industrial and commercial patents":** Yeadon and Hawkins, *Nazi Hydra.*
86 **"after the defeat of Germany":** Manning, *Martin Bormann.*
86 **"leading coordinator":** Marrs, *Rise of the Fourth Reich.*
86 **"good offices of the Spanish banks":** Manning, *Martin Bormann.*
87 **"It is possible that Germany will be defeated":** Marrs, *Rise of the Fourth Reich.*
88 **Operation Penguin:** Steven J. Zaloga, *V-2 Ballistic Missile 1942–52* (Oxford: Osprey, 2003).
88 **V-2 attacks in London:** A4/V2 Resource Site, www.V2rocket.com.
88 **"under rocket attack for some weeks":** Michael J. Neufeld, *The Rocket and the Reich: Peenemünde and the Coming of the Ballistic Missile Era* (New York: Free Press, 1995).
89 **"We have invaded space":** Walter Dornberger, *V-2* (New York: Viking, 1954).
89 **"first actual record on film":** Roy M. Stanley II, *V Weapons Hunt: Defeating German Secret Weapons* (Barnsley, UK: Pen and Sword, 2010).
90 **"Polish Home Army partisans":** Marek Ney-Krwawicz, *The Polish Home Army 1939–1945*, trans.

Antoni Bohdanowicz (London: Polish Underground Movement (1935–1945) Study Trust, 2001). See also www.polishresistance-ak.org/2 Article.htm, courtesy of the Polish Institute and Sikorski Museum, London.

90 **Operation Hydra:** Neufeld, *Rocket and the Reich.* Tragically, the majority of the casualties were press-ganged Polish workers, although the head of engine development, Dr. Walter Thiel, was also among some 735 people who were killed. Forty RAF aircraft were lost.

91 **slave laborers:** Ibid.

91 **"far exceeds anything ever done in Europe":** Ibid.

91 **Operation Penguin:** Zaloga, *V-2 Ballistic Missile.* One of the worst incidents occurred on November 25, 1944, when a V-2 fell on a Woolworth's store in New Cross, East London, killing 168 people. The final V-2 directed against London landed in Orpington, Kent, on March 27, 1945, killing Mrs. Ivy Millichamp—the last of the 60,595 British civilians to be killed in World War II. The greatest single loss of life was the 571 people killed on December 16, 1944, when a V-2 struck the Rex Cinema on Avenue De Keyserlei in Antwerp, Belgium.

91 **"sixty missiles per week":** Tooze, *Wages of Destruction.*

92 **"Confidence was so high":** Davies, *Europe at War.*

92 **Chartres Cathedral and the Bruges Madonna:** Edsel, *Monuments Men.* Along with a vast repository of Hitler's fabulous art collection, the Madonna of Bruges was stored in a salt mine at Altaussee in the Bavarian Alps, where it was primed for destruction by high explosives on Bormann's orders. The Madonna of Bruges was rescued by the Monuments Men on July 10, 1945, and returned to its home in the Church of Our Lady in Bruges, Belgium, where it resides to this day.

93 **"apparent imminence of German defeat":** Thacker, *End of the Third Reich.*

93 **Arnhem:** Lewin, *Ultra Goes to War;* Stephen Badsey, *Arnhem 1944: Operation Market Garden* (Oxford: Osprey, 1993).

93 **"another grueling battle":** Steven J. Zaloga, *The Siegfried Line 1944–45: Battles on the German Frontier* (Oxford: Osprey, 2007).

94 **"electromagnetic separation calutrons":** Kelly, *Manhattan Project.*

94 **"Gen. Groves was still not satisfied":** It is indicative of Groves's influence that he was able to demand specific bombing missions to hamper Germany's nuclear researches. At his request, the Berlin suburb of Dahlem—home to the Kaiser Wilhelm Institute for Physics—was included in the bombing plan for the night of February 15–16, 1944. During this heaviest RAF raid against the city of Berlin, the laboratory of leading Uranverein scientist Otto Hahn was hit and all his papers were destroyed. Thereafter, the Uranverein facilities were dispersed around Germany—but by now Alsos knew most of these locations across the country.

95 **"Deny the enemy his brain":** Baggott, *Atomic.*

95 **"Nothing spelled out":** Ibid.

96 **"pistol remained in Moe Berg's pocket":** Ibid.

Chapter 10: THE FOG OF WAR

97 **"There is no reason why":** Arieh Kochavi, *Prelude to Nuremberg* (Chapel Hill: University of North Carolina, 1998).

98 **Morgenthau Plan:** Yeadon and Hawkins, *Nazi Hydra.*

98 **Dr. Harry Dexter White:** Whiting, *Hitler's Secret War.*

98 **"Two of the Abwehr agents":** Ibid.

98 **"potato field":** *Berliner Morgenpost,* October 5, 1944, reporting a speech by Goebbels that concluded with the words, "The enemy's destructive desires make us even harder and more determined to fight."

99 **"ten fresh German divisions":** William J. Bennett, *America: The Last Best Hope,* 2 vols. (Nashville, TN: Thomas Nelson, 2007).

99 **"barely able to contain his indignation":** Franklin D. Roosevelt Presidential Library and Museum, Hyde Park, NY; OSS Official Dispatch Ref No. 250.

99 **"process of money-laundering":** Loftus and Aarons, *Secret War Against the Jews.*

99 **Operation Safehaven:** Loftus and Aarons, *Secret War Against the Jews;* Higham, *Trading with the Enemy.* See also Yeadon and Hawkins, *Nazi Hydra in America,* for Roosevelt's plans to use British illegal wiretaps against corporate villains in postwar trials of treason.

100 **Federal Economic Administration:** von Hassell et al., *Alliance of Enemies.*

101 **"embarrassment to the Swiss government":** Whiting, *Hitler's Secret War.*

101 **"National Redoubt":** Srodes, *Allen Dulles.*
101 **"another conduit to the Nazi leadership":** Breitman, *U.S. Intelligence and the Nazis.* Following the German occupation of Hungary in March 1944, Wilhelm Höttl had organized the transportation of 440,000 Hungarian Jews to Auschwitz-Birkenau, where they were put to death in the gas chambers between April and June 1944. Höttl was employed by various Allied intelligence services after the war as a reward for the part he played in Operation Crossword (see Chapter 12). He proved to be a useless informant and agent in the Cold War period.
102 **"Luftwaffe code-breaking unit":** Loftus and Aarons, *Secret War Against the Jews.*
102 **"Dulles also exposed Henry Wallace":** Srodes, *Allen Dulles.*
103 **"we must fish in troubled waters":** NARA, College Park, Maryland; NA RG 226 Entry 134, Records of the Office of Strategic Services (OSS), Director's Office and Field Station Records.
103 **"similar remit":** OSS Art Looting Investigation Unit Final Report (Washington, DC: U.S. Government Printing Office, May 1946).
103 **Madonna of La Gleize:** Edsel, *Monuments Men.*
104 **"Eagle's Nest":** Franz W. Seidler and Dieter Zeigert, *Hitler's Headquarters: The Führer's Wartime Bases, from the Invasion of France to the Berlin Bunker* (London: Greenhill Books, 2004).
105 **German battle group in La Gleize:** Bruce Quarrie, *The Ardennes Offensive: VI Panzer Armee* (Oxford: Osprey, 1999).
105 **"We can still lose this war":** Martin Blumenson, *The Patton Papers, 1940–1945* (New York: Houghton Mifflin, 1974).
105 **"If Germany beats us":** *The Eventful 20th Century: The World at War 1939–1945* (London: Reader's Digest Association, 1998).
105 **"Hitler's last gamble":** Michael Veranov, *The Third Reich at War: The Rise and Fall of Hitler's Military Machine* (London: Magpie Books, 1997).
106 **"She stood just as he had seen her":** Edsel, *Monuments Men.*

Chapter 11: RAIDERS OF THE REICH

107 **"too much reliance on Ultra":** Lewin, *Ultra Goes to War.*
108 **"return cylinder that made decryption much more difficult":** Ibid.
108 **"Enigma Hour":** Cornwell, *Hitler's Scientists.*
108 **"TICOM teams":** Richard J. Aldrich, *GCHQ: The Uncensored Story of Britain's Most Secret Intelligence Agency* (London: Harper Press, 2010).
109 **"German intellectual property":** John Gimbel, *Science, Technology and Reparations: Exploitation and Plunder in Postwar Germany* (Stanford, CA: Stanford University Press, 1990).
110 **"thanks to Ultra":** Lewin, *Ultra Goes to War.* The Me 262 gained its first victim on July 26, 1944, in an action against an RAF de Havilland Mosquito photoreconnaissance aircraft. It was not until February 1945 that it became truly operational as a fighter, but by then it was too late to have any significant effect on Allied air operations.
110 **"Hitler's *Wunderwaffen*":** Steven J. Zaloga, *Remagen 1945: Endgame against the Third Reich* (Oxford: Osprey, 2006).
110 **"considerable lead in weapons technology":** Zaloga, *V-2 Ballistic Missile.*
110 **"Occupation of German scientific and industrial establishments":** "Operation Paperclip," from "History of Rocketry" at http://www.daviddarling.info/encyclopedia/P/Paperclip.html.
110 **Operation Lusty:** Gimbel, *Science, Technology and Reparations.*
111 **"exploitation of German technology":** Ibid.
111 **"The Big Three":** Jonathan Fenby, *Alliance: The Inside Story of How Roosevelt, Stalin and Churchill Won One War and Began Another* (London: Simon & Schuster, 2006).
112 **"our inflexible purpose":** Thacker, *End of the Third Reich.*
112 **"their common hate":** von Hassell et al., *Alliance of Enemies.*
112 **"Auergesellschaft plant in Oranienburg:"** Baggott, *Atomic.*
113 **Operation Big:** Kelly, *Manhattan Project.*
113 **"all the German scientists":** Rhodes, *Making of the Atomic Bomb.*
113 **"Soviet atomic research facility":** Baggott, *Atomic.*
113 **"unidentified black substance":** The National Archives, Kew, London; File ADM 223/214.
114 **"To hell with the Russians":** After-action report by Col. John Lansdale Jr., quoted in Rhodes, *Making of the Atomic Bomb.*
114 **"advanced aviation designs":** After the war, the renowned German aircraft designer Prof. Kurt

Tank, famous as the creator of the Focke-Wulf Fw.190 fighter, emigrated to Argentina under the name of Pedro Matthies to avoid prosecution by the Allies. There he was engaged to design the Pulqui II or Arrow jet aircraft at the Instituto Aerotécnico in Córdoba, first flown on June 27, 1950, soon after the outbreak of the Korean War. Although largely successful, the Pulqui project was canceled in 1960 due to escalating costs and the availability of surplus F-86 Sabre jet aircraft. After the Perón regime fell in September 1955, the German design team was disbanded, and many of its members found employment in the U.S. aeronautical industry.

Similarly, soon after Bormann's arrival in Argentina, the Perón government hired Nazi scientist Dr. Ronald Richter in October 1948 to develop a nuclear fission reactor for peaceful objectives. Instead, Richter persuaded Perón to fund the more advanced technology of nuclear fusion with the promise of producing limitless nuclear energy in milk-bottle-size containers to power all manner of household devices and vehicles. Construction of the fusion facility began in June 1949 on isolated Huemel Island in cold-water Nahuel Huapí Lake, not far from Hitler's lakeside house at Inalco. On March 24, 1951, the Perón government announced that "On February 16, 1951, in the . . . Isla Huemel . . . thermonuclear reactions under controlled conditions were performed on a technical scale." This would have made Argentina the first country in the world to harness nuclear energy for peaceful applications. It was, of course, all nonsense; controlled nuclear fusion remains the holy grail for scientists to this day. Richter and his team were sacked in November 1952 after Argentina had spent the equivalent of approximately $1 billion in today's money and some 150 times the amount that the United States was spending on nuclear fusion research at the time. Nevertheless, the Centro Atómico in nearby Bariloche remains the focal point of Argentine nuclear research. Proyecto Huemel or Project Huemel lives on in the Argentine pun *Huele a mula*, which means "It's a rip-off!"

115 **"massive discrepancies in military funds"**: Baggott, *Atomic.*

Chapter 12: BORMANN, DULLES, AND OPERATION CROSSWORD

116 **"Eagle's Nest"**: Seidler and Zeigert, *Hitler's Secret Headquarters.*
116 **"33,000 telex messages"**: von Lang, *Bormann.*
117 **"The more difficult the situation"**: Seidler and Zeigert, *Hitler's Secret Headquarters.*
117 **"I will have you shot"**: Seidler and Zeigert, *Hitler's Secret Headquarters.*
117 **"Germany will rise like a phoenix"**: Ibid.
117 **"whole senior Nazi hierarchy was present "**: Ibid.
117 **"Operation North Wind"**: Ken Ford, *The Rhineland 1945* (Oxford: Osprey, 2000).
118 **"the Führer was unhappy"**: Seidler and Zeigert, *Hitler's Secret Headquarters.*
118 ***"treue* Heinrich"**: von Lang, *Bormann.*
119 **"Uncle Heinrich's offensive did not work out"**: Ibid.
119 **Heinrich Hoffmann:** Ibid.
119 **Dr. Karl Brandt:** Ibid. After his trial at the Nuremberg International Tribunal, Brandt was hanged for crimes against humanity.
120 **"National Socialists! Party comrades!":** Ibid.
121 **"best news we have had in years"**: Ibid.
121 **"clear and present danger"**: Srodes, *Allen Dulles.*
122 **"last physical barrier"**: William I. Hitchcock, *Liberation: The Bitter Road to Freedom, Europe 1944–1945* (London: Faber and Faber, 2008).
123 **Operation Sunrise:** Srodes, *Allen Dulles.*
123 **"Soviet spies in the OSS"**: Robert W. Stephan, *Stalin's Secret War: Soviet Counterintelligence against the Nazis 1941–1945* (Lawrence: University Press of Kansas, 2004).
123 **"Germans have on the Eastern Front 147 divisions"**: Susan Butler, ed., *My Dear Mr. Stalin: The Complete Correspondence of Franklin D. Roosevelt and Joseph V. Stalin* (New Haven: Yale University Press, 2005).
124 **"U.S. Joint Chiefs of Staff expressly forbade"**: Srodes, *Allen Dulles.*
124 **Ernst Kaltenbrunner:** Peter R. Black, *Ernst Kaltenbrunner: Ideological Soldier of the Third Reich* (Princeton, NJ: Princeton University Press, 1984).
124 **"ingratiate themselves with the Americans"**: Breitman, *U.S. Intelligence and the Nazis.*
124 **"transportation of Hungary's Jewish population"**: NARA, College Park, Maryland; Hüttel [Höttl], SS Officer File, NA-BDC RG 242, A-3343.

125 "valuable crates were offloaded": Ronald W. Zweig, *The Gold Train: The Destruction of the Jews and the Looting of Hungary* (London: Harper Collins, 2003). At this time, it was common practice for gauleiters to hijack trains going through their territories—particularly coal trains, to provide for their freezing populations. This was often at the expense of the power stations supplying the war industries.

125 **"fanatical anti-Russian"**: Breitman, *U.S. Intelligence and the Nazis.*

125 **Dulles and Donovan quotes**: Ibid.

125 **"guerrilla movement known as *Werwolf*"**: Timothy J. Naftali, "Creating the Myth of the Alpenfestung: Allied Intelligence and the Collapse of the Nazi Police State," in *Austrian Historical Memory and National Identity*, ed. Günter Bischof and Anton Pelinka (New Brunswick, NJ: Transaction, 1997). The National Redoubt was intended as the last bastion of Nazi resistance even after conventional hostilities ceased with the capture of Berlin. Because of Allied airpower, a lack of troops, and little fuel to move supplies, it never materialized except in the fevered imaginations of Joseph Goebbels and other fanatical Nazi diehards. Known as the Alpenfestung or Alpine Fortress, it supposedly extended across the Alpine regions of Bavaria, Austria, and Italy with Hitler's home of Berchtesgaden at its heart. With the collapse of Germany, the Nazi hierarchy was to retreat to the Alpenfestung where they would be protected by Skorzeny's zealous Werewolves, but in fact Hitler never endorsed the plan and the idea faded as Nazi Germany crumbled. Thanks to Martin Bormann and Operation Feuerland, Hitler had no intention of hiding in the Alps.

126 **"their last stand"**: "Eisenhower's Six Great Decisions," *Saturday Evening Post*, July 13, 1946. In retrospect, it is difficult to understand how the Allied High Command was so thoroughly duped by the notion of the National Redoubt. In his autobiography, Gen. Omar Bradley ruefully recalled, "The Redoubt existed largely in the imagination of a few fanatical Nazis. It grew into so exaggerated a scheme that I am astonished we could have believed it as innocently as we did. But while it persisted, this legend . . . shaped our tactical thinking." In reality, the "tactical thinking" deliberately overstated the threat of the National Redoubt so that the U.S. armies could occupy the region with its vast caches of Nazi loot and high technology facilities and so deny them to the Soviets.

126 **"three cables"**: Dwight D. Eisenhower, *Crusade in Europe* (New York: Doubleday, 1948).

128 **Campione d'Italia**: Dulles, *Secret Surrender.*

129 **"tried to seek peace"**: Richard Breitman and Shlomo Aronson, "The End of the Final Solution? Nazi Plans to Ransom Jews 1944–1945," *Central European History* 25, no. 2 (1992).

129 **"White Buses"**: Meredith Hindley, "Negotiating the Boundary of Unconditional Surrender: The War Refugee Board in Sweden and Nazi Proposals to Ransom Jews 1944–1945," *Holocaust and Genocide Studies* 10, no.1 (1996).

129 **"no black occupation troops"**: NARA, College Park, Maryland; NA RG 266. This grotesque condition is to be found in Walter Schellenberg's draft autobiography, written in Sweden in June 1945.

129 **"The Hungarian Gold Train"**: Zweig, *Gold Train.*

130 **"looted artworks"**: NARA, College Park, Maryland; NA RG 263, Wilhelm Hüttel [Höttl], CIA Name File, Vol. 1.

130 **"Villa Kerry"**: Robert E. Matteson, *The Capture and the Last Days of SS General Ernst Kaltenbrunner, Chief of the Nazi Gestapo, Criminal Police, and Intelligence Services* (Saint Paul, MN: Private publication, 1993). Matteson was a member of the 80th Company, Counter Intelligence Corps, U.S. Army, who led the team that captured Kaltenbrunner on May 12, 1945, after searching the Villa Kerry.

130 **"acrimonious exchange of cables"**: von Hassell et al., *Alliance of Enemies.*

130 **"Dulles fidgeted in his chair"**: William J. Casey, *The Secret War Against Hitler* (Washington, DC: Regnery, 1988).

130 **"It is easy to start a war"**: Peter Grose, *Gentleman Spy: The Life of Allen Dulles* (Boston: Houghton Mifflin, 1994).

130 **"The air was opaque"**: Kim Philby, *My Silent War: The Story of Kim Philby* (London: Modern Library, 2002).

Chapter 13: "Wo bist Adolf Hitler?"

131 **Hitler's fifty-sixth birthday**: Bernd Freytag von Loringhoven, *In the Bunker with Hitler* (London: Weidenfeld & Nicolson, 2006).

131 **"Third Army Memorials"**: Charles Whiting, *Patton's Last Battle* (New York: Stein & Day, 1987).

132 **"Hitler's personal air transport unit"**: Glen Sweeting, *Hitler's Squadron: The Fuehrer's Personal Aircraft and Transport Unit 1933–1945* (Dulles, VA: Brassey's, 2001).

132 **"burning wreckage"**: Geoffrey J. Thomas and Barry Ketley, *KG 200: The Luftwaffe's Most Secret Unit* (Crowborough, UK: Hikoki, 2003).

133 **"Karl Wolff indicated to Dulles"**: Srodes, *Allen Dulles*.

133 **Hummel and Operation Crossword**: Consolidated Interrogation Report regarding Hans Helmut von Hummel, by Capt S. L. Faison Jr., OSS Art Looting Investigation Unit, dated October 11, 1945; from Prisoner of War Papers, Combined Services Detailed Interrogation Center, Bad Nenndorf, Germany. At the time of his arrest by the Americans, Hummel was carrying a hoard of gold reichsmark coins from the largest bank robbery in history. Intriguingly, so was Martin Bormann's wife, Gerda, when she was apprehended, but she was grievously ill with cancer and died on March 23, 1946, poisoned by the mercury used as part of her medical treatment.

133 **"personal meeting between Dulles and Kaltenbrunner"**: NARA, College Park, Maryland; Wilhelm Hüttel [Höttl], Third Army Preliminary Interrogation Report No. 17, June 1945, NA RG 263, Wilhelm Hüttel CIA Name File, Vol. 1.

133 **"purely a stooge"**: Dulles, *Secret Surrender*.

134 **"national treasure of Germany"**: Ian Sayer and Douglas Botting, *Nazi Gold* (Edinburgh: Mainstream, 1998).The final reserves of the Reichsbank arrived at the "Bormann Bunker" in Munich from Berlin and outlying branches, by two special trains and a road convoy, on April 28—just two days before the city was captured by Patton's Third Army.

134 **"most modern weapons technology"**: Neufeld, *Rocket and the Reich*. The principal scientists and technicians of the ballistic missile program, together with fourteen tons of documentation, were moved from Peenemünde by road to Nordhausen. They were under the close guard of SS troops commanded by the ruthless SS Gen. Dr. Hans Kammler, who was under strict orders from Bormann to kill the scientists and destroy the documentation if need be.

134 **"weapons of mass destruction"**: Cornwell, *Hitler's Scientists*. Although the Allies maintained large stocks of chemical weapons such as chlorine, phosgene, and mustard gas, they lagged far behind in the procurement of biological agents based on organophosphate compounds. In 1936 Dr. Gerhard Schrader of IG Farben had developed a highly lethal substance called tabun that attacks and paralyzes the human nervous system, resulting in death from asphyxiation in some twenty minutes. Production of an even more lethal agent known as sarin began in September 1939. By 1945, some 12,500 tons of tabun had been manufactured at Dyhernfurth in Silesia (present-day Brzeg Dolny, Poland) for a variety of delivery systems, including mines and artillery shells, many of which were stored in the underground tunnels of Mittelwerk at Nordhausen, where the V-2 missiles were assembled. A tabun and sarin payload was also developed for the V-1 flying bomb; this was the potential weapon to be used against the United States, launched from U-boats (see Chapter 16). It would also have been used in the A-9/A-10, the first intercontinental ballistic missile, which was still on the drawing board at Peenemünde. Its design specifications formed part of the fourteen tons of research documentation in the hands of SS Gen. Kammler—see previous note.

134 **Hitler's "Nero Decree"**: William L. Shirer, *The Rise and Fall of the Third Reich: A History of Nazi Germany* (New York: Touchstone, 1959). Hitler was utterly merciless toward a German people that he believed had failed him. In a conversation with Albert Speer, he stated: "If the war is lost, the nation perishes. This fate is inevitable. There is no necessity to take into consideration the basis which the people will need to continue a most primitive existence. On the contrary, it will be wiser to destroy those things ourselves because this nation will have proved to be the weaker one and the future will belong solely to the stronger Eastern nation. Besides, those who remain after the battle are only the inferior ones, for the good ones have been killed." Not everyone agreed with the Führer's monstrous nihilism; some tried to countermand the Nero Decree, including Albert Speer and many in the Wehrmacht. Foreseeing this opposition, Hitler declared in the decree that "All directives opposing this are invalid." Bormann saw Speer's disobedience as an opportunity to have him dragged before a court-martial but was unsuccessful. Enough of Bormann's gauleiters followed his orders to make his threat to the Allied agents credible, including gauleiter August Eigruber of Oberdonau, who ensured that bombs were placed in the Altaussee art repository so that it did not "fall into the hands of Bolsheviks or International Jewry." Ironically, Hitler's Nero Decree was a remarkably similar concept to the Morgenthau Plan for reducing Germany to pastoral status.

135 **Bormann's letter to his wife**: Sayer and Botting, *Nazi Gold*.

136 **"Kaiseroda potassium mine"**: Greg Bradsher, "Nazi Gold: The Merkers Mine Treasure," *Prologue: Quarterly of the National Archives and Records Administration* 31, no. 1 (1999).

136 **"134 repositories"**: Whetton, *Hitler's Fortune*.

136 **"Do Not Drop"**: Edsel, *Monuments Men*. Oddly, the stencils on the crates were misspelled: they should have read *stürzen*, not *stürtzen*.

137 **"one of the most important intelligence hauls"**: The National Archives, Kew, London; File ADM 223/214.

137 **Allied seizures of Nazi assets and recovery of loot**: see notes, passim. In the final week of the war, numerous Allied Special Forces units descended on selected sites across the length and breadth of the Third Reich. In the north, 30 Advance Unit stormed into the port of Kiel ahead of the frontline troops to acquire the secrets of sophisticated U-boat designs and high-speed underwater propulsion devices. To the south, they captured Nazi V-2 rocket engineers and many tons of ballistic missile data and plans that formed the basis for the development of ICBMs during the Cold War and the race to the moon. Further east, a TICOM unit reached Hitler's home at Berchtesgaden to seize the latest secure encoding machines that allowed the Nazi high command to communicate in total secrecy. Later, they discovered German interception equipment that was capable of decrypting Soviet radio traffic: a vital tool in the coming Cold War. Fifty miles east of Berchtesgaden, several Special Forces detachments, including OSS and British Special Operations Executive teams, code-named Historian, landed at Altaussee to secure Hitler's fabulous hoard of artworks buried a mile below the surface of the earth in the labyrinthine Kaiser Josef salt mine before they were blown to smithereens by Bormann's fanatical henchman, Gauleiter Adolf Eigruber. Among the hoard were 15 Rembrandts, 23 Bruegels, two Vermeers, 15 Canalettos, 15 Tintorettos, 8 Tiepolos, 4 Titians, and 2 da Vincis as well as sublime sculptures such as Michelangelo's Madonna of Bruges. Days later, the Monuments Men arrived with the first American troops to retrieve all the priceless artifacts before the area became part of the Soviet zone of occupation.

137 **"the Führer flew into a rage"**: von Hassell et al., *Alliance of Enemies*.

137 **"cement submarine"**: Blaine Taylor, *Hitler's Headquarters: From Beer Hall to Bunker 1920–1945* (Washington, DC: Potomac Books, 2007). SS Capt. Helmut Beermann of the SS Begleit Kommando des Führers—Hitler's personal bodyguard—gave a graphic description of life underground: "The whole atmosphere down there was . . . like being stranded in a cement submarine, or buried alive in some charnel house. People who work in diving bells probably feel less cramped. It was dank and dusty. . . . The ventilation could now be warm and sultry, now cold and clammy. . . . Then there [were] the fetid odors of boots, sweaty woolen uniforms and acrid coal-tar disinfectant. Toward the end, when the drainage packed in, it was as pleasant as working in a public urinal."

139 **"Führer's only unquestionably trusted deputy"**: von Lang, *Bormann*.

139 **"useless as a bolt-hole"**: Farago, *Aftermath*.

139 **"Bormann Bunker"**: Sayer and Botting, *Nazi Gold*.

140 **"Ernst is still looking out for Ernst"**: Manning, *Martin Bormann*.

140 **"war criminals fleeing justice"**: Sayer and Botting, *Nazi Gold*. Kaltenbrunner was captured by the Allies on May 12, 1945 (see note for Chapter 12, "Villa Kerry," page 304), condemned by the Nuremberg International Tribunal, and hanged on October 16, 1946.

140 **"highest priority signals"**: von Hassell et al., *Alliance of Enemies*.

140 **"ceasefire came into effect in northern Italy"**: On April 27, 1945, Benito Mussolini and his mistress Clara Petacci were captured by Italian communist partisans; the next day they were shot dead and their bodies mutilated before being strung up by the feet on the forecourt of a gas station on the Piazzale Loreto in Milan. The news of his ally's gruesome fate was a significant factor in Hitler's late decision to flee from Berlin.

140 **"The Führer is dead"**: Antony Beevor, *Berlin: The Downfall 1945* (London: Viking, 2002).

141 **"Where is Adolf Hitler?"**: O'Donnell, *The Bunker* (Boston: Houghton Mifflin, 1978.) O'Donnell interviewed Johannes Hentschel, who recalled the senior doctor well. Her fluency in German was impressive: "*die Klamotten*" is typical Berlin slang for "duds" or "party clothes" and not found in the average German language schoolbook.

141 **"an identifiable corpse"**: The Soviet authorities instituted a thorough investigation, code-named Operation Myth, of the events in the Führerbunker during the final days of the Third Reich and the supposed death of Adolf Hitler. All the surviving captured eyewitnesses from the bunker were subject to intense, prolonged interrogation by the NKVD/MVD. An interim report was completed in late 1946 but it did not satisfy Joseph Stalin. A more comprehensive investigation was then undertaken, resulting in *The Hitler Book*, which was submitted to Stalin on December 29, 1949. The Soviet leader read the 413-page report and, after appending some annotations, locked the single copy of the file in his desk drawer, where it remained until his death in March 1953.

141 **"fascist trick"**: Beevor, *Berlin*.

Chapter 14: THE BUNKER

146 **"general layout of the Führerbunker"**: *After the Battle* magazine, "The Reich Chancellery and the Berlin Bunker Then and Now," 61 (1988).

147 **"emergency exit"**: Seidler and Zeigart, *Hitler's Secret Headquarters*; see also "Politicization of the Construction Industry 1933–1945," pp. 3–4, from the history section of Hochtief website http://www.hochtief.com/hochtief_en/97.jtml; also http://berliner-unterwelten.de/fuehrerbunker. 328.1.html. The escape tunnel's exit into the U-bahn near Mohrenstrasse is still there, although the Chancellery buildings were finally destroyed in 1950 and the Führerbunker in 1989.

150 **"speaking as if"**: *Time* magazine, "As Long As I Live . . . ," May 28, 1945, quoting a Berlin dispatch dated May 1, 1945, http://www.time.com/time/magazine/article/0,9171,775644,00.html. This dispatch was based on an interview with Maj. Ivan Nikitine, who is believed to have been the deputy commander of the SMERSH team from 3rd Shock Army, which had entered the bunker immediately after the first assault troops and interrogated many of the captured survivors. Nikitine reported that, under questioning, Germans who had told of Hitler's death "twisted their stories, clashed in detail," and finally admitted that no one had actually seen the Führer die.

150 **"powerful and dangerous men"**: On two points the description of the scene on April 27 is problematic. One is trivial: the eyewitness was described by a nonexistent rank, "SS-Untergruppenführer." However, a number of members of the SS-Begleit Kommando des Führers holding the rank of SS-Untersturmführer (second lieutenant) were present in the bunker. More puzzlingly, the original *Time* article has Bormann entering with Heinrich Himmler, not Müller. On May 1, Maj. Nikitine's interrogatee might not have known that Himmler had left Berlin months earlier, retiring to a sanatorium on March 13; or it may simply have been a slip of the tongue—hardly impossible, under SMERSH questioning. In any case, Müller, always one of the least visible members of the hierarchy, would have been unknown by sight to a junior officer. Under U.S. interrogation, Erich Kempka, head of the motor pool in the Chancellery, said that he had never seen Müller and was even uncertain of his exact job.

151 **"to secure Hitler's escape from the capital"**: Weidling to Soviet interrogators, 1945. *Descent into Nightmare* (The Third Reich series) (New York: Time-Life Education, 1992).

151 **"sent and signed the message"**: Michael Bar-Zohar, *The Avengers* (London: Arthur Barker, 1968).

151 **T43 *Schlüsselfernschreibmaschine***: Josef Langer, "SFM T-43," online research paper, Vienna, June 2001, http://www.alpenfestung.com/funk_sfm_t_43.htm. See also Jack B. Copeland et al., *Colossus: The Secrets of Bletchley Park's Codebreaking Computers* (Oxford: Oxford University Press, 2006). The T43 had been in development since before the war, and an earlier version had been on the warship *Admiral Graf Spee* when it was scuttled off Uruguay in December 1939.

151 **Hans-Erich Voss**: In 1942, as commander of the heavy cruiser *Prinz Eugen*, Voss had been handpicked by Joseph Goebbels to act as the navy's representative in Hitler's inner circle. He was wounded in the bomb attempt on Hitler's life at the Rastenburg Wolf's Lair headquarters on July 20, 1944.

151 **Villa Winter**: Robert H. Whealey, *Hitler and Spain: The Nazi Role in the Spanish Civil War, 1936–1939* (Lexington: University Press of Kentucky, 1989).

152 **Hermann Fegelein**: When Anni Winter—Hitler's housekeeper at his Munich apartment at Prinzregentenplatz 16—was interrogated in Nuremberg on November 6, 1945, she spoke scathingly about both Bormann—whom she described as a brutal, heartless cynic—and Fegelein. She suggested that the latter had an affair with Eva Braun. Cornell University Law Library, "Frau Anni Winter," in Donovan Nuremberg Trial collection, Subdivision 8/Hitler, section 8.02 German (English translation available); see http://library2.lawschool.cornell.edu/donovan/show.asp?id=567&query=.

152 **"In the city as a whole"**: Beevor, *Berlin*.

152 **Wilhelm Mohnke**: Ian Sayer and Douglas Botting, *Hitler's Last General: The Case Against Wilhelm Mohnke* (London: Bantam Press, 1989). The term *Begleit* is translated here as "escort." Identifying exact units is complicated by parallel titles. The original Führer Begleit Bataillon was composed of men from two elite units, the army's Wachregiment Berlin and the air force's Regiment Hermann Göring. This was later expanded, and most of its elements were transferred to the fighting front, although a company remained. The SS-Begleit Kommando des Führers was the handpicked team of bodyguards directly responsible for Hitler's day-to-day safety and providing his valets and orderlies, which in 1945 numbered about 140 officers and men commanded by SS-Untersturmführer Franz Schädle.

154 **Oskar Schäfer**: http://www.ritterkreuztraeger-1939-45.de/Waffen-SS/S/Schaefer-Oskar.htm. He had volunteered in 1938 and fought as an infantryman with the SS Regiment "Deutschland" before being transferred into the 5th SS Armored Division "Wiking" in 1943 and becoming a tank soldier.

154　**Fegelein's capture:** Joachim Fest, *Inside Hitler's Bunker: The Last Days of the Third Reich* (New York: Farrar, Straus and Giroux, 2004); see also William B. Breuer, *Feuding Allies: The Private Wars of the High Command* (Edison, NJ: Castle Books, 2007).

154　**Peter Högl:** Anton Joachimsthaler, *The Last Days of Hitler: The Legends, the Evidence, the Truth* (London: Arms & Armour Press, 1999).

155　**interview with Fegelein's father:** Kenneth D. Alford and Theodore P. Savas, *Nazi Millionaires: The Allied Search for Hidden SS Gold* (Havertown, PA: Casemate, 2002).

156　**"A lone pilot was standing by in the shadows":** O'Donnell, *Bunker*.

156　**"myth of Fegelein's execution":** Ibid.

156　**"light concrete panel":** *Time* magazine, "As Long As I Live . . . "

157　**"deceived even those quite close to him":** Facial analysis by Alf Linney, professor of medical physics, University College London, commissioned by the authors, August 2010. The leading British expert on facial identification, Prof. Linney is regularly consulted by the Metropolitan Police as an expert witness. Professor Linney has proven scientifically that the man depicted in frames from Walter Frentz's footage of the Hitler Youth presentation on March 20 is not Adolf Hitler. (The presentation did not take place, as frequently claimed, on April 20—the film was released as a newsreel on March 22.)

157　**"later be found on the floor":** *Time* magazine, "As Long As I Live . . . "; Maj. Nikitine mentioned the charred note.

157　**"fitted perfectly":** www.mp44.nl/equipment/gas_mask.htm.

159　**Ilse Braun:** United Press, Warsaw, "Hitler Escaped in U-Boat, Says German Pilot," December 12, 1947, published in the *St. Petersburg Times*, December 13, 1947, http://news.google.com/newspapers?id=fyNPAAAAIBAJ&sjid=504DAAAAIBAJ&pg=4293,888260&dq=hitler-escaped-in-u-boat-says-german-pilot&hl=en. For her disagreement with Eva, see Beevor, *Berlin*. In his testimony to a Warsaw court in 1947, the pilot Baumgart refers to Eva's sister as one of the escape party.

159　**Joachim Rumohr:** Axis Biographical Research, www.geocities.com/~orion47/. See also The Associated Press, "Flier Claims Hitler Escaped," Warsaw, December 18, 1947, for the report of Baumgart's testimony; http://news.google.com/newspapers?id=hSNPAAAAIBAJ&sjid=504DAAAAIBAJ&pg=4258,4339256&dq=baumgart+hitler+warsaw&hl=en. See also reproduction of this article on page 163 in Chapter 15. Baumgart refers to a General "Rommer" or "Roemer" and his wife being with the escape party. The only Nazi general with a name similar to this was Fegelein's close friend Rumohr.

159　**Tiger II tanks:** Oskar Shäfer's testimony; see http://www.ritterkreuztraeger-1939-45.de/Waffen-SS/S/Schaefer-Oskar.htm.

Chapter 15: THE FLIGHT

160　**Kampfgeschwader 200:** Thomas and Ketley, *KG 200*. Officially formed on February 20, 1944, KG 200 had brought together a number of existing sensitive or clandestine Luftwaffe operations—testing and employing captured Allied aircraft, inserting Abwehr agents behind Allied lines, testing "pathfinder" and radar-jamming techniques, flying unconventional bomber missions, and carrying out long-range flights to Japan. Despite its new umbrella identity, KG 200 comprised different groups and squadrons operating from separate bases, and for security reasons they were kept ignorant of each other's activities. Rechlin was the base for KG 200's 6th and 7th Squadrons (Staffeln), equipped with "Mistletoe" unconventional bomber aircraft; on March 6, 1945, these, and Hs 293 radio-guided bombs, had been used against Soviet-held bridges on the Oder river. The long-range specialists of KG 200 were the 1st Squadron, based at Finow.

160　**Peter Erich Baumgart:** The Associated Press, "Luftwaffe Pilot Sent to Gaol for Five Years," Warsaw, August 8, 1949, published in *Canberra Times*, August 9, 1949, http://trove.nla.gov.au/ndp/del/page/690899.

161　**"Baumgart's orders were":** The Associated Press, "Flier Claims Hitler Escaped"; see also note "Baumgart's account," below.

161　**"just four days earlier":** The Associated Press, "RAF's Jets Slash German Airfield," London, published in the *New York Times*, April 24, 1945, http://select.nytimes.com/gst/abstract.html?res=F40E1FFB3C5F1B7B93C7AB178FD85F418485F9.

163　**Baumgart's account:** The Associated Press, "Flier Claims Hitler Escaped." Baumgart's trial in Warsaw was covered extensively by international news agencies, which published regular updates.

Baumgart had been psychiatrically assessed when he first made his claims about flying Hitler out of Berlin; he was declared sane. When he repeated the claims in court, his trial was adjourned for forty-two days; he was once again sent for psychiatric assessment and again was declared sane. According to research carried out by Holocaust groups concerning Auschwitz, the pilot was released in December 1951 after serving three years of his five-year sentence. Nothing is ever heard of him again.

164   **Friedrich von Angelotty-Mackensen:** Interrogation of Friedrich Arthur Rene Lotta von Angelotty-Mackensen, Nuremberg Palace of Justice, March 18, 1948 (Gumberg Library Digital Collections of Duquesne University, "Musmanno Collection—Interrogation of Hitler Associates"). See also http://digital.library.duq.edu/cdm-musmanno; see also The Associated Press, Stockholm, May 8, 1945. Mackensen's three-hour interrogation by Michael Musmanno, one of the American jurists, is rambling, and he repeatedly confuses dates. Mackensen was by then using a wheelchair, having suffered a broken spine in a forced landing in southern Sweden on May 8 after his attempted flight to Malaga, Spain (his was one of eleven German aircraft that were shot down or force-landed that day during such attempts). He had recovered consciousness in a hospital at POW Camp 404 in Marseille, France, on May 16. Throughout his interrogation Mackensen states that he had been delirious for much of his time on the ground in Berlin and Denmark. Although it was dismissed as "fantastic" by Musmanno, close reading of Mackensen's story reveals details that coincide with Baumgart's account. Mackensen, too, seems to have vanished from sight after the war.

164   **"20,000 reichsmarks":** The Associated Press, December 19, 1947.

164   **"message canister":** Interrogation of Angelotty-Mackensen.

164   **Werner Baumbach:** Werner Baumbach, *Broken Swastika: The Defeat of the Luftwaffe* (Munich: Pflaum, 1949; London: Robert Hale, 1960). Baumbach never explains why he was at Travemünde on April 29, but his diary notes speak for themselves. He went to Argentina after the war, working on aviation projects and becoming a friend of Col. Perón. He eventually died in a crash while flying an Argentine-bought British Avro Lancaster bomber over the Andes on October 20, 1953.

164   **Blohm & Voss Bv 222:** Nick Fielding, *Sunday Times*, London, December 28, 2003, http://forum.axishistory.com/viewtopic.php?f=34&t=39672. Reporter Nick Fielding's interview with a ninety-three-year-old former German navigator, Capt. Ernst Koenig, described a plan to evacuate Nazi leaders "to Greenland" by flying boat. Koenig stated that he had just finished preparing two of the Bv 222s for the escape flight when they were attacked on the water by Allied aircraft and destroyed. "We had another in the workshop, and that, too, was made ready. It required a lot of work, but it was done, and once again stores arrived for loading on board." KG 200 is known to have included the Bv 222 among its thirty-two different types of Axis and Allied aircraft. With a payload of some 34.5 tons (nearly three times that of the Ju 290), the flying boat could carry ninety-two fully equipped troops, at a speed of 240 miles per hour. It could stay aloft for up to twenty-eight hours, making it ideal for long-distance flights.

166   **Junkers Ju 290:** Baumbach, *Broken Swastika*; see also The Associated Press, Travemünde, June 16, 1945 (delayed dispatch).

166   **"flight plan":** Thomas and Ketley, *KG 200*.

168   **"I must stay with my men":** Baumbach, *Broken Swastika*.

168   **"dismantled":** On June 19, 1945, the London *Daily Express*—under the headline "Is Hitler in Spain?"—described the arrival of a German trimotor aircraft carrying a mysterious passenger who was "saluted deferentially despite his civilian clothes. . . . His face muffled in a raincoat, the passenger stepped from the plane to the smart Nazi salute of its crew, then took off in a Spanish plane to an unknown destination. The German plane reportedly was dismantled." See "Claim Nazi Officials Arrive in Spain," *Telegraph Herald*, June 21, 1945, http://news.google.com/newspapers?id=XidiA AAAIBAJ&sjid=OXYNAAAAIBAJ&pg=4599,2831598&dq=hitler-in-spain&hl=en.

169   **"recognizable figure":** Interrogation of Angelotty-Mackensen. There is no official record of Degrelle's plane stopping at Tønder, but details of the flight remain obscure, and it is plausible that it could have landed there to top up its fuel tanks before the long flight south. There is a photograph of Degrelle in Oslo, standing next to a Heinkel with the identification letters "CN" visible on the fuselage.

169   **"flown by Albert Duhinger":** http://home.arcor.de/sturmbrigade/Wallonie/Wallonie.htm; see also *Revista Española de Historia Militar* magazine, October 2004.

169   **"crash-landed":** The Associated Press, Donostia-San Sebastián, Spain, May 8, 1945.

169   **"Degrelle had spoken":** The Associated Press, Madrid, May 25, 1945.

169   **Vidkun Quisling:** The Associated Press, Oslo, August 25, 1945.

169   **Pierre Laval:** The Associated Press, Madrid, May 2, 1945.

169   **Filippo Anfuso:** *L'Unità*, Communist Party official publication, Rome, May 25, 1945.

170 **Gen. José Moscardo:** The Associated Press, Moscow, June 16, 1945. Gen. José Moscardo Ituarte was the head of Franco's Casa Militar or military household.

170 **Robert Ley:** Interrogation of Robert Ley, Nuremberg, 1945, Interrogation Records Prepared for War Crimes Proceedings at Nuremberg, 1945–47, page 101; http://www.footnote.com/document/231909201/.

170 **Albert Speer:** Interrogation of Albert Speer, Flensburg; USSBS Special Document, May 22–23, 1945.

170 **Rochus Misch:** Interview, *Secret History: Hitler of the Andes*, Barking Mad Productions for Channel 4 (British public television), 2003. Only two prototypes of the six-engined Junkers Ju 390, designed as part of the so-called America-Bomber project, were ever built. One was test-flown by the Luftwaffe's Long-Range Reconnaissance Squadron 5, but rumors of a test flight that nearly reached the U.S. coast are no longer given any credence.

170 **Zhukov and Berzarin quotes:** Eddy Gilmore, The Associated Press, "Reds Believe Hitler Alive," Berlin, June 9, 1945, published in *Herald-Journal*, June 10, 1945, http://news.google.com/newspapers?id=DV8sAAAAIBAJ&sjid=_soEAAAAIBAJ&pg=4259,3091076&dq=hitler+eddy+gilmore&hl=en.

171 **Hitler's alleged cremation:** Erich Kempka was interrogated by U.S. agents at Berchtesgaden on June 20 and July 4, 1945; see also The Associated Press, "With the British Second Army," May 8, 1945. The Soviets were handed or shown no fewer than six "Hitlers" in the days after the fall of Berlin. One of them had worked as a cook in the Führerbunker.

171 **the dogs:** O'Donnell, *Bunker*.

171 **Högl's death:** Joachimstaler, *Last Days of Hitler*.

172 **Müller's funeral:** O'Donnell, *Bunker*.

172 **"Bormann made his own escape":** Beevor, *Berlin*.

172 **Tiburtius's account:** Interview published in *Der Bund*, Bern, Switzerland, February 17, 1953, and quoted extensively in Manning, *Martin Bormann*.

173 **Bormann's evasion:** Manning, *Martin Bormann*.

Chapter 16: GRUPPE SEEWOLF

175 **Gruppe Seewolf:** Clay Blair, *Hitler's U-Boat War*, vol. 2: *The Hunted, 1941–1945* (London: Cassell, 2000).

176 **"robot bombs":** The Associated Press, London, July 25, 1944.

176 **U-1229:** *Maine Sunday Telegram*, Portland, October 29, 2000. "Commander" is our translation of the rank of *Korvettenkapitän*—see "Treatment of Military Ranks" on page xiv.

176 **"corroborated Mantel's story":** Report on the Interrogation of German Agents, Gimpel and Colepaugh, Landed on the Coast of Maine from U-1230, dated January 13, 1945. Op-16-Z (SC) A1-2(3)/ EF30 Serial 00170716. Located in the archives of the National Museum of the U.S. Navy, Washington, DC, http://www.ibiblio.org/hyperwar/USN/rep/U-1230/.

176 **Speer broadcast:** James P. Duffy, *Target America: Hitler's Plan to Attack the United States* (Westport: Praeger, 2004); see also www.bbc.co.uk/ww2peopleswar/stories/92/a3641492.shtml.

177 **"robots from submarine, airplane or surface ship":** The Associated Press, "An East Coast Port," published in *Deseret [Utah] News*, January 8, 1945.

177 **"V-1 scare":** *New York Times*, "Robot Bomb Attacks Here Held 'Probable' by Admiral," January 8, 1945, http://select.nytimes.com/gst/abstract.html?res=FA0C16F93A5C1B7B93CBA9178AD8 5F418485F9&scp=2&sq=V-1&st=p.

177 **"British Admiralty cable":** Duffy, *Target America*.

177 **sea-launched V-1:** "Hitler's Rocket U-boat Program: History of WW2 rocket submarine," http://www.Uboataces.com. It was not surprising that the United States took the threat seriously; it had managed to reverse engineer the V-1 in just four months, producing the JB-2 Thunderbug. Personnel from the Special Weapons Branch at Wright Field launched a first prototype in October 1944 at Eglin Field, the USAAF base in southwest Florida. The USAAF were enthusiastic about the results achieved by air launches with the B-17 and B-29, but their large production order was cancelled on VJ-Day. Of some thousand JB-2s produced, three hundred were converted for naval use; the improved KUV-1 Loon was first launched from the submarine USS *Cusk* in January 1946. See Mark Fisher, "American Buzz Bombs: An Incomplete History," http://mcfisher.0catch.com/scratch/v1/v1-0.htm.

179 **"U-boat Command's transmissions":** The radio traffic from each U-boat can be found in The National Archives, Kew, London, filed under HW 18. For U-880, see HW 18/400; for U-530, see

HW 18/406; for U-518, see HW 18/410; and for U-1235, see HW 18/431.The weekly antisubmarine situation reports are in D. Syrett, *The Battle of the Atlantic and Signals Intelligence: U-boat Situations and Trends* (Farnham, UK: Ashgate, 1998).

179 **"well documented and correct"**: Blair, *Hitler's U-boat War.*

180 **"treated with great and repeated brutality"**: Philip K. Lundeberg, "Operation Teardrop Revisited," in Timothy J. Runyan and Jan M. Copes, *To Die Gallantly: The Battle of the Atlantic* (Boulder, CO: Westview Press, 1994).

180 **"no physical evidence of its destruction"**: Syrett, *Battle of the Atlantic*; also Michael Gannon, *Operation Drumbeat: The Dramatic True Story of Germany's First U-boat Attacks Along the American Coast in World War II* (New York: Harper Perennial, 1991).

181 **Rodger Winn memorandum:** Gannon, *Operation Drumbeat.* Sir Charles Rodger Noel Winn, CB, OBE, QC (1903–72)—a prewar judge, crippled by childhood polio—made a whole range of probably unparalleled contributions to Allied victory in the Second Battle of the Atlantic, but there is no room here for more than the briefest note on his extraordinary career. While still a civilian, he was reassigned from prisoner interrogation to the Submarine Tracking Room (part of the Operational Intelligence Centre), where he quickly mastered the U-boats' tactics and could frequently predict their actions. Consequently, he was promoted to command the Tracking Room with the temporary rank of commander in the Royal Naval Volunteer Reserve—unprecedented for someone without formal naval officer's training.

182 **"surrendered to the authorities"**: Good histories of Operation Teardrop can be found in Blair, *Hitler's U-boat War*, and Lundeberg, "Operation Teardrop Revisited."

183 **"recovered the Enigma machine"**: http://www.iwm.org.uk/upload/package/10/enigma/enigma12.htm. Francis Harry Hinsley, OBE (1918–98) was an English cryptanalyst at Bletchley Park, who among his other contributions helped initiate a program of seizing Enigma machines and documents from German weather ships. This facilitated the resumption of the decryption of Kriegsmarine Enigma traffic after the interruption in 1942–43.

184 **"massive intelligence-gathering advantage"**: F. H. Hinsley and Alan Stripp, *Codebreakers: The Inside Story of Bletchley Park* (Oxford: Oxford University Press, 1993); see also http://www.bletchleypark.org.uk.

184 **Berchtesgaden:** Arthur H. Mitchell, *Hitler's Mountain: The Führer, Obersalzberg, and the American Occupation of Berchtesgaden* (Jefferson, NC: McFarland, 2007).

184 **Oscar Oeser:** Arthur G. Bedeia, ed., "Guilty of Enthusiasm," in *Management Laureates*, vol. 3 (London: JAI Press, 1993); also see online history of St. Andrews University School of Psychology.

184 **Colossus:** Peter Thorne and John McCutchan, *The Path to Colossus . . . an historical look at the development of the electronic computer.* A presentation to Engineering Heritage Victoria, June 19, 2008, www.consuleng.com.au/The%20Path%20to%20Colossus%20080827%20revcomp.pdf.

185 **"Prof. Oeser was amazed at what he found"**: http://www.ellsbury.com/enigmabombe.htm; see also Lewin, *Ultra Goes to War.* There are references to this machine being introduced for Abwehr signal traffic in December 1944 that refer to it by the designation Schlüsselgerät 41—SG41. (By that date Adm. Canaris was in Gestapo custody, and the Abwehr had passed under the control of the SS Reich Main Security Office.) The Abwehr's original Enigma system had been broken at Bletchley Park in December 1941 by Alfred Dillwyn "Dilly" Knox, and that used by the Sicherheitsdienst (SD) in August 1942 by Keith Batey, but Batey's obituary (London *Times*, September 10, 2010) confirms that neither he nor anyone else was able to reconstruct the working system of this new Siemens & Haske machine.

186 **"Bormann's reply"**: Bar-Zohar, *Avengers.*

186 **"fishing expedition"**: Whealey, *Hitler and Spain.*

186 **Gustav Winter:** Juan Luis Calbarro, "Vida y leyenda de Gustav Winter," *Historia* magazine, 16, April–May 2005.

187 **"peninsula of Jandía"**: "Fuerteventura: geología, naturaleza y actividad humana." A presentation to Canaries Association for Scientific Education, Fuerteventura, December 5–9, 2007; PDF available online, http://docs.google.com/viewer?a=v&q=cache:pjgK76W-XcUJ:www.vierayclavijo.org/html/pdf/cuadernillos/07/0712_fuerteventura.pdf+%22Fuerteventura:+geolog%C3%ADa,+naturaleza+y+actividad+humana%22&hl=en&gl=us&pid=bl&srcid=ADGEESiaB_KX2fCx0XOM4pKP-cXpXS96Uc-62bJnkDFsj58b06zmhrQdQ264BUDbJ0x2w3LW14C69671ZXNYdyiOL_Q2Nhoq9rPQ9fckQyYWQCH1HCIh5aMlXPD3VhZpNrfOqybAii_9&sig=AHIEtbRrbZszO9TEPoIlRji_uOMXYk-aZA. Quotations from interview with Isabel Winter, Gustav Winter's wife, are taken from this presentation. In 1984, an extremely colorful tale about the accidental discovery of a "U-boat pen" tunneled into the island was published by a

German magazine. This fiction has been exploded by the U-boat historian Jak P. Mallmann Showell in his book *U-Boats At War: Landings on Hostile Shores* (Hersham, UK: Ian Allan, 2000), for which he carried out field research and a comprehensive analysis of U-boat orders, logs, and mission reports relevant to the Canary Islands. There are detailed records of the U-boat supply base run from an "interned" German freighter in Las Palmas harbor on Gran Canaria, but no suggestion that U-boats visited Fuerteventura. This is hardly surprising: Villa Winter was designed for a single purpose, and anything that might draw attention to it before 1945 was deliberately avoided.

187 **"dark tales"**: Elizabeth Nash, "Germans Helped Franco Run Civil War Death Camps," London Independent, February 22, 2002, http://www.independent.co.uk/news/world/europe/germans-helped-franco-run-civil-war-death-camps-661623.html.

187 **"near Bordeaux"**: Interview with Isabel Winter.

187 **"built a runway"**: Enrique Nácher, Gran Canaria. "La Leyenda de Gustav Winter: ¿Espía nazi en Fuerteventura?" Historia 16, April–May 2005, republished at http://hispanismo.org/reino-de-las-canarias/5643-la-leyenda-de-gustav-winter-espia-nazi-en-fuerteventura.html.

188 **"relocations to the Canaries"**: The Associated Press, Moscow, February 1, 1944.

188 **Walter Winchell:** "A Reporter's Report to the Nation," syndicated, October 26, 1944. Winchell was scathing about Carlton Hayes, who was appointed U.S. ambassador to Spain in 1942. In spring 1944, Hayes was reportedly obstructive to Operation Safehaven, the U.S. operation designed to find and eliminate German industrial and commercial assets throughout the world. According to Donald P. Steury—a CIA officer in residence at the University of Southern California, writing on the agency's website—Samuel Klaus, the Federal Economic Administration team leader in Spain, indicated that Hayes was unwilling to cooperate and that for several months the embassy would not allow OSS Madrid to pass Safehaven material or even background economic reporting to Washington.

188 **"Hitler's change of aircraft"**: "Is Hitler in Spain?" *Daily Express*, London, June 19, 1945.

189 **experience of the crews**: Jak P. Mallmann Showell, *U-Boat Commanders and Crews 1935–45* (Ramsbury, UK: Crowood Press, 1998).

190 **"augmented by nonregulation items"**: http://www.uboataces.com/articles-life-uboat.shtml.

190 **"The usually relaxed atmosphere" to the end of Chapter 16:** This section of chapter 16 constitutes one of the very few sections in this book that cannot be documented but is based on our own extensive researches and those of our U-boat expert, Innes McCartney, and in consultation with our Luftwaffe expert, Tony Holmes. The types of aircraft employed by the Spanish air force and the military air routes to Fuerteventura and the Jandía Peninsula are based on rigorous knowledge down to which Ju 52s were passed to the Spanish air force by the Condor Legion, and their respective bases. We have established that the Jandía Peninsula was a secret Abwehr facility that had been planned well before the war and built under severe duress by Franco's Republican political prisoners at great human cost. Such a massive investment in an area of barren, hostile terrain begs the question: what other purpose did it have but as a staging post for an elaborate escape plan? The airstrip at the southern tip of the peninsula was capable of taking the Luftwaffe's largest aircraft, such as the Fw-200 Condor or a Ju-290. It is still visible on Google Earth. The whole Jandía Peninsula was a forbidden military zone throughout the war and for years thereafter.

The Allies were seriously concerned that the Canary Islands were being used by the Germans to support U-boat operations. This suspicion was based on the interception of a secret Kriegsmarine document titled *U-Plätze*, or "U-Places," which became interpreted as "U-Bases" with the presumption that they were U-boat bases. The "U" in fact related to *Unterkunft*, or "refuge," and there were scores of them dotted around the world, intended to shelter all types of Kriegsmarine vessels—places to undertake repairs or find fresh water. Similarly there were consistent rumors among the Allies that there were U-boat bases along the South American coastline, even as far south as Tierra del Fuego. There is no evidence to support such a proposition, but the list of locations in the *U-Plätze* does mention a tiny island off the coast of Rio de Janeiro. Nevertheless, the Canary Islands were used by the Nazis to support U-boats; a German tanker was permanently moored at Las Palmas on Gran Canaria to allow U-boats to sneak in at night and refuel clandestinely. Accordingly, Fuerteventura and Jandía in particular were not designed and never acted as a support facility for U-boats or any other activity until April 1945, yet the Villa Winter complex and airstrip had been constructed at vast expense.

As to the actual circumstances of Hitler's journey by U-boat, they have perforce to be a matter of conjecture and informed speculation based on solid research as to the realities of living over long periods of time in the claustrophobic world of the submariner. In particular, we have drawn on the experiences of the Yanagi, the secret underwater trade between Germany and Japan conducted by German and Japanese submarines for the transfer of vital strategic resources, such as tungsten, tin, quinine, coffee, opium, high technology, and VIPs, between 1942 and 1945. These voyages between Europe and Japan were immensely long and, with much time spent underwater, tedious in the extreme. They did, however, show us how U-boats and Japanese submarines were modified for the passage of VIPs.

191 **toilets:** U.S. Navy report, "Sanitation aboard Former German Type IXC," March 1946, www.uboat archive.net/DesignStudiesTypeIXC.htm.

191 **food:** http://www.uboataces.com/articles-life-uboat.shtml.

191 **"arrived off the Argentine coast aboard U-880":** Stanley Ross, Overseas News Agency, "U-Boats Base Spy Surge in Latin America," *Christian Science Monitor*, January 24, 1945.

192 **"Koehn was back":** The Associated Press, Montevideo, Uruguay, August 18, 1945.

192 **Curtiss Condor II:** Peter M. Bowers, *Curtiss Aircraft 1907–1947* (London: Putnam, 1987).

Chapter 17: ARGENTINA—LAND OF SILVER

194 **"when war broke out in 1939":** http://www.archives.gov/research/holocaust/finding-aid/ civilian/rg-84-argentina.html.

195 **Hasse quote:** Michael Sayers and Albert Kahn, *The Plot Against the Peace: A Warning to the Nation* (New York: Dial Press, 1944).

195 **Wilhelm Canaris:** Richard Bassett, *Hitler's Spy Chief: The Wilhelm Canaris Mystery* (London: Cassell, 2005).

195 **Estancia San Ramón:** Patrick Burnside, *El Escape de Hitler* (Buenos Aires: Editorial Planeta, 2000).

196 **"standing joke":** Jorge Camarasa, *Puerto Seguro: Desembarcos clandestinos en la Patagonia [Safe Haven: Clandestine Landings in Patagonia]* (Buenos Aires: Norma Editorial, 2006).

196 **"mansion on Fuerenstrasse":** Sayers and Kahn, *Plot Against the Peace*.

196 **Falange:** Allan Chase, *Falange: The Axis Secret Army in the Americas* (New York: G. P. Putnam's Sons, 1943).

197 **"obviously Central European":** Authors' travels through Patagonia, 2007–09.

197 **Nazi Party membership:** The Associated Press, Berlin, October 17, 1945. See also http://www. archives.gov/research/holocaust/finding-aid/civilian/rg-84-argentina.html.

197 **"to celebrate the Anschluss":** U.S. War Department file, MID 2093, Buenos Aires, April 1938.

198 **"ready to strike":** Report to Argentine Congress by Deputy Raúl Damonte Taborda, chair of a congressional committee to investigate Nazi activities, September 1941, cited in Chase, *Falange.*

198 **"Wherever you turn":** Chase, *Falange.*

198 **Freude, Perón, Duarté:** *New York Times,* "Argentina Evades Its Nazi Past," March 22, 1997, http:// query.nytimes.com/gst/fullpage.html?res=9E02E2DD153BF931A15750C0A961958260.

199 **"number one Nazi":** U.S. Government, *Blue Book on Argentina, Consultation among the American Republics with Respect to the Argentine Situation; Memorandum of the United States Government,* Washington, DC (New York: Greenberg, 1946).

199 **Perón's early career:** Multiple sources consulted by researcher Nahuel Coca, Buenos Aires, 2010. *Time* magazine, "Argentina: Boss of the GOU," November 27, 1944, http://www.time.com/time/ magazine/article/0,9171,796883,00.html.

199 **Perón in Paris:** "O Holocausto, Perón e la Argentina," http://www.arlindo-correia.com/140402. html.

199 **"direct pay of Berlin":** In 1945, the former diplomat Prince Stephan of Schaumburg-Lippe (an SS lieutenant colonel—who thus outranked the German ambassador to Argentina, Edmund von Thermann) would tell the war crimes commission in Berlin of some specific checks among many such payments: check number 463803, dated June 26, 1941, made out to Eva Duarté in the amount of $33,600; and check number 682117, dated June 30, to Col. Juan Domingo Perón in the sum of $200,000. In 1942, "Evita" was able to buy her own apartment at 1567 Calle Posadas in the exclusive Buenos Aires neighborhood of Recoleta; see Roberto Vacca, *Eva Perón* (Buenos Aires: Centro Editor de América Latina, 1971). Von Thermann, the former German ambassador, would confirm the handing over of such payments. He told war crimes investigators that one of the embassy's messengers was the personal representative of Reichsführer-SS Heinrich Himmler and that one of Thermann's own valets—he was never able to find out which—was the highest-ranking officer in the spy service, in direct communication with Reichsleiter Martin Bormann at the Reich Chancellery. See Silvano Santander, *Técnica de una Traición [The Technique of Treachery]: Juan D. Perón y Eva Duarté—Agentes del Nazismo en la Argentina* (Montevideo, Uruguay: Editorial Antygua 1953);

see two notes down, and Von Thermann's testimony detailed in online PDF entitled "Vier Prinzen zu Schaumburg-Lippe," listing Supplement of January 15, 1946 to the Consolidated Interrogation Report No. 4, Attachment 76: "Partial List of Purchases for Linz Made in Germany," http://edocs. fu-berlin.de/docs/servlets/MCRFileNodeServlet/FUDOCS_derivate_000000000030/vierprin zen_letzte_fassung_copia.pdf;jsessionid=452DFAE5507E3516FFD859EB792902B6?hosts=, hosted by Freie Universität, Berlin. The "authorized version" of Evita's life has her meeting Juan Perón only in May 1944 during relief work following the San Juan earthquake; the documents studied by Santander refute this date.

201 **"tirelessly in exile"**: Ladislas Farago, *Aftermath: Martin Bormann and the Fourth Reich* (New York: Simon & Shuster, 1974). Santander, like other Argentine politicians opposed to the Péron regime, had to go into exile on several occasions. After the war he worked closely with the Nazi hunter Simon Wiesenthal and was hailed as a "staunch and liberal friend of the Jews" (Jewish Telegraph Agency, Buenos Aires, December 3, 1964).

201 **Santander's published work:** After publication, in Montevideo in 1953, of Santander's book *Técnica de una Traición*, there was a concerted effort to silence him. His work was dismissed by several Argentine historians, and the (U.S.-authenticated) documents that he quoted were denounced as "communist fakes"; however, none of the libel suits against him succeeded. In 1956, Santander went back to West Germany to look for further proof of the Nazis' transfer of their wealth to Argentina with Perón's complicity. On December 26 that year, the German news magazine *Der Spiegel* published a virulent attack on him titled "The Painstaking Forger." Many of Santander's 1953 accusations in *Técnica de una Traición* have subsequently been proved true by the work of researchers, including the authors of this book, as well as by the testimony of contemporary sources such as Von Thermann and Gerda von Arenstorff.

201 **Von Thermann's memorandum:** Santander, *Técnica de una Traición*.

201 **"Siemens & Haske T43 encryption machine":** Based on the reports that the final messages from Berchtesgaden were to agents in South America, discussed in Mitchell, *Hitler's Mountain*.

202 **"We always let them win":** Santander, *Técnica de una Traición*. Also "Final Interrogation Report of Edmund Freiherr von Thermann," July 11, 1945, NARA, Record Group 59, Records of the Department of State, 862.20235/7-1145. Regarding Niebuhr's naval rank, "captain" is our translation of *Kapitän zur See*—see "Treatment of Military Ranks" on p. xiv.

202 **Delfino shipping:** Manning, *Bormann*; also "Axis Espionage and Propaganda in Latin America," NARA, Record Group 319, Records of the Army Staff, Records of the Office of the Assistant Chief of Staff, G-2, Military Intelligence Division. Separate Binder. Quoted in R. L. McGaha, "The Politics of Espionage: Nazi Diplomats and Spies in Argentina, 1933–1945" (PhD dissertation, Ohio University, 2009): "The F.B.I. suspected that the Delfino company and Sandstede's office were a cover for the movement of German agents, funds, and propaganda materials from Europe to South America. . . . Sandstede used his cover as a Casa Delfino employee to spy for the Nazis."

203 **"recalled to Berlin":** *Time* magazine, "Argentina: Hunting a Nazi," September 8, 1941. See also http://www.time.com/time/magazine/article/0,9171,849464,00.html.

203 **"simply waved through":** Santander, *Técnica de una Traición*.

203 **Damonte report:** Damonte Taborda, cited in Chase, *Falange*. *Time* magazine (see two notes above) suggested that it would not be long before Ambassador von Thermann would have to "pack his trunks." This expectation was premature by a year.

203 **"enjoy the trust of the Nazi agents":** Santander, *Técnica de una Traición*.

204 **Faupel's voyage:** Paul Meskil, *Hitler's Heirs* (New York: Pyramid Books, 1961); Santander, *Técnica de una Traición*.

204 **Scasso:** Marysa Navarro Gerassi, "Argentine Nationalism of the Right," *Studies in Comparative International Development* 1, no. 12 (1965).

204 **"maintain it at all costs":** Santander, *Técnica de una Traición*.

205 **Meynen-Niebuhr correspondence:** Ibid.

206 **"To hell with the U.S.":** *Time* magazine, "The Americas: Misunderstood Argentina," September 20, 1943, http://www.time.com/time/magazine/article/0,9171,774570,00.html.

206 **"Vice President Perón moved into overdrive":** Joseph Page, *Perón: A Biography* (London: Random House, 1983).

207 **Goebbels's article:** *Das Reich*, March 26, 1944, from Sayers and Kahn, *Plot Against the Peace*.

207 **Perón's vision:** Sayers and Kahn, *Plot Against the Peace*.

207 **"threat of an Allied trade embargo":** *Time* magazine, "Argentina: Action Ahead," July 10, 1944, http://www.time.com/time/magazine/article/0,9171,791494,00.html. See also Roosevelt's letter to Winston Churchill at docs.fdrlibrary.marist.edu/PSF/BOX37/a335bb02.html. Britain's

continuing desperate need for food imports in the immediate postwar years, when food rationing was even more severe than during the war, may explain the unwillingness of British governments to draw attention to Argentina's postwar dealings with Nazis refugees.

208 **1944 Freude-Faupel correspondence:** Santander, *Técnica de una Traición.*

209 **"he would meet Martin Bormann there":** Authors' conversation with Jorge Silvio Adeodato Colotto, Perón's former police bodyguard, Buenos Aires, 2008.

209 **Paul Ascher:** "German Disembarkation at San Clemente del Tuyu," declassified Argentine document, Coordinación Federal CF-OP-2315 from Central de Reunión to Navy Ministry, April 18, 1945, Argentine National Archive in Buenos Aires. For facsimile copy, see Farago, *Aftermath.* Captain junior grade is our translation of *Fregattenkapitän*—see "Treatment of Military Ranks" on p. xiv.

209 **Hermann Göring:** U.S. State Department report, 1945. Cited in Chesnoff, *Pack of Thieves.* See also Corky Siemaszko, "Memo Hit Swiss Over Nazi Loot," *New York Daily News*, December 5, 1996, http://www.nydailynews.com/archives/news/1996/12/05/1996-12-05_memo_hit_swiss_over_nazi_loot.html.

209 **"weapons to Spanish Republicans":** Antony Beevor, *The Battle for Spain: The Spanish Civil War 1936–1939* (London: Phoenix, 2006).

209 **$10 million of Göring's loot:** Declassified MI5 (Security Service) document, 2007; interrogation of Ernesto Hoppe, KV 2/ 2636, The National Archives, Kew, London. Following a tip from an MI6 (Secret Intelligence Service) agent in Argentina, Hoppe, a naturalized Argentinean of German birth, was arrested in Gibraltar aboard a ship sailing from Bilbao to Buenos Aires and interrogated at length. Hoppe, code-named "Herold," eventually told his interrogators that his mission was to receive about forty boxes of Nazi contraband that were to be delivered at a coastal landing point by the crew of a U-boat and then loaded into a truck for transport to Buenos Aires. There, depending on the markings on the boxes, they were to be delivered to a bank, to a house in the suburb of Villa Ballester in Buenos Aires—owned by two Nazi brothers—and to another address. While conceding Hoppe's courage and resourcefulness, MI5 concluded that he was an unprincipled rogue equally willing to take pay from Argentina, Germany, or Britain. Hoppe was repatriated to Argentina in October 1945. See also https://www.mi5.gov.uk/output/german-intelligence-agents-and-suspected-agents-5.html and Michael Evans, "'Unprincipled Ruffian' Told MI5 of Nazi Plot to Get Gold to Argentina," *Sunday Times*, September 4, 2007, http://www.timesonline.co.uk/tol/news/uk/article2381177.ece.

209 **Joachim von Ribbentrop:** Santander, *Técnica de una Traición.* See also interrogation of Otto Reinebeck, February 4, 1946, NARA, Record Group 59, Records of the Department of State, File 862.20235/4-2646.

210 **"The gold alone came to $1.12 billion":** Estimates of value come from multiple sources; see notes passim.

210 **"deposits of gold and various currencies":** "German Disembarkation at San Clemente del Tuyu"; for facsimile copy, see Farago, *Aftermath.*

210 **"more than two hundred German companies":** U.S. Government *Blue Book on Argentina.*

211 **"Nazi considered dangerous":** The Associated Press, Washington, DC, April 27, 1946.

211 **"Gerda von Arenstorff":** Santander, *Técnica de una Traición.*

211 **Ludwig Freude memo:** Ibid.

211 **transfers of assets to Argentina:** Ibid.

212 **"state of siege . . . retained . . . and improved on":** *Time* magazine, "Argentina: End of a Siege," August 20, 1945, http://www.time.com/time/magazine/article/0,9171,797675,00.html.

212 **"Argentina was back to normal":** *Time* magazine, "Argentina: Back to Normalcy," October 8, 1945, http://www.time.com/time/magazine/article/0,9171,776258,00.html.

212 **"revelations":** Santander, *Técnica de una Traición*; "Vier Prinzen zu Schaumburg-Lippe."

Chapter 18: THE U-BOAT LANDINGS

217 **San Carlos de Bariloche:** Authors' multiple visits, 2007–8.

217 **"place of exile":** Drew Pearson, "Washington Merry-Go-Round," Bell Syndicate, December 15, 1943. Until July 1942, Pearson's syndicated column had been cowritten with Robert S. Allen, who at that time obtained a major's commission in the U.S. Army.

218 **Estancia Moromar near Necochea:** Declassified FBI document, August 1, 1945; see page 222. Declassified FBI documents here supplied via http://www.paperlessarchives.com/hitler.html.

218 **"Kay normally ran his operation"**: Authors' multiple visits to Buenos Aires, 2007–8. See also Juan Salinas and Carlos De Napoli, *Ultramar Sur: La Última Operación secreta del Tercer Reich* (Buenos Aires: Grupo Editorial Norma, 2002), and Jorge Camarasa, *Puerto Seguro (Safe Haven)* (Buenos Aires: Grupo Editorial Norma, 2006).

218 **Schultz, Dettelmann, Brennecke:** Depositions to Commission of Enquiry into Nazi Activities in Argentina (CEANA). This was set up by President Carlos Menem in May 1997, with both Argentine and international membership and a broad remit to investigate all aspects mentioned in Parts III and IV of the present book. Schultz, Dettelmann, and Brennecke were engineering and radio ratings, all of whose grades came under the category of *Unteroffiziere ohne Portepee*—roughly, "junior petty officers." From documents contained in Camarasa, *Puerto Seguro*. Original Argentine documents available at http://admiral-graf-spee.blogspot.com.

218 **"eight trucks"**: Depositions to CEANA; from documents contained in Camarasa, *Puerto Seguro*.

221 **"Interrogated though the night"**: Salinas and De Napoli, *Ultramar Sur.*

222 **"Commissioner Mariotti telephoned the chief of police"**: Depositions to CEANA; from documents contained in Camarasa, *Puerto Seguro.*

222 **"FBI message"**: Declassified FBI documents, Buenos Aires, August 1945.

223 **Petty Officer Heinrich Bethe and Capt. Manuel Monasterio:** Jeff Kristenssen, *Hitler murió en la Argentina [Hitler Died in Argentina]: Operacion Patagonia (El Dios Abandonado)* (Buenos Aires: Ediciones Lumiere, 1987). "Jeff Kristenssen" is the pen name of an Argentine former merchant navy officer, congressman, and successful businessman, Capt. Manuel Monasterio. We interviewed Monasterio several times in 2007 and 2008. The retired merchant skipper was then an imposing figure in his mid-eighties, lucid, with a sharp wit, fluent in English, and still involved in the welfare of the elderly in Buenos Aires. Monasterio was convinced by Bethe's story and promised he would wait ten years until after Bethe's death before publishing the account. His *Hitler murió en la Argentina* is a strange book, as it appears almost to have been written by three separate authors. He insists, however, that the main characters, a "Pablo Glocknik" and Dr. Otto Lehmann, were real.

Jorge Camasara, in his book *Puerto Seguro*, identifies "Glocknik" as Heinrich Bethe. On the *Admiral Graf Spee* crew list there is a Heinrich Bethe, born October 26, 1912, working as a mechanic's mate in the 6th Division. Capt. Monastero says that he met "Glocknik" in 1967 at Caleta Olivia on the Patagonian coast; he was looking for someone to fix his car when a local suggested he try the *"gringo loco"* (mad European), a German mechanic who lived up the road. Possibly because of their shared maritime background, the two men soon hit it off. The captain admits that he made up the name "Pablo Glocknik" to protect his German acquaintance. Patrick Burnside, in his book *El Escape de Hitler*, gives the false name that Bethe actually used as "Juan Paulovsky," who is confirmed as having lived and died at Caleta Olivia.

Monasterio and *Hitler murió en la Argentina* are discussed at greater length in the first note for Chapter 23, page 324.

223 **"Bethe's recollections of the U-boat landings"**: Kristenssen (Manuel Monasterio), *Hitler murió en la Argentina.*

223 **"Ingeborg Schaeffer replied"**: Television interview, Eyeworks Quatre Cabezas, Berlin, 2007.

224 **Wermuth's interrogation report:** Interrogation of Otto Wermuth by Argentine authorities. Full reports on U-530, including Wermuth's interrogation, are available at http://www.uboatarchive.net/U-530NAReport.htm. There is a "Miramar" on the coast of Argentina, some thirty miles from Mar del Plata, but there would be no reason to surrender at this tiny coastal village. It is most likely that this was a typing error for "Moromar," the estancia near Necochea that housed Hitler on his first night in Argentina. Official translations and documents, such as the interrogation reports from the Nuremberg investigations, are littered with typos far more obvious than this.

224 **"within a week of his own arrival"**: Ibid.

226 **Television interviews with Wilfred von Oven:** Unused interview for Channel 4 UK documentary, *Secret History: Hitler of the Andes*, Barking Mad Productions; also Argentine documentary *Oro Nazi en Argentina* (Nazi Gold in Argentina), Rodolfo Pereyra (see http://www.independent.co.uk/news/world/americas/nazi-gold-shipped-by-uboat-to-argentina-532304.html); and Patrick S. Burnside, *El Escape de Hitler: Su vida invisible en la Argentina—Las conexiones con Evita y Perón* (Buenos Aires: Editorial Planeta, 2000).

226 **Argentine government memorandum:** Dirección de Coordinación Federal, Estrictamente Secreto y Confidential, document DAE 568, October 14, 1952.

227 **"described as the commander of U-235"**: William Stevenson, *The Bormann Brotherhood* (London: Corgi, 1975).

226 **"lost with all hands"**: Contemporaneous German signals decoded from Enigma traffic at Bletchley

Park prove beyond doubt that this was a Kriegsmarine action that destroyed its own submarine by accident. It is also significant that even the British Admiralty muddled the number when releasing data into the public domain—see HW18/421 (U2325 [sic]) at The National Archives, Kew, London. Five U-boats have been raised from the Kattegat, though U-235 is not among them—see http://www.uboat.net/boats/u235.htm.

227 **Lt. Cdr. Franz Barsch:** Stevenson, *Bormann Brotherhood.*

228 **"in a letter dated as early as August 7, 1939":** Santander, *Técnica de una Traición.* Material on Niebuhr's activities up until his expulsion in 1942 is to be found in KV 2/3301 in the British National Archives at Kew. This deals substantially with Nazi operations in Brazil, but leaves many questions unanswered about activities in Argentina.

228 **"seeking a secret U-boat":** Declassified FBI report, Buenos Aires, August 1943.

228 **"Argentine navy carried out antisubmarine operations":** Salinas and De Napoli, *Ultramar Sur.*

228 **"in a rubber boat":** Joseph Newman, "Two Mystery Figures Landed by U-boat," *New York Herald-Tribune,* Buenos Aires, July 14, 1945.

229 **Stanley Ross report:** Overseas News Agency, "U-Boats Base Spy Surge in Latin America," *Christian Science Monitor,* January 24, 1945.

229 **"Koehn was already back":** The Associated Press, Montevideo, Uruguay, August 18, 1945.

229 **Colonel Bustos's recollections:** Ernesto G. Castrillon and Luis Casabal, "Historia Viva Busquedas and Yo Fui Testigo," *La Nación,* Buenos Aires, March 23, 2008.

230– **U-234:** Wolfgang Hirschfield, *The Secret Diary of a U-Boat,* trans. Geoffrey Brooks (London:
31 Cassell, 2000).

231 **"Call off all coastal patrols":** Salinas and De Napoli, *Ultramar Sur.*

231 **"Along the coast of Patagonia":** Drew Pearson, Bell Syndicate, July 24, 1945.

232 **Raúl Damonte Taborda:** United Press, Rio de Janeiro, Brazil, October 20, 1945.

232 **"Not long after the German army was defeated":** Ernesto Guevara Lynch, *Young Che: Memories of Che Guevara by His Father,* trans. Lucía Álvarez de Toledo (London: Vintage/Random House, 2008).

Chapter 19: To Patagonia

234 **Descriptions:** Authors' travels to San Carlos de Bariloche, 2007–8.

234 **Prince Stephan zu Schaumburg-Lippe:** McGaha, "Politics of Espionage." Prince Stephan is not to be confused with his brother, Prince Friederich Christian, also a committed Nazi, who was an aide to Joseph Goebbels and held rank in the SA.

235 **"Abwehr agents in Turkey":** Gerald Reitlinger, *The SS: Alibi of a Nation* (London: William Heinemann, 1956).

235 **"Adm. Canaris was hanged":** Geoff Sullivan and Frode Weierud, "Breaking German Army Ciphers," *Cryptologia* 29, July 2005. The article mentions a four-part message called No. 69, sent at 4:33 p.m. on April 9, 1945, from Walter Huppenkothen. The message was marked *Geheim* (Secret) and was addressed to SS-Gruppenführer Glücks. The article notes: "Glücks [was] kindly requested to immediately inform the chief of Gestapo, SS-Gruppenführer Müller, by telephone, telex or through messenger that his mission has been completed as ordered. The mission he had accomplished was the summary execution of the last prominent members of the German resistance movement connected with the assassination attempt on Hitler on 20 July 1944." SS-Standartenführer Walter Huppenkothen was chief of *Gruppe E–Spionageabwehr* (Group E–counterespionage) in the RSHA department IV, Gestapo. Otto Thorbeck was a legal officer.

236 **"thorough investigation as to Hitler's whereabouts":** Drew Pearson, Bell Syndicate, July 24, 1945.

236 **Carmen Torrentuigi:** Television news magazine *La Cornisa,* Channel 7 Argentina, reporter Martin Jáuregui, 2005. In the television piece the crew members are filming a building on the estancia when Angela Soriani, Carmen's niece, arrives and asks them what they are doing. When they reply that they are filming the house where Hitler was said to have lived, Angela shakes her head and then points to another spot on the estate and says, "He lived there." The house where the Hitlers had lived was pulled down in the 1980s.

236 **"liver dumplings and squab":** Ryan Berry, *Hitler: Neither Vegetarian Nor Animal Lover* (New York: Pythagorean, 2004).

237 **"Hitler and Eva Braun stayed in the main house":** Carmen Torrentuigi via her niece, who said that the staff at the Estancia San Ramón were told that the Hitlers had died in a car crash in March 1946.

237 **"dark-haired, buxom Eva Braun"**: *Time* magazine, "Italy: Spring in the Axis," May 15, 1939, http://www.time.com/time/magazine/article/0,9171,761275,00.html.

237 **"born in San Remo"**: Reuters, Bad Godesburg, Rhineland, January 19, 1946; published in *Baltimore Sun*, January 20, 1946. A German journalist, Bernard Lescrinier, quoted this date and place to a press conference for the launch of his book *Behind the Scenes in the Third Reich* (apparently never actually published). "Fatty" Lescrinier was a notoriously shady character, who fed material mainly to the London *Daily Telegraph* and United Press; according to Michael Tracy, biographer of Sir Hugh Carleton-Greene, Fatty's value lay in his close contacts with Göring's circle and the Reich Chancellery. When his story is followed backward, it does not stand up in detail. However, a young man who had followed Eva in the job of studio assistant to Hitler's "court photographer" Heinrich Hoffman did say that she had a child. This claim was allegedly backed up by Eva Braun's father, who was quoted as saying, "The important thing is that Hitler will not die now without a successor."

237 **"three-day trip to Bavaria"**: United Press, Stockholm, June 11, 1945. A former member of the Swedish Legation in Berlin, Erik Wesslen—who said he had been in close contact with Hitler's headquarters during the siege of the city—believed that the reported marriage of Hitler and Eva in the bunker was to legitimize both a boy and a girl born to Eva during their long relationship. Wesslen said that prominent Germans believed the children to be living in Bavaria with distant relatives of Eva Braun's mother and that the Hitlers left for a three-day trip to Bavaria on April 8 or 9. Hitler and Eva moved into the Führerbunker on April 12 or 15 (historians differ). There is no historical record to prove or disprove that they were in Berlin between April 8 and 12.

237 **"many happy hours"**: In late fall of 1945, The Associated Press reported that U.S. intelligence officers had found Eva Braun's "treasure chest," including "beneath its hoard of jewelry and money, dozens of photographs showing family pictures of her and Adolf Hitler and a mysterious baby girl called Uschi [the diminutive of Ursula]," which were displayed "as normally as they would be in any family album." See "Americans Find Treasure Chest of Eva Braun," Frankfurt, published in *St. Petersburg Times* on November 16, 1945, http://news.google.com/newspapers?id=gBIwAAAAIBAJ&sjid=pE4DAAAAIBAJ&pg=4925,2133570&dq=eva+braun%27s+treasure-chest&hl=en.

On many of the snapshots, which show the little girl from infancy to about three years of age (the last was dated 1944), Eva had handwritten the words, "and here is Uschi again." Eva's personal home-movie library was found in 1945. The library is archived at NARA, Record Group 242.2, Motion Pictures Branch, Archives II, and was eventually released commercially on DVD to the public in 2004. The movies feature Uschi on dozens of occasions, with many scenes showing the great affection in which Hitler and Eva held her. After the war there were many theories about who Uschi was, the prevailing view being that she was the daughter of Eva's best friend Herta Ostermeyer, née Schneider. However, in the newspaper archives there is no mention of the child after this time, and the story seems to have been closed off. Intriguingly, this little girl who features so prominently in Eva's personal life, photographs, and home movies is not even mentioned by Eva's biographer Angela Lambert.

238 **"Eva Braun was again pregnant"**: London *Sunday Chronicle*, June 17, 1945.

238 **"a stillborn child in 1943"**: Interview with Eva Braun's mother, North American Newspaper Alliance, February 18, 1946.

238 **"car crash close to the property"**: *La Cornisa*, Channel 7 Argentina, reporter Martin Jáuregui, 2005.

239 **"none of them were submariners"**: Contemporary newspaper reports describe the extra prisoners aboard the *Highland Monarch* as former Nazi diplomats, spies, and other "undesirables" being thrown out of the country under the instructions of Foreign Minister Juan Cooke. Details of the "passengers" on the *Highland Monarch* are contained in Admiralty files ADM 116/ 5474 and 116/ 5475 at The National Archives, Kew, London.

239 **"neuralgic pain"**: North American Newspaper Alliance, New York, March 3, 1947.

239 **"Hitler needed surgery"**: Dr. Otto Lehmann, Hitler's personal physician, quoted in Jeff Kristenssen (Manuel Monasterio), *Hitler murió en la Argentina*. See note "Petty Officer Heinrich Bethe and Capt. Manuel Monasterio" on page 316.

239 **Gran Hotel Viena**: Authors' visit to hotel, 2007. While visiting Córdoba and staying at one of the city's hotels, the authors' interpreter asked for directions to Mar Chiquita. The young receptionist behind the front desk obliged, recommending the saltwater fish available from the inland sea. She then blithely suggested that if we had nothing better to do we should visit the Gran Hotel, where "Hitler and his wife used to stay after the war."

239 **Max Pahlke:** James Stewart Martin, *All Honorable Men* (Boston: Little and Brown, 1950). Pahlke's ostensible reason for building the complex at a cost of US$25 million was personal: the eldest of his two children, Máximo Junior, was said to suffer severely from psoriasis, and Pahlke's wife Melita

suffered from asthma. The "cure" was apparently found in the saline waters and therapeutic mud of the Mar Chiquita. The story that the motive for building the facility was a relieved father's gratitude was contradicted after the war by a family member, who said that young Max had never had the disfiguring skin disease.

240 **"he then left"**: Fernando Jorge Soto Roland, "Hotel Viena," research paper, January 2010, http://letras-uruguay.espaciolatino.com/aaa/soto_fernando/gran_hotel_viena_y_el_hotel_baln.htm. Roland is a professor of history at the University of Mar del Plata. It has been suggested that the hotel was a money-laundering operation for part of the huge amount of Nazi loot that had arrived in Argentina, but this seems illogical. "Laundering" is a process by which "dirty" money becomes "clean" and available again for use. It would make little sense to pour millions into a huge hotel complex in the middle of nowhere and then just leave it to stagnate.

240 **"the Hitlers' stay at the medical facility"**: Conversations between authors' researcher (anonymous) and Mrs. M., Argentina, 2008. Mrs. M. was a visitor to the hotel who said she met the Hitlers numerous times after the war. Mrs. M. agreed to ask friends if they had kept photographs of the Führer from after the war. After making some enquiries, she received a telephone call from an unknown man. He said that "the Gestapo were still active," threatened her life, and told her that curiosity was dangerous since "she" was still alive—the "she" being Eva Hitler. Mrs. M. has refused to speak to us since. We must presume that during this visit the Hitlers left both Ursula and her infant sister in the care of others at San Carlos de Bariloche.

240 **"lost in thought"**: Ibid.
241 **"wonderful sunsets"**: Researcher's conversations with Claudio Correa, Argentina, 2008.
241 **"would return to plague him"**: Dr. Otto Lehmann, quoted by Kristenssen (Manuel Monasterio), *Hitler murió en la Argentina*.
241 **"huge tracts of land"**: Researcher's conversations with Mrs. M., Argentina, 2008.
241 **"saw him there in October 1945"**: Meskil, *Hitler's Heirs*.
241 **"saw his old boss in a car"**: The Associated Press, Nuremberg, July 29, 1946.
242 **"Frenchman claimed"**: Letter to Director Hoover, FBI, from Los Angeles bureau, June 5, 1947; see page 293.
242 **"more detail"**: Letter, EX 39, from Director Hoover, FBI, to Legal Attaché, Rio de Janeiro, Brazil, dated July 9, 1947.
246 **"even more positive"**: Report marked "Secret—Air Courier from Legal Attaché, Rio de Janeiro, Brazil, to Director Hoover," dated August 6, 1947. Released FBI files are available from http://vault.fbi.gov/adolf-hitler.

Chapter 20: ADOLF HITLER'S VALLEY

247 **"Donitz had declared"**: Bar-Zohar, *The Avengers*.
247 **"The following year Dönitz told"**: Tim Swartz, *Evil Agenda of the Secret Government* (New Brunswick, NJ: Global Communications, 1999).
247 **"The region extends"**: Authors' travels through Chilean and Argentine Patagonia, 2007–8.
247– **"barren, wind-swept . . . other-planetary"**: Philip Hamburger, "Winds across the Pampas,"
48 *New Yorker*, December 1948.
249 **Schmidt's" account:** Quoted from "Hitler's Valley in Argentina," in the Polish weekly news magazine *Przekrój*, March 1995.
249 **"described by Heinrich Bethe"**: Kristenssen (Manuel Monasterio), *Hitler murió en la Argentina*.
249 **"Martin Bormann's hideout in Patagonia"**: Manning, *Martin Bormann: Nazi in Exile*.
249 **"Adolf Hitler's Valley"**: "Hitler's Valley," *Przekrój* magazine.
250 **"described his more modest dwelling"**: Kristenssen (Manuel Monasterio), *Hitler murió en la Argentina*.
250 **"sent to the German school"**: "Hitler's Valley," *Przekrój* magazine.
251 **"a large black truck"**: Hamburger, "Winds across the Pampas."
251 **"He fled with his family"**: BBC Television documentary "Children of the Master Race," part of the series *The Last Nazis*, Minnow Films, London, broadcast 2010. Various halfhearted attempts were made by the West German government to extradite Alvensleben on charges of murdering 4,247 people in the autumn of 1939. These approaches were spurned by the Argentine government, and the SS general lived undisturbed in Argentina until his death in 1970.
252 **"Inalco, their new mansion"**: Abel Basti, *Bariloche Nazi: Sitios históricos relacianados al Nationalsocialismo* (San Carlos de Bariloche, Argentina, privately published, 2005); Burnside, *El escape de Hitler*.

252 **"boathouse next to the jetty"**: Authors' research trips to Inalco, Bariloche, and Villa La Angostura, 2007–8, including Argentine Civil Aviation records.

253 **"along unmade roads and tracks"**: "Hitler's Valley," *Przekrój* magazine; Kristenssen (Manuel Monasterio), *Hitler murió en la Argentina*.

253 **"now covered with trees"**: Authors' multiple visits to Inalco, 2007–8.

253 **"underground steel-lined chambers"**: Authors' conversations with "Jeff Kristenssen" (Manuel Monasterio), Buenos Aires, 2007–8.

253 **"caretaker on the property"**: "Hitler's Valley," *Przekrój* magazine.

253 **"Bustillo also designed"**: for Alejandro Bustillo, see biography in *Revista arquitectura Andina* 4, http://www.arquitecturaandina.com.ar/anterior.php. The "Saracen tower": Researcher conversation with Río Negro province minister of tourism Omar Contreras, Buenos Aires, 2008.

253 **Friedrich Lantschner:** Joachim Lilla, *Statisten in Uniform: Die Mitglieder des Reichstages 1933–1945* (Düsseldorf: Droste Verlag, 2004); Andreas Schulz and Günter Wegmann, *Die Generale der Waffen-SS und der Polizei, Band 1* (Bissendorf: Biblio-Verlag, 2003); Ruth Bettina Birn, *Die Höheren SS- und Polizeiführer: Himmlers Vertreter im Reich und in den besetzten Gebieten* (Düsseldorf: Droste Verlag, 1986). Lantschner, implicated for his involvement in the 1938 Kristallnacht pogroms against the Jews, was a senior Nazi Party official in the Tyrol. In 1945 he fled with his brother Gustav ("Guzzi"—a silver medalist at the 1936 Winter Olympics) along the Vatican ratline run by Cardinal Alois Hudal. Installed in San Carlos de Bariloche, Lantschner set up a thriving building business to which the Perón regime awarded many government contracts.

254 **"Hitler's main residence"**: Kristenssen (Manuel Monasterior), *Hitler murió en la Argentina*. As part of our research in 2008, Capt. Monasterio asked the widow of an old friend, Oswaldo R., if she had kept any of her husband's papers. Oswaldo, a key figure in the ratline operation based in Genoa, had once shown Monasterio a postwar letter from Martin Bormann thanking him for his help. Monasterio's and Oswaldo's wives had been friends and neighbors for years, living next to each other in a small town in the province of Chubut in Patagonia. Mrs. R. agreed to look for the papers. That night the eighty-three-year-old Monasterio received a telephone call from an unknown man, who threatened to kill him and his family and burn down his home unless he dropped this line of enquiry. When Monasterio tried to contact Mrs. R. the next day, he was told that she had gone overseas, to Germany. Capt. Monasterio's book exposed him to a number of death threats over the years; he has also been interviewed by the FBI.

254 **Club Andino Bariloche:** Authors' visits to San Carlos de Bariloche, 2007–8. See Seamus Mirodan, "Nazis' Argentine Village Hide-Out Pulls in Tourists," London *Daily Telegraph*, February 14, 2004, http://www.telegraph.co.uk/news/worldnews/southamerica/argentina/1454352/Nazis-Argentine-village-hide-out-pulls-in-tourists.html.

254– **Josef Schwammberger:** The Associated Press, Berlin, December 3, 2004; see also www.holocaust
55 researchproject.org/ghettos/przemysl.html.

255 **"President Juan Perón explained"**: Authors' visits to San Carlos de Bariloche. See Mirodan, "Nazis' Argentine Village Hide-Out."

Chapter 21: GREEDY ALLIES, LOYAL FRIENDS

256 **"Evita was accompanied by"**: "Wiesenthal Says Evita Likely Stashed Nazi Loot," Reuters, June 26, 1997, published in *Página 12* newspaper, Buenos Aires; *U.S. News & World Report*, "Cry for Them, Argentina, Nazi Loot from Holocaust Victims Enriched Eva Perón," November 15, 1999; Chesnoff, *Pack of Thieves*. See also Nicholas Fraser and Marysa Navarro, *Evita: The Real Life of Eva Perón* (London: Andre Deutsch, 2003; New York: W. W. Norton, 1996).

256 **Alberto Dodero:** *Time* magazine, "Abdication of a Tycoon," May 16, 1949, http://www.time.com/time/magazine/article/0,9171,853719,00.html. See also Jane Shuter, *Aftermath of the Holocaust* (Chicago: Heinemann Library, 2003); Holger M. Meding, *Ruta de los Nazis en los Tiempos de Perón* (Buenos Aires: Emecé Editores, 1999). See also references to Eichmann and Meding's status in "The Long Road to Eichmann's Arrest," *Spiegel Online*, April 1, 2011, http://www.spiegel.de/international/germany/0,1518,754486,00.html, and Nicolás Cassese, "La rama nazi de Perón," *La Nación*, Buenos Aires, February 16, 1997, http://www.lanacion.com.ar/202464.

257 **"French war criminals"**: Uki Goñi, *The Real Odessa: How Perón Brought the Nazi War Criminals to Argentina* (London: Granta Books, 2002).

257 **Benítez in Rome:** Alicia Dujovne Ortiz, *Eva Perón: A Biography* (New York: St. Martin's Griffin, 1997).

257 **Papal Commission of Assistance:** Karlheinz Deschner, *Ein Jahrhundert Heilsgeschichte*, vol. 2

(Cologne: Leck, 1983); Peter Godman, *Hitler and the Vatican* (New York: Free Press/Simon & Schuster, 2004).

257 **Franz Stangl:** Gitta Sereny, *Into That Darkness* (London: Andre Deutsch, 1974; New York: McGraw-Hill, 1974).

257 **"through the Nazi bishop's hands":** Michael Phayer, *Pius XII, the Holocaust and the Cold War* (Bloomington: Indiana University Press, 2007); Goñi, *Real Odessa*. See also Shuter, *Aftermath of the Holocaust*; Meding, *Ruta de los Nazis*; also see references to Eichmann and Meding's status in http://www.spiegel.de/international/germany/0,1518,754486,00.html and http://www.lanacion. com.ar/202464.

258 **"Hudal wrote to President Perón":** Greg Whitlock, "Alois Hudal: Clero-Fascist Nietzsche Critic," in *Nietzsche-Studien* 32 (2003). Hudal would be the "guardian" of Father Adolf Martin Bormann, the Reichsleiter's eldest son; Adolf Martin later resigned the priesthood, married a former nun, and became a teacher of theology in South America. See also L. Bezymensky, *Tracing Martin Bormann* (Honolulu: University Press of the Pacific, 2001); Farago, *Aftermath*; and Stevenson, *The Bormann Brotherhood*. Hudal was also the bishop under whose patronage Jesuit father Avery Dulles, son of John Foster Dulles and nephew of Allen, trained at a monastery in Villach, Austria. Avery Dulles became a cardinal in 2001. See Bezymensky, *Tracing Martin Bormann*.

258 **"Evita left Spain for Rome":** Fraser and Navarro, *Evita*.

258 **"arranged to meet Bormann":** Santander, *Técnica de una Traición*.

258 **"no honor among thieves":** Chesnoff, *Pack of Thieves*, 243.

259 **Ricardo Staudt:** *Time* magazine, "Argentina: The Coddled," December 17, 1945, http://www. time.com/time/magazine/article/0,9171,776519,00.html.

259 **"had no option but to accept":** Farago, *Aftermath*.

259 **"far more intelligent than her husband":** Interview with Araceli Méndez, published in *La Mañana del Sur*, part of the Diario Ambito Financiero news group, Buenos Aires, 1996; also researcher conversations with Araceli Méndez, Buenos Aires, 2008.

259 **"when Müller based himself in Córdoba":** Personal papers of Hans-Ulrich Rudel, auctioned by Signature House, Lot 236, www.signaturehouse.net/.

259 **"a string of untimely deaths":** *Time* magazine, "Milestones," May 7, 1956, http://www.time.com/ time/magazine/article/0,9171,937348,00.html; Gérald L. Posner and John Ware, *Mengele: The Complete Story* (Lanham, MD: Cooper Square Press, 2000); Bar-Zohar, *Avengers*.

259 **Duarte's suicide:** *Life* magazine, "A Dictator Goes A-Wooing," May 25, 1953.

260 **"in the morning gave her a substantial check":** Fraser and Navarro, *Evita*.

260 **Jacques-Albert Cuttat and Instituto Suizo-Argentino:** Grank Garbely, *Evitas Geheimnis: Die Nazis, Die Schweiz, und Perón's Argentinien* (Zurich: Rotpunktverlag, 2003).

260 **"information the FBI took seriously":** FBI report, D. M. Ladd to Hoover, May 15, 1948, NA, RA RG 65 65-55639 (1-24) Box 38, cited in Breitman, *U.S. Intelligence and the Nazis*.

260 **"a guide led him and his bodyguards":** In August 1961, the West German magazine *Revue* published an interview with an Austrian Alpine guide who claimed he guided Bormann over a secret route through the Alps to Italy on August 16, 1947.

260– **"Udine in Italy" and Capt. Bell:** Ian Bell, *No Place to Hide* (London: Minerva Press, 1998). Bell
63 was also interviewed about his work, and sighting of Bormann, in "Nazi Hunter," a program in the documentary series *War Stories* on Granada Television (a British television network), 1999.

263 **Giovanna C:** The *Giovanna C* was built in Japan as the *Eastern Trader* for the U.S. Shipping Board in 1919. It was sold in 1922 to the Luckenbach Steamship Company in New York, serving as the *Horace Luckenbach* until bought by Linea C (part of the Costa Crociere S.p.A. shipping line) in 1947. It plied routes to South and North America until 1953. See http://www.simplonpc.co.uk/ CostaPCs.html#anchor559191 and http://www.theshipslist.com/ships/lines/costa.htm.

263 **"Bormann was now known":** Farago, *Aftermath*. There have been claims that Farago was duped by being shown fake papers. We are not convinced; there is still a complete disinformation opera- tion in Argentina led by staunch Perónists who want nothing to sully the memory of their fascist First Couple. Farago's documentation came from many sources, including the Catholic Information Agency of Argentina (AICA), Argentine senators Silvano Santander and Julio Busaniche, Argen- tine naval intelligence, and Spruille Braden, former U.S. ambassador to Argentina.

264 **Nazi treasure and "major factor in the economic life":** Farago, *Aftermath*. Separately, the respected French daily newspaper *Le Figaro* published corroborating evidence of the details of the physical treasure and investments in 1970. There are suggestions that, before Perón's return from exile in 1972, he offered the ruling junta a slice of what was left of the Nazi treasure he controlled as part of what Farago calls his "admission fee" back to power in Argentina.

264 **"Bormann once again met with his Führer":** Kristenssen (Manuel Monasterio), *Hitler murió en la Argentina.*

265 **"the necessary preparations":** Letter via U.S. Army Courier Service from Legal Attaché, American Embassy London, to Director Hoover, September 17, 1945. Letter from Director Hoover to the American Embassy in Buenos Aires, November 13, 1945. FBI Files on Hitler available online at http://vault.fbi.gov/adolf-hitler.

265 **Gold Party Badge:** Research carried out for authors by www.oocities.com/goldpartypin/index.html.

265 **"since joining in 1924":** Documentary film *Hotel Eden* by Cuini Amelio Ortiz, Deutschland 1995 / 3sat / MDR. Ms. Ortiz had suggested the story of Hitler possibly being in Argentina to her German commissioning editors, but they decided not to run with it.

265 **"when they first met Hitler":** Ortiz, *Hotel Eden.*

268 **Hotel Eden:** Authors' visit, 2007, and various articles by historian Carlos Panozzo, La Falda. Also Carlos Panozzo, *El Hotel Edén de La Falda* (La Falda, Argentina: privately published, n.d.). See also Jorge Camarasa, "La Falda tiene también su secreto nazi," *La Nación*, Buenos Aires, July 27, 1998, www.lanacion.com.ar/nota.asp?nota_id=104816; Ortiz, *Hotel Eden.* During this visit, author Gerrard Wiliams spoke to Ida Eichhorn's great-nephew through the iron gate of the Eichhorns' old house near the hotel: "He told me that he had burned all of the material shown in Cuini's film [see note about documentary film *Hotel Eden* by Cuini Amelio Ortiz above] and accused her of betraying his confidence; he also mistakenly accused Catalina Gomero of being paid for her interviews, which both she and her interviewers denied [see note about video interview with Catalina Gomero below]. He denied the stories about Hitler staying with his great-aunt and great-uncle. On turning away to end our conversation, he stopped, looked back at me, and said, 'One day the truth will come out.' He has since refused to talk further."

268 **Prince of Wales:** Simon Edge, "The Nazi King," London *Daily Express*, May 23, 2011, http://dailyexpress.co.uk/posts/view/113232.

268 **"German School in La Falda":** Various articles by historian Carlos Panozzo, La Falda. Nazi doctrine in schools: Ronald C. Newton, *The "Nazi Menace" in Argentina, 1931–1947* (Palo Alto, CA: Stanford University Press, 1992).

269 **"commemorative ceremony":** Various articles by historian Carlos Panozzo.

269 **"police and armed German sailors":** Ibid.

269 **Acción Argentina:** Lynch, *Young Che*; also authors' conversations with Dr. Floreal Vajlis, Buenos Aires, 2008. Dr. Vajlis, now in his eighties, was Gerrard Williams's landlord in Buenos Aires and is still vehemently antifascist. Dr. Vajlis was present outside the Hotel Eden on this occasion.

269 **"Hotel Eden was seized":** Various articles by historian Charles Panozzo, La Falda; Panozzo, *El Hotel Edén de La Falda*; Alfredo Ferrarassi, *Edén Hotel y Pueblo La Falda* (Córdoba, Argentina: privately published, 2006). Japanese internment: Ayako Tomii, *A Japanese Diplomat's Daughter: An Outsider's Childhood in the 1930s and 1940s* (iUniverse, 2004).

269 **"told her closest circle":** Video interview with Catalina Gomero in *Secret History: Hitler of the Andes*, Barking Mad Productions.

269 **Horst Eichmann:** Ernesto Bohoslavsky, *Contra la Patagonia judía: La familia Eichmann y los nacionalistas Argentinos y Chilenos frente al Plan Andinia . . .* (Santiago de Chile, 2008, PDF online), http://ungs.academia.edu/ebohos/Papers/86439/Contra_la_Patagonia_judia._La_familia_Eichmann_y_los_nacionalistas_argentinos_y_chilenos_frente_al_Plan_Andinia_de_1960_a_nuestros_dias_; *Time* magazine, "Milestones," September 1, 1961, http://www.time.com/time/magazine/article/0,9171,939852,00.html.

270 **"they owned a property":** Authors' visit to Miromar, Mar Chiquita, Córdoba province, Argentina, 2007. We were shown around the hotel by one of its "guardians" from the local community; she had heard many uncorroborated rumors of the Hitlers' presence at the hotel. See also "Hitler's Ghost," *Ghost Hunters International*, U.S. television series on the SyFy channel, January 2010, shot at Hotel Viena.

270 **"head of security, Col. Krueger":** Roland, "Hotel Viena."

270– **Catalina Gomero's account:** Authors' conversations with documentary-maker Cuini Amelio Ortiz
71 (see note above), Rome, 2008; also video interview courtesy of Diario Ambito Financiero news group, and in the Howard and Roberts documentary, *Secret History*. See third note for Chapter 22, on page 323, for further provenance.

271 **John Walsh's account:** Howard and Roberts, *Secret History*.

271– **Jorge Batinic and Mafalda Batinic's account:** Video interview with Jorge Batinic, courtesy
73 Ricardo D'Aloia, editorial director, Diario Ambito Financiero news group, Buenos Aires, 2008. See also *Hoy en la Noticia*, "El Pais: Hitler en Chubut," La Plata, Argentina, July 24, 1997, pdf.diariohoy.net/1997/07/240797CU.PDF.

Chapter 22: DEPARTURES

274 **Ante Pavelić:** IV/D/4 RSHA Gestapo report to Reichsführer-SS Heinrich Himmler, February 17, 1942. See also Srđa Trifković, "The Real Genocide in Yugoslavia: Independent Croatia of 1941 Revisited," Center for Peace in the Balkans, April 21, 2000, http://www.balkanpeace.org/index. php?index=article&articleid=13742.

274 **"Croats in the years after the war":** Yossi Melman, "Tied Up in the Rat Lines," *Haaretz*, Tel Aviv, January 17, 2006; also U.S. Army file on Ante Pavelić, report by Capt. Marion Scot, http://www. jerusalim.org/cd/biblioteka/pavelicpapers/pavelic/ap0015.html.

274– **Ancin's testimony:** Video interview, courtesy Ricardo D'Aloia, editorial director, Diario Ambito
76 Financiero news group, Buenos Aires, 2008. The video interviews with Catalina Gomero and Jorge Batinic (see Chapter 21) and with Hernán Ancin have never been broadcast. An unfinished program made by the newspaper group's TV arm in the 1990s was shown by the group's owner to his friend, Argentine president Carlos Menem. Menem requested that nothing further be done with it. See also "Man Says He Saw Hitler After War," Agence France Presse, May 31, 1997; see http://www. indianexpress.com/Storyold/2523/.

276 **"Carlos Luecke":** Michael D. Miller with Andreas Schulz and Ken McCanliss, *Leaders of the SS & German Police*, vol. 1 (San Jose, CA: R. James Bender, 2008).

277 **Hans-Ulrich Rudel:** One of only twenty-seven men to be awarded the Knight's Cross with Oak Leaves, Swords and Diamonds, Col. Rudel was unique in that a version with Golden Oak Leaves was created specifically for him.

277 **Rudel's postwar activities:** Meskil, *Hitler's Heirs*; also United Press, Bonn, August 28, 1953; see also http://www.pilotenbunker.de/Stuka/Rudel/rudel.htm; for Euphorion Books, see Anne de Courcy, "The Dazzling Beauty with a Poison Pen," *Daily Mail*, UK, January 9, 2009, http:// www.dailymail.co.uk/home/books/article-1109382/The-dazzling-beauty-poison-pen-DIANA-MOSLEY-THE-PURSUIT-OF-LAUGHTER.html.

278 **"Eva finally left Inalco":** Researcher Nahuel Coca's conversations in Buenos Aires, 2008, with Alicia Oliveira, who claimed to have met one of the Hitlers' daughters in that city. Normally such stories can be discounted easily, but Alicia Oliveira was a senior lawyer in the Ministry of Human Rights and had been the first female ombudsman of Buenos Aires. In 1985, Ms. Oliveira was working at a nongovernmental human rights center, the Centro de Estudios Legales y Sociales (CELS). She was consulted on several occasions by a woman who was contemplating a divorce, apparently because of domestic violence, and who had problems with her documents because both she and her German husband were living under false identities. (Ms. Oliveira has refused to break lawyer-client confidentiality by disclosing names.) After several meetings the lawyer gained her client's trust, and the woman—whom Ms. Oliveira judged to be sane and lucid—revealed that she was the daughter of Eva Hitler, who had apparently left Adolf at some time in the 1950s. She did not speak fondly of either parent; she said that her father was dead but her mother was still alive. She had "grown up in the Cordillera, I think in Mendoza [sic], near Neuquén [Neuquén province, not Mendoza]. What she said sounded plausible to me. I asked her to come again, but she never did." The lawyer said that when she saw a photo of Eva Braun she was struck by the resemblance to her client.

278 **"financial dealings across the world":** Interview with Araceli Méndez, *La Mañana del Sur*, 1996; also researcher conversations with Araceli Méndez, Buenos Aires, 2008.

278– **Bormann, Colotto, and Perón:** Authors' conversations with Jorge Colotto, Buenos Aires,
79 2008.

279 **"luxurious Plaza Hotel":** Argentine government document, Dirección Coordinación Federal, Estrictamente Secreto y Confidential, CF "A" No. 9976, October 5, 1960. Report received September 1953.

280 **Círculo Mílitar:** Authors' visits to Buenos Aires, 2008; see also http://www.circulomilitar.org/ Re.htm and http://www.frommers.com/destinations/buenosaires/A34264.html#ixzz0wx55TjO.

280 **"four or five different passports":** Incidentally, the facial analysis expert Professor Alf Linney, of University College London (see note for Chapter 14, "deceived even those quite close to him," page 308), has proved by scientific comparison that the photograph in one alleged Uruguayan passport of Martin Bormann's from Argentina, discovered in the 1990s, cannot be his. A fingerprint on the passport has also been examined; it is not Bormann's.

280 **"financial dealings":** Interview with Araceli Méndez, *La Mañana del Sur*, 1996; also researcher conversations with Araceli Méndez, Buenos Aires, 2008.

281 **"placed the Führer in Colombia":** Declassified CIA report A02592, October 3, 1955. See page 282.

281 **Rodolfo Freude:** Report of investigation by the Delegación de Associaciones Israelitas Argentinas (DAIA), Annual Report, 1997.

281 **"Evita died of cancer"**: Fraser and Navarro, *Evita*.
283 **"The Tyrant"**: David Crassweller, *Perón and the Enigmas of Argentina* (New York: W.W. Norton, 1987).
283 **"I'm not superstitious"**: Tomás Eloy Martínez, *La novela de Perón* (London: Vintage Books, 1997). See also *Time* magazine, "The Hemisphere: Daddykins & Nelly," October 10, 1955, http://www.time.com/time/magazine/article/0,9171,937225,00.html; Charles Keely, "Peronism Still Strong in Argentina," Copley News Service, Buenos Aires, December 5, 1964, reprinted in *The News and Courier*, Charleston, South Carolina, December 6, 1964.
284 **"president fled the country"**: *Time* magazine, "The Hemisphere: Daddykins & Nelly."
284 **"move to a smaller house"**: Kristenssen (Manuel Monasterio), *Hitler murió en la Argentina*.

Chapter 23: GHOSTS IN THE SHADOWS

285 **Heinrich Bethe and the "Lehmann papers"**: Kristenssen (Manuel Monasterio), *Hitler murió en la Argentina* (excerpted throughout chapter); authors' conversations with Kristenssen (Monasterio), Buenos Aires, 2008. See also Chapter 18, page 223, and note, "Petty Officer Heinrich Bethe and Capt. Manuel Monasterio," on page 316). At the beginning of Monasterio's own book is a quotation from Pablo Glocknik/Heinrich Bethe (see note, "Petty Officer Heinrich Bethe and Capt. Manuel Monasterio," on page 316 for more on Glocknik/Bethe) describing a funeral. It reads, in part: "The men move thoughtfully forward, dragging with them an old darkness with memories of glory, of defeat, and of crimes. I watch them silently, from behind, removed, observing expressions, gestures, movements. . . . I am sure that when the pastor said his words, they all imagined a mausoleum in Berlin . . . a strong army, hardened and victorious, parading and bidding farewell to the pain of his death with clarinets. . . . I see them defeated, by the fear and the cowardly pain of having to [keep] closed and silent lips—unable to shout, to demand silence, and to tell the world: Adolf Hitler died yesterday?"
    Capt. Monasterio recalled spending many hours talking with "Glocknik," who wanted to tell someone his secrets before he died. The German sailor revealed details of the Nazi spy network in Argentina, the arrival of two submarines, and his life with Hitler "near Bariloche" until the Führer's death on February 13, 1962. As noted, he also handed over to Monasterio's keeping the Lehmann papers, apparently lost during one of many house moves since the 1970s. These documents, recounted in *Hitler murió en la Argentina*, detailed Dr. Otto Lehmann's life while treating the aging Hitler as his personal physician. Intriguingly, one reference can be found to a man who might fit the doctor's profile, in a genealogy site hidden in the depths of the Internet. This Dr. Otto Lehmann was born in Stettin in 1894 and later practiced in Buenos Aires. We have discovered no more about him, and anyway "Lehmann" may well have been a pseudonym.
286 **"magical battle"**: For more on this supposed conflict, see http://www.foreantimes.com/features/articles/4435/the_magical_battle_of_britain.html.
289 **Gisela Heuser**: Gisela Heuser and Philippe Mervyn, *Adolf Hitler Mon Père* (Paris: ALE Impressions, 1966). See *Der Spiegel*, "Hitler," July 18, 1966, http://www.spiegel.de/spiegel/print/d-46407960.html. Gisela Heuser, on the basis of a "confession" by her mother, published with her husband Philippe Mervyn—who appears to have ghostwritten it on her behalf—a book in which she claimed to be the daughter of the Führer. Mervyn was the son of a rabbi who had died in a concentration camp, and he met Gisela while carrying out research in Germany for his 1964 book *À chacun son juif (Everyone Has His Jew)*. When the young woman told her mother that she was going to marry the son of a rabbi, Frau Heuser suffered a panic attack. "You can't marry a Jew," she protested; when Gisela demanded why not, she replied, "Because you're the daughter of Adolf Hitler. Your father was the Führer." Gisela left home, left Germany, converted to Judaism, and married Philippe Mervyn in a small town near Paris. In the book she writes: "My mother resides in Frankfurt, West Germany, and was as much against my marriage as she was against my decision to enter the Jewish faith. I believe she is still a staunch Nazi and is still in love with the father of her daughter. But I am of a sufficient age to judge my parents objectively and to decide my own way." When last heard of, Gisela and Philippe Mervyn were contemplating emigrating to Israel. Her mother denied the whole story.
289 **Helmut Goebbels**: The Associated Press, Munich, October 7, 1946.
290 **Heinrich Bethe's death**: Authors' conversations with Jeff Kristenssen (Manuel Monasterio), Buenos Aires, 2008.
290– **Bormann and Müller trail**: Robert Taylor, "Nazi Martin Bormann Is Alive in Paraguay, Says
91 Israeli Ex-spy," *Boston Globe*, July 26, 1971; also Farago, *Aftermath*, and Manning, *Martin Bormann*.
291 **"There are two possibilities for me"**: Speer, *Inside the Third Reich*.

BIBLIOGRAPHY
AND OTHER SOURCES

BOOKS

Aarons, Mark. *Sanctuary: Nazi Fugitives in Australia.* Port Melbourne, Victoria: William Heinemann Australia, 1989.

Aarons, Mark, and John Loftus. *Unholy Trinity: The Vatican, the Nazis, and the Swiss Banks.* New York: St. Martin's Press, 1991.

Aldrich, Richard J. *GCHQ: The Uncensored Story of Britain's Most Secret Intelligence Agency.* London: Harper Press, 2010.

Alford, Kenneth D. *Nazi Plunder: Great Treasure Stories of World War II.* Cambridge, MA: Da Capo Press, 2001.

Alford, Kenneth D., and Theodore P. Savas. *Nazi Millionaires: The Allied Search for Hidden SS Gold.* Havertown, PA: Casemate, 2002.

Allen, Martin. *The Hitler/Hess Deception: British Intelligence's Best-Kept Secret of the Second World War.* London: HarperCollins, 2003.

Altner, Helmut. *Berlin Dance of Death.* Staplehurst, UK: Spellmount, 2002.

Aly, Götz. *Hitler's Beneficiaries: How the Nazis Bought the German People.* London: Verso, 2007.

Badsey, Stephen. *Arnhem 1944: Operation Market Garden.* Oxford: Osprey, 1993.

Baggott, Jim. *Atomic: The First War of Physics and the Secret War of the Atom Bomb 1939–1949.* London: Icon Books, 2009.

Bar-Zohar, Michael. *The Avengers.* London: Arthur Barker, 1968.

Bascomb, Neal. *Hunting Eichmann: Chasing Down the World's Most Notorious Nazi.* London: Quercus, 2009.

Bassett, Richard. *Hitler's Spy Chief: The Wilhelm Canaris Mystery.* London: Cassell, 2005.

Basti, Abel. *Bariloche Nazi: Sitios Historicos Relacianados Al Nationalsocialismo.* San Carlos de Bariloche, Argentina: privately published, 2005.

Baumbach, Werner. *Broken Swastika: The Defeat of the Luftwaffe.* London: Robert Hale, 1960.

Bedeia, Arthur G., ed. "Guilty of Enthusiasm." In *Management Laureates,* vol. 3. London: JAI Press, 1993.

Beevor, Antony. *Berlin: The Downfall 1945.* London: Viking, 2002.

——. *The Battle for Spain: The Spanish Civil War 1936–1939.* London: Phoenix, 2006.

Behrman, Greg. *The Most Noble Adventure: The Marshall Plan and the Reconstruction of Post-War Europe.* London: Aurum Press, 2008.

Bell, Ian. *No Place to Hide.* London: Minerva Press, 1998.

Bellamy, Chris. *Absolute War: Soviet Russia in the Second World War.* London: Macmillan, 2007.

Bennett, William J. *America: The Last Best Hope.* 2 vols. Nashville, TN: Thomas Nelson, 2007.

Bergen, Doris. *The Holocaust: A New History.* Stroud, UK: Tempus, 2003.

Berry, Ryan. *Hitler: Neither Vegetarian nor Animal Lover.* New York: Pythagorean, 2004.

Bessel, Richard. *Nazism and War.* London: Phoenix, 2004.

——. *Germany 1945: From War to Peace.* London: Simon & Schuster, 2009.

Best, Geoffrey. *Churchill and War.* London: Hambledon & London, 2005.

Bezymensky, L. *Tracing Martin Bormann.* Honolulu: University Press of the Pacific, 2001.

Biddiscombe, Perry. *The DeNazification of Germany: A History 1945–1950.* Stroud, UK: Tempus, 2007.

Birn, Ruth Bettina. *Die Höheren SS- und Polizeiführer: Himmlers Vertreter im Reich und in den besetzten Gebieten.* Düsselforf: Droste Verlag, 1986.

Black, Edwin. *Nazi Nexus: America's Corporate Connections to Hitler's Holocaust.* Washington, DC: Dialog Press, 2009.

Black, Ian, and Benny Morris. *Israel's Secret Wars: A History of Israel's Intelligence Services.* New York: Grove Press, 1991.

Black, Peter R. *Ernst Kaltenbrunner: Ideological Soldier of the Third Reich.* Princeton, NJ: Princeton University Press, 1984.

Blair, Clay. *Hitler's U-Boat War,* vol. 2: *The Hunted, 1941–1945.* London: Cassell, 2000.

Blumenson, Martin. *The Patton Papers, 1940–1945.* New York: Houghton Mifflin, 1974.

Bowers, Peter M. *Curtiss Aircraft 1907–1947.* London: Putnam, 1987.

Breitman, Richard. *U.S. Intelligence and the Nazis.* Cambridge, UK: Cambridge University Press, 2005.

Breuer, William B. *Feuding Allies: The Private Wars of the High Command.* Edison, NJ: Castle Books, 2007.

Broszat, Martin. *The Hitler State: The Foundation and Development of the Internal Structure of the Third Reich.* Harlow, UK: Longman, 1981.

Burleigh, Michael. *The Third Reich: A New History.* London: Macmillan, 2000.

———. *Sacred Cause: Religion and Politics from the European Dictators to Al Qaeda.* London: Harper Perennial, 2006.

Burnside, Patrick. *El Escape De Hitler: Su vida invisible en la Argentina—Las conexiones con Evita y Perón.* Buenos Aires: Editorial Planeta, 2000.

Butler, Rupert. *An Illustrated History of the Gestapo.* Shepperton, UK: Ian Allan, 1992.

Butler, Susan, ed. *My Dear Mr. Stalin: The Complete Correspondence of Franklin D. Roosevelt and Joseph V. Stalin.* New Haven, CT: Yale University Press, 2005.

Camasara, Jorge. *Puerto Seguro: Desembarcos clandestinos en la Patagonia [Safe Haven: Clandestine Landings in Patagonia].* Buenos Aires: Norma Editorial, 2006.

Capote, Truman. *Answered Prayers.* London: Random House, 1987.

Carr, Jonathan. *The Wagner Clan.* London: Faber and Faber, 2007.

Casey, William J. *The Secret War Against Hitler.* Washington, DC: Regnery, 1988.

Cesarani, David. *Eichmann: His Life and Crimes.* London: William Heinemann, 2004.

Chase, Alan. *Falange: The Axis Secret Army in the Americas.* New York: G.P. Putnam's Sons, 1943.

Chesnoff, Richard Z. *Pack of Thieves: How Hitler and Europe Plundered the Jews and Committed the Greatest Theft in History.* London: Weidenfeld & Nicolson, 2000.

Churchill, Winston. *The Second World War,* vol. 2, *Their Finest Hour.* London: Cassell, 1949.

Citino, Robert M. *The German Way of War: From the Thirty Years' War to the Third Reich.* Lawrence: University Press of Kansas, 2005.

Conant, Jennet. *The Irregulars: Roald Dahl and the British Spy Ring in Wartime Washington.* New York: Simon & Schuster, 2008.

Cookridge, E. H. *Gehlen: Spy of the Century.* London: Corgi Books, 1972.

Copeland, Jack B., et al. *Colossus: The Secrets of Bletchley Park's Codebreaking Computers.* Oxford: Oxford University Press, 2006.

Cornwell, John. *Hitler's Scientists: Science, War and the Devil's Pact.* London: Penguin Books, 2004.

Crassweiler, David. *Perón and the Enigmas of Argentina.* New York: W.W. Norton, 1987.

Dalzel-Job, Patrick. *Arctic Snow to Dust of Normandy: The Extraordinary Wartime Exploits of a Naval Special Agent.* Barnsley, UK: Pen & Sword, 2005.

Davies, Norman. *Europe at War 1939–1945: No Simple Victory.* London: Macmillan, 2006.

Davis, Brian L. *The German Home Front 1939–45.* Oxford: Osprey, 2007.

de Camara, Andrea M. *Moral Courage: Robert "Rosie" Rosenthal's WW2 Experience.* Maxwell Air Force Base, AL: Air Command & Staff College Air University, 2006.

Delaforce, Patrick. *The Hitler File.* London: Michael O'Mara Books, 2007.

Delattre, Lucas. *Betraying Hitler: The Story of Fritz Kolbe, the Most Important Spy of the Second World War.* London: Atlantic Books, 2005.

Delize, Jean. *U-Boote Crews: The Day-to-Day Life Aboard Hitler's Submarines.* Paris: Histoire

& Collections, 2007.

Deschner, Karlheinz. *Ein Jahrhundert Heilsgeschichte*, vol. 2. Cologne: Leck, 1983.

Doerries, Reinhard R. *Hitler's Intelligence Chief: Walter Schellenberg*. New York: Enigma Books, 2009.

Dornberger, Walter. *V-2.* New York: Viking, 1954.

Duffy, James P. *Target America: Hitler's Plan to Attack the United States.* Westport, VA: Praeger, 2004.

Dujovne Ortiz, Alicia. *Eva Perón: A Biography.* New York: St. Martin's Griffin, 1997.

Dulles, Allen W. *The Secret Surrender.* Guilford, CT: Lyons Press, 2006.

Eberle, Henrik, and Matthias Uhl, eds. *The Hitler Book: The Secret Dossier Prepared for Stalin.* London: John Murray, 2006.

Edsel, Robert M. *Monuments Men: Allied Heroes, Nazi Thieves and the Greatest Treasure Hunt in History.* London: Arrow Books, 2009.

Eisenhower, Dwight D. *Crusade in Europe.* New York: Doubleday, 1948.

Ellis, John. *Brute Force: Allied Strategy and Tactics in the Second World War.* London: André Deutsch, 1990.

———. *The World War II Data Book.* London: Aurum Press, 1993.

Evans, Richard J. *The Third Reich at War: How the Nazis Led Germany from Conquest to Disaster.* London: Allen Lane, 2008.

Farago, Ladislas. *Aftermath: Martin Bormann and the Fourth Reich.* New York: Simon & Schuster, 1974.

Farrell, Joseph P. *Nazi International.* Kempton, IL: Adventures Unlimited Press, 2008.

Feliciano, Hector. *The Lost Museum: The Nazi Conspiracy to Steal the World's Greatest Works of Art.* New York: Basic Books, 1997.

Felton, Mark. *Yanagi: The Secret Underwater Trade Between Germany and Japan 1942–1945.* Barnsley, UK: Pen and Sword Books, 2005.

Fenby, Jonathan. *Alliance: The Inside Story of How Roosevelt, Stalin and Churchill Won One War and Began Another.* London: Simon & Schuster, 2006.

Fest, Joachim C. *The Face of the Third Reich.* New York: Da Capo Press, 1999.

———. *Inside Hitler's Bunker: The Last Days of the Third Reich.* New York: Farrar, Straus and Giroux, 2004.

Fitzgerald, Michael. *Adolf Hitler: A Portrait.* Stroud, UK: Spellmount, 2006.

Foley, Charles. *Commando Extraordinary: Otto Skorzeny.* London: Cassell, 1998.

Ford, Ken. *The Rhineland 1945.* Oxford: Osprey, 2000.

Fraser, Nicholas, and Marysa Navarro. *Evita: The Real Life of Eva Perón.* London: Andre Deutsch, 2003; New York: W. W. Norton, 1996.

Friedländer, Saul. *Nazi Germany and the Jews.* London: Phoenix, 2009.

Gannon, Michael. *Operation Drumbeat: The Dramatic True Story of Germany's First U-Boat Attacks Along the American Coast in World War II.* New York: Harper Perennial, 1991.

Garbely, Frank. *Evitas Geheimnis: Die Nazis, Die Schweiz, und Perón's Argentinien.* Zurich: Rotpunktverlag, 2003.

Gimbel, John. *Science, Technology and Reparations: Exploitation and Plunder in Postwar Germany.* Stanford, CA: Stanford University Press, 1990.

Godman, Peter. *Hitler and the Vatican.* New York: Free Press/Simon & Schuster, 2004.

Goldhagen, Daniel Jonah. *Hitler's Willing Executioners: Ordinary Germans and the Holocaust.* London: Abacus, 1997.

Goñi, Uki. *The Real Odessa: How Perón Brought the Nazi War Criminals to Argentina.* London: Granta, 2002.

Grose, Peter. *Gentleman Spy: The Life of Allen Dulles.* Boston: Houghton Mifflin, 1994.

Harper, Stephen. *Capturing Enigma: How HMS Petard Seized the German Naval Codes.* Stroud, UK: Sutton, 1999.

Hastings, Max. *Armageddon: The Battle for Germany 1944–45.* London: Macmillan, 2004.

Haynes, John Earl, Harvey Klehr, and Alexander Vassiliev. *Spies: The Rise and Fall of the KGB in America.* London: Yale University Press, 2009.

Heuser, Gisela, and Philippe Mervyn. *Adolf Hitler Mon Père.* Paris: ALE Impressions, 1966.

Higham, Charles. *Trading with the Enemy: The Nazi-American Money Plot 1933–1949.*

New York: Delacorte Press, 1983.

Hillblad, Thorolf. *Twilight of the Gods: A Swedish Waffen-SS Volunteer's Experiences with the 11th SS-Panzergrenadier Division "Nordland," Eastern Front 1944–45*. Solihull, UK: Helion, 2004.

Hinsley, F. H., and Alan Stripp. *Codebreakers: The Inside Story of Bletchley Park*. Oxford: Oxford University Press, 1993.

Hirschfield, Wolfgang. *The Secret Diary of a U-Boat*. London: Cassell, 2000.

Hitchcock, William I. *Liberation: The Bitter Road to Freedom, Europe 1944–1945*. London: Faber and Faber, 2008.

Hoffmann, Peter. *Hitler's Personal Security: Protecting the Führer, 1921–1945*. New York: Da Capo Press, 2000.

Hyland, Gary, and Anton Gill. *Last Talons of the Eagle: Secret Nazi Technology Which Could Have Changed the Course of World War II*. London: Headline, 1998.

Jeffreys, Diarmuid. *Hell's Cartel: IG Farben and the Making of Hitler's War Machine*. London: Bloomsbury, 2008.

Joachimstaler, Anton. *The Last Days of Hitler: The Legends, the Evidence, the Truth*. London: Arms & Armour Press, 1999.

Johnson, Brian. *The Secret War*. Barnsley, UK: Pen & Sword, 2004.

Jones, Nigel. *The Birth of the Nazis: How the Freikorps Blazed a Trail for Hitler*. London: Constable & Robinson, 2004.

Judt, Tony. *Postwar: A History of Europe since 1945*. London: Pimlico, 2007.

Kelly, Cynthia C., ed. *The Manhattan Project: The Birth of the Atomic Bomb in the Words of Its Creators, Eyewitnesses, and Historians*. New York: Atomic Heritage Foundation, 2007.

Kershaw, Ian. *Hitler, the Germans, and the Final Solution*. London: Yale University Press, 2008.

Kitchen, Martin. *The Third Reich: A Concise History*. Stroud, UK: Tempus, 2007.

Knopp, Guido. *Hitler's Holocaust*. Stroud, UK: Sutton, 2001.

———. *Hitler's Hitmen*. Stroud, UK: Sutton, 2002.

———. *Hitler's Women*. New York: Routledge, 2003.

Kochavi, Arieh. *Prelude to Nuremberg*. Chapel Hill: University of North Carolina, 1998.

Kopleck, Maik. *Berlin 1933–1945*. Berlin: Christoph Links Verlag, 2005.

Kristenssen, Jeff (Manuel Monasterio). *Hitler Murió en la Argentina: Operación Patagonia (El Dios Abandonado)*. Buenos Aires: Ediciones Lumiere, 1987.

Lambourne, Nicola. *War Damage in Western Europe: The Destruction of Historic Monuments during the Second World War*. Edinburgh: Edinburgh University Press, 2001.

Le Tissier, Tony. *Slaughter at Halbe: The Destruction of Hitler's 9th Army*. Stroud, UK: Sutton, 2005.

———. *The Battle of Berlin*. Stroud, UK: Tempus, 2007.

———. *Berlin Then and Now*. Old Harlow, UK: Battle of Britain International, 2007.

———. *Death Was Our Companion: Final Days of the Third Reich*. Stroud, UK: Sutton, 2007.

———. *Berlin Battlefield Guide: Third Reich & Cold War*. Barnsley, UK: Pen & Sword, 2008.

Lewin, Ronald. *Ultra Goes to War*. Barnsley, UK: Pen and Sword Books, 2008.

Lilla, Joachim. *Statisten in Uniform: Die Mitglieder des Reichstages 1933–1945*. Düsseldorf: Droste Verlag, 2004.

Liptak, Eugene. *Office of Strategic Services 1942–1945: The World War II Origins of the CIA*. Oxford: Osprey, 2009.

Loftus, John, and Mark Aarons. *The Secret War against the Jews*. New York: St. Martin's Press, 1994.

Longden, Sean. *To the Victor the Spoils: Soldiers' Lives from D-Day to VE-Day*. London: Constable & Robinson, 2007.

———. *T-Force: The Race for Nazi War Secrets 1945*. London: Constable, 2009.

Lucas, James. *Kommando: German Special Forces of World War Two*. London: Cassell, 1998.

Lundeberg, Philip K. "Operation Teardrop Revisited." In Timothy J. Runyan and Jan M. Copes, *To Die Gallantly: The Battle of the Atlantic*. Boulder, CO: Westview Press, 1994.

Lynch, Ernesto Guevara. *Young Che: Memories of Che Guevara by His Father*. London: Vintage Books/Random House, 2008.

MacDonnell, Francis. *Insidious Foes: The Axis Fifth Column and the American Home Front.* Guilford, CT: Lyons Press, 2004.

MacDonogh, Giles. *After the Reich: From the Liberation of Vienna to the Berlin Airlift.* London: John Murray, 2007.

———. *1938: Hitler's Gamble.* London: Constable & Robinson, 2009.

Mallmann Showell, Jak P. *Das Buch der deutschen Kriegsmarine.* Stuttgart: Motorbuch Verlag, 1992.

———. *U-Boat Commanders and Crews 1935–45.* Ramsbury, UK: Crowood Press, 1998.

———. *Enigma U-Boats: Breaking the Code.* Hersham, UK: Ian Allan, 2000.

———. *U-Boats at War: Landings on Hostile Shores.* Hersham, UK: Ian Allan, 2000.

———. *U-Boat Century: German Submarine Warfare 1906–2006.* London: Chatham, 2006.

Manning, Paul. *Martin Bormann: Nazi in Exile.* Secaucus, NJ: Lyle Stuart, 1981.

Marrs, Jim. *The Rise of the Fourth Reich.* New York: William Morrow, 2008.

Marsh, David. *The Bundesbank: The Bank That Rules Europe.* London: Mandarin Paperbacks, 1993.

Martin, James Stewart. *All Honorable Men.* Boston: Little, Brown, 1950.

Martínez, Eloy Tomás. *La novela de Perón.* London: Vintage Books, 1997.

Matteson, Robert E. *The Capture and the Last Days of SS General Ernst Kaltenbrunner, Chief of the Nazi Gestapo, Criminal Police, and Intelligence Services.* Saint Paul, MN: privately published, 1993.

Mauch, Christof. *The Shadow War Against Hitler: The Covert Operations of America's Wartime Secret Intelligence Service.* New York: Columbia University Press, 2002.

Mazower, Mark. *Hitler's Empire: Nazi Rule in Occupied Europe.* London: Allen Lane, 2008.

McCartney, Innes. *Lost Patrols: Submarine Wrecks of the English Channel.* Penzance, UK: Periscope, 2003.

———. *British Submarines 1939–1945.* Oxford: Osprey, 2009.

Meding, Holger M. *Ruta de los Nazis en los Tiempos de Perón.* Buenos Aires: Emecé Editores, 1999.

Meskill, Paul. *Hitler's Heirs: Where Are They Now?* New York: Pyramid Books, 1961.

Miller, David. *U-Boats: The Illustrated History of the Raiders of the Deep.* Limpsfield, UK: Pegasus, 1999.

Miller, Michael D., with Andreas Schulz and Ken McCanliss. *Leaders of the SS & German Police,* vol 1. San Jose, CA: R. James Bender, 2008.

Mitchell, Arthur H. *Hitler's Mountain: The Führer, Obersalzburg and the American Occupation of Berchtesgaden.* Jefferson, NC: McFarland, 2007.

Moorhouse, Roger. *Berlin at War: Life and Death in Hitler's Capital 1939–45.* London: Bodley Head, 2010.

Naftali, Timothy J. "Creating the Myth of the Alpenfestung: Allied Intelligence and the Collapse of the Nazi Police State." In *Austrian Historical Memory and National Identity,* ed. Günter Bischof and Anton Pelinka. New Brunswick, NJ: Transaction, 1997.

Neufeld, Michael J. *The Rocket and the Reich: Peenemünde and the Coming of the Ballistic Missile Era.* New York: Free Press, 1995.

Ney-Krwawicz, Marek. *The Polish Home Army 1939–1945,* trans. Antoni Bohdanowicz. London: Polish Underground Movement (1935–1945) Study Trust, 2001.

Nicholas, Lynn H. *The Rape of Europa: The Fate of Europe's Treasures in the Third Reich and the Second World War.* New York: Alfred A. Knopf, 1994.

Nicosia, Francis R., and Jonathan Huener, eds. *Medicine and Medical Ethics in Nazi Germany: Origins, Practices and Legacies.* Oxford: Berghahn Books, 2004.

Nutting, David, and Jim Glanville, eds. *Attain by Surprise: The Story of 30 Assault Unit Royal Navy/Royal Marine Commando and of Intelligence by Capture.* London: David Glover, 1997.

O'Donnell, James P. *The Bunker: The History of the Reich Chancellery Group.* Boston: Houghton Mifflin, 1978.

Owen, James. *Nuremberg: Evil on Trial: The Extraordinary Story of How the Nazis Were Brought to Justice.* London: Headline, 2006.

Page, Joseph. *Perón: A Biography.* London: Random House, 1983.

Panozzo, Carlos. *El Hotel Edén de La Falda.* La Falda, Argentina: privately published, n.d.

Parrish, Thomas. *The Ultra Americans: The U.S. Role in Breaking the Nazi Codes.* New York: Stein and Day, 1986.

Paterson, Michael. *The Secret War: The Inside Story of the Code Breakers of World War II.* Cincinnati: David & Charles, 2007.

Patton, George S. *War, As I Knew It.* Cambridge, MA: Riverside Press, 1947.

Pawly, Ronald. *Hitler's Chancellery: A Palace to Last a Thousand Years.* Ramsbury, UK: Crowood Press, 2009.

Payne, Stanley G. *Franco and Hitler: Spain, Germany and World War II.* New Haven, CT: Yale University Press, 2008.

Petropoulos, Jonathan P. *The Faustian Bargain: The Art World in Nazi Germany.* London: Allen Lane, 2000.

Phayer, Michael. *Pius XII, The Holocaust and the Cold War.* Bloomington: Indiana University Press, 2007.

Philby, Kim. *My Silent War: The Story of Kim Philby.* London: Modern Library, 2002.

Pool, James. *Hitler and His Secret Partners: Contributions, Loot and Rewards 1933–1945.* New York: Pocket Books, 1997.

Posner, Gerald. *Hitler's Children: Inside the Families of the Third Reich.* London: Mandarin Paperbacks, 1992.

Posner, Gerald, and John Ware. *Mengele: The Complete Story.* Lanham, MD: Cooper Square Press, 2000.

Preparata, Guido Giacomo. *Conjuring Hitler: How Britain and America Made the Third Reich.* London: Pluto Press, 2005.

Price, Alfred. *The Last Year of the Luftwaffe May 1944 to May 1945.* London: Greenhill Books, 1991.

——. *Aircraft versus Submarine in Two World Wars.* Barnsley, UK: Pen and Sword Books, 2004.

Quarrie, Bruce. *The Ardennes Offensive: VI Panzer Armee.* Oxford: Osprey, 1999.

Rawson, Andrew. *In Pursuit of Hitler: Battles Through the Nazi Heartland March to May 1945.* Barnsley, UK: Pen and Sword Books, 2008.

Reitlinger, Gerald. *The SS: Alibi of a Nation.* London: William Heinemann, 1956.

Rhodes, Richard. *The Making of the Atomic Bomb.* London: Penguin Books, 1986.

——. *Masters of Death: The SS Einsatzgruppen and the Invention of the Holocaust.* Oxford: Perseus Press, 2002.

Rudel, Hans Ulrich. *Stuka Pilot.* London: Euphorion Books, 1952; rpt. Barbarossa Books, 2006.

Ryan, Cornelius. *The Last Battle: Berlin 1945.* London: William Collins, 1966.

Salinas, Juan, and Carlos De Napoli. *Ultramar sur la Ultima Operación Secreta del Tercer Reich.* Buenos Aires: Grupa Editorial Norma, 2002.

Santander, Silvano. *Técnica de una Traición [The Technique of Treachery]: Juan D. Perón y Eva Duarté—Agentes del Nazismo en la Argentina.* Montevideo, Uruguay: Editorial Antygua, 1953.

Saunders, Tim. *Operation Plunder: The British and Canadian Rhine Crossing.* Barnsley, UK: Pen and Sword Books, 2006.

Sayer, Ian, and Douglas Botting. *Hitler's Last General: The Case Against Wilhelm Mohnke.* London: Bantam Press, 1989.

——. *Nazi Gold.* Edinburgh: Mainstream, 1998.

Sayers, Michael, and Albert Kahn. *The Plot Against the Peace: A Warning to the Nation.* New York: Dial Press, 1944.

Schmidt, Ulf. *Karl Brandt, the Nazi Doctor: Medicine and Power in the Third Reich.* London: Hambledon Continuum, 2007.

Schulz, Andreas, and Günter Wegmann. *Die Generale der Waffen-SS und der Polizei,* vol. 1. Bissendorf: Biblio-Verlag, 2003.

Seidler, Franz W., and Dieter Zeigert. *Hitler's Secret Headquarters: The Führer's Wartime Bases, from the Invasion of France to the Berlin Bunker.* London: Greenhill Books, 2004.

Sereny, Gitta. *Into that Darkness.* London: Andre Deutsch, 1974; New York: McGraw-Hill, 1974.

Shepherd, Ben. *The Long Road Home: The Aftermath of the Second World War.* London: Bodley Head, 2010.

Shirer, William L. *The Rise and Fall of the Third Reich: A History of Nazi Germany.* New York: Touchstone, 1959.

Shuter, Jane. *Aftermath of the Holocaust.* Chicago: Heinemann Library, 2003.

Simpson, Bill. *Spitfire Dive-Bombers versus the V-2: Fighter Command's Battle with Hitler's Mobile Missiles.* Barnsley, UK: Pen and Sword Books, 2007.

Sinclair, David. *Hall of Mirrors.* London: Century, 2001.

Smith, Arthur L. *Hitler's Gold: The Story of the Nazi War Loot.* Dulles, VA: Berg, 1996.

Speer, Albert. *Inside the Third Reich.* London: Weidenfeld and Nicolson, 1970.

Srodes, James. *Allen Dulles: Master of Spies.* Washington, DC: Regency, 1999.

Stafford, David. *Endgame 1945: Victory, Retribution, Liberation.* London: Little, Brown, 2007.

Stanley, Roy M., II. *V Weapons Hunt: Defeating German Secret Weapons.* Barnsley, UK: Pen and Sword Books, 2010.

Steinweiss, Alan E., and Daniel E. Rogers. *The Impact of Nazism: New Perspectives on the Third Reich and Its Legacy.* Lincoln: University of Nebraska Press, 2003.

Stephan, Robert W. *Stalin's Secret War: Soviet Counterintelligence against the Nazis 1941–1945.* Lawrence: University Press of Kansas, 2004.

Stevenson, William. *The Bormann Brotherhood.* London: Corgi, 1975.

Stoker, Donald J., Jr., and Jonathan A. Grant, eds. *Girding for Battle: The Arms Trade in a Global Perspective, 1815–1940.* Westport, CT: Praeger, 2003.

Strawson, John. *Hitler as Military Commander.* London: Sphere Books, 1973.

Swartz, Tim. *Evil Agenda of the Secret Government.* New Brunswick, NJ: Global Communications, 1999.

Sweeting, C. G. *Hitler's Squadron: The Fuehrer's Personal Aircraft and Transport Unit, 1933–45.* Washington, DC: Brassey's, 2001.

Syrett, D. *The Battle of the Atlantic and Signals Intelligence: U-Boat Situations and Trends.* Farnham, UK: Ashgate, 1998.

Taylor, Blaine. *Hitler's Headquarters: From Beer Hall to Bunker 1920–1945.* Washington, DC: Potomac Books, 2007.

———. *Hitler's Engineers, Fritz Todt and Albert Speer: Master Builders of the Third Reich.* Newbury, UK: Casemate, 2010.

Thacker, Toby. *The End of the Third Reich.* Stroud, UK: Tempus, 2008.

Thomas, Geoffrey J., and Barry Ketley. *KG 200: The Luftwaffe's Most Secret Unit.* Crowborough, UK: Hikoki, 2003.

Thomas, Gordon. *Inside British Intelligence: 100 Years of MI5 and MI6.* London: JR Books, 2009.

Thuermer, Angus M. *Fairly True Reports from a CIA Man.* Middleburg, VA: unpublished manuscript.

Tomii, Ayako. *A Japanese Diplomat's Daughter: An Outsider's Childhood in the 1930s and 1940s.* iUniverse, 2004.

Tooze, Adam. *The Wages of Destruction: The Making and Breaking of the Nazi Economy.* London: Allen Lane, 2006.

Trevor-Roper, Hugh. *The Last Days of Hitler.* London: Pan Books, 2002.

Turner, John Prayn, and Robert Jackson. *Destination Berchtesgaden: The Story of the United States Seventh Army in World War II.* London: Ian Allan, 1975.

Tutaev, David. *The Consul of Florence.* London: Secker & Warburg, 1966.

Twigge, Stephen, Edward Hampshire, and Graham Macklin. *British Intelligence: Secrets, Spies and Sources.* London: The National Archives, 2008.

U.S. Government. *Blue Book on Argentina: Consultation among the American Republics with respect to the Argentine situation: Memorandum of the United States Government.* Washington, DC. New York: Greenberg, 1946.

U.S. Government. *Report of the American Commission for the Protection and Salvage of Artistic and Historic Monuments in War Areas.* Washington, DC: U.S. Government Printing Office, 1946.

Vacca, Roberto. *Eva Perón*. Buenos Aires: Centro Editor de América Latina, 1971.

Veranov, Michael. *The Third Reich at War: The Rise and Fall of Hitler's Military Machine*. London: Magpie Books, 1997.

von Hassell, Agostino, and Sigrid MacRae with Simone Ameskamp. *Alliance of Enemies: The Untold Story of the Secret American and German Collaboration to End World War II*. New York: Thomas Dunne Books, 2006.

von Lang, Jochen. *Bormann: The Man Who Manipulated Hitler*. London: Weidenfeld & Nicolson, 1979.

von Loringhoven, Bernd Freytag. *In the Bunker with Hitler*. London: Weidenfeld & Nicolson, 2006.

Weindling, Paul Julian. *Nazi Medicine and the Nuremberg Trials: From Medical War Crimes to Informed Consent*. Basingstoke, UK: Palgrave Macmillan, 2006.

Weitz, John. *Hitler's Banker: Hjalmar Horace Greely Schacht*. London: Little, Brown, 1999.

Welch, David. *The Hitler Conspiracies: Secrets and Lies Behind the Rise and Fall of the Nazi Party*. Shepperton, UK: Ian Allan, 2001.

Whealey, Robert H. *Hitler and Spain: The Nazi Role in the Spanish Civil War 1936–1939*. Lexington: University Press of Kentucky, 1989.

Whetton, Cris. *Hitler's Fortune*. Barnsley, UK: Pen & Sword, 2004.

White, John F. *The Milk Cows: The U-Boat Tankers 1944–1945*. Barnsley, UK: Pen & Sword, 2009.

Whiting, Charles. *Patton*. New York: Ballantine Books, 1970.

———. *Skorzeny*. New York: Ballantine Books, 1972.

———. *Patton's Last Battle*. New York: Stein & Day, 1987.

———. *Bloody Bremen*. Barnsley, UK: Leo Cooper, 1998.

———. *Hitler's Secret War: The Nazi Espionage Campaign Against the Allies*. Barnsley, UK: Leo Cooper, 2000.

———. *Bounce the Rhine*. Stapleford, UK: Spellmount, 2002.

———. *Hitler's Warriors: The Final Battles of Hitler's Private Bodyguard, 1944–45*. York, UK: Eskdale, 2005.

Williamson, Gordon. *U-Boat Crews 1914–45*. London: Osprey, 1995.

———. *Wolf Pack: The Story of the U-Boat in World War II*. Oxford: Osprey, 2005.

———. *German Special Forces of World War II*. Oxford: Osprey, 2008.

———. *U-Boat Tactics in World War II*. Oxford: Osprey, 2010.

Willmott, H. P., Charles Messenger, and Robin Cross. *World War II*. London: Dorling Kindersley, 2004.

Wistrich, Robert S. *Hitler and the Holocaust: How and Why the Holocaust Happened*. London: Phoenix Press, 2002.

Wright, Michael, ed. *The World at Arms: The Reader's Digest Illustrated History of World War II*. London: Reader's Digest Association

Wynne, Frank. *I Was Vermeer: The Forger Who Swindled the Nazis*. London: Bloomsbury, 2006.

Yeadon, Glen, and John Hawkins. *The Nazi Hydra in America*. Joshua Tree, CA: Progressive Press, 2008.

Zaloga, Steven J. *Bagration 1944: The Destruction of Army Group Centre*. Oxford: Osprey, 1996.

———. *V-2 Ballistic Missile 1942–52*. Oxford: Osprey, 2003.

———. *V-1 Flying Bomb 1942–52: Hitler's Infamous "Doodlebug."* Oxford: Osprey, 2005.

———. *Remagen 1945: Endgame against the Third Reich*. Oxford: Osprey, 2006.

———. *The Siegfried Line 1944–1945: Battles on the German Frontier*. Oxford: Osprey, 2007.

———. *The Liberation of Paris 1944*. Oxford: Osprey, 2008.

Zhukov, Georgi K. *Marshal Zhukov's Greatest Battles*. London: Sphere, 1969.

Ziemke, Earl F. *Battle for Berlin: End of the Third Reich*. London: Macmillan, 1969.

Zweig, Ronald W. *The Gold Train: The Destruction of the Jews and the Looting of Hungary*. London: Harper Collins, 2003.

MULTIVOLUME SERIES

The Center of the Web (The Third Reich series). Alexandria, VA: Time-Life Books, 1990.
Descent into Nightmare (The Third Reich series). New York: Time-Life Education, 1992.
The Secret War (World War II series). Alexandria, VA: Time-Life Books, 1998.
Wolf Packs (The Third Reich series). Alexandria, VA: Time-Life Books, 1989.
The World at War 1939–1945 (The Eventful 20th Century series). London: Reader's Digest Association, 1998.
The World in Flames 1939–45 (The Illustrated History of the World series). London: Reader's Digest Association, 2007.

MAGAZINE AND JOURNAL ARTICLES

CONTEMPORARY

Das Reich, Berlin, March 26, 1944.
Der Bund, Bern, February 17, 1953.
Der Spiegel. "The Painstaking Forger." December 26, 1956.
Hamburger, Philip. "Winds across the Pampas." *New Yorker*, December 1948.
Life magazine. "A Dictator Goes A-Wooing." May 25, 1953.
L'Unita, Rome, May 25, 1945.
Revue magazine, West Germany, August 1961.
Saturday Evening Post. "Eisenhower's Six Great Decisions." July 13, 1946.
Time magazine. "Abdication of a Tycoon." May 16, 1949. http://www.time.com/time/magazine/article/0,9171,853719,00.html.
Time magazine. "Argentina: Action Ahead." July 10, 1944. http://www.time.com/time/magazine/article/0,9171,791494,00.html.
Time magazine. "Argentina: Boss of the GOU." November 27, 1944. http://www.time.com/time/magazine/article/0,9171,796883,00.html.
Time magazine. "Argentina: End of a Siege." August 20, 1945. http://www.time.com/time/magazine/article/0,9171,797675,00.html.
Time magazine. "Argentina: Hunting a Nazi." September 8, 1941. http://www.time.com/time/magazine/article/0,9171,849464,00.html.
Time magazine. "Argentina: The Coddled." December 17, 1945. http://www.time.com/time/magazine/article/0,9171,776519,00.html.
Time magazine. "As Long As I Live . . . " May 28, 1945, Berlin dispatch dated May 1, 1945. http://www.time.com/time/magazine/article/0,9171,775644,00.html.
Time magazine. "Italy: Spring in the Axis." May 15, 1939. http://www.time.com/time/magazine/article/0,9171,761275,00.html.
Time magazine. "Milestones." May 7, 1956. http://www.time.com/time/magazine/article/0,9171,937348,00.html.
Time magazine. "Milestones." September 1, 1961. http://www.time.com/time/magazine/article/0,9171,939852,00.html.
Time magazine. "The Americas: Misunderstood Argentina." September 20, 1943. http://www.time.com/time/magazine/article/0,9171,774570,00.html.
Time magazine. "The Hemisphere: Daddykins & Nelly." October 10, 1955. http://www.time.com/time/magazine/article/0,9171,937225,00.html

MODERN

After the Battle. "The Reich Chancellery and the Berlin Bunker Then and Now." 61 (1988).
Bellucci, Alberto. "The Bariloche Style." *Journal of Decorative and Propaganda Arts, Argentine Theme Issue* (1992).
Bradsher, Greg. "Nazi Gold: The Merkers Mine Treasure." *Prologue: Quarterly of the National Archives and Records Administration* 31, no. 1 (1999).
Breitman, Richard, and Shlomo Aronson. "The End of the Final Solution? Nazi Plans to

Ransom Jews 1944–1945." *Central European History* 25, no. 2 (1992).

Calbarro, Juan Luis. "Vida y leyenda de Gustav Winter." *Historia* 16, April–May (2005).

Gerassi, Marysa Navarro. "Argentine Nationalism of the Right." *Studies in Comparative International Development* 1, no. 12 (1965).

Guyatt, David. "Princes of Plunder." *Nexus* 12, no. 2 (2005).

Hindley, Meredith. "Negotiating the Boundary of Unconditional Surrender: The War Refugee Board in Sweden and Nazi Proposals to Ransom Jews 1944-1945." *Holocaust and Genocide Studies* 10, no. 1 (1996).

Hodel, Georg. "Evita, the Swiss and the Nazis." *iF Magazine*, January 7, 1999.

Jordan, Jonathan W. "Operation Bagration: Soviet Offensive of 1944." *World War II*, July–August 2006.

Kippax, Steven. "Hitler's Special Forces." *Military Illustrated* 155 (2001).

Nácher, Enrique. "La Leyenda de Gustav Winter: ¿Espía nazi en Fuerteventura?" *Historia* 16, April–May 2005. http://hispanismo.org/reino-de-las-canarias/5643-la-leyenda-de-gustav-winter-espia-nazi-en-fuerteventura.html.

Nash, Elizabeth. "Germans Helped Franco Run Civil War Death Camps." *London Independent*, February 22, 2002. http://www.independent.co.uk/news/world/europe/germans-helped-franco-run-civil-war-death-camps-661623.html.

Przekrój. "Hitler's Valley in Argentina." March 1995.

Sullivan, Geoff, and Frode Weierud. "Breaking German Army Ciphers." *Cryptologia* 29, July 2005. http://www.dean.usma.edu/math/pubs/cryptologia/.

Tyas, Stephen. "British Intelligence and the Nazi Recruit." *History Today* 54 (2004). http://www.historytoday.com/stephen-tyas/british-intelligence-and-nazi-recruit.

Whitlock, Greg. "Alois Hudal: Clero-Fascist Nietzsche Critic." *Nietzsche-Studien* 32 (2003).

NEWSPAPER AND NEWS AGENCY REPORTS

CONTEMPORARY

The Associated Press, Moscow, February 1, 1944.

The Associated Press, London, July 25, 1944.

The Associated Press, "An East Coast Port," published in the *Deseret [Utah] News*, January 8, 1945.

The Associated Press, "RAF's Jets Slash German Airfield," London, published in the *New York Times*, April 24, 1945. http://select.nytimes.com/gst/abstract.html?res=F40E1FF B3C5F1B7B93C7AB178FD85F418485F9.

The Associated Press, Madrid, May 2, 1945.

The Associated Press, Donostia-San Sebastián, May 8, 1945.

The Associated Press, Stockholm, May 8, 1945.

The Associated Press, "With the British Second Army," May 8, 1945.

The Associated Press, Madrid, May 25, 1945.

Eddy Gilmore, The Associated Press, "Reds Believe Hitler Alive," Berlin, June 9, 1945, published in the *Herald-Journal*, June 10, 1945. http://news.google.com/newspapers? id=DV8sAAAAIBAJ&sjid=_soEAAAAIBAJ&pg=4259,3091076&dq=hitler+eddy +gilmore&hl=en.

The Associated Press, Travemünde, June 16, 1945 (delayed dispatch).

The Associated Press, Moscow, June 16, 1945.

The Associated Press, Moscow, June 27, 1945.

The Associated Press, Montevideo, August 18, 1945.

The Associated Press, Oslo, August 25, 1945.

The Associated Press, "Is Hitler Alive?" *Indian Express*, October 14, 1945. http://news. google.com/newspapers?id=orI-AAAAIBAJ&sjid=SEwMAAAAIBAJ&pg=4222,100 7385&dq=eisenhower+hitler+alive&hl=en.

The Associated Press, Berlin, October 17, 1945.

The Associated Press, "Americans Find Treasure Chest of Eva Braun," Frankfurt,

published in *St. Petersburg Times* on November 16, 1945. http://news.google.com/
newspapers?id=gBIwAAAAIBAJ&sjid=pE4DAAAAIBAJ&pg=4925,2133570&dq=
eva+braun%27s+treasure-chest&hl=en.

The Associated Press, Washington, DC, April 27, 1946.

The Associated Press, Nuremberg, July 29, 1946.

The Associated Press, Munich, October 7, 1946.

The Associated Press, "Flier Claims Hitler Escaped," Warsaw, December 18, 1947. http://
news.google.com/newspapers?id=hSNPAAAAIBAJ&sjid=504DAAAAIBAJ&pg=42
58,4339256&dq=baumgart+hitler+warsaw&hl=en.

The Associated Press, "Luftwaffe Pilot Sent to Gaol for Five Years," Warsaw, August 8,
1949, published in *Canberra Times*, August 9, 1949. http://trove.nla.gov.au/ndp/del/
page/690899.

Berliner Morgenpost, October 5, 1944.

British United Press, Hamburg, March 13, 1946.

Daily Express, London, June 19, 1945.

Der Spiegel. "Hitler." July 18, 1966. http://www.spiegel.de/spiegel/print/d-46407960.html.

International News Service, Stockholm, June 11, 1945.

Keely, Charles. "Peronism Still Strong in Argentina." Copley News Service, Buenos Aires,
December 5, 1964, reprinted in the *News and Courier*, Charleston, South Carolina,
December 6, 1964.

La Prensa, Buenos Aires, August 20, 1945.

Newman, Joseph. "Two Mystery Figures Landed by U-boat." *New York Herald-Tribune*,
Buenos Aires, July 14, 1945.

New York Times. "Robot Bomb Attacks Here Held 'Probable' by Admiral." January 8, 1945.
http://select.nytimes.com/gst/abstract.html?res=FA0C16F93A5C1B7B93CBA9178
AD85F418485F9&scp=2&sq=V-1&st=p.

North American Newspaper Alliance, interview with Eva Braun's mother, February 18, 1946.

North American Newspaper Alliance, New York, March 3, 1947.

Pearson, Drew. Syndicated column. July 24, 1945.

Pearson, Drew. "Washington Merry-Go-Round." Bell Syndicate, December 15, 1943.

Reuters, Bad Godesburg, Rhineland, January 19, 1946; published in the *Baltimore Sun*,
January 20, 1946.

Ross, Stanley. "U-Boats Base Spy Surge in Latin America." Overseas News Agency. *Christian
Science Monitor*, January 24, 1945.

Sunday Chronicle, London, June 17, 1945.

Telegraph Herald. "Claim Nazi Officials Arrive in Spain." June 21, 1945. http://news.google.
com/newspapers?id=XidiAAAAIBAJ&sjid=OXYNAAAAIBAJ&pg=4599,2831598
&dq=hitler-in-spain&hl=en.

United Press, Berlin. "Hitler May Have Fled with Bride Before Fall of Berlin." *Miami Daily
News*, June 10, 1945. http://news.google.com/newspapers?id=qE8yAAAAIBAJ&sjid=
yecFAAAAIBAJ&pg=2861,2346002&dq=hitler+fled+berlin+zhukov&hl=en.

United Press, Stockholm, June 11, 1945.

United Press, Rio de Janeiro, October 20, 1945.

United Press, Warsaw. "Hitler Escaped in U-Boat, Says German Pilot," December 12,
1947, published in *St. Petersburg Times*, December 13, 1947. http://news.google.com/
newspapers?id=fyNPAAAAIBAJ&sjid=504DAAAAIBAJ&pg=4293,888260&dq=h
itler-escaped-in-u-boat-says-germanpilot&hl=en.

United Press, Bonn, August 28, 1953.

Walter Winchell, syndicated column, October 26, 1944.

MODERN

Agence France Presse. "Man Says He Saw Hitler After War." May 31, 1997. http://www.
indianexpress.com/Storyold/2523/.

The Associated Press, New York, October 17, 2003.

The Associated Press, Berlin, December 3, 2004.

Cassese, Nicolás. "La Rama nazi de Perón." *La Nación*, Buenos Aires, February 16, 1997. http://www.lanacion.com.ar/202464.

Castrillon. Ernesto G., and Luis Casabal. "Historia Viva Busquedas and Yo Fui Testigo." *La Nación*, Buenos Aires, March 23, 2008.

Daily Telegraph, "Germany and US 'Knew Where Eichmann Was in 1952,'" January 9, 2011. http://www.telegraph.co.uk/news/worldnews/europe/germany/8248965/Germany-and-US-knew-where-Eichmann-was-in-1952.html.

de Courcy, Anne. "The Dazzling Beauty with a Poison Pen." *Daily Mail*, UK, January 9, 2009. http://www.dailymail.co.uk/home/books/article-1109382/The-dazzling-beauty-poison-pen-DIANA-MOSLEY-THE-PURSUIT-OF-LAUGHTER.html.

Edge, Simon. "The Nazi King." London *Daily Express*, May 23, 2011. http://dailyexpress.co.uk/posts/view/113232.

Evans, Michael. "'Unprincipled Ruffian' Told MI5 of Nazi Plot to Get Gold to Argentina." *Sunday Times*, September 4, 2007. http://www.timesonline.co.uk/tol/news/uk/article2381177.ece.

Fielding, Nick. *Sunday Times*, December 28, 2003. http://forum.axishistory.com/viewtopic.php?f=34&t=39672

Hoy en la Noticia. "El Pais: Hitler en Chubut." La Plata, Argentina, July 24, 1997. pdf.diariohoy.net/1997/07/240797CU.PDF.

Jewish Telegraph Agency, Buenos Aires, December 3, 1964.

La Mañana del Sur, Diario Ambito Financiero news group, Buenos Aires, 1996, interview with Araceli Méndez.

Maine Sunday Telegram, Portland, October 29, 2000.

Melman, Yossi. "Tied Up in the Rat Lines." *Haaretz*, Tel Aviv, January 17, 2006.

Mirodan, Seamus. "Nazis' Argentine Village Hide-Out Pulls in Tourists." London *Daily Telegraph*, February 14, 2004. http://www.telegraph.co.uk/news/worldnews/southamerica/argentina/1454352/Nazis-Argentine-village-hide-out-pulls-in-tourists.html.

New York Times. "Argentina Evades Its Nazi Past." March 22, 1997. http://query.nytimes.com/gst/fullpage.html?res=9E02E2DD153BF931A15750C0A961958260.

New York Times. "Demjanjuk Convicted for Role in Nazi Death Camp." May 12, 2011. http://www.nytimes.com/2011/05/13/world/europe/13nazi.html?_r=1&scp=2&sq=Demjanjuk&st=cse.

New York Times, "Nazis Were Given Safe Haven in U.S., Report Says," November 13, 2010. http://www.nytimes.com/2010/11/14/us/14nazis.html?scp=2&sq=nazis&st=cse.

New York Times, Silvano Santander obituary, August 18, 1987.

Reuters. "Wiesenthal Says Evita Likely Stashed Nazi Loot." June 26, 1997, published in *Página* 12 newspaper, Buenos Aires.

Revista Española de Historia Militar magazine, October 2004.

Siemaszko, Corky. "Memo Hit Swiss Over Nazi Loot." *New York Daily News*, December 5, 1996. http://www.nydailynews.com/archives/news/1996/12/05/1996-12-05_memo_hit_swiss_over_nazi_loot.html.

Spiegel Online. "The Long Road to Eichmann's Arrest." April 1, 2011. http://www.spiegel.de/international/germany/0,1518,754486,00.html.

Taylor, Robert. "Nazi Martin Bormann Is Alive in Paraguay, Says Israeli Ex-spy, *Boston Globe*, July 26, 1971.

U.S. News & World Report. "Cry for Them, Argentina, Nazi Loot from Holocaust Victims Enriched Eva Perón." November 15, 1999.

Wiegrefe, Klaus. "The Nazi Criminals Who Became German Spooks." *Der Spiegel*, February 16, 2011. www.spiegel.de/international/germany/0,1518,745640,00.html.

ARCHIVES

The National Archives, Kew, London
File ADM 1/ 15798—Woolforce.
File ADM 116/ 5474 & 5475—*Admiral Graf Spee* crew repatriation.

File ADM 223/ 214—History of 30 Commando Unit, later 30 Assault Unit and 30 Advance Unit.
File ADM 223/ 303—30 Assault Unit War Diary, 1944.
File ADM 223/ 500: Naval Intelligence Commando Unit.
File HW 18/400: U-880.
File HW 18/406: U-530.
File HW 18/410: U-518.
File HW 18/421: U-235.
File HW 18/431: U-1235.
File KV 2/ 3301: Interrogation of Dietrich Niebuhr.
File WO 171/ 1316: 5th King's Regiment War Diary, 1944.

King's College Library Military Archives, London
The History of 30 Assault Unit 1942–1946, Ref GB99.

Franklin D. Roosevelt Presidential Library and Museum, Hyde Park, New York
OSS Official Dispatch Ref No. 250.

U.S. Department of Justice
The Office of Special Investigations: Striving for Accountability in the Aftermath of the Holocaust, Department of Justice, Criminal Division, 2006. http://documents.nytimes.com/confidential-report-provides-new-evidence-of-notorious-nazi-cases?ref=us#p=1.

U.S. National Archives and Records Administration (NARA), College Park, Maryland
"Axis Espionage and Propaganda in Latin America." NARA, Record Group 319, Records of the Army Staff, Records of the Office of the Assistant Chief of Staff, G-2, Military Intelligence Division. Separate Binder.
"Final Interrogation Report of Edmund Freiherr von Thermann." July 11, 1945, NARA, Record Group 59, Records of the Department of State, 862.20235/7-1145.
"Final Interrogation Report of Otto Reinebeck." February 4, 1946, NARA, Record Group 59, Records of the Department of State, 862.20235/ 4-2646.
NA RG 226 Entry 134: Records of the Office of Strategic Services (OSS), Director's Office and Field Station Records.
NA RG 239/ 47: General Patton's conversation re: Agrigento temples, Sicily.
NA RG 263: Wilhelm Hüttel [Höttl] CIA Name File, Vol. 1.
—Correspondence by cable between Donovan and Dulles, March 24, 1945.
—Leslie to Dulles, April 17, 1945.
—Third Army Preliminary Interrogation Report No.17, June 1945.
NA RG 266—Walter Schellenberg's draft autobiography, June 1945.
NA-BDC RG 242, A-3343: Hüttel SS Officer File.
OSS Art Looting Investigation Unit Final Report. Washington, DC: U.S. Government Printing Office, May 1946.

DECLASSIFIED GOVERNMENT DOCUMENTS

Most of the released FBI files are available at http://vault.fbi.gov/adolf-hitler.
Declassified Argentine document, "German Disembarkation at San Clemente del Tuyu," Coordinación Federal CF-OP-2315 from Central de Reunión to Navy Ministry, April 18, 1945, Argentine National Archive in Buenos Aires. For facsimile copy, see Farago, *Aftermath.*
Argentine document, "Strictly Secret and Confidential," Dirección de Coordinación Federal, CF "A" No.9976, October 5, 1960; report received September 1953.
Argentine memorandum, Dirección de Coordinación Federal, DAE 568, October 14, 1952.
CIA report A02592, October 3, 1955.
FBI report and radiograms, Buenos Aires, August 1, 1945.
Letter via U.S. Army Courier Service from Legal Attaché, American Embassy London, to Director Hoover, September 17, 1945.

Letter from Director Hoover to the American Embassy in Buenos Aires, November 13, 1945.
FBI letter to Director Hoover from Los Angeles Bureau, June 5, 1947.
FBI letter, EX 39, from Director Hoover to Legal Attaché, Rio de Janeiro, July 9, 1947.
FBI report, marked "Secret—Air Courier from Legal Attaché, Rio de Janeiro, Brazil, to Director Hoover," dated August 6, 1947.
D. M. Ladd to Hoover, May 15, 1948, NA, RA RG 65 65-55639 (1-24) Box 38, cited in Breitman, U.S. Intelligence and the Nazis.
Gestapo report to Reichsführer-SS Heinrich Himmler, IV/D/4 RSHA, February 17, 1942.
MI5 report, File ref KV/ 2/ 2636, interrogation of Ernesto Hoppe.
Records of the Office of the Secretary of Defense, http://www.archives.gov/iwg/declassified-records/rg-330-defense-secretary/.
U.S. Army report on Ante Pavelić by Capt Marion Scott, http://www.jerusalim.or/cd/biblioteka/pavelicpapers/pavelic/ap0015.html.
U.S. Navy report, March 1946, "Sanitation aboard former German Type IX-C," http://www.uboatarchive.net/DesignStudiesTypeIXC.htm.

OTHER INTERROGATION REPORTS

Friederich von Angellotty-Mackensen, Nuremberg, March 18. 1948. Gumberg Library Digital Collections, Duquesne University, Mussmano Collection. http://digital.library.duq.edu/cdm-musmanno.
Interrogation of German Agents, Gimpel and Colepaugh, Landed on the Coast of Maine from U-1230, dated January 13, 1945. Op-16-Z (SC)A1-2(3)/ EF30 Serial 00170716. Located in the archives of the National Museum of the U.S. Navy, Washington, DC. http://www.ibiblio.org/hyperwar/USN/rep/U-1230/.
Consolidated Interrogation Report regarding Hans Helmut von Hummel, by Capt S. L. Faison Jr., OSS Art Looting Investigation Unit, dated October 11, 1945; from Prisoner of War Papers, Combined Services Detailed Interrogation Center, Bad Nenndorf, Germany.
Erich Kempka, interrogated by U.S. agents at Berchtesgaden, June 20 and July 4, 1945.
Robert Ley, Nuremberg, 1945, Interrogation Records Prepared for War Crimes Proceedings at Nuremberg, 1945–47, page 101. http://www.footnote.com/document/231909201/.
"Vier Prinzen zu Schaumburg-Lippe," listing Supplement of January 15, 1946 to the Consolidated Interrogation Report No. 4, Attachment 76: "Partial List of Purchases for Linz Made in Germany." http://edocs.fu-berlin.de/docs/servlets/MCRFileNodeServlet/FUDOCS_derivate_000000000030/vierprinzen_letzte_fassung_copia.pdf;jsessionid=452DFAE5507E3516FFD859EB792902B6?hosts=, hosted by Freie Universität, Berlin.
Oberleutnant zu See (Naval Lieutenant) Heinz Schaeffer & other prisoners from U-977, surrendered Mar del Plata, Argentina, August 17, 1945. http://www.uboatarchive.net/U-977INT.htm.
Albert Speer, Flensburg. USSBS special document, May 22–23, 1945.
Otto Wermuth, interrogation by Argentine authorities 1945. http://www.uboatarchive.net/U-530NAReport.htm.
Cornell University Law Library, "Frau Anni Winter," November 6, 1945, in Donovan Nuremberg Trial collection, Subdivision 8/Hitler, section 8.02 German (English translation available). http://library2.lawschool.cornell.edu/donovan/show.asp?id=567&query=.

THESES, DISSERTATIONS, AND PAPERS

Bohoslavsky, Ernesto. Contra la Patagonia judía. La familia Eichmann y los nacionalistas Argentinos y Chilenos frente al Plan Andinia (de 1960 a nuestros días). Santiago de Chile, 2008. http://ungs.academia.edu/ebohos/Papers/86439/Contra_la_Patagonia_judia._La_familia_Eichmann_y_los_nacionalistas_argentinos_y_chilenos_frente_al_Plan_Andinia_de_1960_a_nuestros_dias_.
"Fuerteventura: geología, naturaleza y actividad humana." A presentation to Canaries Association for Scientific Education, Fuerteventura, December 5–9, 2007. http://docs.

google.com/viewer?a=v&q=cache:pjgK76W-XcUJ:www.vierayclavijo.org/html/pdf/
cuadernillos/07/0712_fuerteventura.pdf+%22Fuerteventura:+geolog%C3%ADa,+n
aturaleza+y+actividad+humana%22&hl=en&gl=us&pid=bl&srcid=ADGEESiaB_
KX2fCx0XOM4pKP-cXpXS96Uc-62bJnkDFsj58b06zmhrQdQ264BUDbJ0x2w3L-
W14C69671ZXNYdyiOL_Q2Nhoq9rPQ9fckQyYWQCH1HCIh5aMlXPD3VhZp
NrfOqybAii_9&sig=AHIEtbRrbZszO9TEPollRji_uOMXYk-aZA.

Langer, Josef. "SFM T-43," online research paper, Vienna, June 2001. http://www.alpenfes
tung.com/funk_sfm_t_43.htm.

McGaha, R. L. "The Politics of Espionage: Nazi Diplomats and Spies in Argentina, 1933–
1945." PhD dissertation, Ohio University, 2009.

Roland, Fernando Jorge Soto. "Hotel Viena," research paper, January 2010. http://letras-
uruguay.espaciolatino.com/aaa/soto_fernando/gran_hotel_viena_y_el_hotel_baln.htm.

Thorne, Peter, and John McCutchan, *The Path to Colossus . . . an historical look at the
development of the electronic computer.* A presentation to Engineering Heritage Victoria,
June 19, 2008. www.consuleng.com.au/The%20Path%20to%20Colossus%20080827%
2 revcomp.pdf.

OTHER INTERNET REFERENCES

GENERAL

http://www.bletchleypark.org.uk
http://www.cia.gov/library
http://www.circulomilitar.org/Re.htm
http://www.flyingbombsandrockets.com
http://www.gesell.gov.ar/
http://www.geocities.com/~orion47/ (Axis biographical research)
http://www.paperlessarchives.com/hitler.html
http://www.polandinexile.com
http://swissinternees.tripod.com
http://www.trumanlibrary.org/hstpaper/bernsten.htm (Bernard Bernstein Papers)
http://www.uboat.net
http://www.uboataces.com
http://www.v2rocket.com

SPECIFIC WEB PAGES

http://www.30AU.co.uk.
http://admiral-graf-spee.blogspot.com (Depositions to Commission of Enquiry into Nazi
Activities in Argentina [CEANA] in Camarasa, *Puerto Seguro*)
http://www.archives.gov/research/holocaust/finding-aid/civilian/rg-84-argentina.html
http://www.arquitecturaandina.com.ar/anterior.php (biography of architect Alejandro
Bustillo, © Revista Arquitectura Andina, Edición No. 4)
http://www.arlindo-correia.com/140402.html ("O Holocausto, Perón e la Argentina")
http://www.atp.com.ar/verpost.asp?ID=32702
http://www.balkanpeace.org/index.php?index=article&articleid=13742 (Srđa Trifković,
"The Real Genocide in Yugoslavia: Independent Croatia of 1941 Revisited," Center for
Peace in the Balkans, April 21, 2000)
http://www.bbc.co.uk/ww2peopleswar/stories/92/a3641492.shtml
http://berliner-unterwelten.de/fuehrer-bunker.328.1.html
http://www.daviddarling.info/encyclopedia/P/Paperclip.html (Operation Paperclip from
the History of Rocketry)
docs.fdrlibrary.marist.edu/PSF/BOX37/a335bb02.html (FDR letter to Churchill)
http://www.ellsbury.com/enigmabombe.htm

http://www.emporis.com/application/?nav=building&lng=3&id=1149853/
http://www.enotes.com/topic/DKM_Admiral_Graf_Spee
http://en.wikipedia.org/wiki/Nazi_plunder.
http://www.foreantimes.com/features/articles/4435/the_magical_battle_of_britain.html
http://www.frommers.com/destinations/buenosaires/A34264.html#ixzz0wx55TjO
http://www.hochtief.com/hochtief_en/97.jhtml
http://www.holocaustresearchproject.org/ghettos/przemysl.html
http://www.holocaustresearchproject.org/trials/eichmanntrialcapture.html
http://home.arcor.de/sturmbrigade/Wallonie/Wallonie.htm
http://germanhistorydocs.ghi-dc.org/sub_image.cfm?image_id=1874
http://www.iwm.org.uk/upload/package/10/enigma/
http://www.jewishvirtuallibrary.org/jsource/Holocaust/canaris.html
http://www.maritimequest.com/warship_directory/germany/pages/cruisers/ags_crew_
pages/dick_heinrich_rudolf.htm (memoirs of Matrosenobergefreiter Heinrich Rudolf
Dick, Division 1, *Admiral Graf Spee*)
http://mcfisher.0catch.com/scratch/v1/v1-0.htm (Mark Fisher, "American Buzz Bombs:
An Incomplete History")
https://www.mi5.gov.uk/output/german-intelligence-agents-and-suspected-agents-5.html
http://www.mp44.nl/equipment/gas_mask.htm.
http://www.nasenoviny.com/GPREN.html (S.Sgt. Jock Bramah in Normandy)
http://ordorenascendi.blogspot.com/2010/03/operacion-tierra-de-fuego-ii.html
http://www.pilotenbunker.de/Stuka/Rudel/rudel.htm
http://www.polishresistance-ak.org/2 Article.htm (courtesy of the Polish Institute and
Sikorski Museum, London)
http://www.ritterkreuztraeger-1939-45.de/Waffen-SS/S/Schaefer-Oskar.htm
http://www.signaturehouse.net/ (Personal papers of Hans Ulrich Rudel, auctioned by
Signature House Lot 236)
http://www.simplonpc.co.uk/CostaPCs.html#anchor559191
http://www.theshipslist.com/ships/lines/costa.htm.
http://www.uboat.net/boats/u235.htm
http://www.uboataces.com/articles-life-uboat.shtml
http://www.ww2aircraft.net/forum/modern/ejercito-del-aire-spanish-air-force-24156.html
http://www.yadvashem.org (Shoah Resource Center, "Einsatzstab Rosenberg"; also Antonio Louça and Ansgar Schäfer, "Portugal and the Nazi Gold: The 'Lisbon Connection'
in the Sales of Looted Gold by the Third Reich")

ORIGINAL INTERVIEWS

Jorge Luis Bernelli, director, Dirección de Communicación Social, Ministerio de Defensa,
Argentina, 2008.
Jorge Colotto, Juan Domingo Perón's police bodyguard, Buenos Aires, 2008.
Ida Eichhorn's great-nephew, La Falda, Córdoba, 2007.
Jorge Elbaum, executive director, Delegación de Associaciones Israelitas Argentinas (DAIA),
Buenos Aires, 2008.
Ernesto Bernardo Feicher, presidente, DAIA, Córdoba, 2008.
Aníbal Domingo Fernández, Minister of Justice, Security and Human Rights, Buenos Aires, 2008.
David Fletcher, historian, Royal Armoured Corps Tank Museum, Bovington, Dorset, UK,
August 2010.
Innes McCartney, U-boat history and diving consultant, 2008–2010.
Capt. Manuel G. Monasterio ("Jeff Kristenssen"), Buenos Aires, 2008.
Cuini Amelio Ortiz, Rome, 2008.
Juan Angel Serra, Prefecto Mayor, Jefe Servicio de Buques Guardacostas, Prefectura Naval,
Argentina, 2008.
Dr. Floreal Vajlis, Buenos Aires, 2008.
Isabel Winter, 1993; "interview from http://www.philosophie.at/cofete/espanol.htm."

ORIGINAL COMMISSIONED RESEARCH

Facial analysis research carried out by Professor Alf Linney, professor of medical physics, University College London, August 2010.

Original research carried out for authors by www.oocities.com/goldpartypin/index.html.

Researcher conversation with Omar Contreras, Buenos Aires, 2008.

Researcher conversations with Claudio Correa, Argentina, 2008.

Researcher conversations with Araceli Méndez, Buenos Aires, 2008.

Researcher conversations with Mrs. M., Argentina, 2008.

Researcher Nahuel Coca's conversations with Alicia Olivera, Buenos Aires, 2008.

VIDEO, TELEVISION, AND FILM SOURCES

Interviews with Hernán Ancin, Jorge Batinic, and Catalina Gomero, video courtesy of editorial director Ricardo D'Aloia, Diario Ambito Financiero, Buenos Aires, 2008.

Interviews with Catalina Gomero and Rochus Misch, in *Secret History: Hitler of the Andes* by David Howard and Madoc Roberts, Barking Mad Productions, for Channel 4, UK, 2003.

Interview with Ingeborg Schaeffer, Eyeworks Quatre Cabezas, Berlin, 2007.

BBC Television documentary, "Children of the Master Race," part of the series *The Last Nazis*, Minnow Films, London, broadcast 2010.

Channel 7 Argentina. *La Cornisa*. Reporter: Martin Jáuregui, 2005.

Granada Television, "Nazi Hunter," a program in the British documentary series *War Stories*, 1999.

SyFy channel, "Hitler's Ghost," part of the U.S. television series *Ghost Hunters International*, January 2010, shot at Hotel Viena.

Cuini Amelio Ortiz, *Hotel Eden*, documentary film, Deutschland 1995 / 3sat / MDR, 1995.

Rodolfo Pereyra, *Oro Nazi en Argentina (Nazi Gold in Argentina)*, Argentine documentary. http://www.independent.co.uk/news/world/americas/nazi-gold-shipped-by-uboat-to-argentina-532304.html.

U.S. War Department Film, MID 2093, Buenos Aires, April 1938.

AUTHORS' VISITS, NUMBER OF VISITS PER LOCATION

Buenos Aires, Argentina: 14; Estancia San Ramón: 3; San Carlos de Bariloche, Río Negro Province: 5; Villa La Angostura: 3; Inalco Mansion: 3; Córdoba: 1; Hotel Viena, Miromar, Córdoba Province: 1; Hotel Eden and Eichhorn house, La Falda: 1; Eichhorn house, Pan Azucar, Córdoba Province: 1; Caleta de los Loros and Viedma, Río Negro Province: 1; Berlin: 2; Reus Airport, Barcelona: 1

OTHER

Delegación de Asociaciones Israelitas Argentinas (DAIA). Report of investigation by the DAIA, Annual Report, 1997.

INDEX

PICTURE CREDITS

Italic numbers refer to images in book pages; plates are indicated by "PL" and insert number (1 or 2), followed by plate order number within each insert.